Analysis for
Marketing Decisions

IRWIN SERIES IN QUANTITATIVE ANALYSIS FOR BUSINESS

CONSULTING EDITOR   ROBERT B. FETTER   *Yale University*

Analysis for Marketing Decisions

JAMES H. DONNELLY, JR., D.B.A.

Assistant Professor of Marketing and
Quantitative Business Analysis

JOHN M. IVANCEVICH, D.B.A.

Assistant Professor of Management and
Quantitative Business Analysis

Both of the University of Kentucky

1970

RICHARD D. IRWIN, INC., HOMEWOOD, ILLINOIS
Irwin-Dorsey Limited, Georgetown, Ontario

© RICHARD D. IRWIN, INC., 1970

First Printing, February, 1970

Library of Congress Catalog Card No. 74–105917

Printed in the United States of America

This book is dedicated to:

Helene S. Donnelly
Diane, Danny, and Jill Ivancevich

Preface

The application of analytical concepts and tools to marketing problems has been increasing rapidly over the past decade. For example, the available marketing literature today includes numerous articles with an analytical focus. In addition, terms such as decision theory, model building, and linear programming are being increasingly used by marketing executives, teachers, and students. Because of the growing demand in and necessity for quantified approaches to decision making and the utilization of high-speed computers, the use of analytical approaches for solving marketing problems can be expected to increase at an even greater rate in the 1970's.

Consequently, this book has been written for use as an introductory textbook for college and university courses in marketing problems, marketing policy, marketing management, quantitative analysis for marketing, and marketing planning at both the undergraduate and graduate levels. Also, this book may be of interest to marketing executives seeking to acquire a basic understanding of some of the analytical methods being applied in their area.

The book is oriented toward the factors in marketing decision making that can be quantified. However, the book makes no attempt to be an encyclopedia covering every possible quantitative application to marketing. For example, topics such as sales forecasting and attitudinal measurement are not covered since these areas are usually covered in such courses as marketing research and/or statistics. In addition, the book will be of little interest to the professional operations researcher or management scientist. Readers intending to become experts in the various quantitative techniques presented need more training in mathematics than is required for this text. It should be noted that many of the techniques presented require only the ability to follow a chain of logical reasoning. Thus, the emphasis of the book is on an *analytical approach* to marketing decisions and problems rather than a strict mathematical approach. The book, however, assumes that the reader has some understanding of algebra and statistics. Additional materials may be needed for those students with little mathematical background, in order to improve their understanding of various concepts.

Although the framework of the text reflects our experiences in teaching these materials, it has been specifically developed with the needs of students, instructors, and executives in mind. Part I sets the stage for the reader. The importance of the marketing function, the marketing concept, and the increasing complexity of marketing decisions are considered. The analytical approach to marketing decisions and the role of quantitative methods in the analytical approach are discussed. The reader is introduced to the concept of models and model building in marketing, and a conceptual framework is developed for problem analysis and model construction.

Part II provides an introduction to several analytical concepts, tools, and techniques. Chapters Three and Five contain some materials that may have been covered elsewhere in the student's curriculum, but it is assumed that repeating some of the previously learned concepts will not be harmful. The chapters in Part II focus specifically on methodological material which must be understood before the analytical methods can be appreciated. This part is separated from the part on applications to make it easier for an instructor to use Part II in its entirety, in part, or not at all, depending upon the mathematical backgrounds of his students and/or objectives of his course.

Part III is concerned with the applications of various analytical concepts, tools, and techniques to marketing problems. A chapter is devoted to each of the four controllable decision variables open to the marketing manager: product, distribution, promotion, and price. Each chapter examines selected analytical approaches applicable to that particular decision variable.

Part IV considers the impact of computers and simulation in marketing. The reader is introduced to the nature, scope, and potential of simulation as well as the concept of a marketing information system. Finally, the future of analytical methods in marketing is examined.

The authors are grateful to the many individuals who played a part in the development of this text. The graduate and undergraduate students at the Universities of Maryland and Kentucky who endured the preliminary drafts and made many helpful suggestions are due a special note of thanks. Three University of Kentucky graduate students deserve special thanks for their suggestions and comments: Terence A. Shimp, Walt Bergmann, and Arthur R. Thomas.

In addition we would like to acknowledge the contributions of many friends and colleagues. These individuals contributed by reviewing parts of the manuscript and offering constructive suggestions. These friends and colleagues are John K. Ryans, Jr., Assistant Dean, Kent State University; Herbert L. Lyon, University of Kentucky; Dean Lawrence X. Tarpey, Haile Sellassie University; Robert H. Strawser, Pennsylvania State University; and Ted Mattheis, University of Maryland.

Others contributed to this text directly and indirectly either through discussions or encouragement, or as former teachers. Two former teachers— Charles A. Taff, Chairman, Department of Business Administration, University of Maryland and Robert E. Schellenberger, presently Chairman, Department of Management, Southern Illinois University—have had an influence on the authors' academic careers and are due special recognition. In addition, a colleague, Richard T. Hise, Associate Professor and Chairman, Department of Business Administration, Shippensburg State College, provided numerous suggestions, recommendations, and ideas for presenting many of the analytical concepts as well as contributing directly to parts of the text.

We also wish to acknowledge James L. Gibson, Chairman, Department of Business Administration, University of Kentucky, for providing a work atmosphere conducive for preparing this text.

A number of texts have had a significant impact on the authors' teaching and on the framework and approach taken in this text. Thus, thanks are due the authors who have written these texts. The books and authors having the most impact on the development of this text are James E. Howell and Daniel Teichroew, *Mathematical Analysis For Business Decisions* (Homewood, Ill.: Richard D. Irwin, Inc., 1963); David W. Miller and Martin K Starr, *Executive Decisions and Operations Research* (Englewood Cliffs, N.J.: Prentice-Hall, 1960); Richard I. Levin and Charles A. Kirkpatrick, *Quantitative Approaches to Management* (New York: McGraw-Hill Book Company, 1965); and N. Paul Loomba, *Linear Programming: An Introductory Analysis* (New York: McGraw-Hill Book Company, 1964).

The preparation of this text would not have been possible without the technical assistance of our secretaries Mary Sewell and Tharon Eves.

Many thanks are due Professor Robert B. Fetter, editor of this series, whose guidance and editorial assistance has aided us throughout the entire preparation of this text.

Naturally, the authors take full responsibility for any errors which are contained herein.

January, 1970 JAMES H. DONNELLY, JR.
JOHN M. IVANCEVICH

Contents

Analysis: *The Types of Bayesian Analysis. Applied Bayesian Analysis. Prior Analysis: New Power Tool. Introduction to Bayes' Theorem. Preposterior Analysis. Preposterior Analysis Using Imperfect Information.*

PART III. Applications

PART IV. Computers and simulation in marketing

APPENDIXES

PART I
Introduction

chapter one

THE ANALYTICAL APPROACH
TO MARKETING DECISIONS

INTRODUCTION

Marketing is something which affects people everyday of their lives. It affects us physiologically in that it serves our demands for the necessities that keep us alive. It affects us psychologically in that it brings us satisfaction. Finally, it affects us monetarily because in order to obtain the satisfactions desired we must spend money.

If marketing facilitates the flow of goods efficiently, then we all get what we want and need in the way that provides us with the most satisfaction. If the process is accomplished efficiently, then everyone is better off. However, even a housewife who has never studied marketing knows that the system does not always work efficiently. Whenever the local supermarket is out of her favorite brand of frozen vegetables or she becomes offended by a television commercial or finds that the small electrical appliance she recently purchased does not live up to the claims made by the manufacturer, she is aware that various phases of the marketing system are malfunctioning. If she becomes irritated enough by the malfunctioning she may switch to a new supermarket, refuse to buy the brand advertised in the offensive commercial, or switch to another manufacturer of electrical appliances. There is little else the house-wife can do because she does not plan, direct, and control the marketing activities of these firms. The purpose of this text is to provide the prospective business decision maker with knowledge of selected analytical tools and techniques which can help achieve a more efficient marketing system for the firm.

3

THE IMPORTANCE OF THE MARKETING FUNCTION

To understand the importance of marketing in the United States today one must consider the evolution of the American economy. The present state of marketing activity in the United States is a great deal different from that which existed at the beginning of this century. At that time the economy was characterized by a scarcity of goods and services. The major problem facing the firm was production; specifically, how to increase output. For most products a "sellers market" existed; that is, the demand for the product was greater than the supply. The firm concentrated its efforts on improving its productive capacity.

Today, however, the problem faced by most firms is just the opposite of what it was then. Today, the United States economy is characterized not by a scarcity of goods but by a scarcity of markets. The problem of increasing productive efficiency is no longer faced by most firms. The major problem now faced by most firms is to find sufficient numbers of customers for their products. Thus, for most products a "buyers market" exists where the supply of the product is greater than the demand. In addition, the modern American consumer is more affluent and sophisticated than ever before. The basic subsistence needs of his family are well provided for and he has a great deal of leisure time. This motivates him to purchase a whole new range of leisure time products but also gives him the time to shop and choose among the wide range of goods and services competing for his discretionary income. Thus, marketing is indispensable in a highly competitive economy of abundance such as the one in the United States. Marketing managers have managerial responsibility for encouraging the consumption of the vast output of goods and services provided by American business and industry.

The Marketing Concept

From the standpoint of the firm, competition for the consumer's dollar is more intense today than ever before. Not only must firms compete with other firms in the same industry but they must simultaneously compete with firms in other industries which are also vying for consumer dollars. In today's "marketing-oriented" economy the firm must (1) seek to develop demands which it then fulfills and (2) seek to discover insufficiently developed or insufficiently satisfied needs.

This has resulted in an important change in business thinking from one of production orientation to a marketing orientation. In the past, marketing has been perceived as beginning when the product came off the production line. This conception has changed significantly in recent years. With the numerous changes that have occurred in the economy, American firms are beginning to center their attention on the market prior to the design and production of the product. This way of thinking follows the common sense premise that it is easier to adjust the firm's offering to meet the needs and desires of the market rather than to expect the market to adjust to what the firm wishes to produce. This change in business thinking has come to be known as the marketing concept. We can define the marketing concept as a business philosophy, an attitude or a course of business thinking which places the consumer at the *center* of the firm's planning activities. The firm sees the consumer as the controller of corporate destinies and as such derives its strategies and tactics from the market.

This way of thinking does not imply that marketing is the most important business function. Indeed, an automobile could not function without a fuel pump but this does not imply that the fuel pump is the most important component of an automobile engine. In order for an automobile to function effectively, each component in the system must function effectively. In other words the "total system" cannot operate efficiently if the components of the system are not functioning effectively. The same can be said for the business firm. Each function (i.e., purchasing, research and development, personnel management, finance, production, marketing) must perform efficiently if the total system is to operate efficiently.

However, there are two overriding considerations related to marketing that significantly affect management decisions:

1. The marketing function is the primary income producing function of the business firm. When the firm's product leaves the production area and the marketing process begins, the firm has incurred only costs and obtained no income.

2. The firm's market holds veto power over the entire system. A firm can have the finest engineers, the most modern up-to-date production facilities, and a solid financial base but if the market says "no" when the firm presents its offer, then the other activities have been little more than an exercise. In other words, the market sanctions all of the preceding activities prior to the making of a sale.

These two considerations focus on the importance of the *market* to the survival of the firm. Indeed, the market is the lifeblood of a business organization. The firm must view itself as a market entity which can only survive through market orientation. This is more than a marketing philosophy. It is a philosophy around which the entire firm can organize. It stresses the need to center *all* of the functions within the firm around the consumer.

MARKETING DECISIONS

All of the decisions necessary to plan, organize, and execute the activities designed to provide buyers with products can be classified as marketing decisions. The typical marketing decision maker is faced with a myriad of decisions in order to perform his job: "what products to produce," "how much to produce," "how to distribute the products produced," "what price to charge," "when to advertise," "where to advertise," and similar marketing related decisions. In each particular decision situation, the decision maker must be concerned not only with the potential effects of his own actions but also must weigh the potential effects of decisions made by other elements in the firm's external environment such as competitors, channel members, and the government. All in all, he faces an unending sequence of decision problems each of which can have a great impact on the success or failure of a product. It is the marketing decision maker's task to plan marketing programs, direct marketing activities, and monitor their outcomes in order that when dysfunctional deviations occur, corrective measures can be taken immediately. This requires a tremendous amount of planning, organization, coordination, and control or feedback.

THE ANALYTICAL APPROACH TO MARKETING DECISIONS

Traditional Bases for Marketing Decisions

Traditionally the marketing decision maker has resolved the majority of his product, distribution, promotion, and pricing decisions by utilizing one or a combination of the following methods.

1. *Tenacity.* Here the decision maker uses as a basis for a decision a premise that has "always been known to be true." For example, if a toy manufacturer used spot television advertisements because "they have always been the best way to advertise toys," he would be utilizing this method. The unfortunate thing about this method is that frequent repetition of such "truths" often enhances their validity in the eyes of many people.

2. *Authority.* This method centers around "established beliefs." In many industries the channels of distribution have been established over the years. A new firm entering the industry will usually accept these channels of distri-

bution because they are what existing firms utilize. Another example of this method is small or medium sized firms making marketing decisions based on what the larger firms (i.e., the leaders) in the industry have done.

3. *A priori.* This is sometimes referred to as the method of intuition. Many times a decision maker will rely on hunches or intuitions in making his marketing decisions. This may be especially true for an experienced decision maker. Because of his many years of experience he believes he can "feel" when the time is right to introduce a new product.

The marketing executive of today is extremely fortunate if he has some historical data, previous experience, or astute intuition which enables him to make correct and profitable marketing decisions. Unfortunately, the dynamic environment in which most modern marketing decision makers find themselves is such that the problems they face are so complex that they are usually beyond the scope of human intuition and subjective analyses.

The increased complexity of marketing decision problems has not occurred over a short time period. Rather, it has been more of an evolutionary process, the causes of which are many. Most firms have broader product lines than ever before, sell in many more markets than ever before, and face more competition than ever before. All of these factors complicate the environment in which the marketing decision maker operates.

An outside factor which has served to focus attention on the need for more formal problem analysis in marketing has been the development of the electronic computer. The advent of the computer with its phenomenal computational ability and its vast data-generating capacity has provided marketing management with huge amounts of data which would have been too costly to gather only a few years ago. Almost instantly they have at their fingertips sales data, cost data, market information such as demographic and behavioral data, and market share data. The decision maker's problem has now become one of effectively utilizing the available data.

Thus, two developments—the increasing complexity of marketing problems and the growth in electronic computers—have led many marketing managers to move the analysis of decision problems outside the context of their experience, judgment, intuition, and common sense. They have encouraged the marketing manager to take a more *analytical* approach to marketing decisions. This type of approach is generally associated with the application of the scientific method to decision problems. However, it is somewhat broader, since it includes more than solely experimental methods, which to many are synonymous with the scientific method. This is not to imply, however, that the experience or judgment of a marketing decision maker is of no value in solving marketing problems. Obviously, such factors will always play a role in problem solving and in most situations can be a valuable asset. The *analytical* approach taken in this book suggests *a logical and objective process, which to some degree is* (although not so in many cases) *independent of the subjectivity and intangibility which is always included in the decision process.* In other words, the *analytical* approach is a valuable addition to the experience, judgment, intuition, and common sense of the decision maker. The value of the *analytical* approaches presented in this text is that they guarantee logic and consistency in the approach to, and analysis of, marketing problems.

Since the analytical techniques presented are based on scientific methodology, our first task is to acquire an understanding of the nature of the scientific method.

The Scientific Method

The scientific method involves the following four basic phases.

1. *Observation.* Obviously, the purpose of observation is to identify problem areas. Remember a manager's job is to make decisions and if no problems exist then no decisions are needed. The problem may be in the form of an obstacle or an idea. At any rate the detection of problems is most difficult. It often takes a great deal of experience before a marketing manager can distinguish between symptoms of a problem and the basic problem itself.

2. *Problem identification and definition.* The first step in problem solving is to identify the problem. This is clearly a vital step since any analysis or solution arrived at for a poorly defined problem will be worthless. In the following chapter we shall discuss the importance of this phase in the analytical approach to marketing problem solving.

3. *Formulation of a hypothesis.* Once the problem has been identified and clearly defined, a hypothesis or hypotheses can be developed. These are actually possible solutions to the problem. As we shall see later in the marketing framework, this often takes the form of a *model.* Thus, model building is a key factor in the analytical approach taken in this text. It can be considered the hallmark of the analytical approach to marketing decisions. The following chapter will be devoted entirely to a discussion of models and steps in model construction.

4. *Experimentation.* At this point in the strict scientific process the hypothesis formulated in the previous step is either supported or not supported. In the marketing framework this is where the model which has been constructed is manipulated. It is the experimental nature of models which make them useful to business decision makers. Obviously, the marketing decision maker cannot experiment on an actual ongoing marketing system. The practicalities of the business world preclude him from doing this. However, an

accurately constructed model enables the decision maker to experiment with possible solutions without interrupting the ongoing system. If the model accurately depicts the ongoing system it will provide the decision maker with the results of his proposed solutions. In other words it will react as the real system would react.

Thus, the analytical approach taken in this text is based upon the scientific method which has achieved impressive gains in other areas of study. It assures a rational, logical approach to marketing problems rather than relying solely on a decision maker's experience, intuition, and common sense. The analytical approach is characterized by two significant developments: model building and quantitative methods.

Model Building

As we have already mentioned, model building is a basic element of the analytical approach to marketing decisions. In the following chapters we shall examine the basic fundamentals of model construction. In addition, we shall examine several marketing models which are currently being used. These models are designed for specific marketing problem situations such as inventory control, physical distribution, and pricing. Finally, we shall examine other analytical "techniques" which, while they cannot be considered models in the strict sense of the word, have greatly improved the analytical problem-solving ability of marketing decision makers.

The Role of Quantitative Methods

We have stated previously that the need for a more analytical approach to marketing decisions is largely the result of two forces: the increasing complexity of the marketing system and the advent of the electronic computer. However, these two forces would not have created problems if it had not been for the relatively slow development of new methods and techniques of analysis in marketing. While the computer was pouring forth great amounts of data, the development of techniques to analyze the data did not keep pace.

While these changes were occurring in marketing, other areas of business were also experiencing change. However, the transition to more analytical methods occurred more rapidly in many of these areas. Applications, mostly confined to the production segment of the business, began to be made after World War II by operations research staff specialists.[1] These individuals

---

[1] These individuals may also refer to themselves as management scientists or systems analysts. However, we shall assume they are the same since they all share in common the desire to apply scientific analysis to business decision problems.

applied their analytical skills to military problems during World War II and after the war began analyzing business problems. It was not long before these men made a noticeable impact on the results of business decision problems. For the most part, however, their impact was not felt in the area of marketing.

However, it was not long before these individuals turned their interest toward the complex problems faced by the marketing manager. At the same time the marketing manager began to search for aid in solving his marketing decision problems. As a result there has been a great increase in the number of marketing problems which have been subjected to more scientific analysis.

In order to utilize scientific analysis or analytical techniques, one must be "quantitatively oriented." This is because one of the major characteristics and prerequisites of analytical or scientific inquiry is quantitative measurement. Thus, the techniques and models examined in this text are quantitative in nature. Part II presents an introduction to four quantitative techniques: probability theory, decision theory, linear algebra and matrices, and mathematical programming. These quantitative methods are widely used in applying analytical techniques to marketing problems. Part III of the text presents applications of these methods to various marketing problems. In this section the reader will be introduced to the various mathematical models and techniques used in marketing. Part IV concludes the text with discussions of the use of computers and simulation in marketing.

PROBLEMS

1. "Since the marketing function is involved in actually selling the product, it is by far the most important business function." Comment on this statement.

2. "Today, the problem faced by most firms is a scarcity of markets." Comment on this statement. What implications do you feel this situation has for a manufacturing firm?

3. "As the marketing manager in a large consumer products firm I've been making marketing decisions for 25 years based on my experience and sound judgment. This has worked pretty well in the past and I don't see why it shouldn't work in the future." Do you have any advice for the person who made this statement?

4. In what ways has the environment faced by marketing decision makers become more complex over the past several years?

5. Why are we having a great increase in the use of analytical techniques to solve marketing problems? What are the values of such tools and techniques?

6. Discuss the role of quantitative methods in the analytical approach to marketing decisions.

REFERENCES

KELLEY, EUGENE J., and LAZER, WILLIAM. *Managerial Marketing: Perspectives and Viewpoints*. Homewood, Ill.: Richard D. Irwin, Inc., 1960.

KERLINGER, FRED N. *Foundations of Behavioral Research*. New York: Holt, Rinehart and Winston, Inc., 1966.

KOTLER, PHILIP. *Marketing Management*. Englewood Cliffs, N.J.: Prentice-Hall, Inc., 1967.

REWOLDT, STEWART H., SCOTT, JAMES D. and MARTIN R. WARSHAW. *Introduction to Marketing Management*. Homewood, Ill.: Richard D. Irwin, Inc., 1969.

STANTON, WILLIAM. *Fundamentals of Marketing*. New York: McGraw-Hill Book Company, Inc., 1967.

STAUDT, THOMAS A., and TAYLOR, DONALD A. *A Managerial Introduction to Marketing*. Englewood Cliffs, N.J.: Prentice-Hall, Inc., 1965.

chapter two
MODEL BUILDING AND ANALYSIS

INTRODUCTION

In Chapter One we noted that as the task of marketing increases in complexity, marketing managers are being forced to reexamine their methods and techniques for solving marketing problems and developing marketing strategies. Methods which proved successful in the past (i.e., intuition and hunch) are far too risky in the dynamic marketing environment faced in today's economy. The cost of success is high in today's market but the cost of failure is far greater. This has resulted in the development and use of analytical tools of analysis. These tools of analysis are generally referred to as "models."

What Is a Model?

In attempting to determine "What is a Model?" the reader undoubtedly has an intuitive understanding of the term. While he may not have formalized his thinking on such matters, he could, in a few moments, probably provide an acceptable definition. Each of us is familiar with various types of models. As children, we played with models of locomotives, automobiles, and airplanes. In each case these models looked like the real thing but were actually scaled down versions of the thing they represented. A model locomotive is, in most cases, an accurate representation of a real locomotive, at least on the exterior. However, the interior features of the locomotive (i.e., valves and pistons) are not included in the model. This is because in order for the locomotive to serve as a child's toy, the manufacturer needs only to include the exterior features in his model. In other words, some features of the real thing are included and others are excluded. What is included and excluded will depend on the purpose for which the model is constructed. A spacecraft model used to train potential

12

astronauts would differ greatly from a child's model. This is because the purpose of the model is different. In this case, a great deal of attention would be given to constructing an accurate model of the interior aspects of the spacecraft in order that astronaut trainees would be able to simulate an actual space flight.

In the above situations, we have seen that models of the same phenomena can vary, depending on the purpose for which the model is intended. They may not only vary according to the features included in the model but also in the complexity of the model. However, in most cases, the model is a simplified representation. In our discussion, the models constructed were a simplified representation of a physical object (spacecraft, locomotive). However, in marketing we are usually not concerned with physical objects but rather with more abstract phenomena. Thus, for our purposes we shall define a *model* as *a simplified representation of the relevant aspects of an actual system or process.*

At this point the reader may be questioning the value of a simplified representation of a marketing process. This is why we have included the two words "relevant aspects" in our definition. It is obvious that the value of any model depends on how well it represents the system or process under consideration. A highly simplified model that accurately describes a system or process still provides a more clearly understood starting point than a vague conception which a marketing manager creates in his mind. Such a model forces the decision maker to systematically consider the variables in the system and the relationships between the variables, as well as other significant variables in the particular situation. Thus, forcing the decision maker to formalize his thinking reduces the possibility of overlooking important factors or giving too much weight to minor factors.

In reality, the reader is probably more familiar with models for decision making than he thinks. This is because models are more widely used in decision making than is thought at first glance. Unless the reader makes decisions solely by guesswork, it is necessary for him to have in his mind some framework of the various alternatives he faces, the expected results of each alternative, and the relationships between variables. However incomplete they might be, every decision maker utilizes models.

A simple example will illustrate this point. Let us examine the problem of driving to work in the morning. There may be more than one way to arrive at a specific destination (e.g., freeway or through the city). However, there are many factors which must be considered such as driving time, gas expense, traffic conditions, and convenience. As the decision maker analyzes the problem, the process of model building is taking place. He examines each of the two alternative choices in relation to the importance he places on variables such as driving time. This structuring of a problem can be considered a type of model building. Although it is subjective in nature, the decision maker is nevertheless formulating a model in order to reach a decision.

Assume he decides that driving through the city will best serve his purposes. He now formulates in his mind the various alternative routes that are available. He must also understand the relationship among such variables as traffic flow and traffic lights. Here again, what the decision maker is actually doing is formulating a model in his mind to assist him in choosing the best route. Thus, we can see that model building is not something reserved solely for marketing decision makers but rather is done one way or another by anyone who hopes to make a rational decision.

Marketing Models

One of the obvious differences between the physical sciences and social sciences such as marketing is that marketing systems cannot be duplicated in a laboratory. While the physical scientist is able to experiment on a particular system and manipulate independent variables in order to observe the effect on dependent variables, the marketing scientist is unable to do this. This is because the practicalities of the business world preclude the marketing scientist from experimenting on a real-world marketing system. However, this does not do away with the need in marketing decisions for some means to arrive at the kind of conclusion that could be achieved through experimentation. Through the use of models, the marketing decision maker expresses the relationship between various factors in the system under consideration and notes the effect of each factor on the overall performance of the system. Instead of studying the actual system, he studies a model of the system. This enables him to manipulate variables in order to determine the effect such changes will have on the overall performance of the actual system.

If properly constructed, the decision maker can, therefore, experiment on the model and thus predict the effect such changes will have on the actual system. Thus, the complexity of the task facing the marketing manager and the impossibility of experimenting on an actual marketing system makes the use of models highly desirable. However, this same complexity makes the task of building accurate models extremely difficult.

Types of Models

Thus far we have said that the logical analysis of any decision problem is actually based on the idea of models and model building. In order to construct a model, we must have some means to represent the object or system under study. This means can be physical, schematic, symbolic, or a combination of these. For example, a toy locomotive is a *physical* model. The flow chart used to show the complete production of a product is a *schematic* model. It shows all the various activities needed to complete the finished product. Finally, the accounting equation, $A = L + C$, is a *symbolic* model. In this case it is a mathematical model showing the relationship between assets, liabilities, and capital. For that matter we can consider the balance sheet itself a mathematical model. It is an abstraction of the financial condition of a particular enterprise at a given moment of time. On the other hand, the income statement is also a mathematical model in that it is an abstraction of the operations of a business over a period of time.

From the above discussion it is obvious that a scale model of a locomotive is less abstract than a production flow chart, which in turn is less abstract than a mathematical model. The more abstract a model is, the less it will physically resemble the system it represents. In other words, models vary by degree of abstraction. This will help us understand the various types of models. For our purposes we shall use the following two-way classification.

Physical models. These types of models give the appearance of the real thing. Such models as toys and photographs fall in this category. These models are easy to describe and observe but are not easily manipulated. This makes them of little value for the purpose of analysis and prediction. Physical models are also the least abstract of all models.

Symbolic models. These models utilize some set of symbols to represent the object or system under study. They are the most abstract and as such are usually general rather than specific. A mathematical equation is an example of a symbolic model. Symbolic models can be manipulated and are therefore of great value for analysis and prediction purposes.

Thus, we have distinguished between two broad classifications of models based on the degree of abstraction of each. Now let us examine each classification more specifically in order to determine the various types of models in each classification. Generally there are two types of physical models.

1. *Iconic models* look like the real thing but do not act like the real thing. A blueprint drawing of a plant layout is an example of an iconic model. A manager can study such drawings in order to determine possible alternative plant layouts which might prove more efficient.

2. *Analog models* are more abstract than iconic models. They may not look like the real thing but do behave like the real thing. Such models are constructed utilizing some set of properties which are different from what the real

object or system possesses. An organization chart is an example of an analog model which shows authority-responsibility relationships within an organization. Another example are graphs which depict behavior of some variable such as sales volume or selling expenses. Since analog models are more abstract than iconic models, they are usually more general and easier to manipulate.

Since the problems faced by marketing managers typically do not lend themselves to modeling in physical form, symbolic models are of far greater interest to them. There are two types of symbolic models.

1. *Mathematical models* are models in which the object or system under study and the relationships among its parts are expressed in the language of mathematics. Since these models are general, they lend themselves more easily to manipulation of the variables included in the model and therefore, are extremely helpful for analysis and prediction.

2. *Verbal models* are a written version of an individual's thoughts or mental models which the manager may have. Their advantage is that they enable him to place all the relationships and constraints before him as he attempts to solve a problem.

In order to set the stage for further breakdown of mathematical models, let us summarize what we have said thus far in the diagram below.

FIGURE 2–1

Types of Models

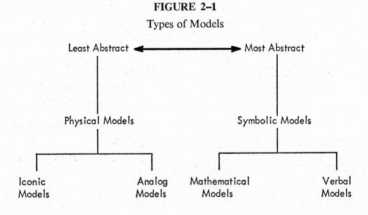

Note that in Figure 2–1 as one moves left to right, the models become more and more abstract. Symbolic models are generally more difficult to construct than physical models. This difficulty in construction of symbolic models is where we must pay for their generality and relative ease of manipulation. In this text we shall be concerned solely with one type of symbolic model, the mathematical model. Such models are easier to manipulate because we may utilize the tools of mathematics when experimenting on such models. While physical models are less abstract in that they look more like the object or system under study, there exists no set of tools which enables experimentation and manipulation of these types of models.

The tremendous growth of the use of quantitative methods for business decision-making purposes is closely tied in with the rapid development of high speed computers. Many of the models we will examine in the succeeding chapters do not require the use of computers. However, extensive use of even relatively simple models can be greatly aided through the use of a computer. Throughout this text most of the models will be solved by manual procedures because the problems presented will be on a relatively small scale. The application of these models to large scale problems is feasible only with the aid of a computer. However, whether a computer is utilized or not, it is necessary for the future marketing decision maker to be familiar with the basic elements and concepts of the particular model being used.

TYPES OF MATHEMATICAL MODELS

The reader must be aware of the major types of mathematical models before he can understand, evaluate, and utilize marketing models.

Descriptive and Normative Models

Mathematical models may be classified according to whether they are descriptive or normative in purpose. A *descriptive model* is one which describes how a system works. That is, it describes things as they are and makes no value judgments about the particular thing being studied. Many times a model is constructed solely to be a description of a real-world phenomenon in mathematical terms. This model can then be used to display the situation more clearly or to indicate how it can be changed. Descriptive models display the alternative choices available to the decision maker and in some cases help the decision maker determine the consequences or outcome of each alternative. However, a descriptive model *does not* select the best alternative.

A *normative model* attempts to provide how things should be. It is one which is specifically constructed to select from among alternatives the best alternative based on some previously determined criteria which are also included in the model. *It tells how the system should be, in order to achieve a particular objective.* These models are also referred to as optimizing models[1] and decision models.[2]

The two classifications—descriptive or normative—describe the purpose of the particular model. These classifications can be further broken down based on the types of variables included in the model.

Deterministic and Stochastic Models

A model is *deterministic* when the law of chance plays no role. In other words, the model contains no probabilistic considerations. All of the factors taken into account in the model are assumed to be exact or determinate quantities. The solution is determined by this set of exact relationships. The linear

FIGURE 2–2

Types of Mathematical Models

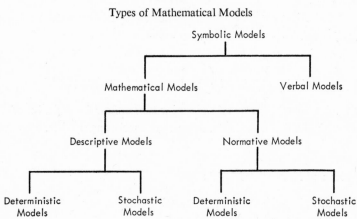

programming model is a deterministic model because all of the relationships are exact ones and all cost data is known. In other words, in a deterministic model we assume conditions of certainty.

Once chance or random variables are introduced, the model is said to be a *stochastic model.* A stochastic model is a model based on the mathematics of statistics and into which conditions of uncertainty are introduced based on observations of real events. Later in the text we shall discuss brand-switching

[1] Clifford H. Springer, Robert E. Herlihy, and Robert I. Beggs, *Advanced Methods and Models* (Homewood, Ill.: Richard D. Irwin, Inc., 1965), p. 12.

[2] Philip Kotler, *Marketing Management: Analysis, Planning, and Control* (Englewood Cliffs, N.J.: Prentice-Hall, Inc., 1967), p. 226.

models, which are stochastic models because the customer's brand choices are presented in probability format. Stochastic models may also be referred to as probabilistic models.

Thus, we can now add to the symbolic model portion of Figure 2–1 by including the various types of mathematical models. This is shown in Figure 2–2.

Through the remainder of this book various marketing models will be presented. In addition, other quantitative techniques will be presented which can prove useful to the marketing executive but cannot truly be considered models. Before proceeding, however, let us briefly examine some of the more popular mathematical models used in marketing. The application of each model to marketing problems will be covered in later chapters.

OPERATIONAL MODELS

Allocation Models

Allocation models are used in a variety of business situations, in which a number of possible candidates or activities are all competing for limited resources. These models enable the decision maker to allocate scarce resources so as to maximize some given objective. For the marketing manager the scarce resource may be salesmen which he must allocate in order to make the most profitable calls, or it may be advertising dollars which must be allocated among several candidate media. In each case the marketing executive wishes to find the optimum way to allocate the scarce resources given certain objectives and constraints. In the case of salesmen, one objective may be to make the most profitable calls, while for advertising it may be to gain the most exposure. He would be constrained by the number of salesmen employed by the organization or the advertising budget. Given these objectives and constraints, the marketing manager must make his decision.

Mathematical programming is one of the methods used in solving this class of problem. We shall see in a later chapter that mathematical programming expresses the objective to be achieved in the form of a mathematical function, the value of which is to be optimized. Constraints are introduced in the form of equations and/or inequalities. The constraints obviously reduce the number of feasible alternatives. A mathematical programming procedure known as the simplex algorithm searches the alternatives in order to find the particular one that optimizes the value of the objective function. Thus, most such models are normative in purpose.

Brand-Switching Models

One of the most important measuring devices used by marketing executives in determining the success or failure of their efforts is the share of the market secured by a product. Obviously, a marketing manager is constantly seeking ways to increase his product's share of the market or to at least prevent the existing share of the market from declining. In order to do this the executive must have some idea of the behavior of consumers in terms of their brand loyalty and their switching from one brand to another. Brand-switching models provide management with such information. Brand-switching models can be considered to be descriptive in purpose.

Waiting-Line Models

In marketing there are many examples of processes which generate waiting lines. These waiting lines are often referred to as queues. For example, housewives often wait in long lines in a supermarket while the husband may have to wait in line at a fuel pump in a service station. In many instances customers become irritable when faced with long periods of waiting, and if it becomes excessive the business may lose customers. In each case the manager faces conflicting problems. He would like to minimize customer ill-will but on the other hand he cannot afford to provide a great number of service facilities. Thus, he must strike a balance between the costs of additional facilities and customer ill-will. Waiting line models, which are descriptive in purpose, enable the manager to reach an optimal decision for facilities planning.

Inventory Models

In short, inventory models provide answers to two questions—"How much?" and "When?" Just as the marketer is concerned with obtaining goods to be sold at the most favorable price, he is also concerned with the point at which orders are placed for repeat goods and the quantity of each order. On one hand he wants enough inventory available at all times to insure that there are no lost sales or loss of customer goodwill, but on the other hand, frequent orders result in increased costs, such as storage costs resulting from carrying an excessive average inventory. Ordering and carrying costs behave in such a way that one set increases while the other decreases. In most cases, ordering costs decrease while storage costs increase as a function of average inventory levels. The inventory model which is normative in purpose enables the marketing executive to determine the economic order quantity (*EOQ*) and the optimum reorder point.

Simulation Models

In many situations marketing problems are so complex that they cannot be depicted by a standard mathematical model. Simulation involves constructing a model which replicates some aspect of the firm's marketing operation and performing step-by-step computations with the model, which duplicates the manner in which the actual system might perform. An individual simulation run can be thought of as an experiment upon a model. Numerous trials or experiments are performed until a workable satisficing solution rather than an optimal solution is reached. This experimental nature of simulation is an important advantage because the system can be studied under a wide variety of conditions which might be impossible to do using the actual real world system. Simulation models are descriptive in purpose.

MODEL CONSTRUCTION

In the first chapter the importance of an analytical approach to marketing problems was stressed. At this time we shall examine the steps that can be taken to insure a logical approach to analytical procedures for formulating and solving a decision problem.

While several approaches are available, we suggest the following series of steps.[3]

1. Define and formulate problem
2. Construct model
3. Solve model
4. Test solution
5. Develop necessary controls for the solution
6. Implement solution

Define and Formulate Problem

This first step in the model building process lays the foundation for all of the following steps. If the problem is ill-defined or loosely formulated, any

---

[3] See C. W. Churchman, R. L. Ackoff and E. L. Arnoff, *Introduction to Operations Research* (New York: John Wiley and Sons, Inc., 1957), chapter 1; and William R. King, *Quantitative Analysis for Marketing Management* (New York: McGraw-Hill Book Co., 1967), p. 105.

model constructed based on such a weak foundation will be of little value. A problem that is well defined and formulated is one in which all of the elements of the problem are clearly delineated. This includes the determination of the objective(s) to be achieved, identification of alternative courses of action, and all components of the problem.

The types of problems faced by the marketing manager vary in complexity. Some may be relatively definable with easily identifiable variables which behave with a high degree of certainty. On the other hand, a problem may contain a great number of interrelated variables which are probabilistic in nature. Thus, we can array problems on a continuum from relatively simple and organized to complex and disorganized with varying degrees of disorganization for each type. This allows us to delineate four general classes of problems.[4] These are presented in Figure 2–3.

1. *Simple and organized.* These problems have only a small number of variables which contain no probabilistic considerations (i.e., they are deterministic). An example of such models in marketing are the inventory models in which all factors are exact or deterministic quantities.

2. *Simple but disorganized.* These types of problems contain many variables but all of the variables are deterministic. Linear programming models and other mathematical programming models are used under these conditions. Such models have a wide variety of use for several types of marketing problems which fall into this classification.

3. *Complex and organized.* These types of problems contain a small number of stochastic variables. Many marketing problems fall into this class. Decision theory is useful for marketing problems of this type.

4. *Complex and disorganized.* These types of problems contain a great number of stochastic variables. Constructing optimizing models for such problems is extremely difficult. One aid to managers facing such problems has been the electronic computer, which has increased management use of such techniques as Pert/CPM and simulation.

Unfortunately, for the marketing executive the majority of the problems he faces tend to lean toward the right side of the continuum in Figure 2–3. That is, they are complex and disorganized. This is caused mainly by two factors. First, most marketing problems consist of a large number of interrelated variables which are probabilistic in nature. Second, because of the

---

[4] This discussion adapted from *Tentative Recommendations for the Undergraduate Mathematics Program of Students of the Biological, Management and Social Sciences* (Berkeley, California: Committee on the Undergraduate Program in Mathematics, 1964), p. 12. Also see Max D. Richards and Paul S. Greenlaw, *Management Decision Making* (Homewood, Ill.: Richard D. Irwin, Inc., 1966), chapter 19.

nature of marketing itself, the majority of marketing problems will involve human behavior variables. Probably no other variable is less predictable than human behavior.

Thus far we have said that the majority of problems faced by the marketing executive are disorganized and complex and that few optimizing models deal with this class of problem. What then can the marketing executive do in order to gain the benefits of these types of models? The only alternative avail-

FIGURE 2–3

Problem (Simple—Complex) Continuum

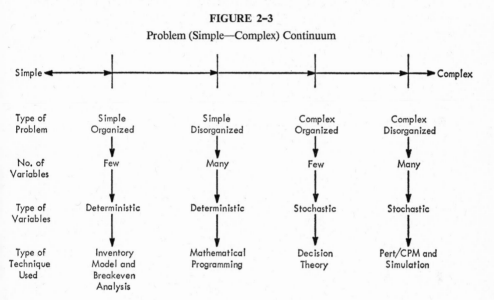

	Simple Organized	Simple Disorganized	Complex Organized	Complex Disorganized
Type of Problem				
No. of Variables	Few	Many	Few	Many
Type of Variables	Deterministic	Deterministic	Stochastic	Stochastic
Type of Technique Used	Inventory Model and Breakeven Analysis	Mathematical Programming	Decision Theory	Pert/CPM and Simulation

able is to attempt to move the problem to the left on the simple-complex continuum in Figure 2–3, that is, reformulate complex disorganized problems into more simple and organized problems. In this way they become more manageable and more readily adaptable to optimizing models. Obviously, this task is not an easy one because in our attempt to simplify a problem we may eliminate one or more important variables, thereby resulting in a model solution which is of little or no practical value. Generally, there are three ways in which complex problems can be redefined into more manageable ones.[5]

1. *Assume certainty.* In some instances it may be permissable to assume certainty in a problem although some of the variables may be stochastic in

---

[5] Richards and Greenlaw, *op. cit.*, pp. 531–32.

nature. This approach is used when facing inventory problems. In such problems the assumption is made that the demand for the product is known. This permits the use of inventory models.

2. *Simplify relationships.* Here we assume that the relationships between variables are much simpler than they are in reality. When linear programming is used, it is assumed that the relationship among variables is linear when in fact it probably is non-linear.

3. *Isolate operations.* Here we attempt to isolate a particular operation or segment of the business. We then seek to optimize the output from that segment and assume that the remaining operations of the firm are not adversely affected.

Thus, the marketing decision maker should, wherever feasible, seek to break down complex problems into more manageable problems where the likelihood is greater that some problem-solving technique can be used. However, great care should be taken whenever this is done.

Construct Model

After the problem has been clearly defined and formulated, the model construction phase can begin. This obviously is a vital phase. Again it should be noted that it is unimportant whether the model superficially looks like the particular system being modeled. What is important is that the model responds in the same fashion as the real system. Whether the model is physical or symbolic is a matter of feasibility. However, as was noted previously, in marketing problem situations it will usually be symbolic. Basically, there are three elements of a model.[6]

1. *Components.* These are the parts of the model. They may be firms, households, warehouses, costs, media, and any other phenomena which are part of the real system.

2. *Variables.* These relate one way or another to the components of the model. They are often classified as *input variables*, which arise outside the component and must be fed into it (e.g., inventory, raw materials); *status variables*, which describe the state of a component (e.g., stage in the family life cycle, income, education, age); and *output variables* which are generated by a component (e.g., costs, demand).

---

[6] Guy Orcutt, "Simulation of Economic Systems," *The American Economic Review*, Vol. L (December, 1960), pp. 893–907.

3. *Relationships.* These specify how the values of different variables are related to each other. For example, inventory models specify the relationship between ordering costs and carrying costs.

The marketing executive is faced with the task of determining all of the relevant components which affect the functioning of the system under study and arrive at measurable variables to represent these factors. Finally he must determine the relationship between the variables.

Solve Model

Once the model has been constructed the next step is to arrive at a solution to the model. For a normative (optimization) model this involves mathematical techniques for ariving at the best strategy or alternative. For tedious computations or iterations the electronic computer has been utilized very successfully. In the case of a descriptive model where there usually is no solution, the model can be termed "solved" when it accurately describes the system under study. This is arrived at by manipulating the model until this point is reached.

Test Solution

Once the model is solved, the solution should be tested before being applied to a large segment of the firm's operations. In this way, the model's effect can be determined on a small scale and if any errors are discovered, the model can be altered accordingly and a new solution obtained. For example, the solution to an inventory problem could be tested on a small scale using perhaps one warehouse or store. The solution to a distribution problem could be tested using only one plant and one warehouse. In this way we can gain insight into the value of the solution and be able to adjust accordingly if changes are necessary.

Develop Controls

In the dynamic environment in which the marketing manager exists change is the rule rather than the exception. Once the model is constructed and solved it must be carefully and continually reexamined in order to insure that the variables and relationships in the model have not changed. There are many forces at work which affect marketing decisions but over which the marketing decision maker has little or no control. Changes in consumer tastes, competitor's actions, changes in government regulations, and economic upswings and downswings can all reduce the validity of the model and its solution. Thus, the need for tight control of the model is vital.

Implement Solution

After the model has been solved and tested, the solution should be implemented by the marketing manager or recommended to the decision maker in cases where staff analysts have constructed the model. In any case the decision maker must be aware of the objective, assumptions, omissions, and limitations of the model. After this is done, further reformulation of the problem may result because of some previously overlooked factor which is deemed important. Once the solution is finally implemented, all personnel who will utilize the solution produced by the model should be made aware of the basic rationale behind the model and the advantages to be gained by implementing the solution.

PROBLEMS

1. Listed below are several types of models. For each one decide whether it is iconic, analog, mathematical, or verbal, and discuss the reason for your choice.
A. A computer program flow chart   B. An aerial map of New York City
C. The equation $y = a + bx$ D. A pilot plant
E. A graph showing the performance of a certain common stock over a six-month period.

2. Clearly define each of the following terms:
A. probabilistic   B. deterministic
C. optimizing   D. stochastic   E. model

3. How can one expect a model based upon assumptions such as certainty and/or linearity to be of value in an actual marketing problem situation?

4. Evaluate the following statement. "The more abstract a mathematical model is the less value it has as a decision aid."

5. In order to break down complex problems, managers will often attempt to break the problem down into more manageable problems which lend themselves to the use of some problem-solving technique. Create a hypothetical marketing problem and then attempt to break it down into more manageable subproblems.

6. Assume that the registrar at your school has asked you to be a consultant on a particular problem. He has become very dissatisfied with the registration system that has been in use for the last several years and has been bombarded with student complaints each semester. He has asked you to attempt to improve the system. You decide first to construct a model of the system. What would be the components, variables, and relationships in your model?

7. Distinguish between descriptive and normative mathematical models. Give an example of each and explain your choice.

REFERENCES

Periodicals

DASH, JOSEPH F. and CONRAD BERENSON. "Techniques in Marketing Research," *Harvard Business Review*, Vol. 47 (September–October, 1969), pp. 14–26, 155.

LAZER, WILLIAM. "The Role of Models in Marketing," *Journal of Marketing*, Vol. 26 (April, 1962), pp. 9–14.

LIPSON, HARRY A. "Formal Reasoning and Marketing Strategy," *Journal of Marketing*, Vol. 26 (October, 1962), pp. 1–5.

STARR, MARTIN K. "Management Science and Marketing Science," *Management Science*, Vol. 10 (April, 1964), pp. 557–573.

Books

CABELL, R. W. and PHILLIPS, A. *Basic Operations Research Methods.* New York: John Wiley & Sons, Inc., 1961.

CHURCHMAN, C. W., ACKOFF, R. L. and E. L. ARNOFF. *Introduction to Operations Research.* New York: John Wiley & Sons, Inc., 1957.

KING, WILLIAM R. *Quantitative Analysis for Marketing Management.* New York: McGraw-Hill Book Co., 1967.

MILLER, DAVID W., and STARR, MARTIN K. *Executive Decisions and Operations Research.* Englewood Cliffs, N.J.: Prentice-Hall, Inc., 1960.

MORRIS, WILLIAM T. *Management Science.* Englewood Cliffs, N.J.: Prentice-Hall, Inc., 1968.

SCHODERBEK, PETER. *Management Systems.* New York: McGraw-Hill Book Co., 1967.

PART II

Analytical concepts, tools, and techniques

chapter three
PROBABILITY

INTRODUCTION

Before a marketing decision maker can comprehend the use of statistics in reaching marketing decisions, he should possess a basic understanding of some of the more important aspects of probability. The development and study of probability began in 17th-Century France, a time when gambling was a popular pastime of the French nobility. One gambler in particular, Chevalier de Mere, was both puzzled and fascinated by the gambling odds which confronted those persons participating in gambling activities. Because of his interest de Mere sought the aid of a noted mathematician of the time, Blaise Pascal, to shed some light on the mysteries of gambling odds. Pascal and a friend, Pierre de Fermat, became interested in the problems of chance and carried on correspondence about these problems. Thus, this interest of two mathematicians in 17th-Century France was the beginning of what today is referred to as the mathematical theory of probability.

Although the ground was broken in studying probability over three centuries ago, business executives and scientists from many different disciplines are just beginning to apply various probability concepts to business-related problems. Some of the currently available presentations of probability utilize highly rigorous mathematics, but we can learn the basic concepts which are of value to the marketing manager without recourse to such sophisticated techniques as differential and integral calculus. Thus, the purpose of this chapter is to introduce the reader to the fundamentals of probability without becoming entangled in mathematical proofs and notation.

PROBABILITY AND OTHER RELATED CONCEPTS DEFINED

Each of the events that a person must cope with and can observe in his everyday activities may be categorized in one of two ways. First, there are

31

events that are absolutely certain to happen. An example of events belonging in this category would be the aging process of man: as each day passes we become chronologically older. Other examples would be obtaining either a head or tail on one flip of an ordinary unbiased coin or the eventual stopping of an automobile that has not been replenished with gasoline in a mileage contest.

The second category consists of all events that may or may not occur at any one specific point in time or over a specified interval of time. Obtaining a head on one flip of a fair coin and the stopping of the automobile exactly 300 miles after the gasoline tank is filled are examples in this category. These types of events are the crux of what is referred to as "probability theory."

It is of interest to those involved in a coin flipping game or the automobile mileage contest to know the probabilities of occurrence of these events. For example, the probability of an automobile traveling a specified distance without refueling with gasoline depends upon such factors as when the tank was previously filled, the engine size, and whether driving occurs within the city limits or on super highways.

The notion of probability has been defined by many scholars and in many different ways. A number of writers have attempted to define probability as a long-run relative frequency. Thus, the probability p of obtaining some event E in an experiment in which the outcome is determined by chance would be defined as

$$p = \lim_{t \to \infty} \frac{t_E}{t}$$

where t_E is the number of times the outcome was E in t trials of the experiment. This mathematical notation is read the probability of E is the limit as t becomes arbitrarily large of the relative frequency of E.[1] This definition of probability has a major limitation. Namely, it only has a conceptual interpretation and no operational one, since in the real world a researcher or decision maker can only perform an experiment a finite number of times.[2] However, the fact that the frequency definition is not adequate does not imply that one cannot think of probabilities intuitively as being numerically equal to long-run relative frequencies when the experiment is capable of repetition. Thus, we are in agreement with Hadley that it is most convenient to think of prob-

---

[1] For an excellent discussion of this concept and its limitations see, G. Hadley, *Introduction to Probability and Statistical Decision Theory* (San Francisco: Holden-Day, Inc., 1967), pp. 10–11.

[2] *Ibid.*

ability as a basic concept and not attempt to provide a rigorous definition for the term. Attempting to define probability leads to mathematical difficulties and no definition can serve to cover all the situations which face a marketing manager. For each situation discussed in the text a specific reference as to what is meant by the probability of occurrence will be made.

BASIC PROBABILITY TERMINOLOGY

In order to understand probability concepts the terminology used by those working in this area of study should be understood. Thus, some of the more basic concepts are presented and discussed in this section.

Experiments, Trials, and Events

Probabilities are related to the outcomes of phenomena that can be observed. These phenomena, together with the actual observation, are called *experiments*. Thus, advertising a product in medium (X_1) or in medium (X_2) and observing the promotional strategy impact on sales are experiments in the probability sense.

When an experiment is carried out one time it is referred to as a *trial*. Thus, although the statement "measure the advertising effectiveness of ads in media X_1 and X_2" defines an experiment, a review of the sales records after advertising for a month, for example, constitutes a trial.

An outcome of a single trial of an experiment is referred to as an *event*. Thus, monthly sales of $10,000 for the product advertised in X_1 is one event associated with a trial of the experiment "observe the December sales of the product advertised in X_1."

Mutually Exclusive Events

The outcomes of a trial or experiment are "mutually exclusive" if the occurrence of any one of them makes the simultaneous occurrence of any other outcome virtually impossible. Assume that an experiment consists of drawing only one card from a normal deck of 52 cards. There are 52 possible outcomes which are both "mutually exclusive" and "equally likely." They are mutually exclusive because if the resulting outcome of the single draw is a ten of hearts, this would make impossible the simultaneous occurrence of the other 51 outcomes. The outcomes are equally likely since each card in the regular deck has an equal chance of being selected.

Chance

The term "chance" is used to denote the process by which an outcome or event is generated from an experiment or trial, assuming no known reasons or assignable causes are available to account for the particular event or outcome observed when the trial or experiment is performed. Trials, experiments, events, and outcomes influenced by chance are described as chance trials, chance experiments, chance events, and chance outcomes. In the quantitative marketing literature today, the terms "probabilistic," "random," and "stochastic" are synonymous with the term "chance."

Independence and Dependence

Events are classified as either independent or dependent. If two events are statistically independent, the occurrence of one of them will not affect the probability of the occurrence of the other.

If a gambler draws a heart from a deck of regular playing cards, replaces the card in the deck, and draws a second card, the probability of the second draw is in no way influenced by the first draw. The events are independent of each other.

Two events are dependent if the occurrence of one of the events will affect the probability of occurrence of the other. If a gambler draws a heart on the first draw and fails to replace this card before drawing a second card, the probability of drawing a second heart is affected by the first draw. The probability of drawing the first heart is 13/52, and the probability of selecting a second heart is 12/51.[3]

Population

In statistics, the word "population," which is synonymous with "universe," refers to the total category under consideration, be it all marketing managers in business firms or all students majoring in marketing at the undergraduate level. For example, assume that a store has sold 1,000 color television sets to 1,000 buyers and the owners are interested in a marketing research study which will provide them with information about the annual incomes of the

---

[3] The probability of selecting the first heart is the ratio defined by the number of ways that a heart may occur, 13 (the number of cards in a suit) divided by the number of possible outcomes, 52 (the number of cards in a deck). Each card has an equal likelihood of being drawn. The probability of selecting the second heart is the number of hearts left in the deck, twelve (assuming of course that the first card was a heart) divided by the number of cards left in the deck, 51.

purchasers of the televisions. Each set sold forms the elementary unit, and hence the population is the 1,000 buyers of the sets. The size of a population is denoted by capital N. A sample is a set of observations which are drawn from the population. If we select 20 percent of the population or 200 buyers, our sample is denoted as $n = 200$.

Interpretation of Probability

The probability of any event, for convenience, is expressed by numbers that lie between zero and one. Impossible events have a probability of 0 and certain events have a probability of one. Uncertain but not impossible events —i.e., events that may or may not occur in any one trial—have a probability (denoted by P) as follows: $0 < P < 1$.[4] The probabilities of uncertain events can be expressed as fractions, decimals, ratios, or percentages.

The closer the probability of an uncertain event is to one, the more likely it is to occur. This is logical since the closer the probability is to one, the greater is the relative number of outcomes in the experiment possessing the characteristic associated with the event, and hence, the greater the chance of one of these outcomes occurring and being observed.

Let us examine a probability problem involving the sale of a product. Assume that the probability of selling exactly 1,000 green Christmas tree lights during the holiday season is calculated, based on past sales experience, to be 1/10. This is the probability of an uncertain event, which can also be expressed as .10, one chance in 10, or as 10 percent.

The event is described as being uncertain because the probability of occurrence lies between zero and one. The probability of .10 does not mean that the store will sell 1,000 green Christmas tree lights every 10 years. Rather it means that if the sales of Christmas tree lights are observed for some time, the long-run ratio of the number of times 1,000 green lights are sold to the number of trials or experiments, will approach .10. Another example of this point is the coin flipping case. The probability of flipping a head on an unbiased regular coin is .5. This does not mean that a head will be observed every two flips, but that over the long-run the number of heads observed will approach the ratio of one out of two or .5.[5]

---

[4] The symbolic representation $0 < P < 1$ denotes that probabilities (P) range from zero to one. The sign $<$ stands for less than.

[5] The long run is emphasized because increased observations increases the accuracy of an estimate by masking chance variances. The person flipping the coin may not flip it with the same force each time. Thus, there may be a run of heads followed by a run of tails. But, for 1,000 flips there should be 500 heads and 500 tails. The apparent bias in the short run is eliminated by the canceling effect of variances in the long run.

A MATHEMATICAL PRESENTATION OF PROBABILITY

Since we are not rigorously defining probability in a universal sense, it is best to specify for each situation what the interpretation is. We will use in this section the following notation for denoting the probability of an event:

$$P \text{ (any event which we are concerned with)} = P(E) \qquad (3\text{–}1)$$

The type of event is usually indicated in an abbreviated manner in parentheses after the notation P. For example, $P(He) =$ probability of a heart from a deck of cards, $P(T) =$ probability of obtaining a tail on one toss of a fair coin, $P(U_s) =$ probability of units of a product being sold by a retail store. The abbreviation in parentheses will always be discussed by the writers before the reader is introduced to the probability equation.

The definition of probability cited can be expressed as follows:

$$P \text{ (event)} = \frac{\text{number of events that can yield the desired outcome}}{\text{total number of equally likely outcomes}}$$

Assume that we are primarily concerned with finding the probability of drawing a heart on a draw from a regular deck of playing cards. What is the proper mathematical formula to use and what is the probability of drawing a heart? If S is a success and F is a failure, symbolically the probability of a success is denoted as:

$$P(S) = \frac{S}{S + F} \qquad (3\text{–}2)$$

Since every unit in the population has an equal chance of occurring on one draw (otherwise it would not be in the particular population in question), then the population must be the sum of successful (desired) outcomes and failures (undesired outcomes) as there is no third alternative and no possibility of a combination. Thus the denominator is $S + F$.

The probability of failure is found by using the formula:

$$P(F) = 1 - \frac{S}{S + F} \qquad (3\text{–}3)$$

One can be certain for a given event that it will either be a success or a failure. Therefore, the sum of the probability of success and the probability of failure must equal one. Thus, given the probability of success, the probability of failure is merely its complement, or one minus the probability of success.

Using our drawing of a heart as an example of a success and substituting in the proper values and abbreviations, we find:

$$P \text{ (heart)} = \frac{13}{13 + 39} = \frac{13}{52} = \frac{1}{4}$$

The probability of a heart not being drawn on the single draw is found by using the following formulas:

$$P \text{ (no heart)} = 1 - \frac{S}{S + F}$$

$$P \text{ (no heart)} = 1 - \frac{13}{13 + 39} = 1 - \frac{13}{52}$$

$$P \text{ (no heart)} = 1 - \frac{1}{4} = \frac{3}{4}$$

Fundamental Theorems of Probability

In order to continue our discussion and improve our knowledge of probability concepts, it is essential to understand two important probability theorems. One of these is called the *addition theorem* and the other is referred

TABLE 3–1

Probability Distribution of Pure Food and Drug Administration
Review Periods and Acceptance Rates

Drug Status Rate: Events	Probability
E_1 = Reviewed one month and accepted	60/100 = .60
E_2 = Reviewed two months and accepted	30/100 = .30
E_3 = Reviewed three months and accepted	8/100 = .08
E_4 = Reviewed four months and accepted	2/100 = .02
Total	1.00

to as the *multiplication theorem.* Before we present the theorems, let us first examine a probability distribution:[6] the distribution of having a new product of a pharmaceutical house accepted as being marketable by the Pure Food and Drug Administration. These are products that have been carefully tested by research and development teams of the company. Assume that all products reviewed by the Federal Agency are accepted, but at different rates. These rates are shown in Table 3–1. The marketing manager would like to estimate approximately when he can begin preliminary promotion of the product throughout the trade.

[6] A probability distribution is a mutually exclusive and exhaustive list of all the events which may result from a chance process and the probability associated with each.

The *addition theorem* of probability is defined as follows:

The probability that one of several mutually exclusive events will occur is equal to the sum of their individual probabilities.

This definition may be presented mathematically by using Equation 3–4. The notations E are used to denote events. Thus,

$$P(E_1 \text{ or } E_2 \text{ or } E_3 \text{ or } \ldots E_n) = P(E_1) + P(E_2) + P(E_3) + \cdots P(E_n)$$
$$= \sum_{i=1}^{n} P(E_i) \tag{3–4}$$

As stated previously, events are mutually exclusive if the occurrence of one of the events makes it impossible for any of the other events to occur at the same time. The following problem may be solved by applying the addition theorem and mathematical formula (3–4). Suppose we are interested in knowing what our chances of having a product accepted in two or three months. This problem may be solved by reviewing Table 3–1, the probability distribution of Pure Food and Drug Administration review periods and acceptance rates or by utilizing the addition theorem.

$P(E_2 \text{ or } E_3)$
$$= P(E_2 \ldots \text{ two months review}) + P(E_3 \ldots \text{ three months review})$$

$$P(E_2 \text{ or } E_3) = .30 + .08 = .38$$

Thus, the chances of having a product reviewed and accepted in either two or three months is .38.

The multiplication theorem is widely employed in discussions of probability. The *multiplication theorem* for independent events may be defined as follows:

The probability that all of several independent events will occur is equal to the product of their separate probabilities.

This definition may be presented mathematically by using Equation 3–5.

$P(E_1 \text{ and } E_2 \text{ and } E_3 \text{ and } \ldots E_n)$
$$= P(E_1) \times P(E_2) \times P(E_3) \times \ldots P(E_n) \tag{3–5}$$

An event is considered independent if its occurrence has no effect upon the occurrence of other events. That is to say that if one particular event occurs, the others may or may not occur. Utilizing Equation 3–5 we can determine the probability of having two new products reviewed separately and both accepted in one month.

$P(E_1 \text{ and } E_1) = P(E_1 \ldots \text{ one month review}) \times P(E_1 \ldots \text{ one month review})$

$P(E_1 \text{ and } E_1) = .6 \times .6 = .36$

Marginal, Joint, and Conditional Probabilities

To explain some additional concepts related to probability let us consider a problem situation. Suppose that a firm produces a living room coffee table in two models (T_1 and T_2) and that each of these models is sold with special accessories (such as a marble top, a slate top, and a formica top). The three accessories are designated as *M*, *S*, and *F*. The marketing manager has studied the sales of the six possible combinations of the models and accessories. The relative frequencies of occurrence of sales are shown in Table 3–2.

TABLE 3–2

Model and Accessory Sales Frequencies

Models	Accessory Groups		
	M(A_1)	S(A_2)	F(A_3)
T_1	.05	.10	.05
T_2	.25	.40	.15

Since the combinations are mutually exclusive, the sum of the entries in the table is one. Also since the table deals in relative frequencies, it may be interpreted as showing the probability of selling the various combinations of tables and tops.

The probability of the two events in each combination occurring together is defined as the joint probability of T_i and A_j. The mathematical notation used to specify the joint probability is:

$$P(T_i A_j) \qquad \text{or} \qquad P(T_i, A_j)$$

The six joint probabilities for the coffee table problem are:

$P(T_1 A_1) = .05 \qquad P(T_1 A_3) = .05 \qquad P(T_2 A_2) = .40$

$P(T_1 A_2) = .10 \qquad P(T_2 A_1) = .25 \qquad P(T_2 A_3) = .15$

These probabilities indicate the chances of selling a particular table with a particular top. For example, $P(T_1 A_1)$ is interpreted as the probability of selling a T_1 model with a marble top. The order inside the joint probability notation does not affect the probability. Thus, $P(A_1 T_1) = .05$.

The data presented in Table 3–2 can also be analyzed as a *conditional probability*. If we ask ourselves what the probability is of selling a marble top table (A_1), given that a T_1 model is sold, we are inquiring about conditional probability. The probability of A_1 occurring, given that T_1 occurs, is presented as

$$P(A_1|T_1)$$

Since the conditional probability is interpreted to mean that it is known that T_1 occurs, only the first row of Table 3–2 needs to be considered in finding the conditional probability. The numbers in the T_1 row indicate that when it is known that

$$
\begin{array}{cccc}
 & M(A_1) & S(A_2) & F(A_3) \\
\hline
T_1 & .05 & .10 & .05
\end{array}
$$

T_1 is sold, the chances that a marble top was sold (A_1) are five out of 20 or 25 percent, the chances that a slate top was sold (A_2) are 10 out of 20 or 50 percent, and the chances that a formica top was sold (A_3) are five out of 20 or 25 percent. If the mathematical formulas are used to represent these conditional probabilities, we have

$$
\begin{aligned}
P(A_1|T_1) &= 5/20 = .25 \\
P(A_2|T_1) &= 10/20 = .50 \\
P(A_3|T_1) &= 5/20 = .25
\end{aligned}
$$

Since A_1, A_2, and A_3 are mutually exclusive, we can combine the conditional probability concept with our knowledge of the addition theorem for mutually exclusive events to generate the following:

$$
\begin{aligned}
P(A_1 \text{ or } A_2 \text{ or } A_3|T_1) &= P(A_1|T_1) + P(A_2|T_1) + P(A_3|T_1) \\
&= .25 + .50 + .25 \\
&= 1.00
\end{aligned}
$$

The result is not unexpected since it is certain that if T_1 is sold, then one of the three tops A_1, A_2 or A_3 will be on the table. Similarly,

$$
\begin{aligned}
P(A_1 \text{ or } A_2|T_1) &= P(A_1|T_1) + P(A_2|T_1) \\
&= .25 + .50 \\
&= .75
\end{aligned}
$$

The concept of *marginal probability* can be derived from Table 3–2. A reproduction of this table with the sums of the row and column probabilities is shown in Table 3–3.

The values which indicate the individual probabilities of T_1, T_2, A_1, A_2, and A_3 are known as marginal probabilities.

TABLE 3–3

Reproduction of Table 3–2 with Marginal Probabilities

	Accessory Groups			
Models	$M(A_1)$	$S(A_2)$	$F(A_3)$	*Marginal Probabilities*
T_1	.05	.10	.05	$P(T_1) = .20$
T_2	.25	.40	.15	$P(T_2) = .80$
Marginal Probabilities	$P(A_1) = .30$	$P(A_2) = .50$	$P(A_3) = .20$	

At the outset of this section it was mentioned that the Table 3–2 values indicated the joint probability for the various combinations of tables and accessory groups. We can show that the following is also true:

$$P(T_iA_j) = P(T_i)P(A_j|T_i)$$

This notation is interpreted to mean that the joint probability of T_i and A_j is the product of the conditional probability $P(A_j|T_i)$ that A_j occurs given that T_i occurs, and the marginal probability $P(T_i)$ that T_i occurs. If we use our data in Table 3–3 we can verify this reasoning.

$$\begin{aligned} P(T_1A_2) &= P(T_1)P(A_2|T_1) \\ &= .20 \times .50 \\ &= .10 \end{aligned}$$

It can also be shown that the following is true:

$$\begin{aligned} P(T_1A_2) &= P(A_2)P(T_1|A_2) \\ &= .50 \times .20 \\ &= .10 \end{aligned}$$

In general, the joint probability of events E_1 and E_2 occurring is given by

$$P(E_1E_2) = P(E_1)P(E_2|E_1)$$
$$P(E_1E_2) = P(E_2)P(E_1|E_2)$$

It then follows that

$$P(E_2|E_1) = \frac{P(E_1E_2)}{P(E_1)}$$

and

$$P(E_1|E_2) = \frac{P(E_1E_2)}{P(E_2)}$$

These are the general formulas for conditional probability.

The marketing decision maker may be concerned with whether the choices made by consumers in purchasing a coffee table with a particular top are independent of each other. If the choice of a top and a table were independent of each other, it would be expected that the probability of choosing a top would be the same regardless of whether table T_1 or T_2 had been chosen. When the choices of tables and tops are independent, the following conditional probability equations would be valid:

$$P(A_1|T_1) = P(A_1|T_2)$$
$$P(A_2|T_1) = P(A_2|T_2)$$
$$P(A_3|T_1) = P(A_3|T_2)$$

and

$$P(T_1|A_1) = P(T_1|A_2) = P(T_1|A_3)$$
$$P(T_2|A_1) = P(T_2|A_2) = P(T_2|A_3)$$

A review of Table 3–3 indicates that these equations are not true and that the choice of a table top is not independent of the choice of a table, or conversely, the choice of a table is not independent of the choice of a table top.

In general, if events E_1 and E_2 are independent of each other

$$P(E_1) = P(E_1|E_2)$$

The probability of E_1 occurring is not affected by the fact E_2 occurs or does not occur. Then,

$$P(E_2) = P(E_2|E_1)$$

We also find that when events E_1 and E_2 are independent, the mathematical notation for joint probabilities is then,

$$P(E_1E_2) = P(E_1)P(E_2|E_1)$$
$$P(E_1E_2) = P(E_2)P(E_1|E_2)$$

These equations are reduced to simply read the following:

$$P(E_1E_2) = P(E_1)P(E_2)$$
$$P(E_1E_2) = P(E_2)P(E_1)$$

Thus, to find the joint probability of independent events, we used the previously discussed multiplication theorem.

$$P(E_1, E_2 \ldots E_n) = P(E_1)P(E_2) \ldots P(E_n)$$

The three forms of probability under conditions of statistical independence are summarized mathematically in Table 3–4.

TABLE 3–4

Summary of Formulas for Marginal, Joint, and Conditional Probability under Conditions of Independence

Probability	Symbolic Format	Formula
1. Marginal	$P(E_1)$	$P(E_1)$
2. Joint	$P(E_1E_2)$	$P(E_1) \times P(E_2)$
3. Conditional	$P(E_1|E_2)$	$P(E_1)$

A brief summary of the formulas used to analyze a situation in which statistical dependence must be coped with is presented in Table 3–5.

TABLE 3–5

Summary of Formulas for Marginal, Joint, and Conditional Probability under Conditions of Dependence

Probability	Symbolic Format	Formula
1. Marginal	$P(E_1)$	$P(E_1)$
2. Joint	$P(E_1E_2)$	$P(E_1|E_2) \times P(E_2)$
3. Conditional	$P(E_1|E_2)$	$\dfrac{P(E_1E_2)}{P(E_2)}$

Integrating the Three Probabilities into a Problem Involving Independence

To acquire a better understanding of marginal, joint, and conditional probabilities under conditions of independence, let us work through a problem. Assume we have three containers which contain yellow and green colored disks in the following proportions:

> Container 1: 2 yellow and 8 green
> Container 2: 4 yellow and 6 green
> Container 3: 7 yellow and 3 green

Suppose we formulate a game in which we draw one disk from Container 1; if it is yellow we draw our second disk from Container 2. If the disk drawn from Container 1 is green, we draw our second disk from Container 3. Figure 3–1 summarizes this hypothetical game.

Applying what we have learned from our discussion of probability concepts, the following type questions about the game can be answered.

1. What is the probability of drawing a green disk from Container 1 on a single draw? This is simply the *marginal* probability of drawing a green disk or

$P(G_1) = \frac{8}{10}$ or .8. The probability of drawing a yellow disk on the first draw is $P(Y_1) = \frac{2}{10}$ or .2.

2. If we select by "chance" a green disk from Container 1, what is the probability of getting a green disk from Container 3? This is an example of *conditional* probability, that is, the probability of a green disk on the second

FIGURE 3–1

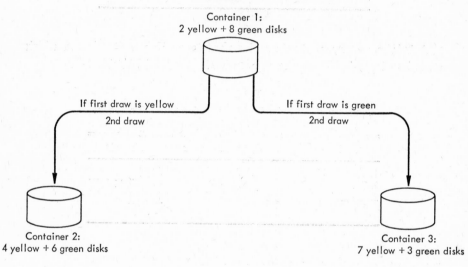

draw if we initially select a green disk from Container 1. The answer is $P(G_2|G_1) = P(G_2) = \frac{3}{10}$ or .3.

3. If you were asked before the game starts to determine the probability of drawing two successive yellow disks, this would simply mean using the *joint* probabilities. The answer to this question is $P(Y_1Y_2) = P(Y_1) \times P(Y_2) = .2 \times .4 = .08$.

The joint probabilities for this problem are as follows:

$$
\begin{array}{rl}
P(Y_1Y_2) = & .08 \\
P(Y_1G_1) = & .12 \\
P(G_1Y_1) = & .56 \\
P(G_1G_2) = & \underline{.24} \\
\text{Total} & 1.00
\end{array}
$$

A tree diagram Figure 3–2 can clearly display this game.

The three probabilities for the possible events can be arranged in tabular format as presented in Table 3–6.

FIGURE 3–2

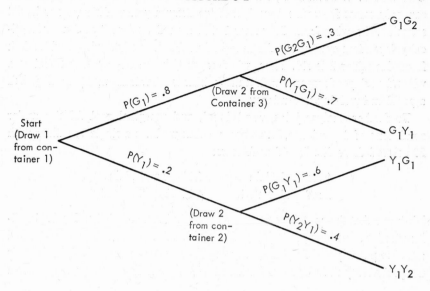

TABLE 3–6

Marginal, Joint, and Conditional Probabilities for Game

Event	Marginal	×	Conditional	=	Joint
Y_1Y_2	$P(Y_1) = .2$		$P(Y_2|Y_1) = .4$		$P(Y_1Y_2) = .08$
Y_1G_1	$P(Y_1) = .2$		$P(G_1|Y_1) = .6$		$P(Y_1G_1) = .12$
G_1Y_1	$P(G_1) = .8$		$P(Y_1|G_1) = .7$		$P(G_1Y_1) = .56$
G_1G_2	$P(G_1) = .8$		$P(G_2|G_1) = .3$		$P(G_1G_2) = .24$
					1.00

Integrating the Three Probabilities into a Problem Involving Dependence

Suppose we alter the game just discussed by adding one white disk to Container 2 and subtracting one yellow disk. The mix of disks in each container would then be as follows:

> Container 1: 2 yellow and 8 green
> Container 2: 3 yellow, 6 green, and 1 white
> Container 3: 7 yellow and 3 green

The rules of the game remain as previously outlined. Is the probability of drawing a white disk affected by the color of the initial disk drawn from

Container 1? It certainly is, since only Container 2 has a white disk and we can only select from this container if we draw a yellow disk on our initial selection. Drawing from Container 1 and then Container 2 or 3 are statistically dependent events; but the marginal probability of drawing a white disk from Container 2 is .10. Thus, whether we have an opportunity to select a white disk depends upon our first draw. This is what is meant by dealing with a problem involving dependency.

To further analyze joint, conditional, and marginal probabilities under conditions of dependence, let us assume that we have a single container with 20 colored disks distributed as follows:

4 red and plain	6 black and plain
6 red and dotted	4 black and dotted

We know that the container contains 10 red and 10 black disks. The probability of red is .5 and the probability of black is .5. A volunteer is blindfolded and asked to participate in a probability exercise. He selects a single disk. What is the probability that his selection is red and dotted? If he utilizes the formula

$$P(RD) = P(R|D) \times P(D)$$
$$P(RD) = .6 \times .5 = .3$$

to find the joint probability of a red and dotted selection, he can solve his problem. The probability of a red and dotted disk under conditions of dependence is .3.

The reader should note that the marginal probability of the events red or black can be formed by summing the probabilities of joint events in which red and black is contained.

$$P(R) = P(RP) + P(RD)$$
$$P(R) = .2 + .3 = .5$$

and

$$P(B) = P(BP) + P(BD)$$
$$P(B) = .3 + .2 = .5$$

Since color affects the probability of plain and dotted, these events can be said to be dependent. Utilizing the container with the 20 colored disks, what is the conditional probability of selecting plain given black, $P(P|B)$? This conditional probability is found by utilizing the general formula

$$P(E_1|E_2) = \frac{P(E_1E_2)}{P(E_2)}$$

Adapting it to this example yields

$$P(P|B) = \frac{P(PB)}{P(B)}$$

where

$$P(PB) = P(B|P) \times P(P) = .6 \times .5 = .3$$
$$P(P|B) = \frac{.3}{.5} = .6$$

The conditional probability of dotted given black is found by using:

$$P(D|B) = \frac{P(DB)}{P(B)}$$
$$P(D|B) = \frac{.2}{.5} = .4$$

The reader should review the terminology, theorems, and other concepts presented in this chapter before attempting to understand and work problems which are covered in the applications chapters of the text. This type of review should allow the reader to comprehend the more sophisticated quantitative models and tools discussed in resolving distribution, product, promotion, and pricing problems facing marketing decision makers.

PROBLEMS

1. Discuss the following statements:

(a) "There is a 1.8 probability that a student will successfully pass the quantitative marketing course."

(b) "The probability of the New York Mets baseball team winning a ball game on any given date is $-.65$."

(c) "There is a probability of .60 that it will snow on Christmas Day this year and a probability of .65 that it will not snow."

2. Discuss whether the following events are independent or dependent:

(a) Procter and Gamble selling over 10,000 tubes of Crest toothpaste in one year.

(b) The Chicago White Sox winning the American League pennant.

(c) The Detroit Tigers winning the World Series in four straight games.

(d) An I.G.A. supermarket running out of bread and milk the day before Thanksgiving.

3. Assume that you are flipping a fair coin. Determine the following:

(a) In one toss the probability of:
   1) One tail

(b) In three tosses the probability of:
   1) Two heads and a tail

     2) Three heads

     3) Three tails

4. Assume that you are flipping an unfair coin which has a .80 probability of heads and a .20 probability of tails. Determine the following:

    (a) In two tosses the probability of:

     1) One tail

     2) One head

     3) Two heads

     4) Two tails

5. Assume that there are two containers with ten colored disks:

Container 1: 7 blue and 3 gold
Container 2: 5 blue and 5 gold

There is an equal probability of choosing each container. You have one draw and find that you have selected a gold colored disk. You want to know which container you have selected from.

    (a) What is the probability that you drew the disk from Container 2?

    (b) If the disk is blue, what is the probability that you drew the disk from Container 1? From Container 2?

6. Assume that there are three containers with the following combinations of colored disks:

Container 1: 8 black and 2 white
Container 2: 4 black and 6 white
Container 3: 6 black and 4 white

The game which you are playing has the following set of rules: You are to select one disk from Container 1. If you pick a black disk, your second draw of a disk will be from Container 2. If you pick a white disk on the first draw from Container 1, your second draw will be from Container 3.

    (a) What is the P (white on second draw, given black on draw one)?

    (b) What is the P (white on second draw, given white on draw one)?

    (c) What is the P (black on second draw, given black on draw one)?

    (d) What is the P (black on second draw, given white on draw one)?

7. Draw a tree diagram presenting the game described in the preceding problem (number 6).

8. What is the probability of getting two diamonds in two successive draws from a regular deck of playing cards if:

    (a) the first card is replaced before the second is drawn.

    (b) the first card is not replaced before the second is drawn.

9. Assume that a marketing manager is interested in learning about the joint, conditional, and marginal probabilities of selling a lamp. The lamp is sold in two forms—metal and plastic. These two types of lamps can be sold with a one-way, two-way, or three-way switch. The relative frequencies of occurrence of sales of the lamps are presented below:

Type of Lamp (L)	Switch		
	1-Way (S_1)	*2-Way* (S_2)	*3-Way* (S_3)
Metal (L_1)	.03	.06	.36
Plastic (L_2)	.10	.30	.15

(a) Establish the mathematical formulas for calculating the six possible joint probabilities for this problem.

(b) What are the conditional probabilities for: $P(S_2|L_1)$; $P(S_3|L_2)$; $P(S_1, S_2,$ or $S_3|L_2)$?

(c) What are the five marginal probabilities for this problem?

(d) Is the choice of buying a particular type of lamp independent of the type of switch? How can you tell if the problem involves independence or dependence?

REFERENCES

Elementary treatments of the theory of probability may be found in:

LEVINSON, H. C. *Chance, Luck, and Statistics.* New York: Dover Publications, Inc., 1963.

NELSON, BOYD L. *Elements of Modern Statistics.* New York: Appleton-Century-Crofts, Inc., 1961.

WESSEL, ROBERT H., WILLETT, EDWARD R., and SIMONE, ALBERT J. *Statistics as Applied to Business and Economics.* New York: Holt, Rinehart, and Winston, Inc., 1966.

More advanced treatments of probability and statistics are found in:

CROXTON, FREDERICK E., and COWDEN, DUDLEY J. *Practical Business Statistics.* Englewood Cliffs, N.J.: Prentice-Hall, Inc., 1960.

HOWELL, JAMES E. and TEICHROEW, DANIEL. *Mathematical Analysis for Business Decisions.* Homewood, Ill.: Richard D. Irwin, Inc., 1963.

PETERS, WILLIAM S. and SUMMERS, GEORGE V. *Statistical Analysis for Business Decisions.* Englewood Cliffs, N.J.: Prentice-Hall, Inc., 1968.

YAMANE, TARO. *Statistics, An Introductory Analysis.* New York: Harper & Row, Publishers, 1967.

chapter four
DECISION THEORY

INTRODUCTION

Decision making is a necessary phase of marketing programs in every proprietorship, partnership, or corporation. In the last decade the systematic analysis of decision problems within a conceptual framework has become known as "decision theory." This term has been associated with sophisticated statistical techniques and there are many writers who project the impression that powerful mathematical and statistical methodologies must be employed to reap maximum benefits from decision theory. These impressions are inaccurate and misrepresent the vast potential of decision theory. The basic concepts of this field of study can be fully comprehended, appreciated, and applied to selected marketing problem situations without a working understanding of high-powered mathematics or elaborate statistical procedures. This chapter is designed so that the concepts of decision theory are presented in such a manner that the reader with a minimum background in mathematics and statistics can comprehend the value and limitations of decision theory.

It is practical to view decision making as an orderly process which involves a number of distinct steps.[1] First, the decision maker has to identify specific problems that require solutions. Second, it is necessary to consider and define the variables affecting the problems. Third, it is necessary to develop one or more feasible strategies which can possibly resolve the problems. Fourth, the decision maker must make a choice and select that strategy which he believes will result in the best outcome. Finally, the strategy must be implemented and evaluated for effectiveness by the decision maker. The fourth step of this five-step process is normally associated with the study of decision theory and will be the main topic covered in this chapter.

---

[1] Herbert Simon, *The Science of Management Decisions* (New York: Harper & Brothers, 1960), p. 1.

The Complex Marketing Environment

The marketing manager, in reaching product, promotion, pricing, or distribution decisions, must cope with environmental forces that are both controllable and uncontrollable. For example, assume that a manager is analyzing a physical distribution situation in which he must ship a large durable product from the West Coast to the East Coast. The manager would consider such factors as the mode of transportation used for shipment, the cost of transportation, and the packaging utilized as controllable factors. Other factors such as the strike potential of unionized personnel involved in transporting the product and the weather conditions and their impact on product movement might be perceived as uncontrollable. The interaction of these two sets of variables are what makes the manager's strategy selection task difficult.

In decision theory the variables that are considered controllable are designated as strategies (S_i). The decision maker usually develops a number of strategies and eventually he must select one strategy. He, of course, can control which strategy is chosen but is not always able to select the most optimum strategy because of the uncontrollable variables operating within his decision-making environment.

Two factors which significantly influence the consequences of selecting a strategy are the states of nature (SN_i) and competitive actions (CA_i). These uncontrollable factors, plus the strategy selected, interact to yield a highly desirable, a highly unattractive, or an unclear and vague end-result.

The states of nature are completely uncontrollable from the vantage point of the decision maker. For example, a manufacturer of military helicopters knows that the accuracy of his production forecasts will depend in large measure upon the military and political attitudes of various East-West political leaders. Similarly, a food processing executive in a firm which specializes in the sale of lemonade who is faced with the problem of how many cases to produce for the coming summer season, knows that the success of his forecasts will depend in large measure upon the summer weather conditions. Generally, there are an overwhelming number of states of nature that can occur. It would be impossible to list them all and to determine the effects that each might have on a problem solving situation and outcome. Normally the decision maker would consider only those states of nature which are most likely to occur and would not become entangled in an endless list of uncontrollable factors which might occur. The opinions and experiences of the decision maker reduces the number of states of nature that are given serious consideration.

A second major category of uncontrollable factors is the competitive actions of market opponents. In many instances, the success of capturing a significant share of the market, improving profit margin, or decreasing the costs of distributing a product will be affected by the actions of competitors. The actions of competitors are, of course, difficult to gauge. Thus, the activities of competitors in response to a particular strategy are perceived as being uncontrollable.

Utility of a Decision

Each decision made by a manager is designed to achieve some objective or set of objectives. The outcome of each decision reached yields some form of utility to the decision maker. The form which the utility of an outcome takes may be psychological or economic.

The main concept to remember when discussing utility is that the reward received from each individual outcome is subjective. That is, each decision maker has his own conception of what each outcome provides him in the form of psychological gratification and/or economic benefits. There is no specific scientific procedure which can compare in an orderly and systematic fashion the utilities of different individuals. If, however, it were possible to accurately determine the utility derived by a decision maker for each outcome, the utility concept could then be expressed mathematically. The outcomes could be viewed as the "payoff" to the decision maker which results from the interaction of strategies, states of nature, and competitive actions. This relationship would then be

$$U = f(S,SN,CA)$$

which is read U is a function (f) of S,SN,CA, where U designates utility, S designates the strategy, SN designates the state of nature, and CA designates competitive actions. The two important factors to consider are that the three major variables—namely, the strategy, state of nature, and competitive action—are highly interrelated and the utility of the "payoff" as perceived by the decision maker is a subjective phenomenon. The opinions, attitudes, and beliefs of human beings may result in different selections of strategy among decision makers because of their different perceptions of the utility of the payoff. In a monetary sense, then, the payoff in dollars can have a different utility to managers faced with similar problems. A dollar to a street beggar has a higher utility than an additional dollar of oil royalties to a Texas millionaire.

The Payoff Matrix

There are many business decisions which result in payoffs and lend themselves to expression in mathematical terms. A commonly used procedure to present monetary payoffs in a matrix format is called a payoff table or matrix. The table presents the payoffs of each interrelationship of the strategies, states of nature, and competitive actions in a two-dimensional array of figures. Each figure in the matrix represents some form of utility (i.e., payoff) to the decision maker for the occurrence of a specific event. A payoff matrix is presented in Table 4–1. The only variable included in the table that was not

TABLE 4–1

Payoff Matrix

	States of Nature			
Strategies	SN_1	SN_2	SN_3	.....................SN_z
S_1	P_{11}	P_{12}	P_{13}	----------------------------------
S_2	P_{21}	P_{22}	P_{23}	----------------------------------
S_3	P_{31}	P_{32}	P_{33}	----------------------------------
.	.	.	.	
.	.	.	.	
S_y				

previously designated are the P's, which are the payoffs to the decision maker, provided the particular state of nature occurs. Thus P_{11} is the payoff to the decision maker if Strategy One (S_1) is selected and State of Nature One (SN_1) occurs. It is found at the intersection of Row 1 and Column 1.

The matrix provides the decision maker with a means for systematically organizing pertinent information in an easy to follow manner. It must be remembered that use of a payoff matrix does not preclude the decision maker from making a strategy choice.

DECISION FRAMEWORKS AND CONDITIONS

There are three types of decision making conditions which may affect the selection of a specific strategy. Depending on the decision maker's knowledge of the states of nature and/or competitive actions, decisions are classified as occurring under conditions of (1) certainty, (2) risk, and (3) uncertainty.

Certainty

If a decision maker knows exactly what state of nature will occur or what his competitor's actions will be, he is said to be operating within a certainty framework. This would mean that only one column of the payoff matrix would be needed to make a decision. Although we would only have to examine the payoffs under one column this does not eliminate the many potential strategies that may have to be investigated. In other words, although only one column is utilized, a large number of strategies or rows may have to be considered before a selection occurs.

Let us illustrate a simple decision situation involving the packaging of a

TABLE 4–2

Packaging Decision: Certainty Condition

Strategies	State of Nature Revenue from Sales (SN₁)
S_1: spend $1	$180
S_2: spend $3	600
S_3: spend $5	⑦⑩⑩
S_4: spend $8	450

product. A marketing decision maker must decide whether to spend $1, $3, $5, or $8 per case to package his product. The range represents different expenditure levels because of the colors and art work used in developing the package. For example, the $1 per case cost would allow the art department of the firm to use only simple designs and black and white colors, while the $8 per case cost would allow the art department to present a colorful and artistic package. The total revenues to be generated are said to be known with certainty. These are presented as a state of nature in Table 4–2.

If the decision maker is primarily concerned with dollars of revenue, he will then select S_3. This example assumes that the ability to identify the revenue generated by using the different package designs is known with certainty. This is, of course, highly unlikely in the normal marketing situation. In the vast majority of marketing problem solving situations, the decision maker s not able to predict infallibly which state of nature or competitor action will transpire if he selects one strategy as opposed to another strategy. When the uncontrollable environmental factors are not known with certainty, the decision maker is said to be operating within an uncertainty or risk framework.

Expected Value, Conditional Value, and Decisions under Risk

In situations where the decision maker does not know for certain the probability of occurrence of the states of nature or competitive actions, he is acting under conditions of risk. For such decisions the concept of expected value is used. The expected value of any event (EV) is the value if the event should occur (the conditional value (CV)), multiplied by its probability of occurrence, (p). Thus, we have $EV = (CV) \times (p)$. Thus, for three possible outcomes the following equation would be utilized:

$$\text{Expected Value} = (CV_1)p_1 + (CV_2)p_2 + (CV_3)p_3$$

where $p_1 + p_2 + p_3 = 1$, since either CV_1, CV_2, or CV_3 must occur.

Suppose a retail store owner is attempting to determine how many loaves of bread to stock for Saturday. The bread is sold for \$.25 a loaf while the costs of purchasing the bread from the bakery is \$.15 a loaf. Any bread that is not sold at the end of the day represents a total loss to the manager. He has observed the following total demand for bread on 10 consecutive Saturdays.

Loaves Demanded	Number of Saturdays The Demand Occurred
61	3
62	3
63	2
64	1
65	1

The conditional values can be calculated by using the following formula for each demand level.

$$CV = (P \times Q_D) - (C \times Q_S)$$

where P designates price per loaf, Q_D designates quantity demanded (up to the quantity stocked since if the bread is not in stock it cannot be sold), C designates cost per loaf, and Q_S designates quantity supplied. The conditional values could then be presented in a conditional value matrix. Table 4–3 shows the conditional values for each supply strategy and demand state of nature.

For example, if 61 loaves are stocked and the loaves demanded are 64, using the formula we would get:

$$CV = (P \times Q_D) - (C \times Q_S)$$
$$CV = (.25 \times 61) - (.15 \times 61)$$
$$CV = 15.25 - 9.15$$
$$CV = 6.10$$

Similarly, if 65 loaves are stocked and 63 loaves are demanded, the conditional value would be:

$$CV = (P \times Q_D) - (C \times Q_S)$$
$$CV = (.25 \times 63) - (.15 \times 65)$$
$$CV = 15.75 - 9.75$$
$$CV = 6.00$$

The conditional value payoff table could be converted to an expected value matrix by using the probabilities of occurrence of each state of nature. These probabilities were obtained by the store manager by keeping accurate records

TABLE 4–3

Conditional Value ($)

Strategy Supply	State of Nature Demand				
	61	62	63	64	65
61	6.10	6.10	6.10	6.10	6.10
62	5.95	6.20	6.20	6.20	6.20
63	5.80	6.05	6.30	6.30	6.30
64	5.65	5.90	6.15	6.40	6.40
65	5.50	5.75	6.00	6.25	6.50

of his Saturday sales volume for the past 10 weeks. We know that $EV = (CV_1)p_1 + (CV_2)p_2 + \ldots (CV_n)p_n$. By constructing an expected value table we can convert the conditional values, which are conditioned in this problem by the demand for bread, to expected values. For example, $EV = (CV_1)(p_1)$, when 61 units are supplied and 61 units are demanded, is found by taking the conditional value from Table 4–3, 6.10, and multiplying it by the probability of occurrence of a demand of 61, which is .3. The expected value is then $(6.10)(.3) = 1.83$. This and other expected values are presented in Table 4–4. If the retail manager is interested in optimizing his monetary payoff from selling bread, he will select the strategy in which 62 loaves of bread are stocked on Saturday. The reason for stocking 62 loaves is that if the manager is faced with this decision for future Saturdays and the conditional values and probabilities remain the same, the average payoff expected over the long run would be greatest. This analysis assumes that the prices and costs of bread do not fluctuate and that the demand for the bread continues at the same level as that which existed during the 10-week observation period.

TABLE 4–4

Expected Value Table ($)

Strategy Supply	Demand States of Nature					Total Expected Value
	61 $p_1 = .3$	62 $p_2 = .3$	63 $p_3 = .2$	64 $p_4 = .1$	65 $p_5 = .1$	
61	1.83	1.83	1.22	.61	.61	6.10
62	1.79	1.86	1.24	.62	.62	6.13
63	1.74	1.82	1.26	.63	.63	6.08
64	1.70	1.77	1.23	.64	.64	5.98
65	1.65	1.73	1.20	.63	.65	5.86

Objective and Subjective Probabilities

The retail store manager determined the probabilities of occurrence of the levels of demand for bread on the basis of past experience. This type of probability is referred to as "objective." The situation under consideration must be a fairly stable one if the experience of the past is to form a valid basis for establishing probabilities that are used to select strategies in the future. For example, if the price and cost of bread fluctuates during different seasons of the year, the probabilities of a particular amount of bread being demanded on a Saturday may not be valid in reaching an optimum stocking decision.

In many marketing decisions the manager will not be able to ascertain from past experience a reliable and valid measure of objective probabilities. Under these circumstances he must resort to making a subjective estimate of the probabilities of occurrence of states of nature and/or competitive actions. For example, if a company is considering marketing one of two products which are in the pilot stage of development and these products are revolutionary and new, the decision maker would have no previous sales experience to aid in the formulation of probabilities of success or failure. Nevertheless, a decision must be made in a reasonable amount of time about which of the products will be marketed. Thus, the decision maker could employ subjective probabilities the same way objective probabilities are used to evaluate alternative strategies.

Decisions under Uncertainty

There exists decision situations in which it is not possible to develop experience based estimates (objective or subjective) for the occurrence of a certain state of nature or competitive action. If this is the case, the expected value derivation cannot occur as shown in Table 4–4. There are, however, a number of decision criteria that have been developed to help explain the decision making procedure followed by managers in selecting among alternative strategies under conditions of uncertainty.

Optimism Criterion: Maximax

Hurwicz[2] suggested that it is best to think optimistically about the occurrence of events influencing a decision. If this philosophy is followed, the decision maker should select that strategy under which it is possible for him to receive the most favorable payoff. In the situation in which the decision maker is completely optimistic, he would first examine the conditional value matrix. Then he would seek to maximize the maximum possible gain (maximax).

TABLE 4–5

Conditional Values for New Power Tool
(in thousands of dollars)

Strategies	Competitor Actions	
	CA_1, Do Nothing	CA_2, Lower Price
*S_1	8	2
†S_2	5	7

* Designates new power tool with safety device and warranty.
† Designates new power tool without any safety features or warranty.

Let us employ, as an example to study decision criteria under conditions of uncertainty, a new product problem. Assume that the management of the Daniel Tool Manufacturing Company is considering two possible new product strategies: (1) market a new power tool with a safety device and a long-term warranty; or (2) market the same power tool without either the safety device or warranty. The management has seriously considered two possible reactions of their main competitor if the new power tool is marketed. The competitor actions are classified as (1) do absolutely nothing; or (2) lower the price of a closely substitutable power tool. After carefully examining the relevant cost and price data, the marketing manager in charge of the new product decision at Daniel develops a conditional payoff matrix which is summarized in Table 4–5.

---

[2] Leonid Hurwicz, "Optimality Criteria For Decision Making Under Ignorance," Cowles Commission Discussion Paper, Statistics, No. 370, 1951 (mimeographed); and R. D. Luce and H. Raiffa, *Games and Decisions* (New York: John Wiley and Sons, Inc., 1957).

The decision maker that is completely optimistic would first arrange the most optimum payoffs for the two strategies.

Strategy	*Most Favor-able Payoff*
S_1	8
S_2	7

Then he would select S_1 because the payoff which is most favorable is 8 as opposed to a smaller payoff of 7 if S_2 were selected.

It would be naive to assume that a decision maker in all situations would be completely optimistic. Thus, Hurwicz developed the concept of the coefficient of optimism. This procedure allows the decision maker to take into account the most and least favorable payoffs and assign weights to them to correspond with his degree of optimism. For example, assume that the decision maker is .8 optimistic and .2 pessimistic about the occurrence of one competitor action versus another competitor action. Each strategy would then be examined separately with these two coefficients in mind. The mathematical procedure used to determine the sum of the weighted values for the two strategies in the new power tool problem is presented in Table 4–6.

Examination of the calculations in Table 4–6 illustrate that it would be more favorable to select S_1. The optimist that is rational and cautious enough to consider unfavorable action would review the sum of the weighted values of 6.8 for S_1 and 6.6 for S_2 and conclude that, on the average, placing a new power tool with the safety device and warranty on the market is most beneficial from a monetary standpoint.

TABLE 4–6
Hurwicz's Coefficients of Optimism and Pessimism Procedure
(in thousands of dollars)

Strategy	Most Favorable	Conditional Value Least Favorable	Coefficient Calculations		Sum of Weighted Values
			Most Favorable .8 +	Least Favorable .2 =	
S_1	8	2	$.8 \times (8) = 6.4$	$.2 \times (2) = .4$	6.8
S_2	7	5	$.8 \times (7) = 5.6$	$.2 \times (5) = 1.0$	6.6

Pessimism Criterion: Maximin

The maximin criterion was introduced by Wald.[3] It is his contention that the decision maker should be completely pessimistic. He should act in his

---

[3] A more complete discussion of the Wald criterion is presented in David W. Miller and Martin K. Starr, *Executive Decisions and Operations Research* (Englewood Cliffs, N.J.: Prentice-Hall, Inc., 1960), chapter 5.

strategy selection process as if all competitive actions and/or states of nature are working against him. Under these completely adverse conditions, the decision maker should select that strategy which allows him to maximize the least favorable payoff. That is, he should maximize the minimum possible gain (maximin). Reexamining Table 4–5 would allow the pessimistic decision maker to organize his minimum payoffs under each strategy. In a pessimistic state of mind the decision maker would select S_2.

Strategy	Least Favor- able Payoff
S_1	2
S_2	5

In the completely optimistic case it was suggested that coefficients of optimism and pessimism would introduce realism into the problem. There are critics who contend that the maximin criterion of Wald is unrealistic because of a failure to introduce a weighted index similar to the Hurwicz coefficient of optimism.

Regret Criterion: Minimax

Another criterion used for decision making under conditions of uncertainty is the Savage[4] criterion of regret. It is his assumption that after a decision has been made and the state of nature and/or competitive action has occurred, the decision maker then receives the given payoff. Savage suggests that, at this point the decision maker may experience regret, because he failed to select the most favorable strategy. This regret takes the form of not select-

TABLE 4–7

Regret Matrix for New Power Tool

Strategies	CA$_1$ Do Nothing	CA$_2$ Lower Price	Maximum Regret
S_1	0	5	5
S_2	3	0	3

ing the most optimum strategy in terms of the uncontrollable factor that actually occurred. Thus, the decision maker should attempt to minimize the maximum regret (minimax). Regret is then defined as the payoff for each strategy under every state of nature and/or competitor action subtracted from

[4] L. J. Savage, "The Theory of Statistical Decision," *Journal of the American Statistical Association,* Vol. 46 (1951), pp. 55–67.

the most favorable payoff that is possible with the occurrence of this event. Table 4–5 would be the starting point in developing a regret matrix shown in Table 4–7. In the original matrix (Table 4–5), the payoffs under CA_1 were 8 and 5. The regret for each strategy under CA_1 is the difference between the maximum payoff (8 for S_1) and its own payoff. Thus, the S_1 regret payoff is 8–8 or 0 and the S_2 regret payoff is 8–5 or 3. The regret for the two strategies under CA_2 is computed in the same manner.

The payoffs presented in Table 4–7 suggest that the decision maker would minimize his regret by selecting S_2. This selection indicates that no matter which competitive action occurs, the decision maker will never have a regret of more than 3.

Criterion of Insufficient Reason

The three preceding decision criteria assumed that, without any previous experience, it is not worthwhile to assign probabilities to the states of nature and/or competitive actions. One well known concept, however, is utilized in introducing probability into decision making under conditions of uncertainty. This is referred to as the LaPlace criterion.[5] This criterion states that, if we do not know the probabilities of occurrence for the various states of nature and competitive actions, we should assume that they are all equally likely to occur. In other words, assign equal probabilities to each competitive action. Symbolically, this is represented for a strategy, S_1, in the general case as follows:

$$EV_{S1} = \frac{1}{n} (P_{11} + P_{12} + \cdots + P_{1n})$$

The symbol n designates the number of competitive actions and the P's designate the payoffs under each of the competitive actions for S_1. If we substitute values from Table 4–5 into this equation, we would find that

$$EV_{S1} = \frac{1}{2}(8 + 2) = \frac{1}{2}(10) = 5.0$$

is the expected value for S_1.

The expected value for S_2 can be calculated using the same format.

$$EV_{S2} = \frac{1}{2}(5 + 7)$$
$$= \frac{1}{2}(12)$$
$$= 6.0$$

Since the largest expected monetary payoff is 6.0 for S_2, this is the strategy which would be selected by the decision maker employing the LaPlace criterion.

[5] This criterion is also referred to as Bayes' postulate. See Robert Schlaifer, *Probability and Statistics for Business Decisions* (New York: McGraw-Hill, Inc., 1959), pp. 445–46.

In reviewing the four most publicized decision criteria, it is interesting to note that both strategies, S_1 and S_2, were adopted depending upon which criterion was being utilized. The completely optimistic and cautiously optimistic decision maker selected S_1 (new power tool with safety device and warranty), the pessimistic decision maker chose S_2 (new power tool without extras), the regretful decision maker selected S_2, and the decision maker adopting the insufficient reason criterion adopted S_2. This simple problem indicates that, under uncertainty conditions, there is no "one best" criterion. The choice of which criterion to employ is dependent upon such phenomena as the personality of the decision maker and the overall company philosophy regarding the achievement of organizational objectives.

BAYESIAN ANALYSIS

The preceding four decision criteria suggest that the marketing decision maker is completely unaware of what his competitors' actions would be if one of the two strategies is undertaken. This degree of uncertainty, however, is not realistic. The decision maker usually possesses some information in a rough form which pertains to the expected actions of his competitors. The work of Schlaifer[6] and Raiffa[7] has concentrated on the use of subjective or personalistic probabilities. The use of prior probability distributions (i.e., objective, subjective, or some combination of these two probabilities) is referred to as the Bayesian approach to decision making under conditions of uncertainty.

The Types of Bayesian Analysis

The Bayesian approach consists of four specific types of analyses. These are the following:

1. *Prior analysis.* In many marketing decision problems the manager must depend upon his business experience and savvy in reaching a decision. The lack of research data or the urgency of making a decision within a relatively short time span may necessitate reaching a decision on the basis of experience. This phase of Bayesian theory is commonly referred to as prior analysis.

2. *Posterior analysis.* In some marketing problem solving situations the decision maker is provided with pertinent data which changes his prior perception about the situation at hand. In the Bayesian framework, when new

---

[6] Schlaifer, *op. cit.*

[7] Howard Raiffa, *Decision Analysis* (Reading, Mass.: Addison-Wesley, 1968).

data is employed to alter previous judgments, the decision maker is performing posterior analysis.

3. *Preposterior analysis.* At times the decision maker will have an opportunity to delay his final decision until more data affecting the problem is gathered. To acquire this information the decision maker has to incur additional costs. That is, the decision maker must pay psychologically and/or monetarily while waiting to receive additional information. The decision maker is faced with a dilemma of finalizing his decision now at time period one (t_1) or collecting additional data and making a decision at time period two (t_2). This phase of the Bayesian approach, the choice between reaching decisions at t_1, t_2, . . . t_n, is referred to as preposterior analysis.

4. *Sequential analysis.* Marketing decisions occasionally may not be reached until a number of data collection and analysis phases transpire. This type of Bayesian decision making, which applies preposterior analysis to multistage decision problems, is referred to as sequential analysis.

Applied Bayesian Analysis

The application of Bayesian Decision Theory can be clarified by using a numerical example. Let us proceed with a problem through some of the phases of the Bayesian approach. Special emphasis will be placed upon prior and preposterior analysis. Assume that the power tool example introduced previously, with two strategies and two competitive actions, is the problem facing the decision maker. In addition, assume that the decision maker believes that all variables except competitive actions can be treated as known. That is, the costs of marketing the product with or without the special features, administrative costs, advertising costs, distribution costs, and customer demand are assumed to be known.

Prior Analysis: New Power Tool

The first step in conducting prior analysis is to prepare a matrix of conditional values. The values presented in Table 4–5 are reproduced again in Table 4–8 for the convenience of the reader.

Suppose now that the marketing manager had to select one of the two strategies. Based on his experiences in the market place in dealing with his competitor he is able to assign probabilities to the two potential competitor actions. He believes that there is a .4 probability that the competitor will do nothing (CA_1) and a .6 probability that the competitor will lower the price of a substitute product. Application of these subjective/objective personalistic

TABLE 4–8

Conditional Values for New Power Tool:
Prior Analysis
(in thousands of dollars)

	Competitor Actions	
Strategies	CA_1, *Do Nothing*	CA_2, *Lower Price*
S_1	8	2
S_2	5	7

probabilities allows the decision maker to calculate the expected value for each strategy and then choose that strategy with the largest payoff.

Table 4–9 presents a summary of the prior analysis calculations. The largest expected value is 6.2 found for S_2, hence the decision maker motivated by monetary gain would recommend marketing the new power tool without the safety device and warranty.

TABLE 4–9

Conditional and Expected Values for Prior Analysis
(in thousands of dollars)

		Competitor Actions			
Strategies	$P(CA_1)$	CA_1 *Do Nothing*	$P(CA_2)$	CA_2 *Lower Price*	*Expected Value*
S_1	.4	8	.6	2	3.2 + 1.2 = 4.4
S_2	.4	5	.6	7	2.0 + 4.2 = 6.2

Introduction to Bayes' Theorem

Before discussing preposterior analysis it is desirable to present the crux of Bayesian Analysis, which is Bayes' Theorem. Assume that two events, A_1 and A_2, exist which are mutually exclusive and exhaustive states of nature. The decision maker knows that one of these events has occurred, but he does not know which one. These are known as *prior events*. Also assume that another event, B, has occurred. Furthermore, this event can only occur after one of the prior events has occurred.

The decision maker can assign $P(A_1)$ and $P(A_2)$, which are the *prior probabilities* or the probabilities of the prior events. He also can estimate the likelihood of B, given either A_1 or A_2, i.e., the *conditional probabilities*, $P(B|A_1)$ and $P(B|A_2)$. What the decision maker wants to know is $P(A_1|B)$ (or $P(A_2|B)$);

the probability of event A_1 given B has occurred. This is known as the *posterior probability*.

In Chapter Three the mathematical formula for conditional probability was designated. Applying it to our present discussion yields:

$$P(A_1|B) = \frac{P(A_1B)}{P(B)} \tag{1}$$

This can be rewritten as

$$P(A_1B) = P(A_1) \times P(B|A_1) \tag{2}$$

$P(B)$ is a marginal probability and, as was shown in Chapter Three, a marginal probability is equal to the sum of the joint probabilities. Therefore

$$P(B) = P(A_1B) + P(A_2B) \tag{3}$$

Extending what was shown in Equation 2 above, we can see that

$$P(B) = P(A_1) \times P(B|A_1) + P(A_2) \times P(B|A_2) \tag{4}$$

Substituting Equation 2 into the numerator of Equation 1 and Equation 4 into the denominator of Equation 1 yields the following

$$P(A_1|B) = \frac{P(A_1) \times P(B|A_1)}{P(A_1) \times P(B|A_1) + P(A_2) \times P(B|A_2)}$$

This equation is Bayes' Theorem and provides the conditional or posterior probability.

To illustrate the use of the theorem and formula, assume that a statistician has developed a demonstration experiment in which three urns, U_1, U_2, and U_3 are utilized. A class of statistics students is told that U_1 contains two expensive pearls, U_2 contains an expensive pearl and a worthless sea rock, and U_3 contains two worthless sea rocks. A student is asked to select one of the three urns and then choose one object from that urn. Assume that the student is blindfolded before he selects the urn and the object. He selects on his first draw an expensive pearl. The statistician would like the student to inform the class what the probability is that the remaining object in the urn from which the pearl was drawn is also a pearl. The probability that either U_1, U_2, or U_3 would be selected initially is .33 respectfully. Let O designate pearl and U designate the urns. Then

$$P(O|U_1) = 1.00$$
$$P(O|U_2) = .50$$
$$P(O|U_3) = .00$$

The statistician would like to know what the probability is that the student drew from U_1 given that he selected a pearl on his one draw. This problem can be solved intuitively because of simplicity, but it can also be answered by using Bayes' Theorem. That is,

$$P(U_1|O) = \frac{P(O|U_1) \cdot P(U_1)}{P(O|U_1) \cdot P(U_1) + P(O|U_2) \cdot P(U_2) + P(O|U_3) \cdot P(U_3)}$$
$$= \frac{1 \cdot 1/3}{(1 \cdot 1/3) + (1/2 \cdot 1/3) + (0 \cdot 1/3)} = 2/3 \text{ or } .667$$

and the student would inform the statistician that the probability is .667 that the remaining object in the urn is a pearl.

This problem clearly indicates that Bayes' Theorem is another way of expressing conditional probabilities. Thus, the probability that the student drew from U_1 is conditioned by the fact that he held a pearl in his hand. If the student held a worthless rock after the draw, the posterior probability that he drew from U_1 would change from 2/3 to 0 since U_1 held no rocks. This type of logic and mathematical procedure is used in Bayesian analysis in revising prior judgments of a decision maker.

Preposterior Analysis

The decision to market the new power tool in one of two different forms can be further investigated under a different set of circumstances. Assume that the decision maker could employ a form of "spy network" which would provide him with perfectly reliable information about the competitor's response to one of the two strategies being considered. This information in the form of "secret data sheets" would cost the decision maker monetarily. The "data sheets" would provide two results: R_1, which designates CA_1 (Do Nothing), is the planned competitor action and R_2, which designates CA_2 (Lower Price), is the contemplated competitor action. These two results indicate the possibility of the following conditional probabilities given the rules of the problem.

$$P(R_1|CA_1) = 1.0 \qquad P(R_1|CA_2) = .0$$
$$P(R_2|CA_2) = 1.0 \qquad P(R_2|CA_1) = .0$$

In the prior analysis section, the decision maker personalistically assigned prior probabilities of .4 to CA_1 and .6 to CA_2. The mathematical derivation of joint and marginal probabilities are presented in Table 4–10. The posterior probabilities for the problem are also included in Table 4–10.

The joint probabilities are found by using the multiplication theorem. For example, for CA_2:

$$P(CA_2) \cdot P(R_2|CA_2) = \text{Joint Probability}$$
$$(.6) \times (1.00) = .6$$

Thus, .6 indicates the joint probability of CA_2 occurring and obtaining reliable spy data informing us that CA_2 will occur. Therefore,

$$P(CA_2) \cdot P(R_1|CA_2) = \text{Joint Probability}$$
$$(.6) \times (0) = 0$$

TABLE 4–10

Joint and Marginal Probabilities: 100% Reliable Spy Data

Spy Results	Joint Probabilities		Marginal Probability	Posterior Probability*	
	$P(CA_1) \cdot$ $P(R_i|CA_1)$ CA_1	$P(CA_2) \cdot$ $P(R_i|CA_2)$ CA_2	$P(CA_i)$	$P(CA_1|R_1)$	$P(CA_2|R_2)$
R_1	.4	0	.4	1.0	0
R_2	0	.6	.6	0	1.0
			1.00		

* The posterior probability is found by dividing the respective joint probability by the appropriate marginal probability.

The next phase of evaluation is to consider the expected value of operating under certainty conditions with regard to CA_1 and CA_2. If the data sheets indicate that R_1 is the situation at hand, the decision maker would select S_1 and if R_2 is the result suggested by the spy sheets, the executive would choose S_2.

The "secret data sheets" can be secured only for a price. The decision maker anticipates a .4 chance of CA_1 occurring and .6 chance of CA_2 occurring. The expected payoff for perfectly reliable information about the competitor's planned action is illustrated in Table 4–11.

TABLE 4–11

Expected Payoff with 100% Reliable Information

Strategies	$P(CA_1) P(R_i|CA_1)$	CA_1	$P(CA_2) P(R_i|CA_2)$	CA_2	Total Expected Payoff*
S_1	.4	8	0	2	3.2
S_2	0	5	.6	7	4.2
					7.4

* The total expected payoff is equal to the sum of the products of the probability of occurrence and the payoff for each strategy.

The total expected payoff of 7.4 indicates that this would be the average outcome over the long run if perfect information is provided. Table 4–9 illustrated that the most favorable payoff in the face of uncertainty (prior analysis) is 6.2 for S_2. The difference between these two payoffs, uncertainty (prior analysis) and certainty (preposterior analysis or 100 percent reliable spy information), represents the monetary value of perfectly accurate information. Thus, 7.4 – 6.2 or $1,200 is what the executive at Daniel should be willing to pay for the information. If the spy charged $1,201, the cost for the secret data would exceed its monetary benefit by $1.00.

Preposterior Analysis Using Imperfect Information

The prior analysis and preposterior analysis discussed thus far has focused upon situations in which perfectly accurate information about competitor actions is provided the decision maker. This, of course, is an unrealistic assumption when dealing with marketing problems. In obtaining information through marketing research surveys or the hypothetical spy arrangement presented in the sample problem, the experienced marketing executive would expect information that is less than 100 percent accurate.

Assume that the marketing decision maker at the Daniel Company can secure spy information that is 70 percent reliable. This spy data can lead to two finds, R_1 or R_2, and the conditional probabilities are

$$P(R_1|CA_1) = .7$$
$$P(R_2|CA_2) = .7$$
$$P(R_1|CA_2) = .3$$
$$P(R_2|CA_1) = .3$$

The decision maker would use the imperfect spy information to develop a table of joint and marginal probabilities. This is done in Table 4–12. The joint probability calculations for the perfect information case (Table 4–10) are the guidelines used in ascertaining the joint probabilities with imperfect information.

The posterior probabilities are found by applying Bayes' Theorem. To find $P(CA_1|R_1)$ we would utilize

$$P(CA_1|R_1) = \frac{P(R_1|CA_1) \times P(CA_1)}{P(R_1|CA_1) \times P(CA_1) + P(R_1|CA_2) \times P(CA_2)}$$
$$= \frac{(.7) \times (.4)}{(.7 \times .4) + (.3 \times .6)} = \frac{.28}{.28 + .18} \text{ or } \frac{.28}{.46}$$
$$= .61$$

The remaining three posterior probabilities would be calculated in the same manner or by dividing each joint probability assigned to R_1 by its marginal probability and each joint probability assigned to R_2 by its marginal probability. Thus,

$$P(CA_2|R_1) = \frac{.18}{.46} = .39$$

$$P(CA_1|R_2) = \frac{.12}{.54} = .22$$

$$P(CA_2|R_2) = \frac{.42}{.54} = .78$$

TABLE 4–12
Joint and Marginal Probabilities: 70% Reliable Information

Joint Probabilities			Conditional Posterior Probabilities	
.4 CA₁	.6 CA₂	Marginal Probabilities	$P(CA_1|R_i)$	$P(CA_2|R_i)$
$R_1(.4) \times (.7) = .28$	$(.6) \times (.3) = .18$	.46	.61	.39
$R_2(.4) \times (.3) = .12$	$(.6) \times (.7) = .42$	.54	.22	.78

After these calculations are completed the decision maker is once again faced with the question of how much he should be willing to spend for the spy information which is 70 percent reliable. A convenient device employed to trace this decision-making process is the decision tree.

The decision tree is a schematic device that presents, in an orderly manner, the Bayesian analysis discussed. The decision tree is presented in Figure 4–1.

The upper path (do not purchase) refers to the prior analysis situation which faced the marketing decision maker at the Daniel Company. The strategy which is most favorable is S_2, which yields an expected payoff of 6.2. The prior probabilities of .4 for CA_1 and .6 for CA_2 are assigned to the conditional values at the terminal locations and these are 8 and 2 for S_1 and 5 and 7 for S_2. A double slash notation is used on the S_1 branch since the most favorable strategy if the decision maker does not purchase the spy information is S_2.

The lower path (purchase spy information) of Figure 4–1 refers to the strategy of purchasing the spy data sheets and then selecting either S_1 or S_2. If the decision maker followed this path, the spy information would result in R_1 or R_2 with associated probabilities for this 70 percent reliable data illustrated in Table 4–12. The probabilities assigned to CA_1 and CA_2 are posterior probabilities (Table 4–12). If the data sheet results are R_1 then the best strategy is S_2 with an expected payoff of 5.78. This payoff is slightly more favorable than

FIGURE 4–1

Decision Tree—New Power Tool Problem 70 Percent Reliable Spy Data
(payoffs in thousands of dollars)

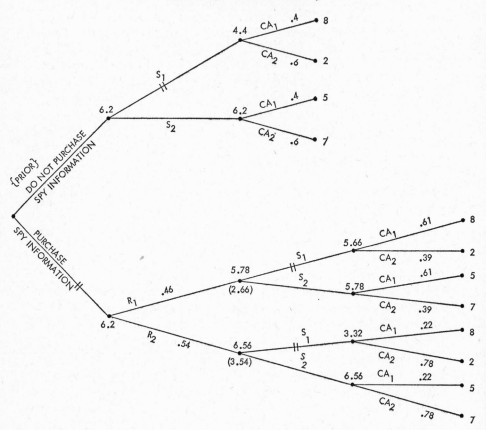

that received from S_1 and consequently S_1 is blocked off with the double slash notation. The same procedure is followed for the R_2 branch and we find that S_2 once again is more favorable. The marginal probabilities of .46 for R_1 and .54 for R_2 when applied to the expected payoffs of 5.78 and 6.56 result in a total expected payoff of 6.2. Thus, any amount of money spent on purchasing the spy information is not warranted since the expected payoff (6.2) of not purchasing (upper path) is identical with the expected payoff of purchasing (lower path). There is no net gain in value from the purchase, so it is useless to make any attempt to get spy information.

The procedures examined above are only a sampling of Bayesian decision theory. The problem of a decision maker faced with the dilemma of which spy to secure his information from is an example of sequential analysis which is not covered in this book.[8] This type of decision problem and others involving continuous prior and sampling distributions can be handled by Bayesian analysis.

Because of the vast amount of computational work, only a small number of business firms are using Bayesian analysis. Despite its limited usage there exists within the procedure itself some promising areas of usage in marketing related problem solving situations. Whether the Bayesian approach will ever be widely employed in business firms is a highly debatable subject. The major critics of the approach complain about its computational complexities and the difficulties in ascertaining conditional values and prior distributions. The examples illustrated above suggest that these criticisms and others may have some validity. Much work is needed in dissecting the human decision process (the personalistic approach) which is an important phenomenon in the Bayesian approach.

PROBLEMS

1. Discuss the following statements.

a) "Most marketing decisions are reached in an environment which is usually considered to be controllable in all facets."

b) "The tree diagram is used most often in solving problems under conditions of certainty."

c) "Posterior analysis is irrelevant in solving marketing problems."

d) "In Bayesian statistics, the probability of occurrence of particular events can and often is greater than one."

e) "Total ignorance of the probabilities of competitor actions or states of nature are taken into consideration in the LaPlace criterion."

2. Describe three areas of marketing where Bayesian analysis could be employed. If the Bayesian approach is to be used, what type of data is needed by the decision maker?

3. What are some of the theoretical and operational weaknesses of the Bayesian approach? Could they be overcome or minimized?

4. Briefly describe the type of marketing decision maker that would be most inclined to use the maximin criterion, the maximax criterion, and the minimax criterion.

5. A manufacturer has three different strategies for placing a new product on the market. The amount and type of competitive reaction to the new product will depend on how secret the development and implementation plans for the new product are kept. The decision maker constructs the following payoff matrix:

---

[8] For an excellent example of sequential analysis see Wroe Alderson and Paul E. Green, *Planning and Problem Solving In Marketing* (Homewood, Ill.: Richard D. Irwin, Inc., 1965), chapter 5.

	CA₁	CA₂
S_1:	6	8
S_2:	9	4
S_3:	5	6

where

$$CA_1 = \text{information is completely secret}$$
$$CA_2 = \text{information is partially secret}$$

The payoff measures are the conditional values in thousands of dollars that the decision maker anticipates. Assume that the decision maker is concerned with optimizing the monetary return for the organization.

(a) If the competitors have received some of the new product information (CA_2), what strategy should be chosen?

(b) If the competitors know nothing about the new product (CA_1), what strategy should be chosen?

(c) What would the maximax choice be?

(d) What would the minimax choice be?

(e) What would the maximin choice be?

(f) What would the insufficient reason choice be?

(g) Assume that a decision maker decides to assign a coefficient of optimism of .80. Which strategy will be chosen?

6. A dairy store manager observes the daily sales of skim milk for a 100-day period. He develops the table of sales presented below.

TABLE 4–A

Skim Milk Sales

Quantities Purchased	Number of Days
40	15
50	20
70	30
100	15
120	20

The milk sells for $.25 a quart and the cost to the store manager of securing the milk from the dairy is $.19.

(a) If 70 units are stocked every day, what will be the firm's expected profit per day over the long run?

(b) Using the data presented in the table, what quantity (40, 50, 70, 100, or 120) should be purchased every day to maximize long-run profits?

7. Suppose that Table 4–8 is revised as shown in Table 4–B.

TABLE 4–B

Conditional Values for New Power Tool:
Prior Analysis (in thousands of dollars)

	Competitor Actions	
	CA$_1$	CA$_2$
Strategies	Do Nothing	Lower Price
S$_1$	5	7
S$_2$	8	2

The .4 probability that the competitor will do nothing and the .6 probability that the competitor will lower the price of the substitute product remain the same.

(a) Develop a set of Tables similar to Tables 4–9 through 4–12 and a tree diagram similar to Figure 4–1 for the revised data. Use all of the information in the chapter regarding probabilities and spy information in developing your new set of data. At each appropriate spot (prior and preposterior) reach a decision as to which strategy should be selected.

REFERENCES

BIERMAN, H., BONINI, C. P., FOURAKER, L. E., and JAEDICKE, R. K. *Quantitative Analysis For Business Decisions*, Rev. ed., Homewood, Ill.: Richard D. Irwin, Inc., 1965.

CHERNOFF, H., and MOSES, L. E. *Elementary Decision Theory*. New York: John Wiley and Sons, Inc., 1959.

CHURCHMAN, C. W., ACKOFF, R., and ARNOFF, E. L. *Introduction to Operations Research*. New York: John Wiley and Sons, Inc., 1957.

KAUFMANN, A. *Methods and Models of Operations Research*. Englewood Cliffs, N.J.: Prentice-Hall, Inc., 1963.

LUCE, R. D., and RAIFFA, H. *Games and Decisions*. New York: John Wiley and Sons, Inc., 1957.

MILLER, D. W., and STARR, M. K. *Executive Decisions and Operations Research*. Englewood Cliffs, N.J.: Prentice-Hall, Inc., 1960.

MORRIS, W. T. *The Analysis of Management Decisions*, Rev. ed., Homewood, Ill.: Richard D. Irwin, Inc., 1964.

SCHLAIFER, R. *Probability and Statistics for Business Decisions*. New York: McGraw-Hill Book Company, 1959.

TIECHROEW, D. *An Introduction to Management Science*. New York: John Wiley and Sons, Inc., 1964.

chapter five
MATHEMATICAL CONCEPTS

INTRODUCTION

In recent years the application of mathematics to problems of business in general and marketing in particular has been increasing at a significant rate. The marketing manager by understanding various mathematical concepts and procedures is better able to cope with complex business problems that often arise in today's environment. Because an understanding of some basic mathematical methods is essential to the implementation of various marketing models, the reader should have a working knowledge of the concepts included in this chapter. Students or practitioners intending to become specialists in mathematics need a more sophisticated coverage than is presented here.

A brief introduction to and discussion of such ideas as functions, inequalities, vectors, matrices, determinants, cofactors, and matrix inversion is included. The reader who finds that his previous mathematical training is inadequate to cope with the topic areas presented is advised to supplement this chapter with an elementary college algebra text.

FUNCTIONS

A function is simply an expression of a relationship between two or more variables. For example, a district sales manager might hypothesize that the sale of a particular product line in his territory is definitely a function of the firm's advertising efforts and the salesman's communicative abilities. If we let S designate sales, A designate advertising effort, and C designate the communicative skills of salesmen, the statement that "sales are a function of advertising and communication" may be expressed symbolically as

$$S = f(A,C)$$

It is convenient to label the "input" variable(s) the independent variable(s), and the "output" variable(s) the dependent variable(s) when expressing a function. In the example above, the dependent variable would be sales of the product line.

Marketing problems usually involve many more variables than two as presented in the hypothetical example. A common practice is to denote different variables, independent and dependent, with subscript notation. The following is a widely used notational system

$$y = f(x_1, x_2, x_3 \ldots , x_n)$$

This is interpreted to mean that the dependent variable y is a function of n independent variables.

INEQUALITIES

Unfortunately, many marketing problems cannot be conveniently expressed in the form of orderly equation systems. Occasionally the problem being examined may necessitate that some minimum or maximum set of constraints be followed. When restrictions upon the variables of an equation or function must be considered, the decision maker must employ inequalities. The concept of inequalities involves a comparison of two or more items or numbers. For example, if d equals j, then it is presented symbolically as an equality

$$d = j$$

If, however, d is not equivalent to j, then it is noted as:

$$d \neq j$$

This notation informs us that one of the two items is greater than or less than the other. In fact, there are four ways of expressing the inequality of d and j. These are:

$$d > j \qquad d < j$$
$$j < d \qquad j > d$$

The reader will recall from elementary mathematics that "$>$" means a strict greater than inequality and "$<$" means a strict less than inequality. The sign "$\geq$" designates a greater than or equal to case and the sign "$\leq$" specifies a less than or equal to case. If in our discussion of d and j the situation warranted introduction of the equal sign, the four ways of expressing the inequality would then become

$$d \geq j \qquad d \leq j$$
$$j \leq d \qquad j \geq d$$

The relationships of items in an inequality system are governed by the following laws:

    a. If $d > j$ and $j > k$, then $d > k$
    b. If $d > j$, then $d + w > j + w$ for every value of w
    c. If $d > j$ and $w > o$, then $dw > jw$
    d. If $d < j$ and $w > o$, then $dw < jw$
    e. If d, j, and w are positive numbers and $d < j$, then

$$\frac{w}{d} > \frac{w}{j} \text{ and } \frac{1}{d} > \frac{1}{j}.$$

The inequality can be solved by procedures which are similar to those followed in solving equalities. For example, the equality $y = 2x$ can be solved for any value of x by substituting the value into the equation. If $x = 10$, the solution of the equation is $y = 20$, for $x = 20$, the solution of the equation is $y = 40$. The inequality $y \geq 2x$ can be solved in the same manner. For $x = 10$, the solution is $y \geq 20$, or y may be 20 or any other number greater than 20.

Another example could be the following situation facing a marketing manager. Suppose that the cost of art work (A) and packaging material (P) for a new product (x) about to be placed on the market must not be in excess of \$180,000. This relationship can be expressed in an inequality format as follows

$$A(x) + P(x) \leq \$180,000$$

Most restrictions in linear programming problems are expressed in an inequality format similar to the example above. More will be said about this in the chapter on mathematical programming.

VECTORS

A vector is a grouping of numbers presented either in a row or column format. The numbers in each row or column are known as the components of the vector. A column vector is written as

$$C_1 = \begin{pmatrix} C_1 \\ C_2 \\ \cdot \\ \cdot \\ \cdot \\ C_m \end{pmatrix} \text{ or } C_1 = \begin{bmatrix} C_1 \\ C_2 \\ \cdot \\ \cdot \\ \cdot \\ C_m \end{bmatrix} \text{ or } C_2 = \begin{pmatrix} 9 \\ 8 \\ 12 \end{pmatrix} \text{ or } C_2 = \begin{bmatrix} 9 \\ 8 \\ 12 \end{bmatrix}$$

The examples cited above are m-component and three-component column vectors, respectively. The notation C_i can be used to specify an entire vector.

Similarly, a row vector can be represented as

$$r_1 = (a_1, a_2 \ldots a_n) \text{ or } r_1 = [a_1, a_2 \ldots a_n]$$

or

$$r_2 = (9, 4, 6) \text{ or } r_2 = [9, 4, 6]$$

These are examples of n-component and three-component row vectors. A row vector that is composed of n columns is said to be an n-component or n-dimensional vector.[1] A vector such as

$$\begin{pmatrix} 9 \\ 3 \\ 6 \end{pmatrix}$$

would be referred to as a 3×1 matrix or a three-component column vector. Similarly, the vector $(9, 8, 6)$ would be referred to as a 1×3 matrix or a three-component row vector. Note that n is used to designate rows and m is used to designate columns.

A vector usually described as a set of numbers is very similar to the coordinates that a map reader employs to find a specific location. For example, the distance from Louisville, Kentucky to Lexington, Kentucky is approximately 75 miles. Graphically this could be shown as follows:

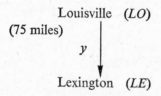

In vector language we would have (75) which indicates (a) that the distance is 75 miles; (b) that we are moving toward (LE); and (c) that we intend to move along the direct Louisville to Lexington route. Thus, a vector graphically can be described as a line with direction and length.

The best method to employ in discussing vectors is the x-axis and y-axis graphical procedure. In vector discussions the x-coordinate is always read or mentioned before the y-coordinate. The vector in Figure 5–1 is symbolically presented as $\begin{pmatrix} 0 \\ 5 \end{pmatrix}$.

---

[1] Jean E. Draper and Jane S. Klingman, *Mathematical Analysis: Business and Economic Applications* (New York: Harper and Row Publishers, 1967), p. 457.

This indicates that we have moved five increments on the positive y-axis and 0 increments on the x-axis. The vector shown in Figure 5–2 is read $\begin{pmatrix} 6 \\ 4 \end{pmatrix}$.

A vector may have one or more negative components. For example, Figure 5–3 illustrates this case. In Figure 5–3 the vector components are $\begin{pmatrix} 3 \\ -3 \end{pmatrix}$.

FIGURE 5–1

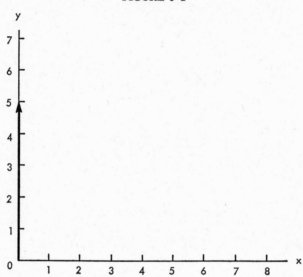

Addition and Subtraction of Vectors

Vectors with the same number of components may be added or subtracted. This is done by adding or subtracting the coordinates of each vector. Suppose that two vectors b and j are to be added. These vectors are

$$b = \begin{pmatrix} 6 \\ 2 \end{pmatrix}$$

and

$$j = \begin{pmatrix} 3 \\ 4 \end{pmatrix}.$$

Symbolically $b + j = k$ and graphically these vectors are presented in Figure 5–4.

FIGURE 5–2

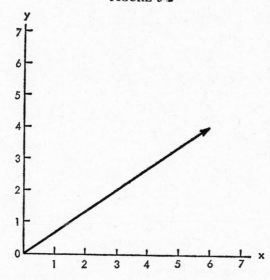

FIGURE 5–3

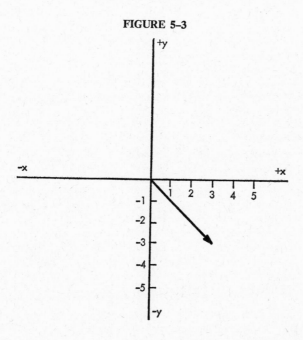

If $b + j = k$, then

$$\binom{6}{2} + \binom{3}{4} = \binom{9}{6}.$$

These same two vectors may be subtracted in a similar manner. The symbols $b' - j' = k'$ and the vectors in Figure 5–5 illustrate the subtraction of

FIGURE 5–4

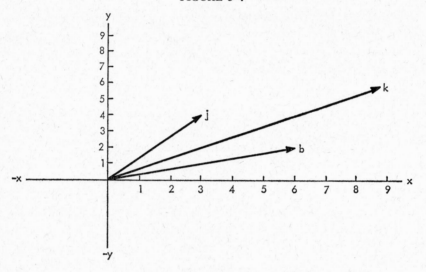

FIGURE 5–5

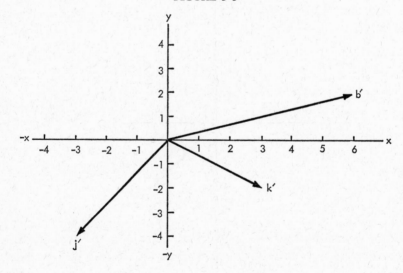

two vectors with the same number of components. The k' vector is derived by subtracting

$$\begin{pmatrix} 6 \\ 2 \end{pmatrix} - \begin{pmatrix} 3 \\ 4 \end{pmatrix} = \begin{pmatrix} 3 \\ -2 \end{pmatrix}.$$

Vector Multiplication

Any vector can be multiplied by any number to form some multiple of the original vector. When a vector is multiplied by a constant, each component of the vector must be multiplied by that constant. The multiplier in vector multiplication is called a scalar. For example, if the vector

$$\begin{pmatrix} 6 \\ 2 \end{pmatrix}$$

is multiplied by 5, the number 5 is the scalar and the resultant vector is

$$5 \times \begin{pmatrix} 6 \\ 2 \end{pmatrix} = \begin{pmatrix} 30 \\ 10 \end{pmatrix}.$$

Note that the original two-component vector which is multiplied by the scalar "5" results in another two-component vector.

A final vector procedure, that of multiplying a vector by another vector can be illustrated by solving a marketing problem. Suppose that a wholesale meat salesman calls on three classes of customers in the Rochester, New York area: independent retail grocers (I.G.A.), chain stores, and small delicatessens. The number of customers called upon during an average month is expressed in the vector designated C.

$$C = \begin{pmatrix} 16 = \text{I.G.A.} \\ 19 = \text{Chains} \\ 6 = \text{Delicatessens} \end{pmatrix} \text{ or } \begin{pmatrix} 16 \\ 19 \\ 6 \end{pmatrix}$$

The district sales manager, after carefully evaluating the total market potential concludes that, on the average, his salesmen in the Rochester region should be able to sell a monthly quota of 200 pounds to each I.G.A. client, 2,000 pounds to each chain store, and 11 pounds to each of the delicatessens. These quotas can be expressed as a row vector S.

$$S = (200, 2000, 11)$$

The total amount of meat expected to be sold monthly in the Rochester area can be ascertained by use of the following vector multiplication procedures.

$$\text{Total meat sales (pounds)} = C \times S$$

$$= \begin{pmatrix} 16 \\ 19 \\ 6 \end{pmatrix} \times (200, 2000, 11)$$

$$= [16(200) + 19(2000) + 6(11)]$$

$$= 41{,}266$$

These multiplication calculations can only be completed if the vectors (i.e., C and S) have the same number of components, although some of the components may be zero. Note that the resultant answer of the vector multiplication is a single number. This would be true regardless of the number of components in each vector. The sample vector multiplication was performed by multiplying each row vector by its corresponding column vector. Symbolically this procedure is

$$C \times S = \begin{pmatrix} y_1 \\ y_2 \\ y_3 \end{pmatrix} \times (x_1 \; x_2 \; x_3)$$

$$= [y_1 x_1 + y_2 x_2 + y_3 x_3]$$

MATRICES

A matrix is a rectangular array of numbers presented in symbolic form as rows and columns in the following manner

$$M = \begin{pmatrix} a_{11} & a_{12} & \ldots & a_{1n} \\ a_{21} & a_{22} & \ldots & a_{2n} \\ \vdots & \vdots & & \\ & & & \\ a_{m1} & a_{m2} & \ldots & a_{mn} \end{pmatrix} \text{ or } M = \begin{pmatrix} 3 & 7 & 8 \\ 4 & 2 & 1 \\ 9 & 8 & 0 \end{pmatrix}$$

The numerical example is a 3×3 or square matrix. A matrix with as many rows (r) as columns (c) is referred to as a square matrix.

A matrix may be thought of as a collection of vectors having the same number of components. The mathematical operations of addition, subtraction, and multiplication for vector analyses are analogous to the procedures used with matrices.

Addition and Subtraction of Matrices

Matrices can be added or subtracted only if they are of the same order. That is, if the number of components in each are equal. If two matrices are to be added, the following procedures would occur

$$M_1\begin{pmatrix} a_{11} & \cdots & a_{1n} \\ & \cdot & \\ & \cdot & \\ & \cdot & \\ a_{m1} & \cdots & a_{mn} \end{pmatrix} + M_2\begin{pmatrix} q_{11} & \cdots & q_{1n} \\ & \cdot & \\ & \cdot & \\ & \cdot & \\ q_{m1} & \cdots & q_{mn} \end{pmatrix}$$

$$= M_3\begin{pmatrix} a_{11} + q_{11} & \cdots & a_{1n} + q_{1n} \\ & \cdot & \\ & \cdot & \\ & \cdot & \\ a_{m1} + q_{m1} & \cdots & a_{mn} + q_{mn} \end{pmatrix}$$

Suppose the following two matrices are to be added. The resultant matrix is a 3×3 matrix.

$$\begin{pmatrix} 4 & 3 & 1 \\ 2 & 0 & 5 \\ 4 & 6 & 6 \end{pmatrix} + \begin{pmatrix} 1 & 2 & 4 \\ 1 & 3 & 2 \\ 0 & 2 & 4 \end{pmatrix} = \begin{pmatrix} 5 & 5 & 5 \\ 3 & 3 & 7 \\ 4 & 8 & 10 \end{pmatrix}$$

    Matrix A Matrix B Resultant
                                                 Matrix

If two matrices that are each 2×2 are added, the resultant matrix will also be 2×2. For example,

$$\begin{pmatrix} 4 & -2 \\ -1 & 0 \end{pmatrix} + \begin{pmatrix} 1 & 8 \\ 6 & -1 \end{pmatrix} = \begin{pmatrix} 5 & 6 \\ 5 & -1 \end{pmatrix}$$

In a manner similar to that used for addition, matrices can also be subtracted from each other. For example,

$$\begin{pmatrix} 6 & 0 & 4 \\ 8 & 4 & 2 \\ 1 & 9 & 3 \end{pmatrix} - \begin{pmatrix} 1 & 9 & 2 \\ 3 & 2 & 2 \\ 4 & 8 & 2 \end{pmatrix} = \begin{pmatrix} 5 & -9 & 2 \\ 5 & 2 & 0 \\ -3 & 1 & 1 \end{pmatrix}$$

Once again the resultant matrix has the same number of elements as the two matrices involved in the subtraction manipulations.

Multiplication of Matrices

Two matrices can be multiplied if, and only if, the number of columns in the first matrix is equal to the number of rows in the second matrix. For example, a 2×3 matrix can be multiplied by a 3×2 matrix or a 2×4 matrix can be multiplied by a 4×2 matrix, but a 2×3 matrix cannot be multiplied by a 5×4 matrix. The symbolic representation of the multiplication of matrices can be illustrated in the following example.

$$W_1 = \begin{pmatrix} a & c & e \\ b & d & f \end{pmatrix} \text{ and } W_2 = \begin{pmatrix} j_1 & j_4 \\ j_2 & j_5 \\ j_3 & j_6 \end{pmatrix}$$

Thus, $W' = W_1 \times W_2$ or

$$W' = \begin{pmatrix} a & c & e \\ b & d & f \end{pmatrix} \times \begin{pmatrix} j_1 & j_4 \\ j_2 & j_5 \\ j_3 & j_6 \end{pmatrix}$$

$$= \begin{pmatrix} (aj_1 + cj_2 + ej_3)(aj_4 + cj_5 + ej_6) \\ (bj_1 + dj_2 + fj_3)(bj_4 + dj_5 + fj_6) \end{pmatrix}$$

$$= \begin{pmatrix} z_1 & z_3 \\ z_2 & z_4 \end{pmatrix}$$

If two matrices placed side by side do not comply with the rule for the multiplication of matrices, a rearrangement of positions may qualify them for multiplication. This is never a problem with "square" matrices which have an equal number of components. For example, matrix (M_1) and matrix (M_2) would be multiplied in the following manner.

$$M_1 = \begin{pmatrix} 1 & 2 \\ 3 & 4 \end{pmatrix} \quad \text{and} \quad M_2 = \begin{pmatrix} 3 & 4 \\ 1 & 2 \end{pmatrix}$$

$$M_1 \times M_2 = \begin{pmatrix} (1 \times 3 + 2 \times 1)(1 \times 4 + 2 \times 2) \\ (3 \times 3 + 4 \times 1)(3 \times 4 + 4 \times 2) \end{pmatrix} = \begin{pmatrix} 5 & 8 \\ 13 & 20 \end{pmatrix}$$

However, suppose that the two matrices being multiplied are presented in the following manner

$$\begin{pmatrix} 3 \\ 2 \\ 1 \end{pmatrix} \times \begin{pmatrix} 1 & 2 & 3 \\ 4 & 5 & 6 \end{pmatrix}$$

Matrix A   Matrix B

This involves multiplying a 3×1 matrix by a 2×3 matrix. The rule that the number of columns in the first matrix being equivalent to the number of rows in the second matrix is clearly violated since matrix A is a 3×1 configuration and matrix B is a 2×3 structure. Thus, $3 \times 1 \neq 2 \times 3$ because the number of columns (1) in matrix A is not equivalent to the number of rows (2) in matrix B. Rearrangement of the two matrices to the following allows us to

$$\begin{pmatrix} 1 & 2 & 3 \\ 4 & 5 & 6 \end{pmatrix} \times \begin{pmatrix} 3 \\ 2 \\ 1 \end{pmatrix}$$

Matrix B   Matrix A

apply the multiplication rule. Matrix B, 2 × 3, has three columns and matrix A has 3 rows, hence 2 × 3 = 3 × 1 and we can then proceed with our calculations.

$$\begin{pmatrix} 1 & 2 & 3 \\ 4 & 5 & 6 \end{pmatrix} \times \begin{pmatrix} 3 \\ 2 \\ 1 \end{pmatrix} = \begin{pmatrix} 1 \times 3 + 2 \times 2 + 3 \times 1 \\ 4 \times 3 + 5 \times 2 + 6 \times 1 \end{pmatrix} = \begin{pmatrix} 10 \\ 28 \end{pmatrix}$$

The number of rows and columns in the answer can be determined from the matrix notation. That is, matrix B is a 2 × 3 form and matrix A is a 3 × 1 form. Placing these notations side by side provides the following

$$2 \times 3 \qquad 3 \times 1$$

The first item in the matrix notation on the left designates the number of rows in the answer and the second item in the matrix notation on the right designates the number of columns in the answer. Thus,

$$\overset{\frown}{}\text{Rows} \qquad \text{Columns}\overset{\frown}{}$$
$$2 \times 3 \qquad 3 \times 1$$

The answer obtained

$$\begin{pmatrix} 10 \\ 28 \end{pmatrix}$$

complies with this guideline.

An Example of Matrix Multiplication

Suppose that a sales manager determines the amount of time per unit spent by three salesmen in selling three different electrical inspection devices at a trade fair. These figures have been tabulated by a careful time review methodology. The calculations are as follows:

Salesmen (hours per device)	Inspection Equipment		
	Model A	Model B	Model C
Johnson	1	2	3
Green	3	2	4
Wilson	2	2	1

At a similar convention next month the company management decides that two Model A devices, three Model B devices, and three Model C devices must be sold. The company is attempting to determine what the salesmen's salaries would be if they closed their exhibition at the time the 2A, 3B, and 3C devices are sold. The anticipated schedule could be presented as

$$\begin{pmatrix} 2 = \text{Model A} \\ 3 = \text{Model B} \\ 3 = \text{Model C} \end{pmatrix}$$

Then multiplication of the salesmen time matrix by the anticipated sales matrix will yield the total number of hours needed from each of the three salesmen to achieve the quota.

$$\begin{pmatrix} 1 & 2 & 3 \\ 3 & 2 & 4 \\ 2 & 2 & 1 \end{pmatrix} \times \begin{pmatrix} 2 \\ 3 \\ 3 \end{pmatrix} = \begin{pmatrix} 17 \\ 24 \\ 13 \end{pmatrix}$$

The company pays its trade fair salesmen on an hourly rate plus a bonus for the sales team, which is divided on the basis of which salesman takes the least amount of time to make a sale. Thus, the man that takes less time could make more in total salary then the others on the team. The hourly rates for the salesmen are as follows:

Johnson	$4.50/hour
Green	$3.00/hour
Wilson	$6.00/hour

The total hourly salary expense expected for this team of three could be calculated as follows:

$$(4.50 \quad 3.00 \quad 6.00) \times \begin{pmatrix} 17 \\ 24 \\ 13 \end{pmatrix} = 226.50$$

The bonus calculations are not included in this example, but they would be considered to derive a total expenditure for salesmen salaries at the second trade fair. This example is presented to show that matrix multiplication can be used to solve business problems. It is, of course, a cumbersome tool and decision makers would have to decide if other arithmetic procedures could provide the same results in less time and by exerting less energy.

Transpose of a Matrix

The transpose of a specific matrix can be conducted by interchanging the rows with the columns of the original matrix. For example, if the original matrix is as follows,

$$\begin{pmatrix} 1 & 2 & 3 \\ 4 & 5 & 6 \end{pmatrix}$$

then the transpose would be

$$\begin{pmatrix} 1 & 4 \\ 2 & 5 \\ 3 & 6 \end{pmatrix}.$$

If the original matrix dimensions are 2 × 3, then the transpose dimensions are 3 × 2. If the original matrix had been square (i.e., 2 × 2, 3 × 3, etc.), then forming the transpose would not alter the dimensions of the original matrix. A transpose is designated by a prime sign (e.g., transpose of A is A').

The Identity Matrix

A square dimensional matrix that has its diagonal elements (i.e., those from the top left-hand corner to the bottom right-hand corner) all equal to one and its non-diagonal elements equal to 0 is known as an identity matrix. A 3 × 3 identity matrix would appear as follows:

$$I = \begin{pmatrix} 1 & 0 & 0 \\ 0 & 1 & 0 \\ 0 & 0 & 1 \end{pmatrix}$$

It is easy to verify that $IM = MI = M$, where M is any matrix being studied and I the identity matrix has the necessary rows and columns. The identity matrix is a valuable concept in discussing the inversion of matrices, which is an important concept in linear programming.

Determinants

A determinant is an array of numbers arranged into rows and columns; each array has a numerical value which may be solved for. The procedures used in determinant analysis are useful in solving simultaneous equation systems. A determinant is normally expressed as follows

$$\begin{vmatrix} 4 & 3 \\ 5 & 2 \end{vmatrix} \quad 2 \times 2 \text{ determinant}$$

$$\begin{vmatrix} 1 & 2 & 3 \\ 4 & 5 & 6 \\ 7 & 8 & 9 \end{vmatrix} \quad 3 \times 3 \text{ determinant}$$

The 2 × 2 and any other determinant network has what are referred to as primary and secondary diagonals. The 2 × 2 example diagonals are designated

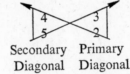

Secondary   Primary
Diagonal   Diagonal

The diagonals are used to find the numerical value of the determinant in the following manner.

$$\begin{vmatrix} 4 & 3 \\ 5 & 2 \end{vmatrix}$$

Determinant = (4)(2) − (5)(3)
value
    = −7

Thus, the value of the determinant

$$\begin{vmatrix} 4 & 3 \\ 5 & 2 \end{vmatrix} \text{ is } -7.$$

The value of the determinant

$$\begin{vmatrix} 9 & 1 \\ -3 & 2 \end{vmatrix} \text{ is } 21.$$

The numerical value of a 3 × 3 determinant is calculated in a similar manner by using multiple primary and secondary diagonal calculations. For example,

$$\begin{vmatrix} 1 & 2 & 3 \\ 4 & 5 & 6 \\ 7 & 8 & 9 \end{vmatrix}$$

is the original determinant. Slight alteration is necessary so that the second and third primary and secondary diagonals pass through three numbers. This is rectified by repeating the first two columns of the determinant.

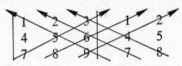

Thus,

3 × 3 Determinant value = $(P_1 + P_2 + P_3) - (S_1 + S_2 + S_3)$
= ([(1)(5)(9)] + [(2)(6)(7)] + [(3)(4)(8)])
    − ([(3)(5)(7)] + [(1)(6)(8)] + [(2)(4)(9)])
= 0

The above should be worked out to verify the 0 answer.

Solving Simultaneous Equations by Use of Determinants

Determinants are occasionally used to solve a set of simultaneous equations. For example, if we are asked to solve for X, Y, and Z in the following equation system by use of determinants we would proceed as follows:

$$3X + 5Y + 2Z = 10$$
$$2X + 3Y + 4Z = 12$$
$$3X + 6Y + 2Z = 14$$

First, the value of each of the unknown variables can be found by solving three separate sets of determinants arranged in a fraction format.

The denominator of the fraction arrangements is nothing more than the coefficients of the three unknowns arrayed in the same format as they appeared in the original equations.

$$\begin{vmatrix} 3 & 5 & 2 \\ 2 & 3 & 4 \\ 3 & 6 & 2 \end{vmatrix} \text{ denominator}$$

The determinant which forms the numerator of a fraction for solving for the unknown X is as follows:

$$\begin{vmatrix} 10 & 5 & 2 \\ 12 & 3 & 4 \\ 14 & 6 & 2 \end{vmatrix} \text{ numerator in solving for } X$$

The column of coefficients for the unknown variable X

$$\begin{pmatrix} 3 \\ 2 \\ 3 \end{pmatrix}$$

has been replaced by the values to the right of the equality sign

$$\begin{pmatrix} 10 \\ 12 \\ 14 \end{pmatrix}$$

in the original system of equations.

The numerator for the fraction in solving for the variable Y is formed by taking the values to the right of the equality sign and placing them in the column of coefficients for the unknown Y.

$$
\begin{vmatrix}
3 & 10 & 2 \\
2 & 12 & 4 \\
3 & 14 & 2
\end{vmatrix}
\quad \text{numerator in solving for } Y
$$

The determinant for the numerator of the fraction in solving for the unknown Z is formed in a similar manner to that used in the X and Y derivations.

$$
\begin{vmatrix}
3 & 5 & 10 \\
2 & 3 & 12 \\
3 & 6 & 14
\end{vmatrix}
\quad \text{numerator in solving for } Z
$$

Thus, the three sets of fraction determinants are solved by the primary and secondary diagonal procedures employed to solve the 3×3 determinant sample cited previously.

$$
X = \frac{
\begin{vmatrix}
10 & 5 & 2 \\
12 & 3 & 4 \\
14 & 6 & 2
\end{vmatrix}
\begin{matrix}
10 & 5 \\
12 & 3 \\
14 & 6
\end{matrix}
\begin{matrix}
[(10)(3)(2) + (5)(4)(14) + (2)(12)(6)] \\
-[(2)(3)(14) + (10)(4)(6) + (5)(12)(2)]
\end{matrix}
}{
\begin{vmatrix}
3 & 5 & 2 \\
2 & 3 & 4 \\
3 & 6 & 2
\end{vmatrix}
\begin{matrix}
3 & 5 \\
2 & 3 \\
3 & 6
\end{matrix}
\begin{matrix}
[(3)(3)(2) + (5)(4)(3) + (2)(2)(6)] \\
-[(2)(3)(3) + (3)(4)(6) + (5)(2)(2)]
\end{matrix}
}
$$

$$
= \frac{40}{-8}
$$

$$
Y = \frac{
\begin{vmatrix}
3 & 10 & 2 \\
2 & 12 & 4 \\
3 & 14 & 2
\end{vmatrix}
\begin{matrix}
3 & 10 \\
2 & 12 \\
3 & 14
\end{matrix}
}{
\begin{vmatrix}
3 & 5 & 2 \\
2 & 3 & 4 \\
3 & 6 & 2
\end{vmatrix}
\begin{matrix}
3 & 5 \\
2 & 3 \\
3 & 6
\end{matrix}
} = \frac{-32}{-8} = 4
$$

$$
Z = \frac{
\begin{vmatrix}
3 & 5 & 10 \\
2 & 3 & 12 \\
3 & 6 & 14
\end{vmatrix}
\begin{matrix}
3 & 5 \\
2 & 3 \\
3 & 6
\end{matrix}
}{
\begin{vmatrix}
3 & 5 & 2 \\
2 & 3 & 4 \\
3 & 6 & 2
\end{vmatrix}
\begin{matrix}
3 & 5 \\
2 & 3 \\
3 & 6
\end{matrix}
} = \frac{-20}{-8} = \frac{20}{8}
$$

To check the accuracy of the findings, substitute the values of X, Y, and Z into one of the equations as follows

$$3X + 5Y + 2Z = 10$$

$$3\left(\frac{40}{-8}\right) + 5\left(\frac{32}{8}\right) + 2\left(\frac{20}{8}\right) = 10$$

$$-\frac{120}{8} + \frac{160}{8} + \frac{40}{8} = 10$$

$$\frac{80}{8} = 10$$

$$10 = 10$$

TWO METHODS OF MATRIX INVERSION

Row and Column Procedures

The inverse matrix is analogous to the reciprocal of a number. It is defined only in relation to something else. If M is a square 2×2, 3×3, or 4×4 matrix, its inverse is designated M^{-1} and is defined as that matrix which will when multiplied by M, result in a product which is simply an identity matrix. Symbolically M^{-1} is the inverse matrix of M if, and only if,

$$M^{-1}M = I = MM^{-1}$$

The inverse will be a square matrix and have the same number of rows and columns as M and the identity matrix I. The inverse does not always exist, even if the original matrix M is dimensionally square. If the determinant of a square matrix is non-zero, an inverse exists, but if the determinant is zero, the inverse does not exist.

Suppose that a vector (2   3) is multiplied by a matrix

$$\begin{pmatrix} 1 & 2 \\ 3 & 4 \end{pmatrix}.$$

This multiplication would result in a new vector as follows:

$$(2 \quad 3) \times \begin{pmatrix} 1 & 2 \\ 3 & 4 \end{pmatrix} = (11 \quad 16)$$

Multiplication of the inverse of the matrix

$$\begin{pmatrix} 1 & 2 \\ 3 & 4 \end{pmatrix}$$

by the resultant vector of the above multiplication (11   16) will return us to the original vector (2   3). There are a number of row and column procedures employed to compute the inverse. The procedures which are employed simultaneously upon the original and the identity matrix are as follows:

1. One row can be interchanged with another row.
2. One column can be interchanged with another column.
3. A row can be multiplied by a constant.
4. A column can be multiplied by a constant.
5. One row can be added to or subtracted from another row.
6. One column can be added to or subtracted from another column.
7. A multiple of a row can be added to or subtracted from another row.
8. A multiple of a column can be added to or subtracted from another column.

The row and column inversion procedure is one of the more tedious of the alternative computational procedures available for inversion. If the matrices being analyzed are quite large, then it would be definitely advantageous to examine the possibilities of utilizing a standard electronic computer program to perform the calculations.

To invert the original matrix presented in this section, we first place beside it an identity matrix of the same size. The eight row and column procedures are then used, when and if appropriate, to convert the original matrix into an identity matrix if an inverse exists. We may either use the row or the column procedures, but not both, in performing the inversion operation on any one problem.

$$\begin{matrix} \text{Original} & \text{Identity} \\ \text{Matrix} & \text{Matrix} \end{matrix}$$

$$\begin{pmatrix} 1 & 2 \\ 3 & 4 \end{pmatrix} \begin{pmatrix} 1 & 0 \\ 0 & 1 \end{pmatrix}$$
1. Place matrices side by side

$$\begin{pmatrix} 1 & 2 \\ \tfrac{3}{4} & 1 \end{pmatrix} \begin{pmatrix} 1 & 0 \\ 0 & \tfrac{1}{4} \end{pmatrix}$$
2. Multiply the 2d row by $\tfrac{1}{4}$ (procedure 3)

$$\begin{pmatrix} 1 & 2 \\ 0 & -\tfrac{2}{4} \end{pmatrix} \begin{pmatrix} 1 & 0 \\ -\tfrac{3}{4} & \tfrac{1}{4} \end{pmatrix}$$
3. Multiply the 1st row by $\tfrac{3}{4}$ and subtract it from the 2d row (procedure 7)

$$\begin{pmatrix} 1 & 2 \\ 0 & -2 \end{pmatrix} \begin{pmatrix} 1 & 0 \\ -3 & 1 \end{pmatrix}$$
4. Multiply the 2d row by 4 (procedure 3)

$$\begin{pmatrix} 1 & 0 \\ 0 & -2 \end{pmatrix} \begin{pmatrix} -2 & 1 \\ -3 & 1 \end{pmatrix}$$
5. Add the 2d row to the 1st row (procedure 7)

$$\begin{pmatrix} 1 & 0 \\ 0 & 1 \end{pmatrix} \begin{pmatrix} -2 & 1 \\ \tfrac{3}{2} & -\tfrac{1}{2} \end{pmatrix}$$
6. Multiply the 2d row by $-\tfrac{1}{2}$ (procedure 3)

Since the original matrix is now an identity, we know our procedural analysis is complete. Thus, the inverse (M^{-1}) of the original matrix (M) is

$$\begin{pmatrix} -2 & 1 \\ \frac{3}{2} & -\frac{1}{2} \end{pmatrix}$$

It is best to check our calculations by multiplying the inverse by the resultant vector we derived to determine if we get the original vector (2   3).

$$(11 \quad 16) \times \begin{pmatrix} -2 & 1 \\ \frac{3}{2} & -\frac{1}{2} \end{pmatrix} = (2 \quad 3)$$

The mathematical calculations indicate that the inverse matrix

$$\begin{pmatrix} -2 & 1 \\ \frac{3}{2} & -\frac{1}{2} \end{pmatrix}$$

represents the array of elements which will revert the resultant vector (11   16) back to its original set (2   3).

The row and column procedures can be employed to conduct inversions of larger square matrices such as a 3 × 3, 4 × 4, 5 × 5, etc. The inversion of a 3 × 3 matrix proceeds exactly in the same manner as used in the sample problem above. It should be remembered that when forming an inverse, one must utilize either row procedures or column procedures; the two procedures must be used separately in forming an inverse. This method is more of a trial and error procedure and use of another method known as cofactor inversion is more systematic, normally faster, and less tedious.

Cofactor Matrix Inversion

Any square matrix which is 2 × 2 or larger may be separated into its cofactors. A cofactor is that element or group of elements which remains when a row and column have been removed from the matrix. An original 2 × 2 matrix is presented below:

Original Matrix

$$\begin{pmatrix} ③ & 2 \\ 5 & 4 \end{pmatrix}$$

If the first row and first column are removed, the cofactor of the circled element, 3, remains and it is 4.

Original Matrix − Row 1, Column 1 = Cofactor

$$\begin{pmatrix} 3 & 2 \\ 5 & 4 \end{pmatrix} \qquad \begin{pmatrix} 3 & 2 \\ 5 & \end{pmatrix} \qquad \begin{pmatrix} & \\ & 4 \end{pmatrix}$$

The original 2 × 2 matrix would contain four cofactors and they would be obtained as follows:

Original Matrix — Row and Column = Cofactor   Sign of
                    Removed   Cofactor

$$\begin{pmatrix} 3 & 2 \\ 5 & 4 \end{pmatrix} \qquad \begin{pmatrix} 3 & 2 \\ 5 & \end{pmatrix} \qquad \begin{pmatrix} & \\ & 4 \end{pmatrix}$$ $\quad$ 1 + 1 = even
                                                                         sign unchanged

$$\begin{pmatrix} 3 & 2 \\ 5 & 4 \end{pmatrix} \qquad \begin{pmatrix} 3 & 2 \\ & 4 \end{pmatrix} \qquad \begin{pmatrix} & \\ -5 & \end{pmatrix}$$ $\quad$ 1 + 2 = odd
                                                                         sign changed

$$\begin{pmatrix} 3 & 2 \\ 5 & 4 \end{pmatrix} \qquad \begin{pmatrix} 3 & \\ 5 & 4 \end{pmatrix} \qquad \begin{pmatrix} & -2 \\ & \end{pmatrix}$$ $\quad$ 2 + 1 = odd
                                                                         sign changed

$$\begin{pmatrix} 3 & 2 \\ 5 & 4 \end{pmatrix} \qquad \begin{pmatrix} & 2 \\ 5 & 4 \end{pmatrix} \qquad \begin{pmatrix} 3 & \\ & \end{pmatrix}$$ $\quad$ 2 + 2 = even
                                                                         sign unchanged

The sign of the cofactor is determined by adding together the location numbers of the row and column which have been removed. If the sum is an even number, the sign of the cofactor is unchanged. If the sum is an odd number, the sign of the cofactor is changed.

If each of the elements in the original matrix is replaced by its cofactor, the matrix of cofactors for the original 2 × 2 matrix is then

$$\begin{pmatrix} 4 & -5 \\ -2 & 3 \end{pmatrix}$$

The matrix of cofactors is used to form the adjoint of a matrix which is useful in the study of business games. Since we already know how to find the transpose of a matrix and the matrix of cofactors, a simple juxtaposition of rows and columns will form the adjoint. Thus, the adjoint is nothing more than the transpose of the matrix of cofactors.

Original Matrix   Matrix of Cofactors   Adjoint Matrix

$$\begin{pmatrix} 3 & 2 \\ 5 & 4 \end{pmatrix} \qquad \begin{pmatrix} 4 & -5 \\ -2 & 3 \end{pmatrix} \qquad \begin{pmatrix} 4 & -2 \\ -5 & 3 \end{pmatrix}$$

The cofactor matrix of a 3 × 3 array of rows and columns is found by using determinants. Suppose that we are asked to find the cofactor matrix of the following original 3 × 3 matrix:

$$\begin{pmatrix} 6 & 8 & 0 \\ 9 & 2 & 1 \\ 5 & 4 & 3 \end{pmatrix}$$

The circled value 6 cannot be replaced in the matrix of cofactors by its entire cofactor

$$\begin{pmatrix} 2 & 1 \\ 4 & 3 \end{pmatrix}.$$

It is replaced by the determinant of its cofactor.

$$\begin{vmatrix} 2 & 1 \\ 4 & 3 \end{vmatrix} = 2 \quad \text{(The sign of the cofactor will reflect the location of the row and column removed.)}$$

The following procedures are then employed to find the cofactor matrix.

Original Matrix

$$\begin{pmatrix} 6 & 8 & 0 \\ 9 & 2 & 1 \\ 5 & 4 & 3 \end{pmatrix}$$

Subtract Row and Column	Cofactors	Numerical Value of Cofactors
$\begin{pmatrix} 6 & 8 & 0 \\ 9 & & \\ 5 & & \end{pmatrix}$	$\begin{pmatrix} 2 & 1 \\ 4 & 3 \end{pmatrix} \begin{vmatrix} 2 & 1 \\ 4 & 3 \end{vmatrix}$	$=$ (2) $1 + 1$ = even sign unchanged
$\begin{pmatrix} 6 & & \\ 9 & 2 & 1 \\ 5 & & \end{pmatrix}$	$\begin{pmatrix} 8 & 0 \\ 4 & 3 \end{pmatrix} \begin{vmatrix} 8 & 0 \\ 4 & 3 \end{vmatrix}$	$= (-24)$ $2 + 1$ = odd sign changed
$\begin{pmatrix} 6 & & \\ 9 & & \\ 5 & 4 & 3 \end{pmatrix}$	$\begin{pmatrix} 8 & 0 \\ 2 & 1 \end{pmatrix} \begin{vmatrix} 8 & 0 \\ 2 & 1 \end{vmatrix}$	$=$ (8) $3 + 1$ = even sign unchanged
$\begin{pmatrix} 6 & 8 & 0 \\ & 2 & \\ & 4 & \end{pmatrix}$	$\begin{pmatrix} 9 & 1 \\ 5 & 3 \end{pmatrix} \begin{vmatrix} 9 & 1 \\ 5 & 3 \end{vmatrix}$	$= (-22)$ $1 + 2$ = odd sign changed
$\begin{pmatrix} & 8 & \\ 9 & 2 & 1 \\ & 4 & \end{pmatrix}$	$\begin{pmatrix} 6 & 0 \\ 5 & 3 \end{pmatrix} \begin{vmatrix} 6 & 0 \\ 5 & 3 \end{vmatrix}$	$= (18)$ $2 + 2$ = even sign unchanged
$\begin{pmatrix} & 8 & \\ & 2 & \\ 5 & 4 & 3 \end{pmatrix}$	$\begin{pmatrix} 6 & 0 \\ 9 & 1 \end{pmatrix} \begin{vmatrix} 6 & 0 \\ 9 & 1 \end{vmatrix}$	$= (-6)$ $3 + 2$ = odd sign changed
$\begin{pmatrix} 6 & 8 & 0 \\ & & 1 \\ & & 3 \end{pmatrix}$	$\begin{pmatrix} 9 & 2 \\ 5 & 4 \end{pmatrix} \begin{vmatrix} 9 & 2 \\ 5 & 4 \end{vmatrix}$	$= (26)$ $1 + 3$ = even sign unchanged

Subtract Row and Column	Cofactors	Numerical Value of Cofactors

$$\begin{pmatrix} & & 0 \\ 9 & 2 & 1 \\ & & 3 \end{pmatrix} \qquad \begin{pmatrix} 6 & 8 \\ 5 & 4 \end{pmatrix} \begin{vmatrix} 6 & 8 \\ 5 & 4 \end{vmatrix} = \quad \begin{array}{l} (16)\ 2 + 3 = \text{odd sign} \\ \text{changed} \end{array}$$

$$\begin{pmatrix} & & 0 \\ & & 1 \\ 5 & 4 & 3 \end{pmatrix} \qquad \begin{pmatrix} 6 & 8 \\ 9 & 2 \end{pmatrix} \begin{vmatrix} 6 & 8 \\ 9 & 2 \end{vmatrix} = (-60)\ 3 + 3 = \begin{array}{l} \text{even sign} \\ \text{unchanged} \end{array}$$

The cofactor matrix is then

$$C_0 = \begin{pmatrix} 2 & -22 & 26 \\ -24 & 18 & 16 \\ 8 & -6 & -60 \end{pmatrix}$$

The determinant of the original matrix

$$\begin{pmatrix} 6 & 8 & 0 \\ 9 & 2 & 1 \\ 5 & 4 & 3 \end{pmatrix}$$

is found to be -164. By using the adjoint of the original, which is the transpose of the cofactor matrix

Cofactor Matrix	Transpose (Adjoint of Cofactor Matrix)

$$\begin{pmatrix} 2 & -22 & 26 \\ -24 & 18 & 16 \\ 8 & -6 & -60 \end{pmatrix} \qquad \begin{pmatrix} 2 & -24 & 8 \\ -22 & 18 & -6 \\ 26 & 16 & -60 \end{pmatrix}$$

and the determinant (-164) of the original matrix, we can find the inverse of the original matrix. Each element in the transposed matrix is divided by the determinant value of the original and we then have the inverse of the original.

$$\begin{array}{l} \text{Inverse of the} \\ \text{original} \end{array} = A^{-1} = \begin{pmatrix} -2/164 & 24/164 & -8/164 \\ 22/164 & -18/164 & 6/164 \\ -26/164 & -16/164 & 60/164 \end{pmatrix}$$

To test and prove that this is in fact the inverse of the original matrix we can multiply the inverse by the original to find the identity matrix.

$$\begin{pmatrix} -2/164 & 24/164 & -8/164 \\ 22/164 & -18/164 & 6/164 \\ -26/164 & -16/164 & 60/164 \end{pmatrix} \times \begin{pmatrix} 6 & 8 & 0 \\ 9 & 2 & 1 \\ 5 & 4 & 3 \end{pmatrix} = \begin{pmatrix} 1 & 0 & 0 \\ 0 & 1 & 0 \\ 0 & 0 & 1 \end{pmatrix}$$

The cofactor approach to matrix inversion is more systematic and less of a "hit or miss" method than the row and column procedures. There are, of course, other inversion procedures and the decision maker would be advised to examine them and select the one which is most appealing.

PROBLEMS

1. Discuss the following statements:

   a) "It is possible for equations to have mathematically correct answers, but some of them cannot be considered as viable solutions to business problems."

   b) "What is the difference between the transpose of a matrix and the adjoint matrix?"

2. Subtract the following matrices:

   a)
   $$\begin{pmatrix} 3 & 2 \\ 8 & -4 \end{pmatrix} - \begin{pmatrix} -6 & -2 \\ -3 & 1 \end{pmatrix}$$

   b)
   $$\begin{pmatrix} 9 & 8 \\ 9 & 8 \end{pmatrix} - \begin{pmatrix} 6 & 3 \\ 6 & 2 \end{pmatrix}$$

3. Multiply the following matrices:

   a)
   $$\begin{pmatrix} 4 & 3 \\ 5 & 6 \end{pmatrix} \times \begin{pmatrix} 1 & 4 \\ 0 & 8 \end{pmatrix}$$

   b)
   $$\begin{pmatrix} 1 & 9 \end{pmatrix} \times \begin{pmatrix} 6 \\ 8 \end{pmatrix}$$

4. Find the transpose of the following matrices:

   a)
   $$\begin{pmatrix} X_1 & X_4 & X_7 \\ X_2 & X_5 & X_8 \\ X_3 & X_6 & X_9 \end{pmatrix}$$

   b)
   $$\begin{pmatrix} 9 & 8 & 7 & 6 \\ 5 & 4 & 3 & 2 \\ 2 & 1 & 9 & 8 \\ 8 & 7 & 6 & 5 \end{pmatrix}$$

5. Find the adjoint of the following matrix:

   $$\begin{pmatrix} 8 & 9 & 3 \\ 7 & 8 & 4 \\ 6 & 1 & 9 \end{pmatrix}$$

6. Find the values of the following determinants:

   a)
   $$\begin{vmatrix} 8 & 6 \\ 7 & 9 \end{vmatrix}$$

b)
$$\begin{vmatrix} -1 & -6 \\ -3 & 5 \end{vmatrix}$$

c)
$$\begin{vmatrix} 8 & 8 & 7 \\ 1 & 6 & 8 \\ 9 & 5 & 4 \end{vmatrix}$$

7. Using column procedures, find the inverse of the following matrix and verify your analysis:

$$\begin{pmatrix} 4 & 8 \\ 6 & 7 \end{pmatrix}$$

8. A glass manufacturing firm has classified all of their accounts into four specific sales regions. The average size of each sale in each region is presented in the vector

$$s = (800,900,500,300)$$

A total of four salesmen sell in each of the regions. The number of times each salesman generates the average size sale is presented in vector (f).

$$f = \begin{pmatrix} 9 \\ 12 \\ 8 \\ 6 \end{pmatrix}$$

a) By vector multiplication, find the total amount of glass which will be sold to each area in a year.

b) If the average glass breakage in shipment per year is approximately 10 percent of the total, what would be the actual amount of usable glass put into the hands of the next link (wholesaler) in the firm's distribution channel?

9. Given the system of equations

$$6X + 4Y + 6Z = 8$$
$$5X + 3Y + 2Z = 10$$
$$7X + 5Y + 3Z = 14$$

find X, Y, and Z, using determinants.

10. Using the cofactor matrix inversion procedure, invert the following matrix:

$$\begin{pmatrix} 8 & 3 & 4 \\ 6 & 2 & 6 \\ 5 & 0 & 1 \end{pmatrix}$$

11. Construct a set of matrices A and B such that $AB = BA$.

12. The dollar level of sales required for the Harvest Food Manufacturers to break even on their new breakfast energy food product depends on fixed costs and the proportion that variable costs are of sales.

a) State this relationship in symbolic mathematical notation in a functional format.

b) State this relationship in terms of a specific equation.

REFERENCES

BOWEN, E. K. *Mathematics with Applications in Management and Economics,* rev. ed. Homewood, Ill.: Richard D. Irwin, Inc., 1967.

CAMPBELL, H. C. *An Introduction to Matrices, Vectors, and Linear Programming.* New York: Appleton-Century-Crofts, 1965.

HADLEY, G. *Linear Algebra.* Reading, Mass.: Addison-Wesley Publishing Company, Inc., 1961.

KEMENY, G., SCHLEIFER, A., JR., SNELL, J. L., and THOMPSON, G. L. *Finite Mathematics with Business Applications.* Englewood Cliffs, N.J.: Prentice-Hall, Inc., 1962.

MOORE, G. E. *Algebra,* rev. ed. New York: Barnes and Noble, Inc., 1961.

RICHARDSON, M. *College Algebra.* Englewood Cliffs, N.J.: Prentice-Hall, Inc., 1958.

SCHWARTZ, JACOB T. *Introduction to Matrices and Vectors.* New York: McGraw-Hill Book Company, Inc., 1961.

chapter six

MATHEMATICAL PROGRAMMING

INTRODUCTION

While linear equations and inequalities such as those discussed in Chapter Five are by no means new mathematical concepts, the integration and development of linear programming is relatively new.[1] In fact, its origin dates back to the years just following World War II. The individual most responsible for the development of linear programming was George B. Dantzig, who at the time was a civilian employed by the United States Air Force. His formal training was as a mathematician and he was working at the time on logistics problems of the Air Force. In attempting to solve these logistics problems, he noted that many of them could be formulated into what we now know as a linear program. Dantzig developed a formal mathematical procedure to solve these problems and entitled his technique the simplex algorithm.[2]

Since that time linear programming models have been used in a wide variety of business problem situations. With the simultaneous growth of operations research and the electronic computer, complex linear programming models can now be used at an increased rate. This chapter will present the basic concepts and rationale of linear programming.

What is Linear Programming?

A linear programming problem occurs whenever the following two conditions arise.

---

[1] There are other types of mathematical programming such as nonlinear programming, quadratic programming, integer programming, and dynamic programming. In this text we will be concerned only with linear programming.

[2] The term algorithm is defined as a rule or procedure for solving a mathematical problem that frequently involves repetition of an operation.

1. When two or more activities compete for limited resources.
2. When it can be assumed that all relationships in the problem are linear.[3]

A sample problem can illustrate the basic fundamentals of linear programming. Assume that the product manager of the Gibson Corporation, a manufacturer of card tables, has the choice of producing two different types—a standard model (*A*) and a more elaborate deluxe model (*B*). Furthermore, let us assume that both models require the same amount of machine time for production, but because of its special features, the deluxe model requires twice as much painting time but less assembling time. The problem the product manager faces is to determine a production "program" for the two products.

TABLE 6–1
Gibson Corporation Resources

Department	Minutes Required per Unit		Capacity per Time Period (*Minutes*)
	Model A	Model B	
Production	6	6	300
Painting	4	8	320
Assembling	5	3	310
Profit contribution per unit	$10	$12	

In this problem, the card tables (*A* and *B*) are the candidates and the three processes (production, painting, and assembling) are the limited resources. If profit is our objective, then we hope to design a program that will maximize profits. This is usually formulated into a mathematical expression known as an objective function or profit function whose value can be computed when the values of all variables are determined. Finally, the capacities of the resources are limited and, if we assume that no plant expansion plans are called for, then this type of limitation is expressed as a set of structural constraints which restrict the values that can be assigned to the candidates. It is essential to remember that the assumption of linearity implies that the set of constraints must be linear. Therefore, the linear programming model is normative and deterministic. We can summarize the above problem in tabular form by introducing numerical values in Table 6–1.

One final important element of linear programming problem solving is the use of inequalities to express relationships. Equations are specific mathe-

---

[3] A linear relationship between two or more variables is one which is directly and precisely proportional. For example, a 10 percent change in one variable will result in a 10 percent change in the other.

matical statements which are represented by an equal sign (=). For example, assuming that profit is our sole objective, we can express this in the following equation:

$$\text{Profit} = \$10(\text{number of Model } A) + \$12(\text{number of Model } B)$$

However, as mentioned in Chapter Five, most problems faced in business cannot be expressed as equalities such as our objective function. Instead of exact specifications, the problem may require only that minimum or maximum requirements be met. For example, in the above problem it is stated that the production time needed to produce one Model A (6 minutes) times the number of Model A's produced plus the time required to produce one Model B (6 minutes) times the number of Model B's produced must be equal to or less than the 300 minutes of available production time per day. Here we must utilize inequalities. The above inequality would be expressed as follows:

$$6A + 6B \leq 300$$

In this case, any amount of time utilized which is equal to or under 300 minutes per day would satisfy the inequality. For example, note that an inequality is much less restrictive than an equation since in an equation $6A + 6B$ would equal 300 minutes. Most constraints faced in a linear programming problem are expressed as greater than or less than inequalities.

In order to acquire a clear understanding of a typical linear programming problem we will work through some problems and solve them by (1) the graphical method, (2) the algebraic method, and (3) the simplex method. Of the three methods, the simplex method represents the most general and powerful method. We shall examine the graphical and algebraic methods because problems which have three or less candidates can be more easily solved by these two methods. Also, an understanding of these two methods will provide a foundation for better understanding the concepts and rationale of the simplex algorithm.

THE GRAPHICAL METHOD

Let us return to the problem we have previously formulated in Table 6–1 and solve it by utilizing the graphical method. Since it is not possible to represent graphically more than three variables, only problems with three or less candidates can be solved by this method. Since our problem has only two competing candidates (Models A and B), it can be solved by the graphical method.

In order to begin solving the problem we must restate it in mathematical form. Since our goal is to maximize profit (P) we can state our objective as follows:

$$\text{Objective Function} = P = \$10A + \$12B$$

This equation reads that profit equals \$10 multiplied by the number of Model A produced plus \$12 multiplied by the number of Model B produced. If we produced ten of each, then profit would equal \$10(10) + \$12(10) or \$220.

The next step is to express our constraints in mathematical form. The time used in producing, painting, and assembling the tables cannot exceed the total time available in each of the three departments. That is, the time needed to make one Model A times the number produced plus the time needed to make one Model B times the number produced must be equal to or less than 300 minutes. The constraints can be expressed in mathematical terms as follows:

$$6A + 6B \leq 300 \text{ minutes of production time}$$
$$4A + 8B \leq 320 \text{ minutes of painting time}$$
$$5A + 3B \leq 310 \text{ minutes of assembling time}$$

Finally, every linear programming problem has a set of non-negativity constraints. This means that there can be no such thing as negative production, since negative production has no physical counterpart. Thus, the optimal solution must have positive values for A and B or

$$A \geq 0$$
$$B \geq 0$$

We can now summarize our problem in mathematical form as follows: Maximize

$$P = 10A + 12B$$

subject to the following constraints:

$$6A + 6B \leq 300$$
$$4A + 8B \leq 320$$
$$5A + 3B \leq 310$$
$$A \geq 0$$
$$B \geq 0$$

Next we designate on a two-dimensional graph Model A on the horizontal axis and Model B on the vertical axis. We can now plot the inequality $6A +$

FIGURE 6–1

Graph of Equation $6A + 6B \leq 300$

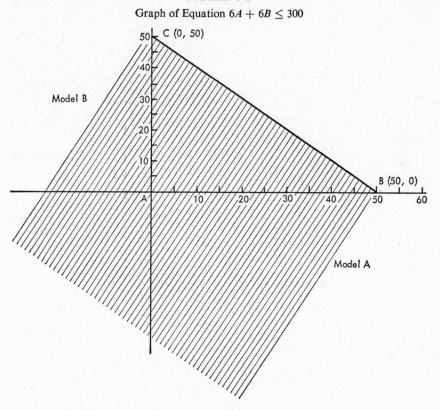

$6B \leq 300$ by locating its terminal points and joining them by a straight line. The terminal points are found by assuming that all available time is devoted to the production of one of the models. Thus, if we did not produce any deluxe models, we could produce 50 regular models and, vice versa, if we produced no regular models, we would be able to produce 50 deluxe models. This is computed as follows:

Let $B = 0$

$$6A + 6B \leq 300$$
$$6A + 6(0) \leq 300$$

Point B $A \leq 50$ regular models when no deluxe models are produced.

and

Let $A = 0$

$$6A + 6B \leq 300$$
$$6(0) + 6B \leq 300$$

Point C $\qquad B \leq 50$ deluxe models when no regular models are produced.

The two points (B,C) are plotted on the graph shown in Figure 6–1.

The region of interest to us is represented in Figure 6–1 by the shaded area. Note that the shaded area includes negative values of A and B which would mean negative production. It is for this reason that we introduced the non-

FIGURE 6–2

Production

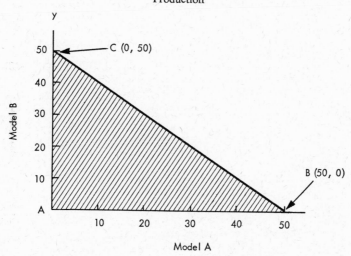

negativity constraints $A \geq 0$ and $B \geq 0$. These constraints restrict us to producing zero or more units of products A and B. Including the non-negativity constraints restricts the area of possible solutions to the first quadrant of the AB plane. This is shown in Figure 6–2.

However, let us assume that the product manager believes he can only sell 30 standard models and 30 deluxe models. This point is not on Line BC but it can be produced without exceeding 300 minutes. In other words, any combination of standard and deluxe models which lies in the shaded area ABC in Figure 6–2 can be produced without exceeding 300 minutes.

We can plot the constraint inequalities for the painting department and assembling department in a similar manner. These constraints are shown in Figures 6–3 and 6–4.

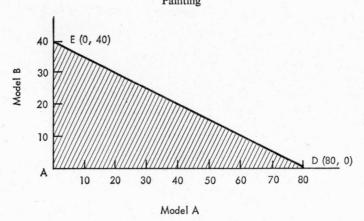

FIGURE 6–3

Painting

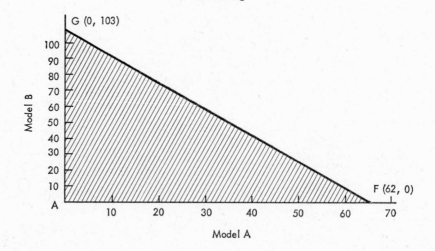

FIGURE 6–4

Assembling

Let $B = 0$

$$4A + 8B \leq 320$$
$$4A + 8(0) \leq 320$$

$$4A \leq 320$$

Point *D* $A \leq 80$ regular models when no deluxe models are produced.

Let $A = 0$

$$4A + 8B \leq 320$$
$$4(0) + 8B \leq 320$$
$$8B \leq 320$$

Point *E* $B \leq 40$ deluxe models when no regular models are produced.

Let $B = 0$

$$5A + 3B \leq 310$$
$$5A + 3(0) \leq 310$$
$$5A \leq 310$$

Point *F* $A \leq 62$ regular models when no deluxe models are produced.

Let $A = 0$

$$5A + 3B \leq 310$$
$$5(0) + 3B \leq 310$$
$$3B \leq 310$$

Point *G* $B \leq 103$ deluxe models when no regular models are produced.

The shaded area in Figure 6–3 represents all combinations of standard and deluxe models which do not exceed 320 minutes of painting time. Any combination falling within the shaded area *ADE* will satisfy this constraint. The shaded area in Figure 6–4 represents all combinations of standard and deluxe models which do not exceed 310 minutes of assembling time. Any combination falling within the shaded area *AFG* will satisfy this constraint.

In order to complete either a standard model or a deluxe model, the production process, painting process, and assembling process must be utilized. In other words, the best combination of standard and deluxe models must fall within the shaded area to the left of Line *BC* in Figure 6–2, within the shaded area to the left of line *DE* in Figure 6–3, and within the shaded area to the left of Line *FG* in Figure 6–4. This combination will not exceed the maximum time in either the production, painting, or assembling departments. Thus, if we combine Figures 6–2, 6–3, and 6–4, we obtain Figure 6–5, the shaded area of which represents the region of all feasible solutions to our problem. The shaded area *ABHE* in Figure 6–5 contains all the combinations of both models which satisfies the inequalities. We can refer to it as a feasibility space.

The construction of Figure 6–5 is the first major step in solving our problem by the graphical method. Our objective is to choose at least one point

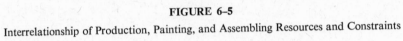

FIGURE 6–5

Interrelationship of Production, Painting, and Assembling Resources and Constraints

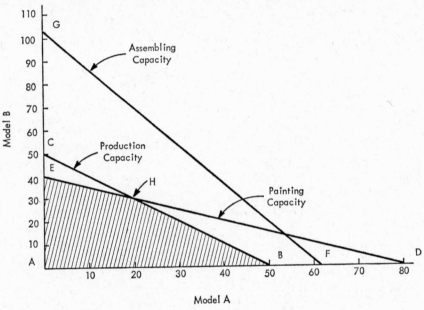

from the shaded area in Figure 6–5 which will maximize our profit (objective) function.

We are now guided by our objective function. If it were possible to plot the objective function in Figure 6–5 and determine the direction of maximum increase, we could continue to move it in this direction until we reached the farthest point on the boundary of the shaded area in Figure 6–5. This would provide us with the optimum solution.

Isoprofit Lines

Since our objective function $10A + 12B$ is not in the form of an equation, we cannot graph it. However, this problem can be solved by selecting an arbitrary profit figure and determining how many units of Model *A* alone (or Model *B* alone) would be needed to reap such a profit.[4] Let us select a profit figure of $400. Since Model *A* contributes $10, we would have to produce 40 units in order to reap a profit of $400. If we produce only Model *B*, we would have to produce 34 units (rounded) in order to reap a profit of $400, since each Model *B* contributes a profit of $12.

FIGURE 6–6

Isoprofit Line

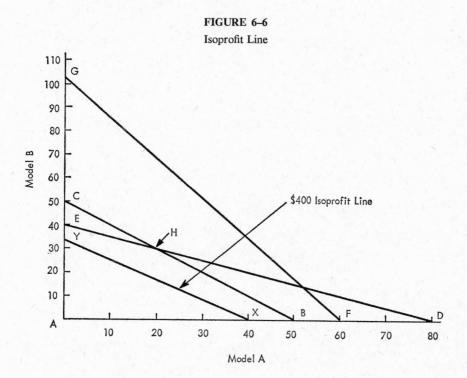

If we locate these two points on our graph ($A = 40$, and $B = 34$) and join them, we obtain the $400 isoprofit line. This appears as Line *xy* in Figure 6–6.

The isoprofit Line *xy* is, therefore, the locus of all points (all combinations of Models *A* and *B*) which yield a profit of $400. We could continue to construct these isoprofit lines for higher and higher profits as long as we remain within the feasibility space. We would be forced to stop when we reach a boundary line or corner point of the feasibility space. When this occurs, we have found (an) optimum solution(s).

---

[4] Any profit figure will suffice but we shall see it will be easier if the point selected falls within the feasibility space in Figure 6–5.

In our problem, we can see that the isoprofit line farthest from the origin and still within the feasibility space is at Point H in Figure 6–6. There are an infinite number of solutions within the feasibility space but Point H provides the optimum solution.

The coordinates of Point H can be read directly from the graph if it is constructed accurately or it can be found by solving simultaneously the equations of the two lines which intersect to form Point H, which is the only point common to both equations. The equations to be solved are

$$\text{Line } BC \qquad 6A + 6B = 300$$
$$\text{Line } DE \qquad 4A + 8B = 320$$

To solve these equations simultaneously we
A. multiply the first equation by 4.
B. multiply the second equation by -3.
C. add the results.

$$4(6A + 6B = 300) = \quad 24A + \quad 24B = \quad 1200$$
$$-3(4A + 8B = 320) = -12A + (-24B) = -960$$
$$12A = 240$$
$$A = \quad 20$$

D. substitute 20 for A in the second equation.

$$4A + 8B = 320 = 4(20) + 8B = 320$$
$$80 + 8B = 320$$
$$8B = 240$$
$$B = \quad 30$$

E. Point H is, therefore (20,30).

We can now test the four points that delineate the feasibility space in order to determine the highest dollar profit.

$$\text{Point } A \quad (0,0) = \quad 10(0) + \quad 12(0) = \$0$$
$$\text{Point } B \quad (50,0) = 10(50) + \quad 12(0) = \$500$$
$$\text{Point } E \quad (0,40) = \quad 10(0) + 12(40) = \$480$$
$$\text{Point } H \ (20,30) = 10(20) + 12(30) = \$560$$

The point that provides us with the most profit is Point H, with a profit of $560.

We have now shown that Point H yields the highest profit contribution, using either the isoprofit line or by solving simultaneously the equations of the two lines which intersect to form Point H and then testing all the points that delineate the feasibility space to determine which yields the greatest profit.

THE ALGEBRAIC METHOD

In this section we shall demonstrate an algebraic solution to the linear programming problem we have just solved through the graphical method. This problem can be stated algebraically as follows: Maximize

$$P = 10A + 12B$$

subject to

$$6A + 6B \leq 300 \text{ (production)}$$
$$4A + 8B \leq 320 \text{ (painting)}$$
$$5A + 3B \leq 310 \text{ (assembling)}$$

As the problem is now stated, it cannot be solved algebraically. We must first convert the inequalities into equations. The above inequalities can be transformed into equations by the addition of non-negative variables, S_1, S_2, S_3. Thus, we now have

$$6A + 6B + S_1 = 300 \text{ (production)}$$
$$4A + 8B + S_2 = 320 \text{ (painting)}$$
$$5A + 3B + S_3 = 310 \text{ (assembling)}$$

The variables S_1, S_2, and S_3 are known as slack variables because they "take up the slack" and serve to form equalities from the inequalities of a linear programming problem. This is because, the nature of the inequality being of the "less than or equal to" type, it is possible that the optimum combination of Models A and B may not necessarily utilize all of the available time in each department. Therefore, we add to each inequality a variable which will take up the time not used in each department. S_1 is equal to the total available time in production less the time used there to produce both models, S_2 is equal to the total available time in the painting department less the time used there to paint both models, and S_3 equals the total available time used in the assembling department less the time used to assemble both models. Mathematically, the slack variables can be expressed as follows:

$$S_1 = 300 - 6A - 6B$$
$$S_2 = 320 - 4A - 8B$$
$$S_3 = 310 - 5A - 3B$$

Thus, by adding slack variables S_1, S_2, and S_3, we have converted the constraint inequalities into equations. The slack variables will take on whatever value is needed to make the equation hold. For example:

1. Assume that in the production department we manufacture 10 Model *A* and 10 Model *B*.

$$S_1 = 300 - 6(10) - 6(10)$$
$$S_1 = 180 \text{ minutes of unused time in the}$$
$$\text{production department.}$$

2. Assume that in the painting department we process 10 Model *A* and 10 Model *B*.

$$S_2 = 320 - 4(10) - 8(10)$$
$$S_2 = 200 \text{ minutes of unused time in the}$$
$$\text{painting department.}$$

3. Assume that in the assembling department we process 10 Model *A* and 10 Model *B*.

$$S_3 = 310 - 5(10) - 3(10)$$
$$S_3 = 230 \text{ minutes of unused time in the}$$
$$\text{assembling department.}$$

Since idle time in the production, painting, or assembling departments can have no profit or loss, the slack variables have no money value and can be included in our objective function with zero profit contributions as follows:

$$P = \$10A + \$12B + \$0S_1 + \$0S_2 + \$0S_3$$

In the graphical method we saw that all the points on or in the feasibility space represented various combinations of Models *A* and *B* which provided a profit. We can now also see that the coordinates (0,0) provide no profit whatsoever. Coordinates (0,0) indicate only unused capacity.

This feasible but nonprofit solution can be shown in the algebraic method by examining the slack variable equations:

$$S_1 = 300 - 6A - 6B$$
$$S_2 = 320 - 4A - 8B$$
$$S_3 = 310 - 5A - 3B$$

These three equations indicate the relationship between the variables S_1, S_2, and S_3, which represent unused time, and *A* and *B*, which represent products. Thus, our first solution is as follows:

$$A = 0$$
$$B = 0$$
$$S_1 = 300 - 6(0) - 6(0)$$
$$S_1 = 300 \text{ minutes not used in production}$$

$$S_2 = 320 - 4(0) - 8(0)$$

$S_2 = 320$ minutes not used in painting

$S_3 = 310 - 5(0) - 3(0)$

$S_3 = 310$ minutes not used in assembling

Our first solution is, therefore, technically feasible but it is certainly not attractive from a profit standpoint. In order to create any profit, we must institute one of the following feasible programs:

1. Produce A alone
2. Produce B alone
3. Produce some combination of A and B.

Produce Only Model A

This means that $B = 0$, $S_1 = 0$, $S_2 = 0$, and $S_3 = 0$. Our equation system thus becomes

for production:

$$6A = 300 \text{ or } A = 50$$

for painting:

$$4A = 320 \text{ or } A = 80$$

for assembling:

$$5A = 310 \text{ or } A = 62$$

Since all three processes are needed to produce A, the production department provides the *limiting* capacity. Therefore, the maximum possible production of A is 50 units. In this case

$$\text{Profit} = \$10(50) + \$12(0) + \$0(S_1) + \$0(S_2) + \$0(S_3)$$
$$= \$500$$

Produce Only Model B

This means that $A = 0$, $S_1 = 0$, $S_2 = 0$, and $S_3 = 0$. Our equation system thus becomes

for production:

$$6B = 300 \text{ or } B = 50$$

for painting:

$$8B = 320 \text{ or } B = 40$$

for assembling:

$$3B = 310 \text{ or } B = 103$$

In this case the painting department provides the limiting capacity. The maximum possible production of B is 40 units. This will yield

$$\text{Profit} = \$10(0) + \$12(40) + \$0(S_1) + \$0(S_2) + \$0(S_3)$$
$$= \$480$$

Produce A and B

Any program that we can devise that will produce a maximum profit utilizing some combination of A and B will be such that it utilizes as much of the resources as possible. We must search for those combinations in which either of the following occur:

1. $S_1 = 0, S_2 = 0$, or
2. $S_1 = 0, S_3 = 0$, or
3. $S_2 = 0, S_3 = 0$

If in our equation system we allow $S_1 = 0$ and $S_2 = 0$, we obtain the following:

$$
\begin{array}{ll}
a) & 6A + 6B = 300 \\
b) & 4A + 8B = 320 \\
c) & 5A + 3B + S_3 = 310
\end{array}
$$

Solving Equations (a) and (b) simultaneously yields $A = 20$ and $B = 30$. Substituting these values into Equation (c) yields:

$$
\begin{aligned}
5(20) + 3(30) + S_3 &= 310 \\
S_3 &= 310 - 100 - 90 \\
S_3 &= 120
\end{aligned}
$$

This means that our solution of $A = 20$ and $B = 30$ will result in 120 minutes of idle time in the assembling department. This program yields a profit of

$$10(20) + 12(30) = \$560$$

Since we have solved this problem by the graphical method, we know that this solution yields the highest profit. However, assuming that this is not known, we must test all the combinations.

Let us assume now that S_1 and $S_3 = 0$

$$a) \qquad 6A + 6B = 300$$
$$b) \ 4A + 8B + S_2 = 320$$
$$c) \qquad 5A + 3B = 310$$

Solving Equations (a) and (c) simultaneously yields $A = 80$ and $B = -30$. We then substitute these values into Equation (b).

$$4(80) + 8(-30) + S_2 = 320$$
$$S_2 = 320 - 320 + 240$$
$$S_2 = 240$$

This solution is not acceptable because of the negative value of B, which we know can have no physical counterpart.

Let us assume now that S_2 and $S_3 = 0$

$$a) \ 6A + 6B + S_1 = 300$$
$$b) \ 4A + 8B \qquad = 320$$
$$c) \ 5A + 3B \qquad = 310$$

Solving Equations (b) and (c) simultaneously yields $A = 54$(rounded) $B = 13$(rounded). Substituting these values into Equation (a) yields:

$$6(54) + 6(13) + S_1 = 300$$
$$S_1 = 300 - 324 - 78$$
$$S_1 = -102$$

This obviously cannot be a solution, for it indicates that we are 102 units short in production capacity. Thus, by utilizing the algebraic method we find that the company should produce 20 of Model A and 30 of Model B to optimize profit.

THE SIMPLEX METHOD (MAXIMIZATION CASE)

In this section the simplex method is used to solve the same problem already solved by the graphical and algebraic methods. As noted previously, the purpose of presenting the graphical and algebraic methods was to give the reader an understanding of the basic concepts, terminology, and underlying rationale of linear programming problems in order to provide a foundation for full appreciation of the simplex method. For easier reference, the data of Table 6–1 are presented again as Table 6–2.

As in the graphic and algebraic methods we must reformulate the data into inequalities.

$$6A + 6B \leq 300$$
$$4A + 8B \leq 320$$
$$5A + 3B \leq 310$$

TABLE 6-2

Department	Model A	Model B	Capacity per Time Period
Production	6	6	300
Painting	4	8	320
Assembling	5	3	310
Profit contribution per unit	$10	$12	

Slack variables are also used in order to convert the inequalities into equations. These slack variables serve the same purpose as they had in the algebraic method. However, in the simplex method, any unknown that occurs in one equation must appear in all equations. The unknowns that do not affect an equation are assigned a zero coefficient. Our problem, then, can be stated in equation format as follows: Maximize

$$\$10A + \$12B + \$0S_1 + \$0S_2 + \$0S_3$$

subject to

$$6A + 6B + 1S_1 + 0S_2 + 0S_3 = 300$$
$$4A + 6B + 0S_1 + 1S_2 + 0S_3 = 320$$
$$5A + 3B + 0S_1 + 0S_2 + 1S_3 = 310$$

and

$$A \geq 0$$
$$B \geq 0$$
$$S_1 \geq 0$$
$$S_2 \geq 0$$
$$S_3 \geq 0$$

The computational routine of the simplex algorithm is an iterative process. To iterate is to repeat mechanical and mathematical operations, and this is what is done in the simplex method. Each iteration moves you toward an optimal solution because each new solution yields a larger profit than the previous solution. The simplex method also indicates when an optimal solution has been reached if one exists.

The simplex method employs matrix algebra. In a previous section simultaneous equations were employed to solve the sample problem. Matrix algebra was covered in Chapter Five. The reader should recall from Chapter Five that any set of simultaneous equations can be solved by using the concept of an inverse. This concept will be utilized in a solution via the simplex method.

Constructing the Initial Program

As in our opening solution to the algebraic method, the initial program in the simplex method is one that involves only the slack variables. Each program is presented in the form of a matrix or tableau. It is vital that the reader fully comprehend the interpretation of the data in what is referred to as a simplex tableau. Let us, therefore, examine the contents of Tableau 6–1.

1. In the "profit" column we list the coefficients of the particular variables in the solution. Since only slack variables are included in the first solution, the coefficients of S_1, S_2, and S_3 are all zero.

2. In the "program" column we list the variables that are included in the solution—that is, the products being produced. In the first solution there are only slack variables or unused time.

3. In the "quantity" column we list the quantities of the variables that are in the solution. In the first solution we have 300 minutes of slack time in production, 320 minutes of slack time in painting, and 310 minutes of slack time in assembling. Thus, total profit can be determined from the program by multiplying the "profit" column and the "quantity" column. In this case it will be zero since slack variables have a zero coefficient in the objective function.

4. The numbers in Columns A and B are the coefficients of the real product variables. For example, the number 6 in Column B means that if we wanted to make one unit of B (bring one Model B into the solution), we would have to give up 6 minutes of S_1 in the production department. The number 5 in Column A means that if we wanted to make one unit of A (bring one Model A into the solution), we would have to give up 5 minutes of S_3 in the assembling department. Thus, the elements in the body matrix represent ratios of substitution.

5. The numbers in Columns S_1, S_2, and S_3 make up the identity matrix. Like the elements of the body matrix, these numbers represent ratios of substitution. For example, the numbers in the S_1 column represent the rate of substitution between S_1 and the variables S_1, S_2, and S_3 in the solution.

6. The objective row contains the coefficients of the variables that are in the objective function. The variable row contains all of the variables in the problem.

INITIAL TABLEAU 6-1

			$10	$12				
Profit (P_i)	Program	Quantity	A	B	S_1	S_2	S_3	
0	S_1	300	6	6	1	0	0	← Objective Row
0	S_2	320	4	8	0	1	0	← Variable Row
0	S_3	310	5	3	0	0	1	3 rows which illustrate the Constraint Equations

Coefficients of Objective Function

The Variables in the Program

The Quantity of the Variables in the Program

Body Matrix

Identity Matrix

Developing Improved Solutions

For easy reference let us reproduce Tableau 6-1 with certain additions.

To find the profit for each solution and to determine if the solution can be improved, we must add two more rows to our initial tableau: a Z_j row and a $P_j - Z_j$ row. These two rows have been added to Tableau 6-1. Let us examine each row.

REVISION—TABLEAU 6-1

Profit (P_j)	Program	Quantity	$10 A	$12 B	0 S_1	0 S_2	0 S_3
0	S_1	300	6	6	1	0	0
0	S_2	320	4	8	0	1	0
0	S_3	310	5	3	0	0	1
	Z_j	0	0	0	0	0	0
Net Evaluation Row	$P_j - Z_j$		$10	$12	0	0	0

The value in the Z_j row in the quantity column indicates the total profit from the particular program. In this case it is zero.

$$\text{Quantity} \times \text{Profit per Unit}$$
$$S_1 = 300 \quad \times \quad 0 \quad = 0$$
$$S_2 = 320 \quad \times \quad 0 \quad = 0$$
$$S_3 = 310 \quad \times \quad 0 \quad = 0$$
$$\text{Total profit} = 0$$

The five values for Z_j which appear in the variable columns represent the amounts by which profit would be reduced if 1 unit of any of the five variables (A,B,S_1,S_2,S_3) are added. For example, if we want to add one unit of Model

B, the elements $\begin{pmatrix} 6 \\ 8 \\ 3 \end{pmatrix}$ in the body matrix indicate we must give up six minutes

of S_1, eight minutes of S_2, and three minutes of S_3. However, it is known that unused capacity is worth nothing so there is no reduction in profit. Thus, profit reduction is computed as follows

$$
\begin{array}{ccccc}
 & \textit{Minutes} & & \textit{Profit} & \\
 & \textit{Given Up} & \times & \textit{per Unit} & = & \textit{Reduction} \\
S_1 = & 6 & \times & 0 & = & 0 \\
S_2 = & 8 & \times & 0 & = & 0 \\
S_3 = & 3 & \times & 0 & = & 0 \\
 & & & \text{Total reduction} & = & 0
\end{array}
$$

We already know that P_j is profit per unit. For Model A it is \$10, for Model B it is \$12. $P_j - Z_j$ represents the *net* profit which will result if we introduce one unit of a particular variable to our program. This we refer to as the net evaluation row in Tableau 6–1. To get a number in the net evaluation row under any particular column, multiply the elements in the column by the corresponding values in the profit (P_j) column and sum the products (this gives us Z_j). We then subtract this value (Z_j) from the number listed in the objective row at the top of the column. This gives us $P_j - Z_j$.

Let us calculate the Z_j's for Tableau 6–1.

$$
\begin{aligned}
Z_j \text{ (total profit)} &= \$0(300) + \$0(320) + \$0(310) = \$0 \\
Z_j \text{ (for variable } A) &= \$0(6) + \$0(4) + \$0(5) = \$0 \\
Z_j \text{ (for variable } B) &= \$0(6) + \$0(8) + \$0(3) = \$0 \\
Z_j \text{ (for variable } S_1) &= \$0(1) + \$0(0) + \$0(0) = \$0 \\
Z_j \text{ (for variable } S_2) &= \$0(0) + \$0(1) + \$0(0) = \$0 \\
Z_j \text{ (for variable } S_3) &= \$0(0) + \$0(0) + \$0(1) = \$0
\end{aligned}
$$

Let us now calculate the net evaluation row ($P_j - Z_j$) or the net profit per unit of each variable.

Variables	Profit per Unit (P_j) $-$	Profit Lost per Unit (Z_j) $=$	Net Profit per Unit ($P_j - Z_j$)
A	\$10	0	\$10
B	\$12	0	\$12
S_1	0	0	0
S_2	0	0	0
S_3	0	0	0

These net profit figures are shown in Tableau 6–1 and are identified as the net evaluation row. These numbers represent the possible improvement in the objective function of the introduction into the program of one unit of each of the column variables. Therefore, these numbers represent the opportunity costs of not having one unit of each of the variables in our program. In other words, our solution could be improved upon by adding one unit of A or B

but not by adding one unit of S_1, S_2, or S_3 since they each have a zero value in the net evaluation row.

Since the initial solution contains only slack variables and therefore a profit contribution of zero, it is definitely not an optimal solution and can be improved upon. The fact that it is not an optimal solution and can definitely be improved upon is determined by the numbers in the net evaluation row.

Let us assume that we have decided to add (produce) one unit of Model A. In order to do this we would be forced to give up six units of S_1, four units of S_2, and five units of S_3. This change would have the following effect on profit.

$$1(\$10) - 6(0) - 4(0) - 5(0) = \$10$$

By introducing one unit of A to our solution we have increased the value of the objective (profit) function by \$10. We could say, therefore, that the opportunity cost of not having this one unit of Model A in our program is \$10. This figure is indicated in the net evaluation row under Column A. The opportunity cost of not having a unit of B in our solution is shown in the net evaluation row as \$12. It was arrived at in the same manner as that of Model A.

The existence of positive values in the net evaluation row is a significant sign. It tells us that a better program can be developed. Thus, we can say that as long as positive values exist in the net evaluation row, then an optimum solution has not been found.[5] For example, by adding one unit of A, our profits can be increased by \$10. On the other hand, a negative value in the $P_j - Z_j$ row (net evaluation row) would indicate the amount by which profits would decrease if one unit of the variable at the head of the column was added to the solution. Thus, we can say that the optimum solution is reached when no positive values remain in the net evaluation row, which indicates that no more profit can be made. If we examine Tableau 6–1, we can see that an optimum solution has not been reached.

Revising the Program

The two positive numbers (10,12) in the net evaluation row indicate the opportunity cost of not adding one unit of A or B to our program. The procedure for improving our solution is basically two steps.

---

[5] This will hold true for linear programming problems in which the objective is to maximize a particular variable such as profit. There are also linear programming problems where the objective is to minimize a variable such as cost. The interpretation of the meaning of values in the net evaluation row of a minimization problem will be covered in another section of this chapter.

1. Determine which variable will be added.
2. Determine which variable will be replaced.

Since the highest opportunity cost falls under Column *B*, then Model *B* should be brought into the program first. Column B, therefore, becomes the key column. Thus, *the column under which the largest opportunity cost falls becomes the key column.*

Since we have decided to bring in Model *B* to replace at least one of the products in the existing program, we must now determine how many units of *B* can be brought in without exceeding the capacity of any of the resources. If we examine Tableau 6–1, we see that if we bring in one unit of *B* we must give up six units of S_1, eight units of S_2, and three units of S_3. We can now determine the maximum number of units of *B* we can bring in without violating the non-negativity constraints.

$$\text{Row } S_1 \text{ (production) } \frac{300}{6} = 50 \text{ units}$$

$$\text{Row } S_2 \text{ (painting) } \quad \frac{320}{8} = 40 \text{ units}$$

$$\text{Row } S_3 \text{ (assembling) } \frac{310}{3} = 103.3 \text{ units}$$

The limiting case arises from row S_2 in Tableau 6–1. This becomes our key row and 40 is the maximum number of Model *B* that can be produced without violating our resource capacities. Thus, *the row in which the smallest replacement ratio occurs becomes the key row.*

For ease of reference we will reproduce Tableau 6–1 in order to indicate the key column and key row.

FINAL REVISION—TABLEAU 6–1

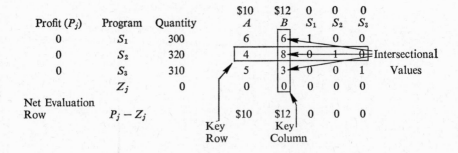

Profit (P_j)	Program	Quantity	$10 *A*	$12 *B*	0 S_1	0 S_2	0 S_3	
0	S_1	300	6	6	1	0	0	
0	S_2	320	4	8	0	1	0	Intersectional
0	S_3	310	5	3	0	0	1	Values
	Z_j	0	0	0	0	0	0	
Net Evaluation Row	$P_j - Z_j$		$10	$12	0	0	0	

Key
Row

Key
Column

Now that the key row and key column have been identified, it is possible to locate the intersectional value. This number can be found at the intersection of the key row and key column. This number is important because dividing the key row by this number gives us the corresponding row in the revised tableau.

Once we have identified the key column and the key row, we are able to develop the second simplex tableau, an improved solution. The first step is to replace the S_2 row (key row) with B, the product we are bringing into the solution. In order to obtain the new row, divide each number in the key row (the row we are replacing) by the intersectional value of the key row, which in this case is eight.

$$\frac{320}{8} = 40 \qquad \frac{4}{8} = .50 \qquad \frac{8}{8} = 1 \qquad \frac{0}{8} = 0 \qquad \frac{1}{8} = .125 \qquad \frac{0}{8} = 0$$

Therefore, the new B row will be 40, .50, 1, 0, .125, and 0. This is shown in Tableau 6–2 (Partial).

TABLEAU 6–2 (PARTIAL)

Profit (P_j)	Program	Quantity	$10 A	$12 B	0 S_1	0 S_2	0 S_3
0	S_1						
$12	B	40	.50	1	0	.125	0
0	S_3						

Note that in the incoming row a dollar figure appears in the profit (P_j) column and that the variables S_1 and S_3 remain with the profit (P_j) per unit of zero. It is now possible to complete our revised tableau. We shall use the following formula to compute the new values for the remaining rows.

$$\begin{pmatrix} \text{Value in} \\ \text{Old Row} \end{pmatrix} - \begin{pmatrix} \text{Intersectional} \\ \text{Value of} \\ \text{Old Row} \end{pmatrix} \times \begin{pmatrix} \text{Corresponding} \\ \text{Value in} \\ \text{Replacing Row} \end{pmatrix} = \begin{pmatrix} \text{New} \\ \text{Row} \end{pmatrix}$$

Let us compute the new values for the S_1 and S_3 rows.

$$
\begin{aligned}
S_1 \text{ row } 300 - (6 \times 40) &= 60 \\
6 - (6 \times .50) &= 3 \\
6 - (6 \times 1) &= 0 \\
1 - (6 \times 0) &= 1 \\
0 - (6 \times .125) &= -.75 \\
0 - (6 \times 0) &= 0
\end{aligned}
$$

$$
\begin{aligned}
S_3 \text{ row } 310 - (3 \times 40) &= 190 \\
5 - (3 \times .50) &= 3.5 \\
3 - (3 \times 1) &= 0 \\
0 - (3 \times 0) &= 0
\end{aligned}
$$

$$0 - (3 \times .125) = -.375$$
$$1 - (3 \times 0) = 1$$

We can now construct a new tableau adding on to Tableau 6–2 (Partial)

TABLEAU 6-2 (PARTIAL)

Profit (P_j)	Program	Quantity	$10 A	$12 B	0 S_1	0 S_2	0 S_3
0	S_1	60	3	0	1	−.75	0
$12	B	40	.50	1	0	.125	0
0	S_3	190	3.5	0	0	−.375	1
	Z_j						

Net
Evaluation Row $P_j - Z_j$

We can now proceed to compute the Z_j row in the new tableau. Remember, these figures indicate the amount of profit we would give up by introducing one unit of these variables into the solution.

$$Z_j \begin{pmatrix} \text{Total Profit} \\ \text{of} \\ \text{Second Solution} \end{pmatrix} = \$10(0) + \$12(40) + \$0S_1 + \$0S_2 + \$0S_3$$
$$= \$480$$

Z_j for A	$0(3)	+ $12(.50)	+ $0(3.5)	= $6.00
Z_j for B	$0(0)	+ $12(1)	+ $0(0)	= $12.00
Z_j for S_1	$0(1)	+ $12(0)	+ $0(0)	= 0
Z_j for S_2	$0(−.75)	+ $12(.125)	+ $0(−.375)	= 1.5
Z_j for S_3	$0(0)	+ $12(0)	+ $0(1)	= 0

We are now able to complete our revised tableau, 6–2

FINAL REVISION—TABLEAU 6-2

Profit (P_j)	Program	Quantity	$10 A	$12 B	0 S_1	0 S_2	0 S_3
0	S_1	60	3	0	1	−.75	0
$12	B	40	.50	1	0	.125	0
0	S_3	190	3.5	0	0	−.375	1
	Z_j	$480	$6	$12*	0	1.5	0
Net Evaluation Row	$P_j - Z_j$		$4	0	0	−1.5	0

In examining the revised solution we note the presence of a positive number in the *A* column in the net evaluation row. This indicates we have not yet

---

* In order to test his comprehension, the reader should be able to answer the question Why does the Z_j row indicate that if one more unit of *B* is produced our profits would be reduced by $12?

reached an optimal solution. Therefore, we must complete another iteration and develop a third solution.

Since the value of $4.00 is present, we will bring variable A into our solution. It becomes the key column. We must now determine how many units of A we can bring in without exceeding the capacity of any of the resources. We compute these values exactly as we did previously and select the row with the smallest ratio to be our key row.

$$\text{Row } S_1 \text{ (Production)} \qquad \frac{60}{3} = 20 \text{ units}$$

$$\text{Row } B \text{ (Model B)} \qquad \frac{40}{.50} = 80 \text{ units}$$

$$\text{Row } S_3 \text{ (Assembling)} \qquad \frac{190}{3.5} = 54.3 \text{ units}$$

Since Row S_1 has the smallest ratio, it becomes the key row (replaced row). Let us now construct a new tableau and include in it the key column, key row, and intersectional values.

TABLEAU 6–3

Profit (P_j)	Program	Quantity	$10 A	$12 B	0 S_1	0 S_2	0 S_3	
0	S_1	60	3	0	1	−.75	0	◄Key row
$12	B	40	.50	1	0	.125	0	
0	S_3	190	3.5	0	0	.375	1	Inter-
	Z_j	$480	$6	$12	0	1.5	0	sectional
Net								Values
Evaluation Row $P_j - Z_j$			$4	0	0	−1.5	0	
			Key Column					

The key row of the third solution is computed by dividing each number in the replaced row by the intersectional value of the replaced row.

$$\frac{60}{3} = 20 \qquad \frac{3}{3} = 1 \qquad \frac{0}{3} = 0 \qquad \frac{1}{3} = .33 \qquad \frac{-.75}{3} = -.25 \qquad \frac{0}{3} = 0$$

We can now begin to construct our revised tableau.

TABLEAU 6–3 (PARTIAL)

Profit (P_j)	Program	Quantity	$10 A	$12 B	0 S_1	0 S_2	0 S_3
$10	A	20	1	0	.33	−.25	0
$12	B						
0	S_3						

To find the new value for the B row and S_3 row we again utilize the formula:

$$\begin{pmatrix} \text{Value in} \\ \text{Old Row} \end{pmatrix} - \begin{pmatrix} \text{Intersectional} \\ \text{Value of} \\ \text{Old Row} \end{pmatrix} \times \begin{pmatrix} \text{Corresponding} \\ \text{Value in} \\ \text{Replacing Row} \end{pmatrix} = (\text{New Row})$$

Row B

$$
\begin{aligned}
40 &- (.50 \times & 20) &= & 30 \\
.50 &- (.50 \times & 1\ ) &= & 0 \\
1 &- (.50 \times & 0\ ) &= & 1 \\
0 &- (.50 \times & .33) &= & -.165 \\
.125 &- (.50 \times & -.25) &= & .25 \\
0 &- (.50 \times & 0\ ) &= & 0
\end{aligned}
$$

Row S_3

$$
\begin{aligned}
190 &- (3.5 \times & 20) &= & 120 \\
3.5 &- (3.5 \times & 1\ ) &= & 0 \\
0 &- (3.5 \times & 0\ ) &= & 0 \\
0 &- (3.5 \times & .33) &= & -1.16 \\
-.375 &- (3.5 \times & -.25) &= & .50 \\
1 &- (3.5 \times & 0\ ) &= & 1
\end{aligned}
$$

We can now add to our third tableau.

TABLEAU 6–3 (PARTIAL)

Profit (P_j)	Program	Quantity	$10 A	$12 B	0 S_1	0 S_2	0 S_3
$10	A	20	1	0	.33	−.25	0
$12	B	30	0	1	−.165	.25	0
0	S_3	120	0	0	−1.16	.50	1
	Z_j						
Net Evaluation Row	$P_j - Z_j$						

We can now proceed to compute the Z_j row in the new tableau.

$$Z_j \begin{pmatrix} \text{Total Profit} \\ \text{of} \\ \text{Third Solution} \end{pmatrix} = \$10(20) + \$12(30) + \$0(120) = \$560$$

$$
\begin{aligned}
Z_j \text{ for } A &= \$10(1) &+ \$12(0) &+ \$0(0) &= \$10 \\
Z_j \text{ for } B &= \$10(0) &+ \$12(1) &+ \$0(0) &= \$12 \\
Z_j \text{ for } S_1 &= \$10(.33) &+ \$12(-.165) &+ \$0(-1.16) &= +1.35 \\
Z_j \text{ for } S_2 &= \$10(-.25) &+ \$12(.25) &+ \$0(.50) &= +.50 \\
Z_j \text{ for } S_3 &= \$10(0) &+ \$12(0) &+ \$0(1) &= 0
\end{aligned}
$$

We can now complete our revised tableau, 6–3.

FINAL REVISION—TABLEAU 6-3

Profit (P_j)	Program	Quantity	$10 A	$12 B	0 S_1	0 S_2	0 S_3	
$10	A	20	1	0	.33	−.25	0	
$12	B	30	0	1	−.165	.25	0	Inverse of
								←—Body Matrix
0	S_3	120	0	0	−1.16	.50	1	
	Z_j	$560	$10	$12	+1.35	+.5	0	
Net Evaluation Row	$P_j − Z_j$		0	0	−1.35	−.5	0	

Since there is no positive $P_j - Z_j$ value, no further profit increase is possible. The optimum solution has been obtained. It is

$$A = 20 \text{ units}$$
$$B = 30 \text{ units}$$
$$S_3 = 120 \text{ minutes}$$

Profit will be maximized by producing 20 units of Model A, 30 units of Model B, and having 120 minutes of slack time in the assembling department (S_3). The variables A, B, and S_3 are shown in the program column with their values represented by the corresponding elements in the quantity column. The variables S_1 and S_2 do not appear in the program and, hence, are equal to zero. Our total profit (Z_j) appears in the quantity column and is equal to $560. This is arrived at by examining our objective function.

$$\text{Total Profit} = \$10(20) + \$12(30) + \$0(S_1) + \$0(S_2) + 120(S_3)$$
$$= \$560 + 120S_3$$

Let us examine our structural constraints.

1) For production

$$6A + 6B \leq 300$$
$$6(20) + 6(30) \leq 300$$
$$300 = 300$$

2) For painting

$$4A + 8B \leq 320$$
$$4(20) + 8(30) \leq 320$$
$$320 = 320$$

3) For assembling

$$5A + 3B \leq 310$$
$$5(20) + 3(30) \leq 310$$
$$190 < 310$$

Thus, we have 120 minutes of slack time in the Assembling Department.

Interpreting the Final Solution

As we have already noted, all the values in the net evaluation row of Tableau 6–3 are either zero or negative. This indicates that an optimal program has been attained. However, our final tableau provides us with some other interesting data.

If we examine the net evaluation row at S_1, we see that introducing one unit of S_1—allowing one unit of the production department capacity to stay idle—will decrease our objective function by \$1.35. On the other hand, if we had one more unit of S_1, the profit function would be increased by \$1.35. Thus, \$1.35 is the shadow price (or accounting price) of one unit of production department capacity. Also, the shadow price of S_2 is equal to \$.50 and S_3 is equal to zero. The total value of all of the available resources can be computed by multiplying the existing capacities of the resources by their shadow prices and summing the products. For example,

$$300(1.35) + 320(.50) + 310(0) = \$565$$

If we compare this total value of the available resources (\$565) with the value of the objective function Z_j in the final tableau (\$560), we see they differ by only \$5. The two values should be equal but differ because of rounding. The fact that the value of the objective function in the final tableau is equal to the imputed value of the available resources is referred to as the fundamental theorem of linear programming.[6]

Summary

The simplex method for a maximization problem can be summarized as follows:

I. Define and clearly formulate the problem.
  1. State the objective function.
  2. Formulate the structural constraints into inequalities.

---

[6] For an excellent discussion and explanation of this concept, see N. Paul Loomba, *Linear Programming* (New York: McGraw-Hill Book Company, 1964), pp. 125–127. The discussion presented here is based on this work.

3. Convert the inequalities into equalities by adding nonnegative slack variables. Remember that any unknown that occurs in one equation must appear in all equations. The unknowns that do not affect an equation are assigned a zero coefficient.
4. Restate the objective function to include the nonnegative slack variables.

II. Construct the initial program.
   1. The first solution will include only the slack variables. The program column in the initial tableau will include only the slack variables, and the profit (P_j) column will include only zeros.

III. Determine optimality of the program.
   1. Examine the elements of the net evaluation row ($P_j - Z_j$). An optimal program has been found if all the elements of the row are either zero or negative. The presence of a positive number in the net evaluation row indicates that a better program can be constructed.

IV. Revise the program.
   1. The first step is to locate the key column. The key column is that column under which the largest positive element in the net evaluation row ($P_j - Z_j$) is found.
   2. Locate the key row. This is achieved by first computing the replacement ratios. The row in which the smallest replacement ratio appears becomes the key row or replaced row.
   3. Transform the key row. This is done by dividing all the elements in the key row starting with the quantity column by the intersectional value of the key row. The intersectional value of the key row is found at the intersection of the key column and key row.
   4. Transfer remaining rows. This is done by utilizing the formula.

$$\begin{pmatrix} \text{Value} \\ \text{in the} \\ \text{Old Row} \end{pmatrix} - \begin{pmatrix} \text{Intersectional} \\ \text{Value of} \\ \text{Old Row} \end{pmatrix} \times \begin{pmatrix} \text{Corresponding} \\ \text{Value in} \\ \text{Replacing Row} \end{pmatrix} = \begin{pmatrix} \text{New} \\ \text{Row} \end{pmatrix}$$

V. Obtain the optimal solution.
   1. This is done by repeating Steps III and IV until an optimal program has been achieved. Remember, this will occur when all the elements in the net evaluation row ($P_j - Z_j$) are either zero or negative.

THE SIMPLEX METHOD (MINIMIZATION CASE)

Linear programming problems may also involve the minimization of an objective function. This type of problem would contain structural constraints of the "greater than or equal to" variety. Outside of these constraint conditions a minimization problem is the same as a maximization problem. In this section we will solve such a problem by the simplex method.[7]

Let us assume that the marketing manager of the Puff Cosmetics Co. has just completed an extensive marketing research study of the firm's wealthiest clients. The purpose of the study was to determine what ingredients to include in a new luxury bath mixture the company is planning to produce and market. The marketing manager wants to include the right ingredients in order to produce a bath mixture with just the right strength and scent but also wants to be sure that the mixture does not exceed certain costs.

Let us assume that the marketing manager decides to prepare some of the new mixture for test marketing purposes. He decides to produce 400 pounds of the new mixture consisting of two different grades of powder (A and B). Powder A costs \$6 per pound and B costs \$16 per pound. No more than 160 pounds of A can be used and at least 120 pounds of B must be used. These constraints are based on the softness and scent requirements that are desired. The problem facing the manager is to determine how much of each ingredient should be used if the company hopes to minimize costs.

We can state the cost function as follows:

$$Cost = 6A + 16B$$

We have three constraints in this problem. The first states that we must produce 400 pounds of the bath mixture blend. We can state this mathematically as

$$A + B = 400 \text{ pounds}$$

The second constraint states that we cannot use more than 160 pounds of A. Stated mathematically, this is

$$A \leq 160 \text{ pounds}$$

This tells us that we may use less than 160 pounds of A but we cannot use more than this amount.

The third constraint states that we must use at least 120 pounds of B. Stated mathematically, this is

$$B \geq 120 \text{ pounds}$$

---

[7] Minimization problems can, of course, also be solved by the graphical method and the algebraic method. We shall only be concerned with a simplex solution. However, the reader should be able to intuitively imagine a graphical solution utilizing isocost lines instead of isoprofit lines. For excellent discussions of the minimization case see Richard I. Levin and C. A. Kirkpatrick, *Quantitative Approaches to Management* (New York: McGraw-Hill Book Company, Inc., 1965), pp. 247–257 and Loomba, *op. cit.*, pp. 130–142.

This statement reads *B* must be "equal to or greater than" 120 pounds. In other words, we can use more than 120 pounds of *B* but cannot use less.

The problem is summarized in mathematical form as follows:
Minimize

$$\text{Cost} = 6A + 16B$$

subject to

$$A + B = 400 \text{ pounds}$$
$$A \leq 160 \text{ pounds}$$
$$B \geq 120 \text{ pounds}$$

We can now proceed to solve the problem via the simplex method. The basic steps involved in solving this problem with a few exceptions are identical to the approach used in solving a maximization problem. Only the procedure for constructing the initial tableau differs.

Constructing the Initial Tableau

In the maximization problem our initial solution contained only slack variables and netted a profit of zero. However, it served as a starting point or base from which we moved toward an improved and finally optimal solution.

In this cost minimization problem we also need a base as a starting point. Here again, it will serve as a point of departure.

Let us allow $A = 0$ and $B = 400$. Notice that this is a feasible solution since it does not violate any of our constraints.

$$
\begin{aligned}
&1)\ A + B\ \ = 400 \\
& 0 + 400 = 400 \\
& 400 = 400 \\
&2)\ A \leq 160 \text{ and } 0 < 160 \\
&3)\ B \geq 120 \text{ and } 400 > 120
\end{aligned}
$$

In this problem finding a first solution by inspection is possible. However, in a blending problem which contains 20 ingredients, finding a solution by inspection would be practically impossible. Thus, we must find a method to arrive at a first solution that can be used in all problems no matter how complex they are. This is achieved through the use of what are known as artificial variables.

Let us begin by not including any of ingredient *A* or *B* in our initial solution. Instead, we begin by including 400 pounds of *C*—an artificial variable which represents a third ingredient. The first constraint equation would then look like this

$$A + B + C \;\; = 400 \text{ pounds}$$
$$0 + 0 + 400 = 400 \text{ pounds}$$
$$400 = 400 \text{ pounds}$$

Our constraint is satisfied. But what does C represent? Let us assume that C is a very special type of skin powder which is extremely expensive ($200 per pound) which we can substitute well for our final blend. Because of its unusually high cost it will not be in our final optimum solution but it is technically feasible and serves as a starting point from which to work.

The variable C is known as an artificial variable which to us is only of value as a computational device since it allows two types of constraints to be treated: the "greater than or equal to" constraint and the equality constraint.

The second constraint is the "less than or equal to" type, with which we are already familiar. In order to convert it into an equation, we must add a slack variable (S_1).

$$A \leq 160 \text{ pounds}$$
$$A + S_1 = 160 \text{ pounds}$$

The third constraint is

$$B \geq 120 \text{ pounds}$$

In order to convert this inequality into an equation, we must subtract a slack variable.

$$B - S_2 = 120 \text{ pounds}$$

In this case, the slack variable S_2 is equal to the amount by which B will exceed 120 pounds in the final optimal solution.

However, $B = 0$ in our first initial solution, then S_2 will equal -120 pounds ($0 - S_2 = 120$, $S_2 = -120$). Obviously, this cannot be feasible because we cannot have -120 pounds of bath powder.

Here again we must make use of the artificial variable in order to prevent S_2 from appearing in the first initial solution. If we want B and S_2 to equal zero in our first solution, then we must add another new ingredient—a substitute for B in the first solution. As in the case of C this new ingredient D will be thought of as an extremely costly powder ($200 per pound). Its high cost precludes it from appearing in the final optimal tableau. Let us summarize what has been done thus far with the third constraint. The original constraint read

$$B \geq 120$$

By subtraction of a slack variable the constraint became

$$B - S_2 = 120$$

By addition of an artificial variable the constraint now becomes

$$B - S_2 + D = 120$$

Now the equation in our initial solution will still hold because $B = 0$ and $S_2 = 0$.

In order to simplify our computations, we will use the letter M to represent the high cost ($200) of the two artificial variables C and D. We are now ready to summarize our problem in mathematical form. Minimize

$$\text{Cost} = 6A + 16B$$

subject to

$$
\begin{aligned}
A + B + C &&&= 400 \\
A && + S_1 &&= 160 \\
B && - S_2 + D &= 120
\end{aligned}
$$

As we already know, any unknown that appears in one constraint equation must appear in all equations. Hence we must show zero cost for the slack variables S_1 and S_2 and M cost for the artificial variables C and D. Once this is done the problem is ready for the initial simplex tableau. Minimize

$$\text{Cost} = \$6A + \$16B + \$MC + \$0S_1 + \$0S_2 + \$MD$$

subject to

$$
\begin{aligned}
A + B + C + \$0S_1 + \$0S_2 + \$0D &= 400 \\
A + 0B + 0C + 1S_1 + 0S_2 + 0D &= 160 \\
0A + B + 0C + 0S_1 - 1S_2 + D &= 120
\end{aligned}
$$

The initial simplex solution is presented in Tableau 6–4. It maintains the same format as the tableau used in the maximization problem. However, note that the first column is labeled cost (C_j). Also note that the total cost of the first solution is an extremely high $520 M$.

The Z_j row and the net evaluation row $(C_j - Z_j)$ are computed in the same manner as in a maximization problem. Since in this example the objective is to minimize costs, the key column is that column which has the largest negative value in the net evaluation row. As long as a negative number exists in the net evaluation row of a minimization problem, the optimal solution has not been obtained. The negative entries in the net evaluation row represent the opportunity cost of not having a unit of the particular variable in the solution. In

INITIAL TABLEAU 6-4

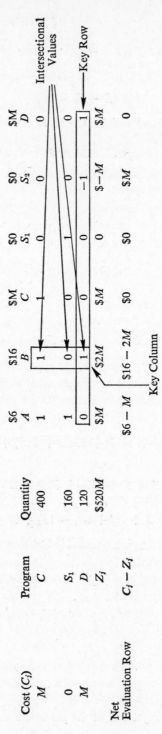

Cost (C_j)	Program	Quantity	$6 A	$16 B	$M C	$0 S_1	$0 S_2	$M D
M	C	400	1	1	1	0	0	0
0	S_1	160	1	0	0	1	0	0
M	D	120	0	1	0	0	-1	1
	Z_j	$520M	$M	$2M	$M	0	$-M	$M
Net Evaluation Row	$C_j - Z_j$		$6 - M	$16 - 2M	$M	$0	$M	0

Key Column

Key Row

Intersectional Values

this case, $16 - 2M$ is a larger negative number than $6 - M$. Thus, B becomes the key column. The necessary computations for arriving at an improved solution are as follows:

$$Z_j \text{ (total cost)} = \$M(400) + \$0(160) + \$M(120) = \$520M$$
$$Z_j \text{ for } A = \$M(1) \quad + \$0(1) \quad + \$M(0) \quad = \$M$$
$$Z_j \text{ for } B = \$M(1) \quad + \$0(0) \quad + \$M(1) \quad = \$2M$$
$$Z_j \text{ for } C = \$M(1) \quad + \$0(0) \quad + \$M(0) \quad = \$M$$
$$Z_j \text{ for } S_1 = \$M(0) \quad + \$0(1) \quad + \$M(0) \quad = \$0$$
$$Z_j \text{ for } S_2 = \$M(0) \quad + \$0(0) \quad + \$M(-1) = \$-M$$
$$Z_j \text{ for } D = \$M(0) \quad + \$0(0) \quad + \$M(1) \quad = \$M$$

Let us now calculate the net evaluation row $(C_j - Z_j)$.

Variables	C_j	$- Z_j$	$= (C_j - Z_j)$
A	$\$6$	$- \$M$	$= \$6 - M$
B	$\$16$	$- \$2M$	$= \$16 - 2M$
C	$\$M$	$- \$M$	$= \$0$
S_1	$\$0$	$- \$0$	$= \$0$
S_2	$\$0$	$- (\$-M)$	$= \$M$
D	$\$M$	$- \$M$	$= \$0$

The next step is to determine the key row, that is, the row that will be replaced in the second tableau. This is computed exactly as it was in the maximization problem.

$$\text{Row } C \quad \frac{400}{1} = 400$$
$$\text{Row } S_1 \quad \frac{160}{0} = \text{undefined}$$
$$\text{Row } D \quad \frac{120}{1} = 120$$

Since Row D has the smallest quotient, it becomes the key row (replaced row). We can now begin computing the second tableau. Again, the first step is to replace the D row (key row) with B, the element we are bringing into the solution. In order to obtain the new row we divide each number in the key row (the row we are replacing) by the intersectional value of the key row, which in this case is one.

$$\frac{120}{1} = 120 \quad \frac{0}{1} = 0 \quad \frac{1}{1} = 1 \quad \frac{0}{1} = 0 \quad \frac{0}{1} = 0 \quad \frac{-1}{1} = -1 \quad \frac{1}{1} = 1$$

We can now begin to construct the second tableau. This is presented in Tableau 6–5.

TABLEAU 6–5 (PARTIAL)

Cost (C_j)	Program	Quantity	$6 A	$16 B	$M C	$0 S_1	$0 S_2	$M D
M	C							
0	S_1							
$16	B	120	0	1	0	0	−1	1

In order to complete Tableau 6–5 the remaining rows must be computed. In order to do this we use the same formula we used in the maximization case.

$$\begin{pmatrix} \text{Value in} \\ \text{Old Row} \end{pmatrix} - \begin{pmatrix} \text{Intersectional} \\ \text{Value of} \\ \text{Old Row} \end{pmatrix} \times \begin{pmatrix} \text{Corresponding} \\ \text{Value in} \\ \text{Replacing Row} \end{pmatrix} = \begin{pmatrix} \text{New} \\ \text{Row} \end{pmatrix}$$

Row C

$$400 - (1 \times 120) = 280$$
$$1 - (1 \times 0) = 1$$
$$1 - (1 \times 1) = 0$$
$$1 - (1 \times 0) = 1$$
$$0 - (1 \times 0) = 0$$
$$0 - (1 \times -1) = 1$$
$$0 - (1 \times 1) = -1$$

Row S_1

$$160 - (0 \times 120) = 160$$
$$1 - (0 \times 0) = 1$$
$$0 - (0 \times 1) = 0$$
$$0 - (0 \times 0) = 0$$
$$1 - (0 \times 0) = 1$$
$$0 - (0 \times -1) = 0$$
$$0 - (0 \times 1) = 0$$

It is now possible to construct a revised tableau adding on to Tableau 6–5.

REVISION—TABLEAU 6–5

Cost (C_j)	Program	Quantity	$6 A	$16 B	$M C	$0 S_1	$0 S_2	$M D
M	C	280	1	0	1	0	1	−1
0	S_1	160	1	0	0	1	0	0
$16	B	120	0	1	0	0	−1	1
	Z_j							
Net Evaluation Row	$C_j - Z_j$							

The final step in arriving at a new tableau is the computation of the Z_j row.

$$Z_j \begin{pmatrix} \text{Total Cost} \\ \text{of} \\ \text{Second Solution} \end{pmatrix} = \$M(280) + \$0(160) + \$16(120) = \$280M + 1,920$$

$$\begin{aligned}
Z_j \text{ for } A &= \$M(1) &&+ \$0(1) &&+ \$16(0) &&= \$M \\
Z_j \text{ for } B &= \$M(0) &&+ \$0(0) &&+ \$16(1) &&= \$16 \\
Z_j \text{ for } C &= \$M(1) &&+ \$0(0) &&+ \$16(0) &&= \$M \\
Z_j \text{ for } S_1 &= \$M(0) &&+ \$0(1) &&+ \$16(0) &&= \$0 \\
Z_j \text{ for } S_2 &= \$M(1) &&+ \$0(0) &&+ \$16(-1) &&= \$M - 16 \\
Z_j \text{ for } D &= \$M(-1) &&+ \$0(0) &&+ \$16(1) &&= \$16 - M
\end{aligned}$$

We can now complete Tableau 6–5.

Examination of the net evaluation row $(C_j - Z_j)$ indicates that an optimum solution has not yet been found. This means that another iteration must be performed. The key column is A since it has the largest negative element. The next step is to find the key row (replaced row).

$$\text{Row } C \quad \frac{280}{1} = 280$$

$$\text{Row } S_1 \quad \frac{160}{1} = 160$$

$$\text{Row } B \quad \frac{120}{0} = \text{undefined}$$

Since it has the smallest quotient, Row S_1 becomes the key row. We can now compute the new row and the remaining rows as we did previously.

$$\frac{160}{1} = 160 \quad \frac{1}{1} = 1 \quad \frac{0}{1} = 0 \quad \frac{0}{1} = 0 \quad \frac{1}{1} = 1 \quad \frac{0}{1} = 0 \quad \frac{0}{1} = 0$$

$$\begin{pmatrix} \text{Value in} \\ \text{Old Row} \end{pmatrix} - \begin{pmatrix} \text{Intersectional} \\ \text{Value of} \\ \text{Old Row} \end{pmatrix} \times \begin{pmatrix} \text{Corresponding} \\ \text{Value in} \\ \text{Replacing Row} \end{pmatrix} = \begin{pmatrix} \text{New} \\ \text{Row} \end{pmatrix}$$

$$\begin{aligned}
\text{Row } C \quad 280 - (1 \times 160) &= 120 \\
1 - (1 \times 1) &= 0 \\
0 - (1 \times 0) &= 0 \\
1 - (1 \times 0) &= 1 \\
0 - (1 \times 1) &= -1 \\
1 - (1 \times 0) &= 1 \\
-1 - (1 \times 0) &= -1
\end{aligned}$$

FINAL REVISION—TABLEAU 6-5

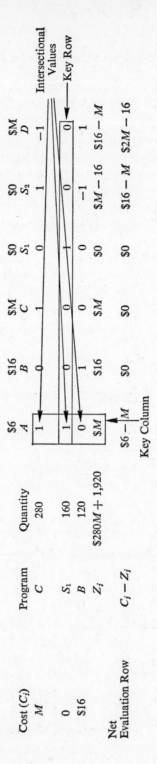

Cost (C_j)	Program	Quantity	$6 A	$16 B	$M C	$0 S_1	$0 S_2	$M D
M	C	280	1	0	1	0	1	-1
0	S_1	160	1	0	0	1	1	0
$16	B	120	0	1	0	0	-1	1
	Z_j	$280M + 1,920$	$M	$16	$M	$0	$M - 16	$16 - M
Net Evaluation Row	$C_j - Z_j$		$6 - M	$0	$0	$0	$16 - M	$2M - 16

Key Column

Intersectional Values

Key Row

$$
\begin{array}{llll}
\text{Row } B & 120 - (0 \times 160) = & 120 \\
& 0 - (0 \times & 1) = & 0 \\
& 1 - (0 \times & 0) = & 1 \\
& 0 - (0 \times & 0) = & 0 \\
& 0 - (0 \times & 1) = & 0 \\
& -1 - (0 \times & 0) = & -1 \\
& 1 - (0 \times & 0) = & 1
\end{array}
$$

$$
Z_j \begin{pmatrix} \text{Total Cost} \\ \text{of} \\ \text{Third Solution} \end{pmatrix} = \$M(120) + \$6(160) + \$16(120) = \$2,880 + \$120M
$$

$$
\begin{array}{lllll}
Z_j \text{ for } A = & \$M(0) & + \$6(1) & + \$16(0) & = \$6 \\
Z_j \text{ for } B = & \$M(0) & + \$6(0) & + \$16(1) & = \$16 \\
Z_j \text{ for } C = & \$M(1) & + \$6(0) & + \$16(0) & = \$M \\
Z_j \text{ for } S_1 = & \$M(-1) & + \$6(1) & + \$16(0) & = \$6 - M \\
Z_j \text{ for } S_2 = & \$M(1) & + \$6(0) & + \$16(-1) & = \$M - 16 \\
Z_j \text{ for } D = & \$M(-1) & + \$6(0) & + \$16(1) & = \$16 - M
\end{array}
$$

The revised solution is presented in Tableau 6–6.

The presence of a negative M value in the net evaluation row indicates that an optimal solution has yet to be found. Examination of the net evaluation row indicates that Row S_2 becomes the key column. The next step is to find the key row (replaced row).

$$
\text{Row } C \quad \frac{120}{1} = 120
$$

$$
\text{Row } A \quad \frac{160}{0} = \text{undefined}
$$

$$
\text{Row } B \quad \frac{120}{(-1)} = -120
$$

Since it has the smallest quotient, Row C becomes the key row. We now compute the new row and the remaining rows as we did previously.

$$
\frac{120}{1} = 120 \quad \frac{0}{1} = 0 \quad \frac{0}{1} = 0 \quad \frac{1}{1} = 1 \quad \frac{-1}{1} = -1 \quad \frac{1}{1} = 1 \quad \frac{-1}{1} = -1
$$

$$
\begin{pmatrix} \text{Value in} \\ \text{Old Row} \end{pmatrix} - \begin{pmatrix} \text{Intersectional} \\ \text{Value in} \\ \text{Old Row} \end{pmatrix} \times \begin{pmatrix} \text{Corresponding} \\ \text{Value in} \\ \text{Replacing Row} \end{pmatrix} = \begin{pmatrix} \text{New} \\ \text{Row} \end{pmatrix}
$$

$$
\begin{array}{llll}
\text{Row } A & 160 - (0 & \times 120) = & 160 \\
& 1 - (0 & \times 0) = & 1 \\
& 0 - (0 & \times 0) = & 0 \\
& 0 - (0 & \times 1) = & 0
\end{array}
$$

TABLEAU 6-6

Cost (C_i)	Program	Quantity	$6 A	$16 B	$M C	$0 S_1	$0 S_2	$M D
$M	C	120	0	0	1	-1	1	-1
$6	A	160	1	0	0	1	0	0
$16	B	120	0	1	0	0	-1	1
	Z_i	$120M + 2,880	$6	$16	M	$6 - M	$M - 16	$16 - M
Net Evaluation Row	$C_j - Z_j$		$0	$0	$0	$M - 6	$M - 16	$2M - 16

← Key Row

Intersectional Values

Key Column

$$1 - (0 \quad \times -1) = \quad 1$$
$$0 - (0 \quad \times \quad 1) = \quad 0$$
$$0 - (0 \quad \times -1) = \quad 0$$

Row B $\quad 120 - (-1 \times 120) = 240$
$$0 - (-1 \times \quad 0) = \quad 0$$
$$1 - (-1 \times \quad 0) = \quad 1$$
$$0 - (-1 \times \quad 1) = \quad 1$$
$$0 - (-1 \times -1) = -1$$
$$-1 - (-1 \times \quad 1) = \quad 0$$
$$1 - (-1 \times -1) = \quad 0$$

$$Z_j \begin{pmatrix} \text{Total Cost} \\ \text{of} \\ \text{Fourth Solution} \end{pmatrix} = \$0(120) + \$6(160) + \$16(240) = \$4,800$$

$$Z_j \text{ for } A = \$0(0) \quad + \$6(1) \quad + \$16(0) \quad = \$6$$
$$Z_j \text{ for } B = \$0(0) \quad + \$6(0) \quad + \$16(1) \quad = \$16$$
$$Z_j \text{ for } C = \$0(1) \quad + \$6(0) \quad + \$16(1) \quad = \$16$$
$$Z_j \text{ for } S_1 = \$0(-1) + \$6(1) \quad + \$16(-1) = \$-10$$
$$Z_j \text{ for } S_2 = \$0(1) \quad + \$6(0) \quad + \$16(0) \quad = \$0$$
$$Z_j \text{ for } D = \$0(-1) + \$6(0) \quad + \$16(0) \quad = \$0$$

The revised solution is presented in Tableau 6–7.

TABLEAU 6–7

Cost (C_i)	Program	Quantity	$6 A	$16 B	$M C	$0 S_1	$0 S_2	$M D
0	S_2	120	0	0	1	−1	1	−1
$6	A	160	1	0	0	1	0	0
$16	B	240	0	1	1	−1	0	0
	Z_j	$4,800	$6	$16	$16	$−10	$0	$0
Net Evaluation Row	$C_j - Z_j$		0	0	$M − 16	$10	$0	$M

Tableau 6–7 contains no negative values in the net evaluation row ($C_j - Z_j$). Therefore, we have reached an optimal solution. We must use 160 pounds of powder A and 240 pounds of powder B. This results in a cost of $4,800, which is the minimum cost combination of A and B, which also satisfies the constraints of the problem. The slack variable S_2 is also in the solution. It represents the amount of B used over the minimum requirement of 120 pounds.

Summary

The simplex method for a minimization problem can be summarized as follows:

I. Define and clearly formulate the problem.
   1. State the objective function.
   2. Formulate the structural constraints into inequalities.
   3. Convert the inequalities into equalities by the subtraction of non-negative slack variables, assuming the inequalities are of the "greater than or equal to" type. These equations are then further modified by the addition of non-negative artificial slack variables. Remember that any slack or artificial slack variable that appears in one equation must appear in all equations with a proper coefficient.
   4. Restate the objective function to include all slack and artificial slack variables.

II. Construct the initial program.
   1. The first solution will include only the artificial slack variables.

III. Determine optimality of the program.
   1. Examine the elements of the net evaluation row $(C_j - Z_j)$. An optimal program has been found if all the elements of the row are either zero or positive. The presence of a negative number in the net evaluation row indicates that a better program can be constructed.

IV. Revise the program.
   1. The first step is to locate the key column. The key column is that column under which falls the largest negative element in the net evaluation row $(C_j - Z_j)$.
   2. Locate the key row. This is achieved by first computing the replacement ratios. The row in which the smallest replacement ratio falls is the key row or replaced row.
   3. Transform the key row. This is done by dividing all the values in the key row starting with the quantity column by the intersectional value of the key row. The intersectional value of the key row is found at the intersection of the key column and key row.
   4. Transform the remaining rows. This is done by utilizing the following formula.

$$\begin{pmatrix} \text{Value} \\ \text{in the} \\ \text{Old Row} \end{pmatrix} - \begin{pmatrix} \text{Intersectional} \\ \text{Value of} \\ \text{Old Row} \end{pmatrix} \times \begin{pmatrix} \text{Corresponding} \\ \text{Value in} \\ \text{Replacing Row} \end{pmatrix} = \begin{pmatrix} \text{New} \\ \text{Row} \end{pmatrix}$$

V. Obtain the optimal solution.

    1. This is done by repeating Steps III and IV until an optimal program has been achieved. Remember, this will occur when all the values in the net evaluation row $(C_j - Z_j)$ are either zero or positive.

DEGENERACY

If we think in terms of vectors (see Chapter Five), it is easy to see that each new simplex program is obtained by selecting a new set of basis vectors. In fact, the simplex method is based upon a set of rules whereby we proceed from one basic feasible solution to the next until an optimal solution is achieved. In terms of vectors, the vector that is introduced is the key column and the vector to be replaced is the key row.

The student will recall that in identifying the key column we select the column containing the largest positive entry or largest negative entry, depending upon whether we are concerned with a maximization problem or a minimization problem. In the problems solved thus far we have had no difficulty in identifying the key column or the key row. However, in choosing the key row we can encounter two problems.

1. One or more of the variables in the quantity column may have a value of zero in the initial solution. Thus, the smallest replacement ratio will be zero, and the replacement process cannot be achieved because the variable to be replaced is zero.

2. The replacement ratios (nonnegative) for two or more variables in the basis vector may be identical. In other words, we cannot choose the key row because there is a "tie."

Whenever either of these two conditions exist, we have what is known as a degenerate[8] linear programming problem. If we were to attempt to solve such a problem, we would find that either after a finite number of iterations an optimum solution would be achieved or we would begin to cycle, that is, keep returning to the same solution. Let us examine a problem where a tie occurs between two replacement ratios.

The marketing manager of the Starr Electronics Company has three products in his line, products *A*, *B*, and *C*. The products yield profits of $7, $10, and $8 respectively. The three products must go through three processes, with each

---

[8] For an excellent discussion of degeneracy, see Loomba, *op. cit.*, chapter 9.

product requiring different amounts of time in each process. The manager has 100 hours of available time in each process. He has formulated his problem in the following manner: Maximize

$$7A + 10B + 8C$$

subject to

$$4A + 4B + 0C \leq 100$$
$$4A + 2B + 2C \leq 100$$
$$2A + 4B + 4C \leq 100$$

with $A \geq 0, B \geq 0, C \geq 0$. Converting inequalities into equalities yields

$$4A + 4B + 0C + 1S_1 + 0S_2 + 0S_3 = 100$$
$$4A + 2B + 2C + 0S_1 + 1S_2 + 0S_3 = 100$$
$$2A + 4B + 4C + 0S_1 + 0S_2 + 1S_3 = 100$$

The initial tableau can now be constructed.

TABLEAU 6–8 (PARTIAL)

Profit (P_j)	Program	Quantity	$7 $A	$10 $B	$8 $C	$0 S_1	$0 S_2	$0 S_3
0	S_1	100	4	4	0	1	0	0
0	S_2	100	4	2	2	0	1	0
0	S_3	100	2	4	4	0	0	1
	Z_j	0	0	0	0	0	0	0
Net Evaluation Row	$P_j - Z_j$		$7	$10	$8	0	0	0

Key Column

Examination of the initial solution reveals that Column B is the key column. Our next step is to choose the key row which is that row which has the smallest replacement ratio. However, in attempting to do this we see that there is a tie between Row S_1 and Row S_3. Thus, we cannot identify the variable that will be replaced by the incoming variable B. The ratios are calculated as follows:

$$\text{Row } S_1 \quad \frac{100}{4} = 25$$

$$\text{Row } S_2 \quad \frac{100}{2} = 50$$

$$\text{Row } S_3 \quad \frac{100}{4} = 25$$

The situation we now face is unlike anything we have encountered thus far since we have never had to replace more than one variable at a time. In fact, the simplex algorithm only allows the replacement of one variable at a time. Thus, we must find a way to break the tie.

Although a number of arbitrary rules have been established for breaking the tie, we shall use the following: *The variable whose subscript is smallest should be removed first.* This will enable us to continue the solution of the problem. In our problem, S_1 will become the key row as shown in Tableau 6–8.

REVISED TABLEAU 6–8

Profit (P_j)	Program	Quantity	$7 A	$10 B	$8 C	$0 S_1	$0 S_2	$0 S_3	
0	S_1	100	4	4	0	1	0	0	← Key Row
0	S_2	100	4	2	2	0	1	0	Inter-sec-
0	S_3	100	2	4	4	0	0	1	tional Values
	Z_j	0	0	0	0	0	0	0	
Net Evaluation Row	$P_j - Z_j$		$7	$10	$8	$0	$0	$0	

Key Column

We are now able to proceed in constructing an improved solution in the same manner followed previously in the chapter. In order to obtain the new row, divide each number in the key row (the row we are replacing) by the intersectional value of the key row.

$$\frac{100}{4} = 25 \quad \frac{4}{4} = 1 \quad \frac{4}{4} = 1 \quad \frac{0}{4} = 0 \quad \frac{1}{4} = \frac{1}{4} \quad \frac{0}{4} = 0 \quad \frac{0}{4} = 0$$

We compute the new values for the remaining rows as usual.

$$\begin{pmatrix} \text{Value in} \\ \text{Old Row} \end{pmatrix} - \begin{pmatrix} \text{Intersectional} \\ \text{Value of} \\ \text{Old Row} \end{pmatrix} \times \begin{pmatrix} \text{Corresponding} \\ \text{Value in} \\ \text{Replacing Row} \end{pmatrix} = \begin{pmatrix} \text{New} \\ \text{Row} \end{pmatrix}$$

$$
\begin{aligned}
S_2 \text{ Row } 100 - (2 \times 25) &= 50 \\
4 - (2 \times 1) &= 2 \\
2 - (2 \times 1) &= 0 \\
2 - (2 \times 0) &= 2 \\
0 - (2 \times \tfrac{1}{4}) &= -\tfrac{1}{2} \\
1 - (2 \times 0) &= 1 \\
0 - (2 \times 0) &= 0
\end{aligned}
$$

$$S_3 \text{ Row } 100 - (4 \times 25) = 0$$
$$2 - (4 \times 1) = -2$$
$$4 - (4 \times 1) = 0$$
$$4 - (4 \times 0) = 4$$
$$0 - (4 \times \tfrac{1}{4}) = -1$$
$$0 - (4 \times 0) = 0$$
$$1 - (4 \times 0) = 1$$

The improved solution is presented in Tableau 6–9.

PARTIAL TABLEAU 6–9

			$7	$10	$8	$0	$0	$0
Profit (P_j)	Program	Quantity	A	B	C	S_1	S_2	S_3
$10	B	25	1	1	0	$\tfrac{1}{4}$	0	0
0	S_2	50	2	0	2	$-\tfrac{1}{2}$	1	0
0	S_3	0	-2	0	4	-1	0	1

We can now calculate Z_j in the new tableau.

$$Z_j \begin{pmatrix} \text{Total Profit} \\ \text{for} \\ \text{Second Solution} \end{pmatrix} = \$10(25) + \$0(50) + \$0(0) = \$250$$

Z_j for A $\$10(1) + \$0(2) + \$0(-2) = \$10$
Z_j for B $\$10(1) + \$0(0) + \$0(0) = \$10$
Z_j for C $\$10(0) + \$0(2) + \$0(4) = \$ \ 0$
Z_j for S_1 $\$10(\tfrac{1}{4}) + \$0(-\tfrac{1}{2}) + \$0(-1) = \$ \ 2.50$
Z_j for S_2 $\$10(0) + \$0(1) + \$0(0) = \$ \ 0$
Z_j for S_3 $\$10(0) + \$0(0) + \$0(1) = \$ \ 0$

The completed tableau can now be constructed.

REVISED TABLEAU 6–9

			$7	$10	$8	$0	$0	$0	
Profit (P_j)	Program	Quantity	A	B	C	S_1	S_2	S_3	Inter-
$10	B	25	1	1	0	$\tfrac{1}{4}$	0	0	sectional
0	S_2	50	2	0	2	$-\tfrac{1}{2}$	1	0	Values
0	S_3	0	-2	0	4	-1	0	1	Key Row
	Z_j	$250	$10	$10	0	$2.50	$0	$0	
Net Evaluation Row	$P_j - Z_j$		$-\$3$	$0	$8	$-\$2.50$	$0	$0	

Key Column

Examination of revised Tableau 6–9 indicates that we have encountered another obstacle. Variable S_3 (the other variable in the tie) is reduced to zero when we compute the replacement ratios. They are

$$\text{Row } S_2 = \frac{50}{2} = 25$$

$$\text{Row } S_3 = \frac{0}{4} = 0$$

In other words, we are unable to introduce the new incoming product (C) because the minimum nonnegative replacement ratio is zero. Nevertheless, we proceed by following the same rules[9] as usual and construct a new tableau. We begin by calculating the new row as follows:

$$\frac{0}{4} = 0 \quad \frac{-2}{4} = -\frac{1}{2} \quad \frac{0}{4} = 0 \quad \frac{4}{4} = 1 \quad \frac{-1}{4} = -\frac{1}{4} \quad \frac{0}{4} = 0 \quad \frac{1}{4} = \frac{1}{4}$$

We follow the usual procedure for computing the remaining rows.

$$\begin{pmatrix}\text{Value in} \\ \text{Old Row}\end{pmatrix} - \begin{pmatrix}\text{Intersectional} \\ \text{Value of} \\ \text{Old Row}\end{pmatrix} \times \begin{pmatrix}\text{Corresponding} \\ \text{Value in} \\ \text{Replacing Row}\end{pmatrix} = \begin{pmatrix}\text{New} \\ \text{Row}\end{pmatrix}$$

B Row
$$25 - (0 \times 0) = 25$$
$$1 - (0 \times -\tfrac{1}{2}) = 1$$
$$1 - (0 \times 0) = 1$$
$$0 - (0 \times 1) = 0$$
$$\tfrac{1}{4} - (0 \times -\tfrac{1}{4}) = \tfrac{1}{4}$$
$$0 - (0 \times 0) = 0$$
$$0 - (0 \times \tfrac{1}{4}) = 0$$

S_2 Row
$$50 - (2 \times 0) = 50$$
$$2 - (2 \times -\tfrac{1}{2}) = 3$$
$$0 - (2 \times 0) = 0$$
$$2 - (2 \times 1) = 0$$
$$-\tfrac{1}{2} - (2 \times -\tfrac{1}{4}) = 0$$
$$1 - (2 \times 0) = 1$$
$$0 - (2 \times \tfrac{1}{4}) = -\tfrac{1}{2}$$

The improved solution is presented in Tableau 6–10.

---

[9] Actually what we do is assume that the variable with a zero value really has a very small magnitude which can be thought of as approaching zero.

PARTIAL TABLEAU 6–10

Profit (P_j)	Program	Quantity	$7 A	$10 B	$8 C	$0 S_1	$0 S_2	$0 S_3
$10	B	25	1	1	0	¼	0	0
$ 0	S_2	50	3	0	0	0	1	−½
$ 8	C	0	−½	0	1	−¼	0	¼

We can now calculate Z_j in the new tableau.

$$Z_j\left(\begin{array}{c}\text{Total Profit}\\ \text{for}\\ \text{Third Solution}\end{array}\right) = \$10(25) + \$0(50) + \$8(0) = \$250$$

Z_j for A $\$10(1)$ + $\$0(3)$ + $\$8(-\frac{1}{2})$ = $6
Z_j for B $\$10(1)$ + $\$0(0)$ + $\$8(0)$ = $10
Z_j for C $\$10(0)$ + $\$0(0)$ + $\$8(1)$ = $8
Z_j for S_1 $\$10(\frac{1}{4})$ + $\$0(0)$ + $\$8(-\frac{1}{4})$ = $.50
Z_j for S_2 $\$10(0)$ + $\$0(1)$ + $\$8(0)$ = $0
Z_j for S_3 $\$10(0)$ + $\$0(-\frac{1}{2})$ + $\$8(\frac{1}{4})$ = $2

The completed tableau can now be constructed.

REVISED TABLEAU 6–10

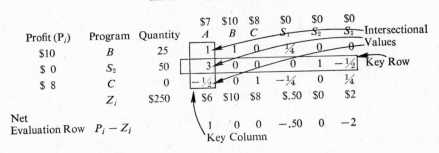

Profit (P_j)	Program	Quantity	$7 A	$10 B	$8 C	$0 S_1	$0 S_2	$0 S_3	Intersectional Values
$10	B	25	1	1	0	¼	0	0	
$ 0	S_2	50	3	0	0	0	1	−½	Key Row
$ 8	C	0	−½	0	1	−¼	0	¼	
	Z_j	$250	$6	$10	$8	$.50	$0	$2	

Net
Evaluation Row $P_j - Z_j$ | 1   0   0   −.50   0   −2
                            Key Column

Examination of Tableau 6–10 reveals that Column A becomes the key column. The key row is determined by the smallest non-negative replacement ratio, which is found in Row S_2.

$$\text{Row } B \quad \frac{25}{1} = 25$$

$$\text{Row } S_2 \quad \frac{50}{3} = \frac{100}{6}$$

The next step is to compute the new row in the usual manner.

$$\frac{50}{3} = \frac{100}{6} \quad \frac{3}{3} = 1 \quad \frac{0}{3} = 0 \quad \frac{0}{3} = 0 \quad \frac{0}{3} = 0 \quad \frac{1}{3} = \frac{1}{3} \quad \frac{-\frac{1}{2}}{3} = -\frac{1}{6}$$

We follow the usual procedure for computing the remaining rows.

$$\binom{\text{Value in}}{\text{Old Row}} - \binom{\text{Intersectional}}{\text{Value of}} \times \binom{\text{Corresponding}}{\text{Value of}} = \binom{\text{New}}{\text{Row}}$$

Row B
$$25 - (1 \quad \times \quad {}^{100}\!/_6) = {}^{50}\!/_6$$
$$1 - (1 \quad \times \quad 1) = 0$$
$$1 - (1 \quad \times \quad 0) = 1$$
$$0 - (1 \quad \times \quad 0) = 0$$
$$\tfrac{1}{4} - (1 \quad \times \quad 0) = \tfrac{1}{4}$$
$$0 - (1 \quad \times \quad \tfrac{1}{3}) = -\tfrac{1}{3}$$
$$0 - (1 \quad \times \quad -\tfrac{1}{6}) = \tfrac{1}{6}$$

Row C
$$0 - (-\tfrac{1}{2} \times {}^{100}\!/_6) = {}^{50}\!/_6$$
$$-\tfrac{1}{2} - (-\tfrac{1}{2} \times 1) = 0$$
$$0 - (-\tfrac{1}{2} \times 0) = 0$$
$$1 - (-\tfrac{1}{2} \times 0) = 1$$
$$-\tfrac{1}{4} - (-\tfrac{1}{2} \times 0) = -\tfrac{1}{4}$$
$$0 - (-\tfrac{1}{2} \times \tfrac{1}{3}) = \tfrac{1}{6}$$
$$\tfrac{1}{4} - (-\tfrac{1}{2} \times -\tfrac{1}{6}) = \tfrac{1}{6}$$

The improved solution is presented in Tableau 6–11.

PARTIAL TABLEAU 6–11

Profit (P_j)	Program	Quantity	$7 A	$10 B	$8 C	$0 S_1	$0 S_2	$0 S_3
$10	B	${}^{50}\!/_6$	0	1	0	$\tfrac{1}{4}$	$-\tfrac{1}{3}$	$\tfrac{1}{6}$
$ 7	A	${}^{100}\!/_6$	1	0	0	0	$\tfrac{1}{3}$	$-\tfrac{1}{6}$
$ 8	C	${}^{50}\!/_6$	0	0	1	$-\tfrac{1}{4}$	$\tfrac{1}{6}$	$\tfrac{1}{6}$

We can now calculate Z_j for the new tableau.

$$Z_j \binom{\text{Total Profit for the}}{\text{Fourth Solution}} = \$10\left(\frac{50}{6}\right) + \$7\left(\frac{100}{6}\right) + \$8\left(\frac{50}{6}\right) = \$267$$

$$Z_j \text{ for } A \quad \$10(0) \quad + \$7(1) \quad + \$8(0) \quad = \$ 7$$
$$Z_j \text{ for } B \quad \$10(1) \quad + \$7(0) \quad + \$8(0) \quad = \$10$$
$$Z_j \text{ for } C \quad \$10(0) \quad + \$7(0) \quad + \$8(1) \quad = \$ 8$$

$$Z_j \text{ for } S_1 \ \$10(\tfrac{1}{4}) \quad + \$7(0) \quad + \$8(-\tfrac{1}{4}) = \$ \ .50$$
$$Z_j \text{ for } S_2 \ \$10(-\tfrac{1}{3}) + \$7(\tfrac{1}{3}) \quad + \$8(\tfrac{1}{6}) \quad = \$ \ .33$$
$$Z_j \text{ for } S_3 \ \$10(\tfrac{1}{6}) \quad + \$7(-\tfrac{1}{6}) + \$8(\tfrac{1}{6}) \quad = \$ \ 1.83$$

The complete tableau can now be constructed.

REVISED TABLEAU 6–11

Profit (P_i)	Program	Quantity	$7 $A	$10 $B	$8 $C	$0 S_1	$0 S_2	$0 S_3
$10	B	$\tfrac{5}{6}$	0	1	0	$\tfrac{1}{4}$	$-\tfrac{1}{3}$	$\tfrac{1}{6}$
$ 7	A	$\tfrac{10}{6}$	1	0	0	0	$\tfrac{1}{3}$	$-\tfrac{1}{6}$
$ 8	C	$\tfrac{5}{6}$	0	0	1	$-\tfrac{1}{4}$	$\tfrac{1}{6}$	$\tfrac{1}{6}$
	Z_j	$267	$7	$10	$8	.50	.33	1.83
Net Evaluation Row	$P_j - Z_j$		0	0	0	−.50	−.33	−1.83

In Tableau 6–11 all of the elements in the net evaluation row are either zero or negative. This indicates that we have found an optimal solution to the problem.

By arbitrarily choosing the variable with the lowest subscript we have broken the tie and solved the problem. However, we should note that arbitrarily selecting one of the tied variables as we have done may result in a longer path to the optimum solution (a greater number of iterations). Also, it may result in what we earlier referred to as cycling. Although cycling is possible, it very rarely occurs in practice. However, general methods of resolving degeneracy have been devised. Such a method has been developed by A. Charnes and W. Cooper which, if utilized, will prevent against falling into the cycling process.[10] This procedure is:

1. Identify the tied variables or rows.

2. For each of the columns in the identity (starting with the extreme left-hand column of the identity and proceeding one at a time to the right), compute a ratio by dividing the entry in each tied row by the key column number in that row.

3. Compare these ratios column by column, proceeding to the right. The first time the ratios are unequal, the tie is broken.

4. Of the tied rows, the one in which the smaller algebraic ratio falls is the key row.

5. If the ratios in the identity do not break the tie, form similar ratios for

---

[10] A. Charnes and W. Cooper, *An Introduction to Linear Programming* (New York: John Wiley and Sons, Inc., 1953), pp. 20–24, 62–69.

the columns of the main body, and select the key row as described in Steps 3 and 4.

PROBLEMS

1. Demonstrate that you understand the following concepts by defining each one.

a. Objective function
b. Structural constraints
c. Inequality
d. Slack variable
e. Shadow price
f. Artificial variable
g. Net evaluation row
h. Feasibility space

i. Isoprofit line
j. Iteration
k. Key column
l. Key row
m. Positive number in net evaluation row
n. Degeneracy
o. Z_i row

2. What is meant by the term linear programming?

3. Utilizing the graphical method, solve the following problem: Maximize
$$\$20x + \$10y$$
subject to
$$4x + 9y \leq 180$$
$$5x + 6y = 150$$
$$5x + 14y \leq 175$$

4. a. Explain the method of assigning coefficients to the slack variables in the objective function.

b. Explain how you arrive at the initial simplex tableau.

c. Why is the element at the intersection of the key column and key row so important?

d. What is the rule for computing the new row?

e. What is the rule for computing the remaining rows?

5. Solve the following problem by the simplex method. Maximize
$$\$4A + \$6B + \$4C$$
subject to
$$2A + 16B + 8C \leq 160$$
$$4A + 8B + 2C \leq 120$$
with $A \geq 0, B \geq 0, C \geq 0$

6. Solve the following problem by the simplex method. Minimize
$$\$2A + \$2B + \$3C$$
subject to
$$10A + 8B + 6C \geq 36$$
$$2A + 3B + 2C \geq 7$$
with $A \geq 0, B \geq 0, C \geq 0$

7. Set up the initial tableau for the following problem: The Apex Record Company is a manufacturer of rock and roll records. At present the firm makes two types of records. The conventional monoral type of 45 rpm records and stereo $33\frac{1}{3}$ rpm records. The 45 rpm records require eight units of raw material A and two units of raw material B per 100 records. The stereo $33\frac{1}{3}$ records require four units of A

and six units of *B* per 100 records. The firm currently has 12,000 units of *A* and 5,000 units of *B*. The company makes $80 per 100 45 rpm records and $150 per 100 33⅓ rpm records. The company has just signed a new rock group and wants to best use the two resources in order to maximize the profit on records made by the group.

8. Set up the initial tableau for the following product mix problem. The Bar-B-Que Company is a manufacturer of outdoor cooking equipment. The three major products now produced are three types of outdoor grills, Models *A*, *B*, and *C*. The grills have a profit of $4, $6, and $8, respectively. To produce Model *A* requires one hour of engineering time, five hours of direct labor, and three hours of clerical time. To produce Model *B* requires two hours of engineering time, six hours of direct labor, and four hours of clerical time. To produce Model *C* requires three hours of engineering time, six hours of direct labor, and four hours of clerical time. The firm has available 400 hours of engineering time, 1,800 hours of direct labor, and 800 hours of clerical time.

9. How can we determine degeneracy during the solution stages of a linear programming problem?

10. What happens when cycling occurs in using the simplex method to solve a linear programming problem?

REFERENCES

CHUNG, A. *Linear Programming* (Columbus: Charles E. Merrill Books, Inc., 1963).

LEVIN, RICHARD I., AND LAMONE, RUDOLPH P. *Linear Programming for Management Decisions* (Homewood, Ill.: Richard D. Irwin, Inc., 1969).

LLEWELLYN, R. *Linear Programming* (New York: Holt, Rinehart and Winston, Inc., 1964).

LOOMBA, N. PAUL. *Linear Programming* (New York: McGraw-Hill Book Company, Inc., 1964).

NAYLOR, T. H., AND BYRNE, E. T. *Linear Programming* (Belmont, Calif.: Wadsworth Publishing Company, Inc., 1963).

STOCKTON, R. S. *Introduction to Linear Programming* (Boston: Allyn and Bacon, Inc., 1960).

PART III

Applications

chapter seven

PRODUCT PLANNING

INTRODUCTION

Before a firm can market a product there must be something to sell—a product or service. From this standpoint product planning is the starting point for the entire marketing program. The firm must develop ideas for new products. Once this is accomplished, management can then determine whether there is an adequate market for the product and decide how the product should be marketed. In this chapter we shall examine two quantitative techniques which can aid the marketing manager in his product decisions. Network methods shall be discussed in relation to new product development projects, and Markov analysis will be utilized in determining market shares and brand switching behavior among consumers.

New Product Planning

The development of new products is essential for sustaining a firm's rate of profit. This is because a firm's profit usually starts to decline while the sales volume curve is still climbing for a given product. In many industries innovation has become the rule rather than the exception. In fact, studies by the consulting firm of Booz, Allen and Hamilton have indicated that growth industries are industries which are new product oriented. In a study of selected industries they concluded that industries which spend the most for new-product development have enjoyed higher rates of growth.

Product innovation is a top management responsibility because the problems encountered in the management of a new product program are such that they require the attention of executives who possess the most influence in an organization. Exactly where new product planning and development falls in the organization structure will vary by firm. Generally, however, one of three approaches is used: 1) appointing a product development and planning

155

committee, 2) organizing a new product department or, 3) selecting product managers.

Product development and planning committee. This is probably the most widely used organizational arrangement for new product development and planning. The firm's top management team as well as individuals from marketing, production, research, finance, and engineering usually participate. An obvious advantage of this approach is the pooling of many talents.

New product department. Recently a greatly increasing number of firms have set up a separate and formally organized department, the purpose of which is to plan and develop new products. In some firms it may consist of only one person while in others there may be as many as five or six people in the department. These departments are usually responsible for developing and screening new product ideas, determining objectives, and planning and co-ordinating the many activities involved in launching a new product. When these activities have been accomplished, the new product is usually assigned to a specific operating department. The obvious advantage of this arrangement is that the responsibility for new product development and planning becomes a full-time activity.

Product manager. In some firms a product manager is used for product development and planning. However, a product manager's responsibility is not limited to new products. The scope of his activities varies widely by company depending upon the product and market requirements of the firm. In some firms this individual is known as a "brand manager," and he is responsible for developing and planning the complete marketing program for his particular brand or group of products. As such, he may be responsible for new product development in addition to the improvement of existing products. Some of the largest consumer product manufacturers, such as Procter and Gamble, Pillsbury, and Colgate-Palmolive, utilize this approach.

No matter which approach is used, the complexities of launching a new product are still present. The many related and unrelated tasks and activities that must be organized and coordinated make the job of new product introduction a difficult operation. Each task must be performed in the proper sequence and must be coordinated with other independent tasks in order for the entire program to jell. Some of the activities necessary in launching a new product are the following:

1. Preliminary marketing research
2. Development of prototype model
3. Preliminary advertising ideas
4. Market test of model

5. Financial analysis
6. Production feasibility reports
7. Modified product design
8. Launching of product

A brief examination of these activities should indicate the great need for some type of coordination of the entire process in order to insure that certain tasks that must be completed prior to another task are actually completed. Some idea is also needed of approximately how long the entire process will take. In summary, some method is needed to avoid unnecessary conflicts and delays by keeping track of all events and activities and their interrelationships on a specific project. Fortunately for the marketing manager, network methods provide the means to achieve this goal.

NETWORK METHODS (PERT)

PERT stands for Program Evaluation and Review Technique. It was developed through the cooperation of the U.S. Navy and Booz, Allen and Hamilton, a management consulting firm. What exactly is PERT? It is a method by which conflicts, delays, and interruptions in a project are minimized by coordinating and synchronizing the various parts of the overall job in order to complete the project on schedule. It does not solve a manager's problems but it does help him see what his problems are and what solutions are realistic.

PERT is especially useful to management in nonrepetitive problem areas. A nonrepetitive process is one which the manager has not previously encountered in the past and is not likely to encounter again in the future. These are opposed to repetitive processes such as periodic reorders of inventory about which management has past experience, standards, and costs. However, management must still plan and coordinate nonrepetitive operations. Obviously, this is more difficult because there is no past experience on which to rely. PERT is extremely helpful in such situations. It enables a manager to think through a project in its entirety and at the same time informs him of possible delays. As such, it usually leads to a more optimum utilization of resources.

Fundamentals of PERT

PERT is developed around two fundamental concepts: activities and events. An *activity* is the work necessary to complete a particular event. An *event* is an accomplishment at a particular point in time. In PERT diagrams or networks, we designate an event with a circle and an activity as an arrow connecting the two circles. For example, in Figure 7–1 there are two events, which are assigned numbers, connected by one activity, which we designate with an arrow. Each of the two events occur at a specific point in time. Event

FIGURE 7–1

Two Events and One Activity

1 could represent the specific point in time "marketing research project begun" and Event 2 could represent the specific point in time "marketing research project completed." The arrow connecting the two events represents the activity—the actual work done—and the time necessary to complete the work. Thus, the two events in Figure 7–1 designate the beginning and end of the activity which is marketing research. The activity is what requires time, not the events.

Above we referred to a PERT diagram or network. The term network is used when several events and activities are combined in a diagram. Figure 7–1

FIGURE 7–2

PERT Network

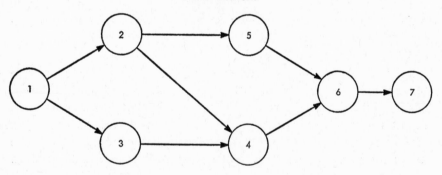

is a very simple PERT network involving two events and one activity. A more complex PERT network is presented in Figure 7–2.

Examination of Figure 7–2 indicates that Event 1 is the network beginning event since there are no activities leading to it and Event 7 is the network ending event since there are no activities leading away from it. Note also that

Event 2 is the beginning event for two activities and Events 4 and 6 are the ending events for two activities as well as the beginning event for one activity.

The paramount variable in a PERT system is time. Time is obviously the basic measure of how long a project will take. Estimating how long each activity will take is extremely difficult since the manager has no experience to rely on in most cases. This results in uncertainty in making estimates of the time needed to complete the entire network. However, probability theory provides a means of reducing some of the uncertainty involved in our estimate of time.

ESTIMATING ACTIVITY TIME REQUIREMENTS

As we mentioned previously, PERT projects are usually unique and are, therefore, subject to a great deal of uncertainty. PERT is designed to deal specifically with this problem of uncertainty through the application of statistical analysis in determining the job time estimates.

For example, assume we are estimating how long it will take to complete a marketing research study. We must collect, tabulate, and analyze certain data. We know that at times our firm's computer facility is greatly overworked and a tremendous backlog of job orders exist. If such a situation occurred, the chances would be greater that our market research study would take longer to complete.

However, at other times, no backlog of job orders exists and in fact the firm's computer facility has much idle time. If this situation occurred, we would have a greater chance of completing our study earlier than expected. Thus, we could estimate a variety of possible completion times for the market research study.

For PERT projects, three time estimates are required for each activity. The individual or group chosen to make each time estimate should be that individual or group who is most closely connected with and responsible for the particular activity under consideration. The three time estimates needed are:

Optimistic time (*a*). This is the time the project can be completed in if everything goes exceptionally well and we encounter no obstacles or problems.

Most likely time (*m*). This is the most realistic estimate of how long an activity might take. This is the time we would expect to occur most often if the activity was repeated numerous times.

Pessimistic time (*b*). This is the time that would be required if everything went wrong and we encountered numerous obstacles and problems.

Obviously, we cannot in PERT be concerned with three times for every activity. It would be extremely impractical to try to deal simultaneously with the most optimistic time, the most likely time, and the most pessimistic time. Fortunately, a way has been developed which enables us to arrive at one time estimate. An expected time (t_e) and its standard deviation[1] (σ) can be estimated satisfactorily for each activity by using the following formulas:

$$t_e = \frac{a + 4m + b}{6}$$

$$\sigma = \frac{b - a}{6}$$

Let us examine these formulas in relation to the marketing research study mentioned above. Assume that the marketing research staff estimates that eight weeks is the most likely completion time (m). However, the staff feels that there is a small chance (perhaps one time in 10) that the study might be completed in two weeks. Therefore, the optimistic time (a) is 2. Finally, the staff feels there is also a slight chance that things could go wrong and the

FIGURE 7–3

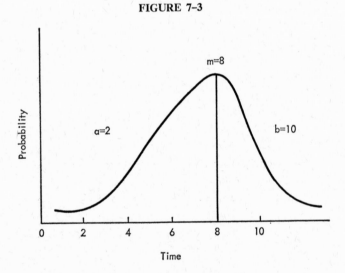

project would take 10 weeks to complete. Therefore, the pessimistic time (b) is 10. The probability that the project will be completed in a given amount of time can be illustrated graphically as shown in Figure 7–3. We can see that there is a greater probability that the project will take eight weeks than any other time. This is shown as the highest point on the curve in Figure 7–3. In

---

[1] If necessary, the reader can refresh his memory concerning the standard deviation and its properties by consulting any basic statistics text.

order to compute the expected time (t_e) from the three time estimates that have been provided, we must determine what time will divide the total area under the curve in half, in other words, where there is a 50–50 chance of completing the job at that time. We use the previously mentioned formulas to arrive at the expected time and variation.

$$t_e = \frac{a + 4m + b}{6}$$

$$\sigma = \frac{b - a}{6}$$

Substituting our time estimates into the formulas yields:

$$t_e = \frac{2 + 4(8) + 10}{6}$$

$$= \frac{44}{6}$$

$$t_e = 7.33$$

and

$$\sigma = \frac{10 - 2}{6}$$

$$= \frac{8}{6}$$

$$\sigma = 1.33$$

Figure 7–4 indicates the 50–50 dividing line.

FIGURE 7–4

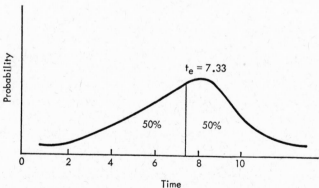

Note that in our formula for computing the expected time (t_e), the weight that is given to the most likely time is much greater than the weight given to the optimistic and pessimistic times, since each of them has only a small chance of occurring. Also, note that the optimistic and pessimistic times each receive the same weight.

In conclusion, it should be clear that the expected time (t_e) may be either to the right or to the left of the most likely value (m), depending on the three time estimates. To illustrate an expected time value (t_e) to the right of the most likely time, let us now assume that the marketing research staff provided the following three time estimates:

$$
\begin{aligned}
\text{Optimistic time } (a) &= 6 \text{ weeks} \\
\text{Most likely time } (m) &= 8 \text{ weeks} \\
\text{Pessimistic time } (b) &= 16 \text{ weeks}
\end{aligned}
$$

Substituting these values into the formulas yields:

$$
t_e = \frac{a + 4(m) + b}{6}
$$
$$
= \frac{6 + 4(8) + 16}{6}
$$
$$
t_e = 9
$$

and

$$
\sigma = \frac{b - a}{6}
$$
$$
= \frac{16 - 6}{6}
$$
$$
\sigma = 1.67
$$

In this case the expected time (t_e) lies to the right of the most likely time (m).

DEVELOPING PERT NETWORKS

There are four basic phases in constructing a PERT network.

1. Define each task that must be done.
2. Estimate how long each task will take.
3. Construct the network.
4. Find the critical path—i.e., the longest path from the beginning event to the ending event.

In this section we will solve a simplified problem using PERT in order to gain an understanding of the mechanics of constructing a PERT network.

Assume you are the marketing vice president of the Grimes Electric Company. You have just been informed by Engineering that the new Electro-Whiz combination electric toothbrush and water pic has just passed the final series of tests and will be ready for public sale in about three months. It is your task to prepare the field sales force to promote this new product. You would like to have your salesmen begin as soon as possible to call on retail dealers.

The first step is to define each task that must be done. After spending time thinking the project through, you come to the conclusion that the project consists of nine activities.

1. Obtain as much information as possible on the new product.
2. Prepare a short product presentation on the operation of the Electro-Whiz. This can be done as soon as Activity 1 is completed.
3. At the same time obtain test models of the product.
4. Having completed Activity 2, you are able to develop your marketing plan.
5. After the test models have been obtained you can develop some materials for the salesmen on the features and uses of Electro-Whiz which they will keep for their own use.
6. Once the marketing program has been developed and approved, you can call in the sales force for training sessions on the operation of Electro-Whiz.
7. When all the salesmen are at the home office, you can present the product program.
8. Upon completion of 7, you can present the marketing program to the sales force.
9. Once 8 is completed, the salesmen can return to their territories.

The network for the project is shown in Figure 7–5, and a detailed description of the activities and events in the network is provided in Table 7–1.

Let us now reconstruct Figure 7–5 and insert the expected time (t_e) for each activity. We shall assume that the expected time for each event was calculated by inserting the optimistic time estimate, the most likely time estimate, and

FIGURE 7–5

PERT Network for Electro-Whiz

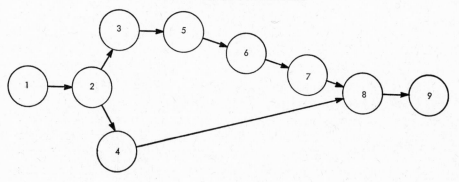

TABLE 7–1

Description of Activities and Events for Figure 7–5

Activity Description	Prerequisite Activities	Event Description
1–2 Obtain new product information	—	2—Information obtained
2–3 Prepare presentation on Electro-Whiz	1–2	3—Presentation completed
2–4 Obtain test models of the product for demonstration	1–2	4—Test models obtained for demonstration
3–5 Develop marketing plan	2–3	5—Marketing plan completed
5–6 Call in salesmen from the field	3–5	6—Salesmen arrive at home office
6–7 Product program presented	5–6	7—Product program presented
4–8 Develop material for use	2–4	8—Material developed
7–8 Marketing program presented	6–7	8—Material developed and marketing program presented
8–9 Salesmen return to their territories	7–8 and 4–8	9—Salesmen back in assigned territories

the pessimistic time estimate into the weighted average formula presented earlier. This is shown in Figure 7–6. The time figures represent weeks.

Calculation of Earliest Expected Date

Once the PERT network has been constructed and the expected time (t_e) has been calculated for each event, we can turn our attention to calculating the *earliest expected date* (T_E) in which the project can be completed. Examination of Figure 7–6 reveals that there are two paths through this network—Path 1–2–3–5–6–7–8–9 and Path 1–2–4–8–9. The work on Path 1–2–3–5–6–7–8–9 will take a total of nine working weeks, while performance of the work on Path 1–2–4–8–9 will require a total of 11 working weeks. The earliest expected date for the completion of the network is 11 weeks and completion of the network can be expected no sooner than 11 weeks if we began the project today. It is clear that the earliest expected date of an event is found by calculating the *longest* path from the network beginning event to the particular event in question, whether it is the network ending event or some other event.

Let us suppose that the manager wants to determine how soon he can complete a particular event which is not the network ending event. For example, when can he expect to have Event 6 completed? To determine this

FIGURE 7–6

PERT Network for Electro-Whiz with t_e for Each Activity

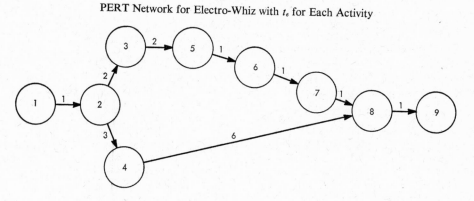

we do exactly as we did previously; sum the paths from the network beginning event to the particular event in question and choose the longest path if there is more than one path. Thus, the (T_E) for Event 6 is (Path 1, 2, 3, 5, 6) 6 weeks.

We can calculate the earliest expected date (T_E) for each event in the network by utilizing the same rule, by taking the longest path from the network beginning event to each of the other events in the network. This is shown in Figure 7–7.

The importance of the *earliest expected time* (T_E) is that it provides us with the dates on which certain work will be completed. If the computed date is unsatisfactory, it gives us an opportunity to adjust our operations.

In Figure 7–7 the T_E is computed for each event as follows. The network beginning event is assigned a zero. Since there is only one path to Event 2, the

FIGURE 7–7

PERT Network for Electro-Whiz with T_E for Each Event

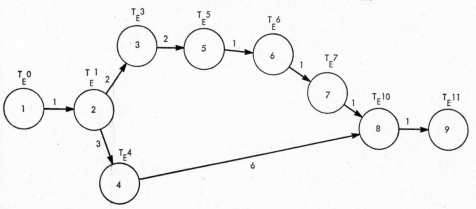

earliest expected date is one week. The T_E for Event 3 is found by adding the T_E for Event 2 and the expected time for Activity 2–3. Thus the T_E for Event 3 equals $1 + 2$ or 3. The T_E for Event 4 is found by adding the T_E for Event 2 and the expected time of Activity 2–4. This gives us $1 + 3$ or 4. It is easy to see that the earliest expected time for events 5, 6, and 7 are also calculated by adding the T_E for the preceding event and the expected time for the preceding activity. However, Event 8 is somewhat different since it has two events leading to it—Path 1–2–3–5–6–7–8, which requires eight weeks, and Path 1–2–4–8, which requires 10 weeks. Hence, the T_E of Event 8 is 10 weeks because T_E is the longest path from the network beginning event to the particular event in question.

The Critical Path

We have just seen that the longest path through the PERT network determines the earliest expected date of the network-ending event. This longest path is more commonly referred to as the *critical path*. Thus, we can define the critical path as the most time-consuming path of activities from the network beginning event to the network ending event.

Latest Allowable Date (T_L)

The latest allowable date is the latest date on which an event can occur without creating a delay in the scheduled completion of the project. In Figure 7–6 we determined that the longest path through the network was Path 1–2–4–8–9. We determined this by calculating the earliest expected dates for each of the nine events in the network. T_L for an ending event is equal to the date directed by management for completion of the project. If a directed date is not specified, then $T_L = T_E$ for the network ending event.

Let us examine Event 7. We expect that it will be completed seven weeks after the network is begun. If we began Activity 7–8 immediately thereafter, we would be ready for Event 8 to occur in eight weeks after the network was begun. However, we see that Event 8 cannot occur until 10 weeks after the start of the network because of other activity paths. Thus, we really do not have to complete Event 7 in seven weeks, we could actually complete it in nine weeks after the start of the network and still not interfere with our scheduled completion time of 11 weeks. This is the importance of the latest allowable date.

Now let us examine the T_L for Event 5. In order for our network to be completed on time (11 weeks), we must complete Event 5 within seven weeks after the network beginning event or we shall be late. Hence, the T_L for Event 5 is seven weeks.

Let us now compute the T_L for Event 4 on the critical path. We expect that it will be completed four weeks after the network is begun. If we began Activity 4–8 immediately thereafter, we would be ready for Event 8 in 10 weeks after the network was begun. In order for our network to be completed on time (11 weeks), we must complete Event 4 within four weeks after the network beginning event or we shall be late. Thus, the T_L for Event 4 is the same as its T_E.

Examine Event 2. Between Event 2 and the network ending event there are two paths. Path 2–4–8–9 involves 10 weeks and Path 2–3–5–6–7–8–9 involves eight weeks. If we expect to complete the network in 11 weeks, Event 2 must be completed one week after the network beginning event in order to allow 10 additional weeks for the completion of the network.

By now the reader should note that when we calculated the T_E's, we found (by addition) the longest path from the network beginning event to the particular event in question. When calculating the T_L's, we subtract in order to find the longest path from the network ending event back to the particular event in question.

In Figure 7–8 our network is presented with both the T_E's and the T_L's calculated.

FIGURE 7–8

PERT Network for Electro-Whiz with T_E and T_L for Each Event

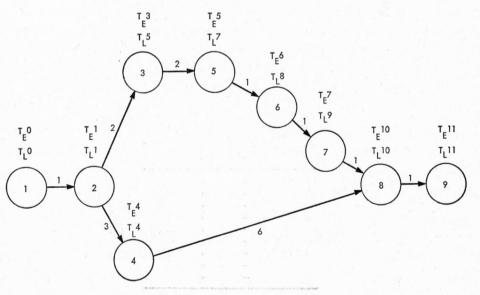

In Figure 7–8 we see that the T_L of an event is found by subtracting the expected elapsed time for the activity from the previous T_L. For example, the T_L for Event 3 is found by subtracting the T_E of Activity 3–5 from the T_L of Event 5 or $7 - 2 = 5$. Examine Event 2 once again. Note that when two or more paths yield different values, we always choose the smaller when calculating the T_L of an event. Remember that in calculating the T_E of an event, we always chose the larger value. Calculating the T_L of Event 2 we get

$$\text{Path } 2\text{–}3 = 5 - 2 = 3$$
$$\text{Path } 2\text{–}4 = 4 - 3 = 1$$

Since we choose the smaller value, the T_L for Event 2 is one.

Finally, observe that for the events on the critical Path 1–2–4–8–9 the T_E equals the T_L for each event. All this means is that the latest allowable date on which these events can be completed equals the earliest date on which we can expect to have them completed. This is understandable since the critical path is the longest path through the network.

Slack Time

Slack time is obviously time to spare in the completion of certain events. In Figure 7–8 we noted that Event 8 cannot occur until 10 weeks after the start of the network. However, Event 7 is expected to be completed seven weeks after the beginning of the network. Since Activity 7–8 takes one week, we can see that Event 7 does not have to be completed in seven weeks. We could actually take nine weeks to complete it and still meet our scheduled completion time of 11 weeks. Thus, we can say there is slack on Path 1–2–3–5–6–7–8–9 and if we fall slightly behind, we do not have to worry. Slack time is calculated utilizing the following formula.

$$\text{Slack Time} = S = T_L - T_E$$

We can calculate the slack time in our network as follows:

TABLE 7–2

Slack Time for PERT Network

Event	T_L	$-$	T_E	$=$	Slack Time
1	0	$-$	0	$=$	0
2	1	$-$	1	$=$	0
3	5	$-$	3	$=$	2
4	4	$-$	4	$=$	0
5	7	$-$	5	$=$	2
6	8	$-$	6	$=$	2
7	9	$-$	7	$=$	2
8	10	$-$	10	$=$	0
9	11	$-$	11	$=$	0

Notice that four events, 3, 5, 6, 7, have slack time. They have a slack time of two weeks. From a practical standpoint this indicates that we could fall two weeks behind somewhere on these four events and still not jeopardize our completion date at its earliest expected date. It also indicates that we can shift resources, if possible, to the critical path, thereby perhaps shortening the time of the entire project. This is an important use of the slack time computation.

Notice that there is no slack time on the critical path. The T_L of each event is equal to the T_E for the event. Can we have slack time on the critical path? The answer is yes. Imagine a network in which the T_L of the network ending event is less than the T_E for the same event. This would occur when we have allowed the project less time than it is expected to take us to complete the project. In such cases which are atypical, the network has negative slack, which would mean we are behind schedule. A case could also arise where we have allowed more time than we need and T_L is greater than T_E.

COMPUTING THE PROBABILITY OF ACHIEVING THE COMPLETION DATE

The reader will recall that when we began our discussion of PERT, we pointed out that there was uncertainty involved in our answers. The reason for this is that the entire PERT system is based upon estimates of time. Specifically, there were three estimates of time, each with some degree of uncertainty attached to them. Even the t_e value is uncertain because it was calculated using the three time estimates. In this section we will examine methods for dealing with these uncertainties with the objective of estimating the probability that a project will be completed by T_L.

Earlier, in addition to calculating the expected time (t_e), we also provided a formula for calculating its standard deviation. This formula was:

$$\sigma = \frac{b - a}{6}.$$

The reader should recall from an elementary statistics course that the standard deviation is a statistical measure which indicates the tendency for data to disperse around the mean. In PERT projects it will aid us in calculating the probability of achieving the completion date of the project. In order to illustrate how this is done, let us examine the simplified PERT network in Figure 7–9.

The most optimistic time, most likely time, and most pessimistic time estimates are listed for each activity. First we shall compute the estimated time

FIGURE 7–9

PERT Network

(t_e) and the standard deviation for each individual activity. Finally we shall compute the standard deviation for the network ending event.

The expected times (t_e) for each of the activities and the earliest expected date (T_E) for the network ending event are shown in Table 7–3.

Our next step is to calculate the standard deviations for each individual activity. This is shown in Table 7–4.

TABLE 7–3

Expected Times for PERT Network in Figure 7–9

Activity	Most Optimistic Time (a)	Most Likely Time (m)	Most Pessimistic Time (b)	$\dfrac{a + 4m + b}{6} = t_e$
1–2	4	6	8	$\dfrac{4 + 24 + 8}{6} = 6.0$
2–3	4	10	16	$\dfrac{4 + 40 + 16}{6} = 10.0$
3–4	6	12	16	$\dfrac{6 + 48 + 16}{6} = 11.7$
4–5	4	12	20	$\dfrac{4 + 48 + 20}{6} = 12.0$

T_E (network ending event (5)) = 6.0 + 10.0 + 11.7 + 12.0
T_E = 39.7 weeks

TABLE 7–4

Standard Deviations for PERT Network in Figure 7–9

Activity	Most Optimistic Time (a)	Most Pessimistic Time (b)	$\dfrac{b - a}{6}$	Standard Deviation (σ)
1–2	4	8	$\dfrac{4}{6}$	.67
2–3	4	16	$\dfrac{12}{6}$	2.00
3–4	6	16	$\dfrac{10}{6}$	1.67
4–5	4	20	$\dfrac{16}{6}$	2.67

Now that we have the standard deviations for each of the individual activities, we would like to obtain some probability measure that will indicate what our chances are of finishing on time. In order to obtain this, we must calculate the standard deviation for the network ending event. To calculate the standard deviation for the ending event in a series, we take the square root of the sum of the individual activity standard deviations squared. This is expressed mathematically as

$$\sigma \text{ for Network Ending Event} = \sqrt{\Sigma(\sigma)^2}$$
$$= \sqrt{(.67)^2 + (2.0)^2 + (1.67)^2 + (2.67)^2}$$
$$= \sqrt{.449 + 4.0 + 2.79 + 7.13}$$
$$= \sqrt{14.37}$$
$$\sigma T_E = 3.8 \text{ weeks (rounded)}$$

We now have two specific measures for this network.

1. The earliest expected date (T_E) for the network ending event (39.7) weeks.
2. The standard deviation of the network ending event (3.8) weeks. This can be written (σT_E).

The manager is keenly interested in the likelihood of meeting the scheduled completion date of the project (T_L). He would also prefer to have that likelihood expressed quantitatively in terms of probability. PERT procedures can provide this information.

The difference between the earliest expected completion date (T_E) and the latest allowable date (T_L) is divided by σT_E in order to express the difference in standard deviations $(\sigma T_E\text{'s})$, which has traditionally been denoted by the letter Z. Thus we have

$$Z = \frac{T_L - T_E}{\sigma T_E}$$

Since the earliest expected date (T_E) is the sum of a series of means of probability distributions, T_E will tend to be distributed according to the normal probability distribution, and the Z value which we compute can be evaluated by using the Table of Areas under the Normal Curve shown in Appendix B.

Assume that the network in Figure 7–9 must be completed in 43.7 weeks. We can illustrate the T_E and T_L of the network ending event in Figure 7–10 on the following page.

In order to determine the number of standard deviations (Z) we are from the mean, we subtract the T_E value from the T_L value. This is actually slack time on this particular critical path. We then divide the slack time by the

FIGURE 7–10

Probability Distribution of Network Ending Event

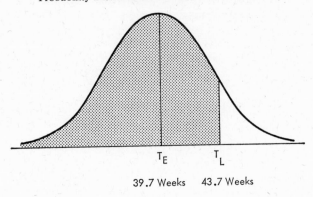

T_E T_L

39.7 Weeks   43.7 Weeks

standard deviation of the network ending event in order to get the number of standard deviations the slack time represents. This is shown as follows:

$$Z = \frac{T_L - T_E}{\sigma T_E}$$

$$Z = \frac{43.7 - 39.7}{3.8}$$

$$Z = \frac{4.0}{3.8}$$

$$Z = 1.05$$

In order to determine what percentage of the curve is contained within 1.05 standard deviations from the mean, we must consult Appendix B, a table of areas under the curve. We find that 1.05 standard deviations from the mean encompasses .3531 percent of the curve from the mean. We know that 50 percent of the area under the curve lies to the left of the mean. Thus, our chances of finishing before the latest allowable date (T_L) is approximately 85 percent. The remaining difference (15 percent) is the probability that we will finish after the latest allowable date.[2]

Before proceeding, let us examine Figure 7–11 and Figure 7–12.

Figure 7–11 illustrates the existence of zero slack on the critical path. In this case Z would equal zero and the probability of meeting the latest allowable date (T_L) equals .50. Figure 7–12 illustrates a case where the T_L value lies to the left of the T_E value, that is, where we have negative slack on the critical path.

---

[2] This calculation assumes that the task times along any path are independent.

In this case we know from the beginning that we have less time available to complete the job than we know we shall need. The shaded area in Figure 7–12 indicates the probability of finishing on time. Here Z will be negative and the

FIGURE 7–11

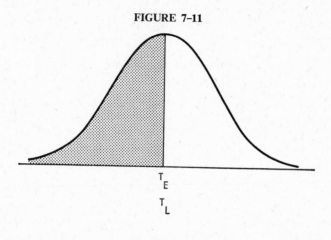

FIGURE 7–12

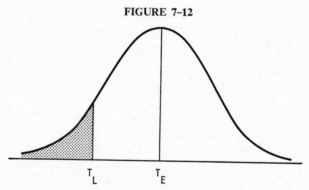

probability value is equal to .5 minus the value in the table. In this case the probability of meeting the latest allowable date will be less than .50. The unshaded area in Figure 7–12 indicates the probability of being late, which in this case is greater than .50.

A Complete PERT Problem

Assume you are the marketing vice president of the Kidds Toy Company. The engineering department has developed preliminary plans for Robo-Man, an electrically powered toy robot. The report received favorable reactions from top management and you have been assigned the task of organizing a new-product development program for the project. If your firm expects to compete in the up and coming selling season, the toy should be on the market in no more than five months.

After some deliberation, you conclude that the project will consist of eight activities:

1. A preliminary marketing research report is made.
2. A prototype model is developed.
3. At the same time the introductory advertising campaign is being developed.
4. The necessary engineering tests are performed to test the strength and durability of the product.
5. The new toy model is tested in order to get children's reactions to the product.
6. A financial analysis is made of both the marketing and production requirements for the product.
7. After engineering and consumer tests any modifications can be made in the product design.
8. Go or stop project decision must be made.

FIGURE 7–13

PERT Network for Robo-Man

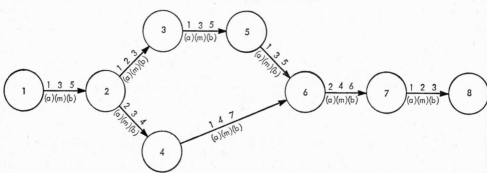

The network for the project is shown in Figure 7–13 with the estimates of the most optimistic, most likely, and most pessimistic times. A detailed description of the activities and events in the network is provided in Table 7–5. Our first step is to calculate the expected time for each activity in Figure 7–13. In Table 7–6 the three time estimates are given and the expected time (t_e) is calculated using the formula

$$t_e = \frac{a + 4m + b}{6}$$

TABLE 7–5

Description of Activities and Events in Figure 7–13

Activity	Description	Prerequisite Activities	Event Description
1–2	Development of preliminary market research report		2—Market research report completed
2–3	Development of prototype model	1–2	3—Prototype model developed
2–4	Development of introductory advertising campaign	1–2	4—Ad Campaign developed
3–5	Engineering tests of new product	2–3	5—Engineering tests completed
4–6	Financial analysis of marketing and production requirements	2–4	6—Financial analysis completed
5–6	Children test initial model	3–5	6—Tests completed
6–7	Modifications in product design	5–6 and 4–6	7—Modifications made
7–8	Determination of stop or go decision	6–7	8—Decision made

TABLE 7–6

Calculation of t_e Values for Figure 7–14

Activity	Most Optimistic Time (a)	Most Likely Time (m)	Most Pessimistic Time (b)	t_e (in weeks)
1–2	1	3	5	3.0
2–3	1	2	3	2.0
2–4	2	3	4	3.0
3–5	1	3	5	3.0
4–6	1	4	7	4.0
5–6	1	3	5	3.0
6–7	2	4	6	4.0
7–8	1	2	3	2.0

Figure 7–14 shows the PERT network with the expected time (t_e) values for each activity.

We can now devote our attention to the calculation of the earliest expected date (T_E) in which the project can be completed. Examination of the network reveals there are two paths through the network—Path 1, 2, 3, 5, 6, 7, 8, which takes a total of 17 weeks, and Path 1, 2, 4, 6, 7, 8, which takes a total of 16 weeks. Thus, if we begin at once, completion of the network can be expected no sooner than 17 weeks. In Figure 7–15 the network is shown with the T_E values for each event. Remember we calculate the earliest expected date for each event in the network by taking the longest path from the network beginning event to each of the other events in the network.

FIGURE 7–14

Expected Time (t_e) for Each Activity

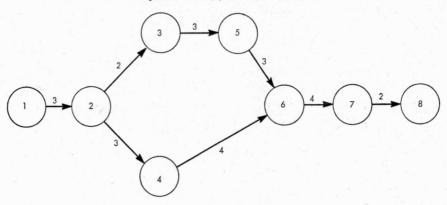

The reader already knows that the longest path through the PERT network determines the earliest expected date of the network ending event. Thus, Path 1, 2, 3, 5, 6, 7, 8 is the *critical path.*

Our next task is to calculate the latest allowable date (T_L) for each event.

FIGURE 7–15

Earliest Expected Date for Each Event in Network

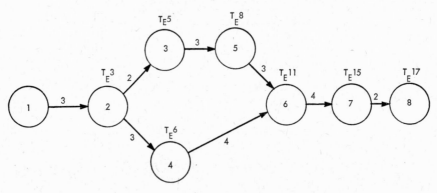

Again this is the latest date on which an event can occur without creating a delay in the completion of the project. To calculate the T_L's, we subtract from the network ending event back to the event in question. In the project we have a directed date of five months (20 weeks) in which the project must be completed. Thus, the T_L for the network ending event is 20 weeks. The T_L values for the entire network are shown in Figure 7–16.

In Figure 7–16 we see that there is slack time on the critical path. Can such a situation exist? The answer we know is yes because we have allowed 20 weeks

FIGURE 7–16

Latest Allowable Date for Each Event in Network

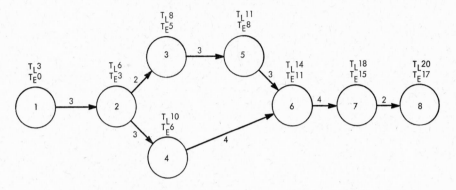

to complete the project, which is three more weeks than we actually need. However, note that the critical path has less slack (three weeks) than Path 1, 2, 4, 6, 7, 8, which has four weeks. The calculations of slack time are shown in Table 7–7.

TABLE 7–7

Calculation of Slack Time for Events
in Network

Event	T_L	—	T_E	= Slack Time
1	3	—	0	=	3
2	6	—	3	=	3
3	8	—	5	=	3
4	10	—	6	=	4
5	11	—	8	=	3
6	14	—	11	=	3
7	18	—	15	=	3
8	20	—	17	=	3

Our next step is to compute the probability of achieving our completion date. First, we must calculate the standard deviations for each individual activity on the critical path. This is shown in Table 7–8.

Now that we have the standard deviation for each activity on the critical path, we can calculate the standard deviation for the network ending event.

$$\sigma T_E = \sqrt{\Sigma \sigma^2}$$
$$= \sqrt{(.67)^2 + (.33)^2 + (.67)^2 + (.67)^2 + (.67)^2 + (.33)^2}$$
$$= \sqrt{.449 + .109 + .449 + .449 + .449 + .109}$$
$$= \sqrt{2.0}$$
$$\sigma T_E = 1.4 \text{ weeks (rounded)}$$

TABLE 7–8

Standard Deviations for Critical Path Activities

Activity	Most Optimistic Time (a)	Most Pessimistic Time (b)	$\dfrac{b-a}{6}$	Standard Deviation
1–2	1	5	$\dfrac{4}{6}$	.67
2–3	1	3	$\dfrac{2}{6}$	.33
3–5	1	5	$\dfrac{4}{6}$	.67
5–6	1	5	$\dfrac{4}{6}$	.67
6–7	2	6	$\dfrac{4}{6}$	.67
7–8	1	3	$\dfrac{2}{6}$	.33

Our next step is to compute the slack time on the critical path. We divide the slack time by the standard deviation of the network ending event (σT_E) in order to get the number of standard deviations (Z) the slack time represents. This is computed as follows

$$Z = \frac{T_L - T_E}{\sigma T_E}$$
$$= \frac{20 - 17}{1.4}$$
$$Z = 2.14$$

Examining Appendix B reveals that a Z value of 2.14 encompasses .4838 percent of the curve from the mean of a normal distribution. We know that 50 percent of the area under the curve lies to the left of the mean of a normal distribution. Thus, our chances of finishing before the latest allowable date (T_L) of 20 weeks is about 98 percent. This is shown as the shaded area under the curve in Figure 7–17.

In conclusion the reader should see that PERT is a valuable planning and control aid for management. It forces managers to think each major program and project through in its entirety. It aids them in identifying possible delays and conflicts before they occur. It helps in achieving earlier deadlines because of continuous, effective control.

FIGURE 7–17

Probability Distribution of Network Ending Event

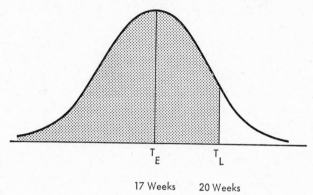

17 Weeks   20 Weeks

NETWORK METHODS (CPM)

A method closely related to PERT is known as CPM (Critical Path Method). Next to PERT, this method of planning and controlling projects is probably the most widely used network method.

CPM departs from PERT in that CPM brings into the planning and control process the concept of cost. However, this is not to say that PERT completely omits the cost concept. In PERT we assumed that cost varied directly with time for all the activities in the project. In other words when a reduction in time had been achieved, we assumed that a reduction in cost had also been achieved. When the earliest expected date (T_E) of the network was reduced, we assumed there had been a reduction in cost.[3]

Another area of departure between PERT and CPM is that CPM uses a single time estimate for each activity; whereas in PERT we used three. The user of CPM is assumed to have a more solid basis when estimating the time required for each activity.

Whether PERT or CPM is used will be determined by the needs of the program or the type of project. When time can be estimated accurately and costs can be determined in advance, CPM is probably the better of the two network methods. A good example of this type of project is a construction project, where material and labor costs can be determined fairly accurately

---

[3] When PERT was originally developed, it did not consider the direct relationship between cost and time. However, the latest versions of PERT present highly sophisticated cost analysis procedures.

and in advance. However, when there is a high degree of uncertainty and/or the need for control over time outweighs control over costs, PERT is probably the better choice of the two. Many marketing projects fall into this latter group.

Development of a CPM network follows the same principles as a PERT network, so there is no need to repeat them. The real difference lies in estimating the times for each activity.

For each activity in a CPM network there are two time estimates and two corresponding cost estimates. There is a *normal time* estimate, which corresponds to the most likely time in a PERT network, and a *crash time* estimate, which is the time that would be needed if no costs were spared. *Normal cost* is, therefore, the cost necessary to finish the project in the normal time and *crash cost* is the cost necessary to complete the job in the *crash time*. We can depict this situation graphically as follows:

FIGURE 7–18

Crash Time and Cost vs. Normal Time and Cost

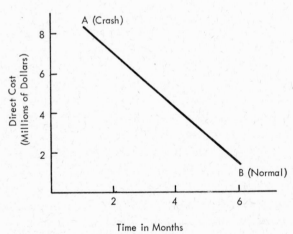

Time in Months

In Figure 7–18 the vertical axis represents the costs associated with completing a particular project and the horizontal axis depicts the time needed for completion. The graph indicates that a crash effort could complete the project in two months at a cost of $6 million, while a normal effort would cost $2 million and take six months to complete. We refer to the line connecting the two points (*A* and *B*) as the approximated time-cost curve because we do not really know exactly how the time-cost relationship behaves without conducting a great deal of research and cost analysis.

Actually, there are two ways that the time-cost relationship could behave. These are shown in Figures 7–19 (I & II). In Figure 7–19(I) curve *C–D* depicts the case where an initial reduction of time can be achieved with a modest increase in cost. In this case the time needed for the project is reduced from Point *X* to Point *Y* and cost increases only from Point *S* to Point *T*. Figure 7–19(II) illustrates the opposite time-cost relationship. In this case Curve *F–G* illustrates that the increase in cost is high when compared to the decrease in time. A reduction in the time needed for the project is reduced from Point *X* to Point *Y* with an increase in cost from Point *S* to Point *T*.

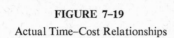

FIGURE 7–19

Actual Time–Cost Relationships

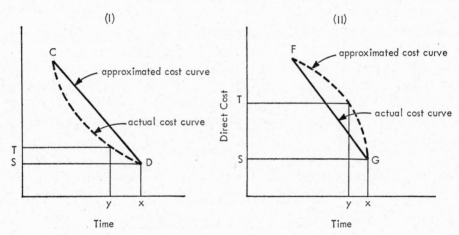

The differences between the actual and approximate curves shown in Figure 7–19 have been exaggerated in order to illustrate the point. In an actual situation a straight line may be an accurate enough approximation of the actual relationship. As was mentioned in Chapter Two, using linear approximations of actual relationships is one method used to simplify complex problems. The purpose here is to enable us to determine rapidly the cost of speeding up a particular activity without getting bogged down in lengthy time-cost studies and complex accounting concepts. For the purposes of the CPM analysis the approximated time-cost curve may be accurate enough. Remember that our goal is to determine where on the critical path reduction in time can be achieved with a minimum of additional expenditure.

Let us illustrate the basics of CPM by examining the network in Figure 7–20.

FIGURE 7–20

Normal Times for all Activities

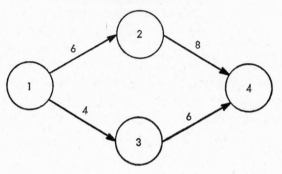

For any set of activities on the critical path of a given network, each will have its own cost per week of crashing and there will be a large number of alternative ways to crash the project with each having its own cost. For Figure 7–20 the normal times are shown on the network and the earliest expected date of the network ending event is 14 weeks. The critical path is Path 1, 2, 4. Now let us calculate the cost of crashing the program. This is shown in Table 7–9.

TABLE 7–9

Calculation of Cost of Crashing Program

	Time in Weeks		Cost		Cost to Crash Per Week
Activity	Normal	Crash	Normal	Crash	
1–2	6	4	$ 8,000	$12,000	$2,000
1–3	4	2	6,000	9,000	1,500
2–4	8	6	6,000	8,000	1,000
3–4	6	4	10,000	16,000	3,000

In Table 7–9 the cost to crash per week is found by using the following formula:

$$\text{Cost to crash} = \frac{\text{crash cost} - \text{normal cost}}{\text{normal time} - \text{crash time}}$$

We can now construct a new network utilizing the crash time for each activity. By crashing all the activities, we see that the earliest expected date for the network ending event is now ten weeks. The critical path remains Path 1, 2, 4 (see Figure 7–21). The direct cost of the project is now $45,000 (a total of the crash cost column) as opposed to $30,000 under the normal time. However, the project is completed four weeks earlier. Our problem now becomes one of determining if we can crash the project without crashing every activity in the network. If this is possible, we may be able to still reduce the earliest expected date to ten weeks without increasing the total cost from $30,000 to $45,000.

Examination of Table 7–9 indicates that Activity 2–4 on the critical path is the least costly activity to crash. It can be reduced two weeks at a cost of $1,000 per week. If this is done, then the earliest expected date would be 12 weeks and the total cost of the program would be $32,000.

The remaining activity (1–2) on the critical path can be reduced two weeks at a cost of $2,000 per week or $4,000. Thus, the earliest expected date is ten

FIGURE 7–21

Crash Times for All Activities

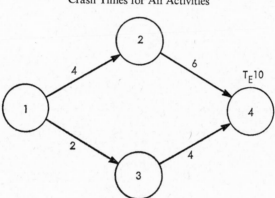

weeks with a total cost of $36,000. Our network now is shown in Figure 7–22. Examination of Figure 7–22 indicates that both Paths 1, 2, 4 and 1, 3, 4 are critical paths. Each path requires ten weeks to complete. Thus, any reduction of the time on one of the paths without a corresponding reduction on the other path will not reduce the earliest expected date (T_E) of the network ending event any further.

For example, why not crash Activity 1–3 or 3–4? Remember that Activities 1–2 and 2–4 have already been crashed and can be crashed no further. Therefore, if we reduced the time of Path 1, 3, 4, it would be a foolish expenditure of money, since Path 1, 2, 4 would have the longest T_E and therefore remain as the critical path. Thus, by closer examination we have managed to reduce the T_E from 14 weeks to 10 weeks with an expenditure of $6,000 rather than $15,-000. The total cost is now $36,000 instead of $45,000, when all activities were crashed.

This discussion of CPM has utilized a very simplified problem. The reader can imagine that a more complex network made up of numerous activities would be more realistic. However, the example provided here presents the

FIGURE 7–22
Crash Times for Activities 1–2 and 2–4

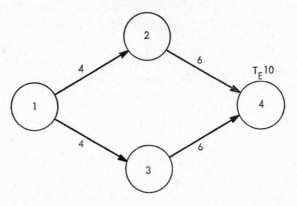

basic underlying rationale and approach of CPM. In addition, we have devoted a great deal more attention to PERT than to CPM. This is because PERT is much more widely used in product planning programs. Finally, the reader can well imagine that for PERT or CPM problems involving numerous events and activities, the use of a computer greatly facilitates the analysis.[4]

MARKOV CHAIN ANALYSIS (BRAND SHARE MODEL)

The Markov process is concerned with analyzing present movement of a variable in order to predict the future movement of the variable. In recent years it has been used by marketing managers in determining market shares for their products and in analyzing switching behavior among consumers.

Importance of Market Share Measurement

The market share of a firm is viewed as a major means of determining its competitive position. Indeed, market share is probably a more effective gauge of a product's success than its sales volume. This is because market share indicates to management whether or not changes in its sales are due to variables

---

[4] For an excellent complete treatment of PERT and CPM see Richard I. Levin and C. A. Kirkpatrick, *Planning and Control with PERT/CPM* (New York: McGraw-Hill Book Company, Inc., 1966).

under its control or outside its control. "If a company's sales fall but its market share remains constant, this implies that the whole industry was affected by similar environmental forces. On the other hand, if a firm's sales increased, but its market share dropped, this could be indicative that its marketing mix or its implementation is ineffective."[5]

One authority goes so far as to suggest that a firm's market share is almost as important as its profits: "Marketing executives must watch their *market share* just as much as their profits. Present customers can never be taken for granted."[6]

Market share can also be used as a control device. "One frequently used standard or measure of overall sales effectiveness is the market share. It is also frequently used as a goal of the sales effort and as a means of controlling sales performance."[7]

Market share can also be utilized in marketing planning and goal setting. For example, a specific market share, either for all the firm's products combined or for individual brands, can be designated as marketing objectives. In this regard, these objectives involve attempting to *maintain* a given market share or *increase* it.

Of course, firms are not only interested in their own market shares, but the market shares of competitive firms as well. Of special significance are the trends of these market shares, since trends often dictate the nature and direction of future competitive strategies.

Of particular interest to marketers is a projection of their market share at some particular future time. If it appears that the market share will decline, then management can take the necessary steps to try and prevent this situation.

There are three major factors which determine an individual firm's future market share. Assuming a static market size, the first of these is the firm's ability to retain its *present* customers. This is called the "retention rate." The second is its ability to draw customers away from competitive firms, that is, the "switching-in rate." The third is the tendency for the firm to lose customers, that is, the "switching-out rate."

One of the earliest studies of these three factors was by the automobile industry prior to World War II. A rather simplified approach was utilized in that the manufacturers attempted merely to ascertain what makes of cars pur-

---

[5] Philip Kotler, *Marketing Management* (Englewood Cliffs, N.J.: Prentice-Hall, Inc., 1967), pp. 583–584.

[6] Philip Kotler, "The Use of Mathematical Models in Marketing," *Journal of Marketing*, Vol. 27 (October, 1963), p. 33.

[7] John R. Matthews, Jr., Robert D. Buzzell, Theodore Levitt, and Ronald E. Frank, *Marketing: An Introductory Analysis* (New York: McGraw-Hill Book Company, Inc., 1964), p. 51.

chasers had owned before their present ones. Shortly after the war, it was not uncommon for the industry to analyze the source of its customers (what competitive products they purchased before) and their destination (which brands were purchased after purchase of a given product ceased).[8]

The Markov Process

A concept from mathematics—the *Markov process*—has received much attention as a method capable of describing brand switching phenomena and enabling the marketer to predict market shares at some future date. It was developed by a Russian mathematician of the same name in the early 1900's. Its first application was that of predicting the movement of gas particles in a closed chamber. Other applications have involved analyses of attitude changes, labor mobility, epidemiology of mental diseases, and social power.[9] However, the process has also been used in the field of marketing, where it is used to predict future market shares based on current brand loyalty and brand switching patterns.

The key feature of a Markov process is that the "state" of the "system" at any given point in time depends only on its state in the immediately previous point in time, and not on any other past events. In strict terms, a Markov process is a stochastic process such that knowing the outcome of the *last* experiment we can neglect any other information about the past in predicting the future.[10]

This assumption is referred to as a *first-order* Markov process. It allows one to compute the probability that a consumer will purchase Brand J on the next purchase, given that Brand I was purchased the previous time. *Higher order* Markov processes are required if the probability of buying Brand J depends on two, three, four, or greater previous purchases.

In summary, it can be said that in order for the Markov process to be useful operationally, it generally embraces the following:

1. A firm's retention rate.
2. Switching-in and switching-out probabilities.
3. An assumption that the last purchase patterns can be used as indicators of the future retention rate and switching-in and switching-out rates.
4. An assumption that the total market is of a constant size, which indicates that every customer makes a purchase in each time period.

---

[8] See Robert Buzzell, *Mathematical Models and Marketing Management* (Boston: Graduate School of Business Administration, Harvard University, 1964), p. 217.

[9] See Frank Harary and Benjamin Lipstein, "The Dynamics of Brand Loyalty: A Markovian Approach," *Operations Research*, Vol. 10 (January–February, 1962), pp. 20–21.

[10] Buzzell, *op. cit.*, pp. 218–219.

A complete coverage of the application of the Markov process to business problems would require intense mathematical training on the part of the reader. However, by utilizing the concepts discussed in Chapter Five we can demonstrate the application of first-order Markov chains to marketing problems.

Let us assume that X, Y, and Z are the only three home delivery bakeries in a town. The managements of each of the bakeries is aware that consumers switch bakeries over time for various reasons such as dissatisfaction with service or because of advertising. To simplify the mathematics in this problem, we will make two assumptions.

1. All three bakeries collect data on the number of their customers and the bakery from which they previously purchased.
2. No new customers enter the market and no old customers leave the market during the period under study.

TABLE 7–10

Movement of Customers Between Bakeries X, Y, and Z

Bakery	January 1 Customers	Movement during January		February 1 Customers
		Gain	Loss	
X	300	140	90	350
Y	600	140	90	650
Z	400	60	160	300

Suppose that Table 7–10 presents the movement of customers between the three bakeries for a one month period. The table indicates that Bakery Z is the only one to end up with a net loss in customers. The data in Table 7–10, while it does indicate the movement of customers and net gains and losses, is not detailed enough for sound management decision-making. Specifically, management needs data in order to

1. Determine the future market share of each firm.
2. Determine the rate of gains and losses in market share.
3. Determine if an equilibrium state of constant market shares will ever exist.

The first major step in utilizing the Markov process is to develop a matrix of transition probabilities. Transition probabilities are the probabilities that a firm will retain, gain and lose its customers. The retention probabilities are computed in Table 7–11.

Our next step is to determine the rates at which all bakeries gain new cus-

TABLE 7–11

Retention Probabilities for Bakeries X, Y, and Z

Bakery	January 1 Customers	Number Lost	Number Retained	Retention Probability
X	300	90	210	210/300 = .70
Y	600	90	510	510/600 = .85
Z	400	160	240	240/400 = .60

tomers each month. In order to achieve this we would need data on the flow of customers. This is shown in Table 7–12.

TABLE 7–12

Flow of Customers Between Bakeries X, Y, and Z

Bakery	January 1 Customers	Gains from			Losses to			February 1 Customers
		X	Y	Z	X	Y	Z	
X	300	0	60	80	0	60	30	350
Y	600	60	0	80	60	0	30	650
Z	400	30	30	0	80	80	0	300

In Table 7–12 all of our available data is in concise form. We can now determine not only the net gains and losses for each of the bakeries but also the interrelationships between the gains and losses of each bakery. We are now able to summarize the probabilities of retaining as well as gaining and losing customers. These probabilities are computed in Table 7–13.

TABLE 7–13

Computation of Transition Probabilities

Bakery	Bakery		
	X	Y	Z
X	210/300 = .70	60/600 = .10	80/400 = .20
Y	60/300 = .20	510/600 = .85	80/400 = .20
Z	30/300 = .10	30/600 = .05	240/400 = .60

We can now reduce Table 7–13 to a matrix in which the gains and losses take the form of transition probabilities. This becomes known as our matrix of transition probabilities.

Matrix of Transition Probabilities

$$
\begin{array}{c}
 \\
X \\
Y \\
Z
\end{array}
\begin{array}{ccc}
X & Y & Z \\
.700 & .100 & .200 \\
.200 & .850 & .200 \\
.100 & .050 & .600
\end{array}
$$

The matrix of transition probabilities contains for each bakery the retention probability and the probability of losses to the other bakeries. The rows of the matrix depict the retention of customers and the gain of customers, while the columns depict the retention of customers and the loss of customers. Let us illustrate how the matrix is read by interpreting two columns and two rows.

1. Column 1 tells us that Bakery X retains .70 of its customers, loses .20 of its customers to Bakery Y and .10 of its customers to Bakery Z.

2. Row 1 tells us that Bakery X retains .70 of its customers, gains .10 of Bakery Y's customers and .20 of Bakery Z's customers.

3. Column 2 tells us that Bakery Y retains .85 of its customers, loses .10 of its customers to Bakery X and .05 of its customers to Bakery Z.

4. Row 2 tells us that Bakery Y retains .85 of its customers, gains .20 of Bakery X's customers and .20 of Bakery Z's customers.

The reader should interpret Column 3 and Row 3 before proceeding.

Remember that a basic assumption of Markov analysis is that consumers do not switch their patronage at random, and we assume that choices of bakeries in the future reflects choices made in the past. As we stated previously, a first order Markov process assumes that the probability that a consumer will purchase Brand J on the next purchase depends upon the outcomes of the last event and not on any earlier buying behavior.

Predicting Future Market Shares

Let us assume that the market shares on February 1 are as follows. These are computed by dividing the number of customers each bakery has on February 1 by the total number of customers (1300).

Bakery X	26.9%
Bakery Y	50.0%
Bakery Z	23.1%

With this data we are now able to calculate the probable market shares for each bakery on March 1. In order to do this we place the February 1 market share figures in a matrix and multiply this matrix by the matrix of transition probabilities.

Transition Probability   *February 1*   *Probable Market*
Matrix   *Market Shares*   *Shares March 1*

$$
\begin{matrix} X \\ Y \\ Z \end{matrix}
\begin{pmatrix} .700 & .100 & .200 \\ .200 & .850 & .200 \\ .100 & .050 & .600 \end{pmatrix}
\times
\begin{pmatrix} .269 \\ .500 \\ .231 \end{pmatrix}
=
\begin{pmatrix} .2845 \\ .5250 \\ .1905 \end{pmatrix}
$$

To arrive at the market shares for March 1, we multiplied the two matrices using the row and column procedures discussed in Chapter Five. They can be explained as follows:

First Column $\times$ First Row

1. X's ability to retain customers $\times$
   X's market share = .700 $\times$ .269   = .1883
2. X's ability to attract Y's
   customers $\times$ Y's market
   share = .100 $\times$ .500   = .0500
3. X's ability to attract Z's
   customers $\times$ Z's market
   share = .200 $\times$ .231   = .0462

   X's market share March 1   .2845

The reader should perform the two remaining column and row multiplications and explain each of them before continuing.

With the existing data it is possible for us to calculate the probable market shares for succeeding months. For example, the probable market shares for April 1 can be determined by squaring the transition probability matrix and multiplying this by the February 1 probabilities.[11]

By squaring the original transition probability matrix, we are, in reality, computing the probabilities of retention, gain, and loss. We multiply this by the original market shares, which gives us the probable market shares for April 1.

$$
\begin{matrix} X \\ Y \\ Z \end{matrix}
\begin{pmatrix} .700 & .100 & .200 \\ .200 & .850 & .200 \\ .100 & .050 & .600 \end{pmatrix}
\times
\begin{pmatrix} .700 & .100 & .200 \\ .200 & .850 & .200 \\ .100 & .050 & .600 \end{pmatrix}
=
$$

In order to arrive at the new matrix, we use the column and row procedures discussed in Chapter Five. The procedure and explanation for one column and row is provided here.

---

[11] There are other methods of doing this. However, the method shown here can calculate probable market shares for some future period without calculating the probabilities for the intermediate periods.

First Row   *First Column*

$(.700 \quad .100 \quad .200)$

$$\times \quad \begin{pmatrix} .700 \\ .200 \\ .100 \end{pmatrix} = \begin{array}{l} \text{New First Column-} \\ \text{First Row Value} \end{array}$$

First Row × First Column:

1. X's ability to retain customers × X's ability to retain customers = the percentage of its customers it retains after two months = $.700 \times .700 = .4900$.

plus

2. X's ability to attract Y's customers × Y's ability to attract X's customers = X's recovery of its own customers from $Y = .100 \times .200 = .0200$

plus

3. X's ability to gain Z's customers × Z's ability to attract X's customers = X's recovery of its own customers from $Z = .200 \times .100 = .0200$

Thus, the new first column-first row value is

$$.4900 + .0200 + .0200 = .5300$$

The remaining values are computed in the same manner. The new matrix is, therefore,

$$\begin{pmatrix} .5300 & .1650 & .2800 \\ .3300 & .7525 & .3300 \\ .1400 & .0825 & .3900 \end{pmatrix}$$

We then multiply this matrix by the original market shares for February 1.

$$\begin{pmatrix} .5300 & .1650 & .2800 \\ .3300 & .7525 & .3300 \\ .1400 & .0825 & .3900 \end{pmatrix} \times \begin{pmatrix} .269 \\ .500 \\ .231 \end{pmatrix} = \begin{pmatrix} .290 \\ .541 \\ .169 \end{pmatrix}$$

The procedure and explanation for one column and row is provided here.

$$(.5300 \quad .1650 \quad .2800) \times \begin{pmatrix} .269 \\ .500 \\ .231 \end{pmatrix} = \begin{array}{l} X\text{'s market share} \\ \text{for April 1.} \end{array}$$

First Row × First Column:

1. X's ability to keep its own customers after two months × X's original share of the market = X's share of its original group of customers on April 1 = $.5300 \times .269 = .1426$.

2. X's ability to attract Y's original group of customers after two months $\times$ Y's original share of the market = X's share of Y's original group of customers on April 1 = .1650 $\times$ .500 = .0825.

3. X's ability to attract Z's original group of customers after two months $\times$ Z's original share of the market = X's share of Z's original group of customers on April 1 = .2800 $\times$ .231 = .0647.

Thus, the probable market share for X on March 1 is

$$.1426 + .0825 + .0647 = .290 \text{ (rounded)}$$

The remaining values are calculated in the same manner. The market shares for March 1 are, therefore,

$$X = .290$$
$$Y = .541$$
$$Z = .169$$

We could in the same manner compute the probable market share in three months by cubing the matrix of transition probabilities and multiplying it by the February 1 market shares, and so on for as many months as we desired.

Thus far we have determined the future market share of a seller and determined the rate of gains and losses in market share. Our next task is to determine if an equilibrium state can exist.

Determination of Equilibrium State

As long as the transition probabilities remain the same, a state of equilibrium in the market shares will eventually be reached. This, of course, assumes that none of the firms engages in any competitive strategies that will alter the original probabilities.

The original transition probability matrix can be written in equation form as follows:

$$X = .700X + .100Y + .200Z$$
$$Y = .200X + .850Y + .200Z$$
$$Z = .100X + .050Y + .600Z$$

where X, Y, and Z represent eventual equilibrium market shares for Firms X, Y, and Z.

Since the final market shares of all three firms must total to 100 percent, we must add a fourth equation:

$$1.0 = X + Y + Z$$

By solving these equations, either simultaneously or by determinants, we arrive at final equilibrium market shares for Bakeries X, Y, and Z.

Simultaneous Equations

$$X = .70X + .10Y + .20Z$$
$$Y = .20X + .85Y + .20Z$$
$$Z = .10X + .05Y + .60Z$$
$$1 = X + Y + Z$$

We subtract X, Y, and Z from both sides of the equations.

$$0 = -.30X + .10Y + .20Z$$
$$0 = .20X - .15Y + .20Z$$
$$0 = .10X + .05Y - .40Z$$
$$1 = X + Y + Z$$

Since we have four equations and three unknowns, one equation is extraneous and is not needed to solve the problem. We have decided to drop the equation $0 = .10X + .05Y - .40Z$. Thus, we now have the following three equations to consider:

$$0 = -.30X + .10Y + .20Z \qquad (1)$$
$$0 = .20X - .15Y + .20Z \qquad (2)$$
$$1 = X + Y + Z \qquad (3)$$

Step 1.   Multiply Equation (2) by 1.5 and add it to Equation (1).

$$0 = -.3X + .1Y + .2Z$$
$$\underline{0 = .3X - .225Y + .3Z}$$
$$0 = \qquad - .125Y + .5Z$$
$$.125Y = .5Z$$
$$Y = 4Z$$

Step 2.   Multiply Equation (1) by 1.5 and add it to Equation (2).

$$0 = .2X - .15Y + .2Z$$
$$\underline{0 = -.45X + .15Y + .3Z}$$
$$0 = -.25X \qquad + .5Z$$
$$.25X = .5Z$$
$$X = 2Z$$

Step 3.   Substitute the values for X and Y into Equation (3).

$$1 = X + Y + Z$$
$$1 = 2Z + 4Z + Z$$
$$1 = 7Z$$
$$Z = 0.143$$

Step 4.   Substitute the value for Z into the equations developed in Steps 1
and 2.

$$X = 2Z$$
$$X = 2(0.143)$$
$$X = 0.286$$

$$Y = 4Z$$
$$Y = 4(0.143)$$
$$Y = 0.571*$$

We can also solve the equations through the use of determinants as follows:

$$X = \frac{\begin{vmatrix} 0 & .10 & .2 \\ 0 & -.15 & .2 \\ 1 & 1 & 1 \end{vmatrix}}{\begin{vmatrix} -.3 & .10 & .2 \\ .2 & -.15 & .2 \\ 1 & 1 & 1 \end{vmatrix}} = \frac{0.050}{0.175} = 0.286$$

$$Y = \frac{\begin{vmatrix} -.3 & 0 & .2 \\ .2 & 0 & .2 \\ 1 & 1 & 1 \end{vmatrix}}{\begin{vmatrix} -.3 & .10 & .2 \\ .2 & -.15 & .2 \\ 1 & 1 & 1 \end{vmatrix}} = \frac{0.100}{0.175} = 0.571$$

$$Z = \frac{\begin{vmatrix} -.3 & .1 & 0 \\ .2 & -.15 & 0 \\ 1 & 1 & 1 \end{vmatrix}}{\begin{vmatrix} -.3 & .1 & .2 \\ .2 & -.15 & .2 \\ 1 & 1 & 1 \end{vmatrix}} = \frac{0.025}{0.175} = 0.143$$

Thus, our equilibrium market shares are

Bakery X	28.6%
Bakery Y	57.1%
Bakery Z	14.3%

Remember that these equilibrium market shares are calculated on the assumption that our matrix of transition probabilities remains fixed. In many cases we may need to change our transition probability matrix when our firm or some competitive firm takes an action which will alter the matrix of transition probabilities. Then new equilibrium market shares can be calculated. In this

---

* Note: Due to rounding error, this value is given so that the sum will be 1. Obviously, the value is 0.572.

way we are using the Markov process as an intermediate-run marketing management tool. To insure that we have achieved equilibrium market shares, we can multiply the matrix of transition probabilities by the equilibrium market shares.

$$\begin{pmatrix} .700 & .100 & .200 \\ .200 & .850 & .200 \\ .100 & .050 & .600 \end{pmatrix} \times \begin{pmatrix} .286 \\ .571 \\ .143 \end{pmatrix} = \begin{pmatrix} .286 \\ .571 \\ .143 \end{pmatrix}$$

The reader should perform the matrix multiplication in order to prove that we have achieved an equilibrium state in the market.

Assumptions of Markov Analysis

There are several assumptions we have implicitly made throughout the discussion of the Markov process. First, we assume that the distribution of market share among brands at any time depends solely on the distribution in the previous time period and the transition probabilities. In other words, we are saying that the probability that a consumer will purchase a given brand at a particular time depends only on his previous purchase.

The reader undoubtedly noticed throughout the discussion that we assumed that the total market is of a constant size. The model assumes that every customer makes a purchase in every time period. This is of course a simplifying assumption. We know that in reality the time interval between purchases will vary widely.[12]

One final assumption is that the model does not consider variations in the quantity purchased by a consumer.

As pointed out in Chapter Two, there will be many times when complex and disorganized marketing problems must be redefined into more manageable ones if models are to be constructed. One method used is to simplify relationships between variables. The assumptions made in Markov analysis are an example of simplifying relationships in order to construct a model.[13]

PROBLEMS

1. Why is PERT expecially useful in nonrepetitive problem areas? Give some examples of repetitive marketing problems and nonrepetitive marketing problems.

---

[12] There is a method of eliminating this problem by introducing an additional state of "no purchase." However, this will not be discussed in this text.

[13] The approach used to demonstrate the application of first-order Markov chains to a marketing problem was adapted from Richard I. Levin and C. A. Kirkpatrick, *Quantitative Approaches to Management* (New York: McGraw-Hill Book Co., Inc., 1965), chapter 11.

2. Discuss the statement "The paramount variable in a PERT network system is time."

3. Assume that you have been assigned a term project in one of your marketing courses. Data for the report will come from both primary and secondary sources. It is your task to collect both types of data. You have a total of 10 weeks in which to complete the assignment. List the activities and their most optimistic, most likely, and most pessimistic times, and construct a PERT network for the project.

4. Illustrate that you understand the following concepts by briefly defining each one.
A. Event
B. Activity
C. Expected time (t_e)
D. Earliest expected date (T_E)
E. Latest allowable date (T_L)
F. Slack time
G. Standard deviation

5. Assume that you are the marketing manager of a college textbook manufacturer. You have just received the completed manuscript of a marketing textbook written by a college professor. The time of issue for such a book has a profound

| | Time Estimates (weeks) | | |
Activity	Most Optimistic Time	Most Likely Time	Most Pessimistic Time
1. Check manuscript for content.	1	2	3
2. Check for legal permissions to reprint from other sources.	2	4	6
3. Obtain needed permissions.	1	3	5
4. At the same time prepare drawings, figures, and charts.	2	4	6
5. Edit entire manuscript for correct grammar, etc.	4	7	10
6. Return manuscript to author for necessary corrections and suggestions for changes.	1	2	3
7. Author sends manuscript back with corrections made.	1	2	3
8. Set type.	1	2	4
9. Check page proofs.	2	3	4
10. At the same time have authors check page proofs.	3	4	5
11. Make corrections and print text.	4	6	8
12. At the same time prepare advertisements for text.	1	2	3
13. Have sales meeting to inform sales force of the nature of the text.	1	1	1

influence on sales and profit. Most professors make adoption decisions in March or April for the following Fall semester. Therefore, missing a March issuance date for a new textbook may cost a whole year's sales in addition to letting a competitive book gain a stronghold in the market. Listed above are the activities and their time estimates you feel must be achieved before the text is ready for publication. Assume it is July 1 and you hope to have the book ready for release by March 1 (35 weeks available). Construct a network for the activities, and compute the probability of completion.

6. CPM is used widely in construction projects but rarely in marketing projects. Why do you think this is so?

7. The first major step in utilizing the Markov process is the development of a transition probability matrix. What does this matrix show?

8. On January 1, each of three home delivery bakeries has an equal (one-third) share of the market in a city. During the previous year Bakery X retained .80 of its customers while losing .10 to Bakery Y and .10 to Bakery Z. Bakery Y managed to retain .90 of its customers while losing .05 to Bakery X and .05 to Bakery Z. Bakery Z retained .85 of its customers while losing .05 to Bakery X and .10 to Bakery Y. Suppose the same pattern of switching holds for the coming year. What will be each bakery's share of the market next January 1?

9. As of July, Bakery X has 50 percent of the market with Bakeries Y and Z equally dividing the remainder. It is known that Bakery X retains .80 of its customers while gaining .05 of Bakery Y's customers and .05 of Bakery Z's customers. Bakery Y retains .90 of its customers while gaining .10 of X's customers and .10 of Z's customers. Bakery Z retains .85 of its customers and gains .10 of X's customers and .05 of Y's customers. Determine the market share of each bakery on September 1. What will each firm's market share be assuming an equilibrium condition is reached?

REFERENCES

Periodicals

BLICKSTEIN, S. "How to Put PERT into Marketing (and Aid Planning)," *Printer's Ink*, Vol. 289 (October 23, 1964), pp. 27–29.

DAVIS, EDWARD W. "Resource Allocation in Project Network—a Survey," *Journal of Industrial Engineering*, Vol. 17 (March–April, 1966), pp. 177–188.

DRAPER, JEAN E. and NOLEN, LARRY H. "A Markov Chain Analysis of Brand Preferences," *Journal of Advertising Research*, Vol. 4 (September, 1964), pp. 33–38.

GISSER, P. "Taking the Chances Out of Product Introductions (Using the PERT Technique)," *Industrial Marketing*, Vol. 50 (May, 1965), pp. 86–91.

EHRENBERG, S. C. "An Appraisal of Markov Brand-Switching Models," *Journal of Marketing Research*, Vol. 1 (November, 1965), pp. 347–362.

MILLER, ROBERT W. "How To Plan and Control with PERT," *Harvard Business Review*, Vol. 40 (March–April, 1962), pp. 93–104.

Books

EVARTS, HARRY F. *Introduction to PERT*. Boston: Allyn and Bacon, Inc., 1964.

FRANK, RONALD E., KUEHN, ALFRED E., and WILLIAM MASSY, EDS. *Quantitative Techniques in Marketing Analysis*. Homewood, Ill.: Richard D. Irwin, Inc., 1962.

KEMENY, J. G. and SNELL, J. L. *Finite Markov Chains*. Princeton, New Jersey: D. Van Nostrand Company, Inc., 1960.

KEMENY, J. G., SNELL, J. L. and G. L. THOMPSON. *Introduction to Finite Mathematics*. Englewood Cliffs, N.J.: Prentice-Hall, Inc., 1957.

LEVIN, RICHARD I. and KIRKPATRICK, CHARLES A. *Planning and Control with PERT /CPM*. New York: McGraw-Hill Book Company, Inc., 1966.

MATHEWS, JOHN B., JR., BUZZELL, ROBERT D., LEVITT, THEODORE, and RONALD E. FRANK. *Marketing: An Introductory Analysis*. New York: McGraw-Hill Book Company, Inc., 1964.

chapter eight
DISTRIBUTION

INTRODUCTION

A major goal of any marketing system is the efficient distribution of goods from production to consumption. To many people, the task of marketing involves the performance of two major tasks: seeking out and stimulating buyers, and physically moving goods to points of consumption. Many feel that marketing executives have spent too great a proportion of their time performing the first task and have relegated the second task to a subsidiary function. They claim that too much attention has been given to developing products, pricing products, and promoting products, and not enough attention has been given to efficiently distributing these products.

The Importance of Distribution

Recently, two factors have forced marketing management to pay greater attention to the problems of distribution. They are:

1. The increased cost for such distribution services as transportation and warehousing.
2. The increased recognition that efficient distribution is a potent weapon in the demand stimulation process.

Many executives are surprised to learn of the high costs of physically moving their product. One expert has stated that transportation and handling costs are the third largest component of the total cost of business operations.[1] Thus, the economic motive of cost reduction should be sufficient support for a closer look at the problems of distribution.

---

[1] John F. Magee, "The Logistics of Distribution," *Harvard Business Review*, Vol. 38 (July–August, 1960), pp. 89–101. Also see John F. Magee, *Physical Distribution Systems* (New York: McGraw-Hill Book Company, 1967).

However, in addition to providing cost savings, a coordinated distribution system can also aid in stimulating demand for a product. A product does not have built-in intrinsic market value. Even a finished product stored in a warehouse has only potential value. A product must be made available when the buyer desires it and where he can obtain it conveniently. Thus, the distribution system adds both time and place utility to a product. Distribution includes not only selection of marketing channels but the logistics problems which arise in the dispersion of the merchandise and the management of inventories.

In this chapter, three analytical techniques will be examined which can aid marketing management in achieving more efficient distribution of their products. These techniques are break-even analysis, the transportation model, and the inventory model. Facility planning or queuing theory is often presented in discussions of distribution, but we will defer this topic area until Chapter Twelve, which deals specifically with simulation.

SELECTING CHANNELS OF DISTRIBUTION

A channel of distribution is the combination of institutions through which a seller markets his products. This structure of institutions may be comprised of many different types and numbers of middlemen. The simplest channel would be one where the goods are moved from the factory directly to the buyer. An example of a direct channel would be the house-to-house distribution of certain household products such as vacuum cleaners and cosmetics. On the other hand, numerous middlemen may comprise the channel, as is usually the case with low unit-value staple products.

The marketing decision maker in a firm usually has many alternatives in choosing the number and type of middlemen to be employed. The firm may decide to use various types of merchant middlemen (wholesalers and retailers) or one of the several types of agents. It is this element of choice that presents the marketing manager with a decision problem.

Most channel selection problems involve three distinct aspects. First, the decision maker must decide on the general type of channel to be used. For example, for industrial products there is a predominance of direct selling. This is understandable since the markets for most industrial goods are highly concentrated, orders are usually of sizable amounts, and many industrial goods require much pre-sale and post-sale service. However, for most consumer products, especially those which are relatively low priced mass-distributed items, more complex or indirect channels are utilized. This is because middlemen perform an economically useful function in the distribution of such products.

Second, if middlemen are going to be utilized, the decision maker must decide on the number of middlemen to use at each level in the channel. This decision will, of course, be determined by the market coverage the firm desires for the product. Specifically, two decisions must be made: the type of outlet which should handle the good, and the intensity of distribution. Obviously, the nature of the product will greatly affect these decisions. If the product needs a certain environment for sale or requires service after purchase, this will reduce the number of available alternatives. Similarly, if the product requires specialized efforts or investment in special facilities or inventories (e.g., paint distributors, shoe retailers), this may dictate that a policy of exclusive distribution—a single outlet in a given area—be followed. Otherwise the decision maker may decide on a policy of selective or intensive distribution.

Third, the decision maker must select the individual firms to carry his product. Of course, in some cases where the firm is young or the product is new, the middlemen will select the firm's product. However, in most cases the decision maker will have to evaluate the capabilities of the various middlemen.

While a great number of problems arise in the selection of channels of distribution, this section will examine the problem of choosing among channel alternatives. To solve the problem, two quantitative tools will be used: break-even analysis and decision theory. While decision theory was discussed in an earlier chapter, this is the students' first exposure to break-even analysis. However, the mathematics utilized for break-even analysis is basic and has been covered in other chapters. This will become readily apparent to the reader as he proceeds working through the sample problem. Before analyzing the problem let us examine the concept of break-even analysis.

BREAK-EVEN ANALYSIS

At the end of an operating period a seller hopes that his income from the period's sales will be sufficient to cover production costs, marketing costs, and administrative costs and to provide some amount of profit. However, if revenue for a particular period is sufficient only to cover the first three items, we can say that the seller in question has broken even or is operating at the break-even point. In other words, if the firm had been able to increase its sales volume by only one item more than the break-even point, it would have shown a profit for the period. The break-even point is the particular scale of operations where total revenue equals total cost.

In order to utilize break-even analysis, we must first become familiar with the types of data needed for the analysis. There are several types of revenue and cost data which are needed.

Total Revenue

This is an estimate of the amount of money expected from sales of the product during the period. First, some estimate is needed of the probable sales volume. This may be in the form of a sales forecast. This figure multiplied by the selling price or the average selling price would give an estimate of total revenue for the period.

Variable Costs

Some costs incurred by the firm will vary directly with output. These are known as variable costs. When output is zero, total variable costs will also be zero. Examples of such costs in marketing would include transportation and salesmen's commissions. Variable costs per unit would, therefore, be constant per unit regardless of the level of volume. For example, variable marketing costs per unit might be $.10 for a particular product. This may consist of transportation and commissions.

Fixed Costs

In manufacturing and selling a product, many of a firm's costs may remain fixed regardless of the level of output. These are known as fixed costs. An example of a fixed marketing cost would be advertising expenditures which are contracted at the beginning of an operating period.

By now many astute students are probably questioning the classification of costs as only variable and fixed. It is true that many semivariable costs and semifixed costs exist. Perhaps sales commissions are increased during seasonal slumps or quantity discounts are increased during off seasons. These would be examples of changing variable costs per unit. Similarly, we recognize that fixed costs do not remain "fixed" indefinitely but rather do vary from time to time. In addition many fixed costs, although remaining fixed for normal variations in output, will vary if output is either exceedingly low or high. An example of such a situation would be hiring additional part-time salespeople during an unusually high peak demand season. These costs we can term "semi-fixed" costs. Thus, when we use the term "fixed" costs, we are actually referring to the short run. In the long run, all costs are subject to variation.

While there are methods of treating semivariable and semifixed costs in break-even analysis, we will disregard such costs in our analysis. Since break-even analysis is most useful only in the short run for forecasting and planning, such an elimination is justified. Thus, in our analysis we will use only variable costs and fixed costs. Now let us proceed to analyze a break-even problem facing a marketing manager.

The Problem

The Gizmo Novelty Company is a manufacturer of inexpensive novelty gift items which are distributed mostly through wholesalers to gift shops, cigar stores, and variety stores. However, one of the firm's executives has developed a new product which top management feels has great potential. This product is an inexpensive plastic seat belt for stadium seats. Originally the firm had planned to market the product as a novelty but then began to consider the product from a more practical viewpoint. After an intensive market research study of sports fans and the number of injuries which occur when fans fall out of bleachers, the firm decided to seriously attempt to market the product. There were two possible alternatives available and management was undecided about which approach to use.

1. Market the product as an industrial product through wholesalers to manufacturers of stadium equipment on a national scale.
2. Market the product as a consumer good through wholesalers to various retail outlets such as variety stores and department stores.

The cost accountants at Gizmo Novelty Company have collected the following data for each of the alternative plans.

Plan 1		Plan 2	
Production costs (fixed)	$15,000	Production costs (fixed)	$ 15,000
Production costs		Production costs	
(per unit variable)	.09	(per unit variable)	.09
Marketing costs		Marketing costs	
(fixed)	25,000	(fixed)	135,000
Marketing costs		Marketing costs	
(per unit variable)	.01	(per unit variable)	.01
Price to wholesaler		Manufacturers selling	
(charged by Gizmo)	.30	price	.40
Selling price	.50	Wholesale price	.50
		Retail price	.75

To solve the problem we shall use break-even analysis and decision theory concepts. The following symbols will be used:

$$BE = \text{break-even point}$$
$$P = \text{selling price per unit}$$
$$TFC = \text{total fixed costs}$$
$$V = \text{variable cost per unit}$$
$$Q = \text{number of units}$$

Using these symbols we can now develop the formula for the break-even point in both dollars and units.

First we define the equation for total cost:

$$TC = V \cdot Q + TFC$$

Then we define total revenue:

$$TR = P \cdot Q$$

At the break-even point the total cost equals the total revenue, therefore, equating these two equations yields:

$$P \cdot Q = V \cdot Q + TFC$$

Solving for Q,

$$
\begin{aligned}
P \cdot Q - V \cdot Q &= TFC \\
(P - V)Q &= TFC \\
Q &= \frac{TFC}{P - V}
\end{aligned}
$$

This is the break-even equation in units.

Proof by dimensional analysis:

$$\text{units} = \frac{\$}{\$/\text{unit}} = \text{units}$$

To get the break-even equation in terms of dollars, divide by the reciprocal of selling price.

$$\frac{Q}{\frac{1}{P}} = \frac{TFC}{\frac{P}{P} - \frac{V}{P}}$$

$$P \cdot Q = \frac{TFC}{1 - \frac{V}{P}}$$

Proof by dimensional analysis:

$$\frac{\text{units}}{\frac{1}{\$/\text{unit}}} = \frac{\$}{\frac{\$/\text{unit}}{\$/\text{unit}}}$$

$$\$ = \frac{\$ \; \text{units}}{\text{units}} = \frac{\$}{1} = \$$$

Summarizing:

$$\text{Break-even point in units} = \frac{TFC}{P - V}$$

$$\text{Break-even point in dollars} = \frac{TFC}{1 - \frac{V}{P}}$$

Applying these formulas to each of the alternatives in our problem gives the following results:

Plan I

Break-even point in units $= \dfrac{\$40,000}{.30 - .10} = 200,000$ units

Break-even point in dollars $= \dfrac{\$40,000}{1 - \dfrac{.10}{.30}} = \$60,000$

Plan II

Break-even point in units $= \dfrac{\$150,000}{.40 - .10} = 500,000$ units

Break-even point in dollars $= \dfrac{\$150,000}{1 - \dfrac{.10}{.40}} = \$200,000$

The above formulas have provided us with break-even points in units and dollars for both of the alternative plans. However, they have not provided us with a complete analysis of the relationships among the four variables: fixed costs, variable costs, output, and revenue. In other words, we do not know how the break-even points will vary with changes in one of the variables. Specifically, it does not show us the relationship of changes in sales to changes in profit, changes in costs to changes in profit, and changes in the scale of our

FIGURE 8–1

Break-even Chart for Plan I

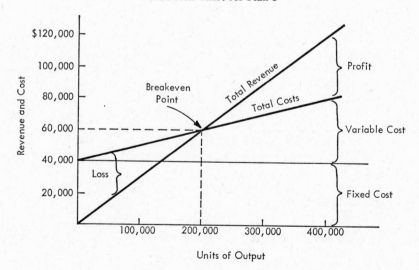

Units of Output

operation to changes in profits. Fortunately, a graphic device has been developed which provides insight into these relationships. This graphic device is known as a break-even chart. The break-even charts for both alternative plans in our problem are presented in Figures 8–1 and 8–2.

Thus, from the break-even chart we can determine the profit possibilities for various levels of output for Plan I. We can summarize them as follows:

TABLE 8–1

Profit Levels of Plan I

Level of Output in Units	Sales	Total Costs	Profit or Loss
100,000	$ 30,000	$50,000	$ − 20,000
200,000	60,000	60,000	−0−
300,000	90,000	70,000	20,000
400,000	120,000	80,000	40,000

We can now proceed in the same fashion to reach a graphical solution for Plan II.

FIGURE 8–2

Break-even Chart for Plan II

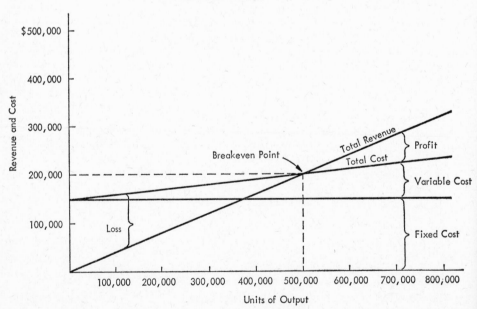

Summarizing the break-even chart for Plan II gives us the following profit potentials:

TABLE 8–2

Profit Levels of Plan II

Level of Output in Units	Sales	Total Costs	Profit or Loss
400,000	$160,000	$190,000	$–30,000
500,000	200,000	200,000	–0–
600,000	240,000	210,000	30,000
700,000	280,000	220,000	60,000
800,000	320,000	230,000	90,000

The break-even charts have shown the relationships between costs, output, and profit. They illustrate that profits will vary depending on output and costs. With this information we may now use various concepts from decision theory to arrive at a solution for our problem.

Let us assume that based on their assessment of the market and past performance data for similar products, the management of Gizmo has estimated the probabilities of the various levels of sales for each alternative plan. These probabilities are presented below.

Plan I

Level of Sales (Units)	Probability of Occurrence
100,000	.15
200,000	.30
300,000	.35
400,000	.20

Plan II

Level of Sales (Units)	Probability of Occurrence
400,000	.20
500,000	.25
600,000	.35
700,000	.15
800,000	.05

Using these probability estimates in conjunction with the data provided by break-even analysis will enable us to determine the expected value (profit) of each of the alternative plans. The reader will recall from Chapter Four that the expected value of a particular event equals the value of the event, if it should occur, multiplied by the probability of the event occurring. The expected value (profit) of each plan is calculated as follows:

TABLE 8–3

Expected Value of Plan I

Level of Output (Units)	Value ×	Probability of Occurrence =	Expected Value
100,000	$−20,000	.15	$−3,000
200,000	−0−	.30	−0−
300,000	20,000	.35	7,000
400,000	40,000	.20	8,000
		Expected Value of Plan I	$12,000

TABLE 8–4

Expected Value of Plan II

Level of Output (Units)	Value ×	Probability of Occurrence =	Expected Value
400,000	$−30,000	.20	$−6,000
500,000	−0−	.25	−0−
600,000	30,000	.35	10,500
700,000	60,000	.15	9,000
800,000	90,000	.05	4,500
		Expected Value of Plan II	$18,000

Thus, if the Gizmo management bases its decision entirely on the profit criterion, then the stadium seat belts will be marketed through wholesalers to variety stores and novelty stores.

In this problem we have utilized a combination of break-even analysis procedures and elementary decision theory concepts to arrive at a decision. This is not the only area where break-even analysis can be utilized. It can be utilized in numerous other areas both related and unrelated to the field of marketing. In this problem we utilized it to provide a sounder basis on which to make distribution channel decisions.

Before leaving break-even analysis it would be wise to note some of the assumptions on which the use of break-even analysis is based. This is not to deter from the value of the tool but rather to strengthen the conditions under which it is used.

Assumptions of Break-Even Analysis

In order for break-even analysis to be properly applied to marketing problems, the decision maker should be aware of the following:

1. Break-even analysis is useful only over relatively short ranges of output. This is because it is assumed that there is a linear relationship among costs, volume, and revenue. Thus, it is not a valuable long-range decision-making tool.

2. Since the break-even model (i.e., the symbolic equation formula) is a deterministic model, it is a static tool. Therefore, it would be more valuable in relatively stable situations than in highly dynamic or volatile situations. It provides a simplified description of the relationship between cost, volume, revenue, and output.

3. Break-even analysis should only be used as a guide for decision making. Its presentation provides a conceptual tool for understanding the relationships between costs, volume, revenue, and output. However, it should not be the determining factor in a decision.

The important point to recognize is that break-even analysis is an aid to decision making. It is definitely not a panacea which can be used mechanistically to reach marketing decisions.[2]

THE TRANSPORTATION MODEL

The transportation method is addressed to and for a special class of linear programming problems for which the basic approach of the simplex technique discussed in Chapter Six is appropriate. However, the transportation method is somewhat easier since it does not call for the development and manipulation of linear equations. Rather, it involves only addition, subtraction, and multiplication. The transportation problem may be solved by the simplex method but the *transportation algorithm* discussed in this section provides a much more efficient method of handling such a problem.

The Problem

The transportation problem may be stated as follows:
Given a number of sources of supply and destinations, and the cost of ship-

---

[2] For another discussion of break-even analysis as applied to distribution see Frank J. Charvat and W. Tate Whitman, *Marketing Management: A Quantitative Approach* (New York: Simmons-Boardman Publishing Corp., 1964), chapter 10.

ping a product from the source of supply to each destination, select those routes that will minimize total shipping costs.

With data concerning the total capacities of the sources of supply, the total needs of the destinations, and the shipping cost per unit of the product, the transportation algorithm may be used to arrive at the optimum shipping program which results in the minimum total shipping costs.

In Chapter Six the assumptions of the basic linear programming model were discussed. As with the algebraic and simplex methods of linear programming, the basic transportation method can be used only with problems which display:

1. Conditions of certainty.

2. Linear relationships between the variables.[3] This would mean that the shipping cost per unit is known in advance and this cost must remain constant regardless of the quantity of goods shipped. However, for the transportation algorithm an additional assumption—one-for-one substitution—must be made. This means that if a marketing manager decides not to ship 100 units of a product from Source *x* to Destination *y*, he must be able to instead substitute 100 units from other sources to be shipped to Destination *y*. It should be remembered from Chapter Six that this is not a prerequisite of the graphical, algebraic, or simplex methods of linear programming.

Let us work through a sample problem so that the methodology can be clearly understood.

Utilizing the Transportation Model

The Hamilton Distributing Corporation is the distributor for a stereophonic speaker manufacturer. Hamilton owns three warehouses as follows:

Warehouse Locations	Speakers in Stock
New York	200
Chicago	150
Denver	50

The corporation has the following monthly demand requirements from three customers:

Customer Location	Monthly Orders
Miami	180
Seattle	150
Omaha	70

---

[3] In more advanced treatments of the transportation algorithm this assumption may be relaxed.

The cost of delivery from each warehouse to each customer is determined largely on the basis of overland mileage. The per unit delivery costs have been determined to be:

TABLE 8–5

Transportation Costs
(in dollars)

| | Destination Demand | | |
Supply Source	Miami	Seattle	Omaha
New York	4	12	7
Chicago	5	8	2
Denver	8	5	3

The management of Hamilton desires to deliver the speakers in good condition and in such a way that their transportation cost would be minimized. In this particular problem it would not be too tedious after acquiring problem-solving experience to arrive at the minimum transportation cost by careful inspection of Table 8–5 and the data on warehouses and customers cited above. If, however, Hamilton was an extremely large distributor with 50 warehouse facilities and 350 customers spread out all over the United States and overseas, then the complexity of the problem would make the inspection solution almost impossible. Thus, to acquire a working understanding of the transportation method, let us proceed to work out the above problem.

The Distribution Matrix

The first step in developing the initial feasible solution is to design a matrix indicating (1) all warehouse stocks and customer requirements and (2) the transportation costs for each unit in the upper portion of the matrix cell. Such a matrix is presented in Table 8–6.

The per unit transportation costs are inserted in the sub-cell as negative values. The sub-cells represent costs and the Hamilton management is interested in minimizing total transportation costs. If the problem involved profit maximization, the cells would contain positive values.

The 400 in the lower right hand cell indicates that supply equals demand. The figures in the requirements (demand) row and supply column are called *rim values*.

The next step is to assign shipments of various numbers of speaker units in the lower left half of the cells in such a manner that the number of units shipped to the demand destination will exactly meet its requirements. One of the more widely known procedures used to reach an initial feasible solution in distribution problems is referred to as the *northwest corner method.* In Table 8–6 this would be the square (cell) in the upper left corner of the matrix. In the northwest corner cell we place the smaller of the rim values for that row and column. The rim value for the row is 200 and for the column is 180. Thus we place 180 in the northwest corner cell. This indicates that 180 speakers are shipped from New York to Miami. Since the rim value of the column was less than that of the row, the next cell to be filled is the one to the right of the cell just filled. There are still 20 speakers available in New York. The customer in Seattle has ordered 150. Thus, we can place the 20 speakers in the New York–Seattle square. We have now depleted the New York supply and cannot make

TABLE 8–6

Initial Distribution Matrix

Supply Source	Destination Demand			Total Supply
	Miami	Seattle	Omaha	
New York	−4	−12	−7	200
Chicago	−5	−8	−2	150
Denver	−8	−5	−3	50
Total Requirements	180	150	70	400

another move to the right. We now drop down one cell and assign the necessary number of units to fill that cell, that is, the Chicago-Seattle cell. Chicago has 150 speakers available and Seattle has an unsatisfied order for 130. Thus, 130 units of the Chicago supply is allocated to Seattle.

We cannot make another move downward because Seattle's demand has been filled. Thus, we move one cell to the right, that is, to the Chicago-Omaha cell. The remaining Chicago supply of 20 speakers is used to fill part of the Omaha demand of 70. Thus, we place 20 in the Chicago-Omaha cell. This leaves Omaha with an unsatisfied demand for 50 speakers. However, Denver has exactly 50 speakers which have not been allocated. We assign these units to the Denver-Omaha cell. This initial feasible solution is presented in Table 8–7.

The total shipping costs of the initial distribution arrangement can be computed. The units to be shipped are multiplied by their related costs and

TABLE 8–7

Northwest Corner Initial Matrix

Supply Source	Destination Demand			Total Supply
	Miami	Seattle	Omaha	
New York	−4 180	−12 20	−7	200
Chicago	−5	−8 130	−2 20	150
Denver	−8	−5	−3 50	50
Total Requirements	180	150	70	400

the products summed to obtain the total shipping cost. This is shown in Table 8–8.

The next step is to determine whether the initial solution of supply and demand shipments is the *optimum solution*. The optimum solution to the management of Hamilton is that solution which minimizes their total trans-

TABLE 8–8

Total Transportation Cost

Supply: Demand	Units × Cost per Unit ($) =	Transportation Cost ($)
New York: Miami	180	4	720
New York: Seattle	20	12	240
Chicago: Seattle	130	8	1,040
Chicago: Omaha	20	2	40
Denver: Omaha	50	3	150
	Total transportation cost	2,190

portation costs. The formal test for optimization requires two steps: (1) determination of row and column values and (2) determination of the values of unoccupied cells.

Evaluation of Occupied Cells

In computing the r (row) and C (column) values, *only occupied cells are given consideration.* A basic rule to follow is:

The sum of the row and column values is equal to the value in the sub-cell of an occupied cell.

A zero (any randomly selected number may be used) is placed to the left of the row of the northwest corner cell (i.e., the first occupied cell, Table 8–7). Following the basic rule:

$$0 + (-4) = -4$$

Therefore, the column value is -4, which is placed over the column (C_1). The next occupied cell to consider is Row 1 (r_1), Column 2 (C_2) or the New York: Seattle shipment.

$$0 + (-12) = -12$$

The -12 value is placed over Column 2 (C_2). The next row and column value to calculate is r_2. Since $C_2 = -12$, the value of Row 2 is

$$-12 + (+4) = -8$$

The $+4$ is found because using the rule that the sum of the row and column values is equal to the value in the subcell of an occupied cell provides the problem solver with two known values, the -12 and -8. Thus, column value (-12) + row value (unknown) equals the sub-cell value (-8). The row value which fulfills the requirements of the equation is $+4$.

Table 8–9 illustrates the necessary computations:

TABLE 8–9

Row and Column Value Computations

Occupied Cell	Row Value	+ Column Value	= Sub-cell Value
r_1C_1	0	-4	-4
r_1C_2	0	-12	-12
r_2C_2	$+4$	-12	-8
r_2C_3	$+4$	-6	-2
r_3C_3	$+3$	-6	-3

The reader should note that a specific pattern must be adhered to when computing the row and column values, going from a known r or C value to the unknown r or C value.

Evaluation of Unoccupied Cells

The second formal step in testing for optimality of a solution is determination of the values of the unoccupied matrix cells. The rule used is:

The value in the sub-cell is subtracted from the sum of the row and column values pertaining to the unoccupied cell being evaluated.

In Table 8–7, Row 1, Column 3 is unoccupied. To evaluate the cell, sum the row and column values,

$$0 + (-6) = -6$$

and then subtract the value in the sub-cell.

$$-6 - (-7) = +1$$

The value of unoccupied cell r_1C_3 equals $+1$, and this computed value is placed in the cell. The values of each unoccupied cell may be computed in a similar manner. Table 8–10 illustrates the values of the unoccupied cells.

TABLE 8–10

Unoccupied Cell Computations

Cell	Row Value	+	Column Value	=	Sum of r and C	−	Sub-cell Value	=	Unoccupied Cell Value
r_1C_3	0		− 6		−6		−7		+1
r_2C_1	+4		− 4		0		−5		+5
r_3C_1	+3		− 4		−1		−8		+7
r_3C_2	+3		− 12		−9		−5		−4

Table 8–11 presents the initial solution with row and column values and unoccupied cell values included in the matrix.

TABLE 8–11

Initial Solution with Row, Column, and Unoccupied Cell Values

Supply Source	Destination Demand						Supply Total
	Miami	−4	Seattle	−12	Omaha	−6	
0 New York	180	−4	20	−12	+1	−7	200
+4 Chicago	+5	−5	130	− 8	20	−2	150
+3 Denver	+7	−8	−4	− 5	50	−3	50
Total Requirements	180		150		70		400

Interpretation and Improvement in Initial Matrix

Once the unoccupied cell values are determined, the signs of the values indicate whether an optimum solution has been found. The signs are interpreted as follows:

1. A (+) value in an unoccupied cell indicates that a poorer solution will result if units are moved into that cell.
2. A (−) value in an unoccupied cell indicates that a better solution can be found by shifting units into the unoccupied cell.
3. A zero value in an unoccupied cell indicates that another solution of equal value is available to the problem solver by moving units into the zero value cell.

Utilizing the sign interpretation and reviewing Table 8–11 reveals that an improved solution can be achieved by moving units into unoccupied cell r_3C_2; all other unoccupied cells have (+) values and moving units into them would result in a poorer solution. If the problem solver is faced with a situation in which there is more than one negative cell, he could move into any one of the cells with negative values but a move into the most negative cell will result in the most improvement.

The cell selected to be moved into is indicated by placing a (+) in it. In our problem this is r_3C_2. The plus sign indicates that units are to be added to r_3C_2. However, if units are added to r_3C_2, then the same number of units must be subtracted from either r_1C_2 or r_2C_2. If this is not done, then Seattle will get more speakers than it has ordered. Therefore, we place a (−) sign in cell r_2C_2 to indicate the necessary reduction in units. (We shall see momentarily that we cannot place the (−) sign in r_1C_2.) This is necessary to maintain the rim values since we have said that the sum of the values in each column and row must be equal to the respective rim values.

However, if the value in r_2C_2 is reduced below 130, then the sum of the units in Row 2 will not equal 150. Thus, we must add units to some cell in Row 2. At first glance it would appear that either of the two remaining cells (r_2C_1 or r_2C_3) would do. However,

> The number of occupied cells must be equal to the number of rows plus the number of columns minus one ($r + C − 1$).

In this problem there are three rows and three columns. Thus, there can be only five occupied cells.

$$3 + 3 − 1 = 5$$

In order to meet this required condition one formerly unoccupied cell is to be occupied, one formerly occupied cell is to become unoccupied, and all other shifts must take place within the already occupied cells. Therefore, the offsetting $(+)$ sign for Row 2 must be placed in r_2C_3 and the same logic dictates that a $(-)$ sign be placed in r_3C_3. Table 8–12 indicates the affected cells with the appropriate signs and dotted lines.

The problem solver must now decide how many units to move into cell r_3C_2. It is evident that the more units that are moved into r_3C_2 the more money we will save. The limiting factor becomes the smallest unit value in the cells in which we have placed $(-)$ signs. In Table 8–12 this is r_3C_3 which has 50 units.

TABLE 8–12

Moving Toward Optimum Solution

Supply Source	Destination Demand						Supply Total
	Miami	−4	Seattle	−12	Omaha	−6	
0 New York	180	−4	20	−12	+1	−7	200
+4 Chicago	+5	−5	(−) 130	−8	(+) 20	−2	150
+3 Denver	+7	−8	(+) −4	−5	(−) 50	−3	50
Total Requirements	180		150		70		400

Therefore, all cells containing $(+)$ or $(-)$ signs are adjusted by adding or subtracting 50 units as the signs indicate.

The reader should note that as a result of the shifting, no speakers are shipped from Denver to Omaha. Previously, 50 speakers were shipped from Denver to Omaha at a cost of $3 per unit. Now, all seventy units required by Omaha are shipped from Chicago at a cost of $2 per unit. This results in a cost reduction of $50. For the Seattle customer we previously shipped 130 units from Chicago at a cost of $8 per unit. Now we ship 80 units from Chicago and the remaining 50 units are shipped from Denver at a cost of only $5 per unit. This results in an additional cost reduction of $150. Thus, total transportation costs are reduced by $200 and each customer still receives his required number of speakers. The improved solution is shown in Table 8–13.

The total transportation cost for the improved solution is $1,990 (see Table 8–14) or $200 under the $2,190 cost of the initial solution. We must now test the new solution for optimality. All row and column values and all unoccupied

TABLE 8–13

Improved Solution: Second Matrix

Supply Source	Destination Demand						Supply Total
	Miami	−4	Seattle	−12	Omaha	−6	
0 New York	180	−4	20	−12	+1	−7	200
+4 Chicago	+5	−5	80	− 8	70	−2	150
+7 Denver	+11	−8	50	− 5	+4	−3	50
Total Requirements	180		150		70		400

TABLE 8–14

Total Transportation Cost: Second Matrix

Supply: Demand	Units	×	Cost per Unit ($)	=	Transportation Cost ($)
New York: Miami	180		4		720
New York: Seattle	20		12		240
Chicago: Seattle	80		8		640
Chicago: Omaha	70		2		140
Denver: Seattle	50		5		250
			Total transportation cost		1,990

TABLE 8–15

Row and Column Value Computations
Second Matrix

Occupied Cell	Row Value	+	Column Value	=	Sub-cell Value
r_1C_1	0		− 4		− 4
r_1C_2	0		−12		−12
r_2C_2	+4		−12		− 8
r_2C_3	+4		− 6		− 2
r_3C_2	+7		−12		− 5

cell values must be recomputed. These values have been inserted in Table 8–13 and the necessary calculations are shown in Table 8–15 and Table 8–16.

A review of Table 8–16 shows that only one iteration is necessary to reach an optimal solution to the problem of distribution facing the Hamilton Corporation. Since in the second matrix the unoccupied cells contain no negative values, the optimum supply and demand combinations have been determined.

TABLE 8–16

Unoccupied Cell Computations
Second Matrix

Cell	Row Value	+	Column Value	=	Sum of r and C	−	Sub-cell Value	=	Unoccupied Cell Value
r_1C_3	0		−6		−6		−7		+ 1
r_2C_1	+4		−4		0		−5		+ 5
r_3C_1	+7		−4		+3		−8		+11
r_3C_3	+7		−6		+1		−3		+ 4

Thus, from a transportation cost standpoint, the firm will minimize its expenses in shipping speakers by using the following network of movement.

New York:Miami	180
New York:Seattle	20
Chicago:Seattle	80
Chicago:Omaha	70
Denver:Seattle	50

The problem which faced the marketing management of Hamilton required only one iteration. This is a relatively small number of manipulations. In some cases in using the "northwest corner method" the problem solver may have to conduct numerous iterations before reaching an optimal solution. In such a situation a computer can be a valuable aid to the marketing decision maker.

A Synopsis of the Northwest Corner Method

1. Study the problem facing the problem solver (e.g., cost, items, and objectives).
2. Set up initial distribution matrix, allowing one column for each demand destination and one row for each supply source.
3. Set up northwest corner initial matrix and proceed to compute the initial solution.
4. Obtain the row and column values using the rule and formula: row value + column value = value in the sub-cell.
5. Evaluate unoccupied cells by using the rule and formula: row value + column value − (value in the sub-cell) = unoccupied cell value.
6. Review signs of values in unoccupied cells and interpret their meaning.
7. Move units to the unoccupied cell with the largest negative value.
8. Repeat Steps 4–7 until all unoccupied cells have positive values.
9. Present supply and demand combinations and the optimal total cost figure in a concise manner.

Introduction of a Slack Variable

Thus far in our discussion of the transportation method we have assumed that total supply was equal to total demand (requirements). In many problems, however, this condition will probably not be true. In other words, in most situations the firm either has more orders than it can fill or its available supply exceeds its demand. In both situations the company will still be interested in obtaining the least cost distribution pattern. This objective can still be achieved by introducing a slight modification into the transportation method as we have presented it thus far.

To illustrate a situation where supply and demand are not equal, let us assume that the Hamilton Distributing Corporation has more orders than it has speakers on hand:

Warehouse Locations	*Speakers in Stock*
New York	200
Chicago	150
Denver	50
	400

Customer Location	*Orders*
Miami	180
Seattle	150
Omaha	120
	450

We shall assume that the shipping costs per unit remain the same. It is obvious that at least one order will not be fully shipped. Thus, we must answer two questions:

1. Which order(s) will not be fully shipped?
2. What is the least cost distribution pattern?

Let us set up this problem in a matrix as described earlier in this section. This is shown in Table 8–17. A brief look at the lower right hand cell indicates that the 400 speakers in stock do not equal the demand for 450 speakers. Since the transportation method will not function unless these two figures are equal, we must make an adjustment in the matrix in order to bring about this necessary condition.

To solve this problem we utilize the same procedure as outlined previously except that a *slack variable* is introduced into the transportation matrix. In our problem this is done by adding a row which represents a hypothetical

TABLE 8–17

Unequal Supply-Demand Situation

Source *Supply*	*Destination Demand*			*Supply* *Total*
	Miami	*Seattle*	*Omaha*	
New York				200
Chicago				150
Denver				50
				400
Total Requirements	180	150	120	450

TABLE 8–18

Unequal Supply-Demand Situation
Initial Solution

Source *Supply*	*Destination Demand*			*Supply* *Total*
	Miami	*Seattle*	*Omaha*	
New York	−4 / 180	−12 / 20	−7	200
Chicago	−5	−8 / 130	−2 / 20	150
Denver	−8	−5	−3 / 50	50
Dummy	0	0	0 / 50	50
Total Requirements	180	150	120	450

warehouse (designated dummy) as shown in Table 8–18. If supply should exceed demand, an additional column for a dummy customer would be provided. The northwest corner method is then used to obtain the initial solution. This is shown in Table 8–18. Note that in our initial solution it is the customer in Omaha whose order will not be fully shipped. This is because in the initial solution he is designated 50 units from the fictitious dummy warehouse, which does not exist. However, note that the rim requirements have been met.

The costs have been entered in the sub-cells as usual. Note that zeros have been placed in sub-cells pertaining to the dummy warehouse. This is because

TABLE 8–19

Total Cost of Initial Solution

Supply: Demand	Units × Cost per Unit($)	= Transportation Cost($)
New York: Miami	180	4	720
New York: Seattle	20	12	240
Chicago: Seattle	130	8	1,040
Chicago: Omaha	20	2	40
Denver: Omaha	50	3	150
Dummy: Omaha	50	0	0
	Total transportation cost	2,190

TABLE 8–20

Row and Column Value Computations

Occupied Cell	Row Value +	Column Value =	Sub-cell Value
r_1C_1	0	− 4	− 4
r_1C_2	0	−12	−12
r_2C_2	+4	−12	− 8
r_2C_3	+4	− 6	− 2
r_3C_3	+3	− 6	− 3
r_4C_3	+6	− 6	0

TABLE 8–21

Unoccupied Cell Computations

Cell	Row Value +	Column Value =	Sum of r + C −	Sub-cell Value =	Unoccupied Cell Value
r_1C_3	0	− 6	−6	−7	+1
r_2C_1	+4	− 4	0	−5	+5
r_3C_1	+3	− 4	−1	−8	+7
r_3C_2	+3	−12	−9	−5	−4
r_4C_1	+6	− 4	+2	0	+2
r_4C_2	+6	−12	−6	0	−6

the dummy warehouse will make no shipments, and therefore will incur no costs. We compute the total cost of the initial solution as we did previously. This is shown in Table 8–19.

We must now test the initial solution for optimality. All row and column values and all unoccupied cell values must be computed as was done previously. These calculations are shown in Table 8–20 and Table 8–21.

Table 8–22 presents the initial solution with row and column values and unoccupied cell values included in the matrix.

TABLE 8–22

Initial Solution with Row, Column, and Unoccupied Cell Values

Source Supply	Destination Demand						Supply Total
	Miami −4		Seattle −12		Omaha −6		
0 New York	180	−4	20	−12	+1	−7	200
+4 Chicago	+5	−5	(−) 130	−8	(+) 20	−2	150
+3 Denver	+7	−8	−4	−5	50	−3	50
+6 Dummy	+2	0	(+) −6	0	(−) 50	0	50
Total Requirements	180		150		120		450

Examination of Table 8–21 reveals that there are two unoccupied cells with (−) values. Since we are interested in making the greatest improvement, we shall move goods into r_4C_2. In Table 8–22 the dotted lines indicate the cells in which the movements will take place.

We shall leave it as an exercise for the reader to decide how many units should be shifted into cell r_4C_2 and to complete the problem. This particular problem requires two iterations to optimize. Table 8–23 presents the final

TABLE 8–23

Optimum Solution

Source Supply	Destination Demand						Supply Total
	Miami −4		Seattle −12		Omaha −6		
0 New York	180	−4	20	−12	+1	−7	200
+4 Chicago	+5	−5	30	−8	120	−2	150
+7 Denver	+11	−8	50	−5	+4	−3	50
+12 Dummy	+8	0	50	0	+6	0	50
Total Requirements	180		150		120		450

optimum solution. The reader is strongly encouraged to carry the problem through the intervening iterations.

The reader should be sure that he can interpret the final solution presented in Table 8–23.

The Degenerate Situation

It was previously mentioned that a basic feasible solution for transportation problems consists of $r + C - 1$ basis variables. This means that the number of occupied cells in a transportation program should be one less than the number of rows and columns in the transportation matrix. If we are working with a 3 x 3 matrix, the number of occupied cells should be five. Whenever the number of occupied cells is less than $r + C - 1$, the problem is said to be degenerate.

A degenerate condition in a transportation problem can occur when the initial matrix is designed. That is, in establishing the initial 3 x 3 northwest corner matrix the number of occupied cells is less than five. To correct the degeneracy condition in this case, we can allocate a value to an unoccupied cell, so that the number of occupied cells meets the $r + C - 1$ condition. The cell into which the value is placed is then considered occupied in the evaluation procedures.

Let us assume that the Hamilton Corporation data is as follows:

Warehouse Location	Speakers in Stock	Customer Location	Monthly Orders
New York	20	Miami	20
Chicago	40	Seattle	15
		Omaha	25

Using the "northwest corner method," we construct the initial matrix given in Table 8–24.

Examination of the initial matrix illustrates that we have three occupied cells. According to the $r + C - 1$ rule, we should have four occupied cells. Hence, the solution offered in Table 8–24 is degenerate. This form of degeneracy arises when, in using the "northwest corner method," both a column requirement and a row requirement are satisfied simultaneously. This occurred in the New York–Miami cell (the northwest cell).

A procedure that can be used to resolve degeneracy is to assign a zero value to one of the unoccupied cells. Although there is a great deal of flexibility in selecting the unoccupied cell for the zero value, the general procedure,

TABLE 8–24

Northwest Corner Initial Matrix:
Degenerate Solution

Source Supply	Destination Demand			Supply Total
	Miami —4	Seattle —7	Omaha —1	
0 New York	20 |—4	|—12	|—7	20
—1 Chicago	|—5	15 |— 8	25 |—2	40
Total Requirements	20	15	25	60

TABLE 8–25

Degeneracy Correction

Supply Source	Destination Demand			Supply Total
	Miami —4	Seattle —7	Omaha —1	
0 New York	20 |—4	|—12	|—7	20
—1 Chicago	0 |—5	15 |— 8	25 |—2	40
Total Requirements	20	15	25	60

when using the "northwest corner method," is to assign it to a cell so as to maintain an unbroken chain.[4] Table 8–25 shows the zero value added to the Chicago-Miami cell, although it could also have been assigned to the New York–Seattle cell.

In Table 8–25 we now have four occupied cells, which satisfies the degeneracy test. The problem can now be solved using the same methodological procedures used in the previous example. The cell with the assigned zero is treated just as any other occupied cell in the solution. The zero that is assigned has no specific meaning in a problem; it is merely a computational device which permits the regular solution method to be applied to the northwest corner initial matrix when degeneracy occurs.[5]

---

[4] Richard I. Levin and Rudolph P. Lamone, *Linear Programming For Management Decisions* (Homewood, Ill.: Richard D. Irwin, Inc., 1969), pp. 165–170.

[5] For an excellent discussion of degeneracy, see N. Paul Loomba, *Linear Programming* (New York: McGraw-Hill, Inc., 1964).

INVENTORY MODELS

A fundamental reason for having goods inventories is to separate manufacturing and distribution into independent, successive activities. The marketing manager, who must cope with inventory problems in a firm, is usually concerned about inventory cost minimization. At times decisions concerning the minimization of inventory costs and fulfilling customer demand for a product are at cross purposes. For example, the firm is concerned about the cost of carrying large inventories but desires to satisfy the buyers' demand for a product at the time of request. This is especially true for retail clothing items. The store owner only has a specified amount of storage space for his clothing inventory. The entrepreneur may fear that by not having an item on hand when requested the customer will become dissatisfied and not return in the future. The desirable course of action is to systematically study the cost components of inventory and the demand for the items so that customer service and goodwill are maintained at a high level.

The Inventory Decision

The seller or manufacturer of goods must cope with two key inventory decisions if a complete and intelligent inventory program is to be developed. These mutually interrelated decisions are: (1) the size of each lot or batch of items to be purchased, and (2) the time to order or request this quantity. By utilizing a basic technique developed by management scientists referred to as the economic order quantity model, the inventory decision process facing the marketing manager can be made easier.

The Cost Components of the Inventory Model

The costs which a business organization may incur as a result of inventory fluctuations are usually classified into two categories. First, there are the *ordering costs* of getting a particular item into the firm's actual inventory. These costs are incurred each time an order is placed. They are the clerical and administrative costs per order. They also include the cost of receiving and placing into inventory the goods ordered.

Second, there are the *carrying costs*. These include the interest on money invested in inventory, storage space, rent, obsolescence, payment of taxes, and insurance on losses due to theft, fire, and deterioration and protection. The carrying cost component is usually expressed as an annual figure and as a percentage of the average inventory figure.

To minimize inventory cost, marketing decision makers attempt to minimize ordering and carrying costs. These two costs are related to each other in opposing directions as shown in Figure 8–3.

The number of orders placed by the manager for a given period of time is equal to demand (D) for the period divided by the size of each order quantity (Q). The total ordering cost per period (week, month, or year) is equal to the cost of placing each order (J) multiplied by the number of orders per period

$\dfrac{D}{Q}$ or $\dfrac{D}{Q}$ (J). It should be evident now that as the order lot size increases (e.g.,

from 10 to 20, or 25 to 67, etc.), fewer orders are required to meet the demand for a period, and consequently the ordering cost component will decrease. This is illustrated graphically by the downward sloping ordering cost curve in Figure 8–3.

The period cost of carrying an item in inventory is calculated by multiplying the value of the item (V) by a percentage figure (E), which is management's educated estimate of taxes, insurance, etc., per period as a percentage of the value of inventory. The total carrying costs are equal to the cost of carrying

FIGURE 8–3

Ordering and Carrying Cost Relationship
(total cost equals ordering cost plus carrying cost.)

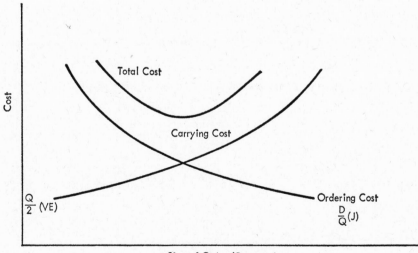

Size of Order (Quantity)

one item *(VE)* multiplied by the average inventory $Q/2$.[6] As the size of the order increases, carrying cost will increase as shown in Figure 8–3.

A number of assumptions are made by the decision maker working with the economic order quantity model. They are:

1. The demand for the item over the period is known with certainty. Thus, we are developing the economic order quantity model *(EOQ)* under conditions of certainty.
2. The rate at which the inventory of the item is depleted is constant. Figure 8–4 below illustrates depletion at a constant rate.

FIGURE 8–4

Constant Depletion

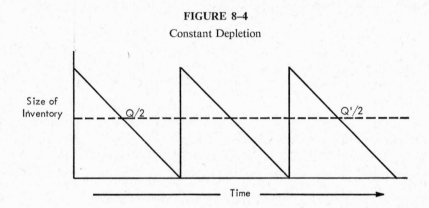

The average inventory is found under conditions of constant usage (i.e., selling same amount monthly for year, 50 or 100 or 200 items per month for full year).

3. The time necessary for acquiring order of item after request is exactly known (e.g., the lead time).

These assumptions are not completely realistic, but they allow us to study in an uncomplicated manner the development of the *EOQ* model. Further sophistication of the basic model can occur only if the simplified form is clearly understood.

---

[6] It is assumed that the quantity goes from Q, the maximum size of the inventory, to zero before the next order arrives, and that the usage rate is constant. Therefore:

$$\text{Average Inventory} = \frac{Q - 0}{2} = \frac{Q}{2}$$

$$\left(\text{e.g., } AI = \frac{100 - 0}{2} = 50 \right)$$

The Tabular Method of Determining EOQ

A sample problem will once again serve as the vehicle for acquiring a working understanding of a quantitative tool applied to a marketing problem.

Let us assume that a large department store in San Francisco is attempting to solve a lot size problem involving men's turtle neck shirts. The marketing manager desires to minimize total inventory cost per instructions of the president. The yearly demand, which is constant for the turtle necks, is estimated at 1,000. The administrative and clerical cost of placing an order is $2.40. The marketing manager estimates insurance and taxes to be 10 percent per year. The value of an item is $6.00. Thus, the components involved are:

$$D = 1,000$$
$$J = \$2.40$$
$$E = \quad 10\%$$
$$V = \$6.00$$

Development of a table of values showing the relationship of the components is presented in Table 8–26.

TABLE 8–26

Tabular Approach

Number of Orders Per Year	Size of Lot Q	Order Cost D/Q(J)	+	Carrying Cost Q/2(VE)	=	Total Cost TC
1	1,000	2.40		300		302.40
2	500	4.80		150		154.80
4	250	9.60		75		84.60
5	200	12.00		60		72.00
10	100	24.00		30		54.00
20	50	48.00		15		63.00

By utilizing the tabular approach we find that an order size of 100 per order will result in the lowest total cost. The marketing manager, however, cannot determine by utilization of this approach if any other lot size is more beneficial to the firm.

The EOQ Equation and Formula

The tabular method involves experimentation and manipulation of costs before the decision maker arrives at the optimum cost. Instead of performing the tabular procedures every time an inventory program is being analyzed, it is possible to utilize what is referred to as the economic order quantity formula.

Referring back to Figure 8–3 we see that the minimum total inventory cost point is at the point directly above the intersection of carrying cost and ordering cost. Thus, the EOQ formula may be derived by using this relationship between total, carrying, and ordering costs. The first step in algebraic derivation is to set carrying and ordering cost equal to each other.

$$\frac{Q}{2}(VE) = \frac{D}{Q}(J) \tag{1}$$

Solving for Q yields

$$Q(VE) = \frac{2DJ}{Q} \tag{2}$$

$$Q^2(VE) = 2DJ \tag{3}$$

$$Q^2 = \frac{2DJ}{(VE)} \tag{4}$$

$$Q = \sqrt{\frac{2DJ}{(VE)}} \tag{5}$$

The final equation is commonly referred to as the economic order quantity formula, which can be used to solve the type of inventory order size problem facing the management of the department store.[7] Using the cost, demand, and estimation data in our problem, we can determine the economic order size, $D = 1,000$, $J = \$2.40$, $E = 10$ percent and $V = \$6.00$.

$$Q = \sqrt{\frac{2(1000)\,(2.40)}{(6.00)\,(.10)}}$$

$$Q = \sqrt{\frac{4,800}{.60}}$$

$$Q = \sqrt{8,000}$$

$$Q = 89.44$$

Reorder Points

Once the decision maker has arrived at the economic lot size, he can very easily determine the number of orders placed per period, $\frac{D}{Q}$, and the average inventory for the particular item, $\frac{Q}{2}$. We have already mentioned that the lead

---

[7] For a review of how calculus is used to derive the EOQ formula, see Max D. Richards and Paul S. Greenlaw, *Management Decision Making* (Homewood, Ill.: Richard D. Irwin, Inc., 1966), p. 473.

time is assumed known and constant. Since this is known, the decision maker can also determine the date to place each order.

For example, let us assume that the economic order quantity for an item is 1000 units. Weekly demand is 250 and the lead time is one week. In this case each reorder would simply be placed one week prior to the depletion of the present inventory—or when the level of inventory had fallen to 250 units. The reorder points in this case are shown in Figure 8–5.

FIGURE 8–5

Reorder Points

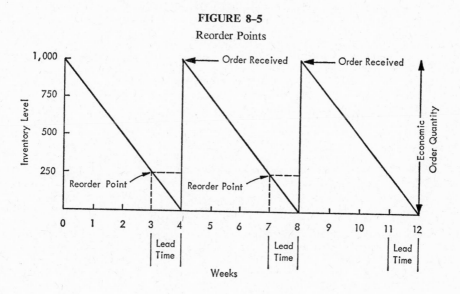

The reader is encouraged to determine the reorder points in the shirt problem previously discussed. Remember that $89 \times 11 = 979$. Therefore, one order will have to be for 110 shirts $(89 + 21)$ to insure that 1000 shirts are ordered. To simplify his task, the reader can assume the department store is closed two weeks per year for vacation. Thus, weekly demand would be 20 shirts (1000 divided by 50 weeks).

The answer derived by using the tabular method was 100 units per order, while utilization of the *EOQ* formula provides us with an answer of 89[8] units per order. The number of orders to be placed during the year can be ascertained by using the *EOQ* of 89 and demand for the turtle necks of 1000. The department store will place $\dfrac{D}{Q}$ orders. If the number of orders to be placed

---

[8] The 89.44 figure is rounded off. This rounding off will create a situation in which all of our figures used are at best only approximations.

is not a whole number, as is the case in this problem, 11 or 12, subjective judgment as to the exact number to order will have to be made by the decision maker. It should be noted that the *EOQ* formula is only a tool to be utilized and it doesn't eliminate the necessity of making a decision.

Quantity Discounts—Take or Reject Them?

A common inventory policy decision that faces marketing managers is determining the economic lot size if one or more price discounts may be obtained from a supplier when specific quantities are purchased. For example, the per unit cost of an item would be reduced 10 percent if the retailer purchases the shirts by ordering 200 or more at a time.

An approach which may be used to aid in solving quantity discount problems is to compare the total annual cost of ordering and carrying inventory under nonquantity and quantity discount conditions. Let us continue using the data of the department store. The annual demand of turtle neck shirts is 1,000; the value of each shirt is $6.00; ordering cost is $2.40; cost of carrying the inventory is 10 percent of the value of inventory. The Style-Rite shirt manufacturer offers the department store an 8 percent discount on purchases if they buy in lots of 200 or more. In order to compare the nonquantity and quantity situation, we first would calculate the *EOQ*.

$$Q = \sqrt{\frac{2DJ}{(VE)}} \tag{1}$$

$$Q = \sqrt{\frac{2(1000)\,(2.40)}{(6.00)\,(.10)}} \tag{2}$$

$$Q = 89.44 \text{ units per order or 89 units.} \tag{3}$$

The optimum number of shirts in each order is 89 and unit price is $6.00, total value per order is 89 × $6.00 = $534.00. Since the sale of the shirts is constant, average worth of inventory is $\frac{\$534.00}{2}$ = $267.00. The carrying cost is 10 percent and 10 percent of $267.00 is $26.70. Each year 11 purchases are made to satisfy demand;[9] thus ordering cost is 11 multiplied by $2.40 or $26.40. The total annual cost under the *EOQ* conditions and nonquantity discount conditions are as follows:

---

[9] The number of orders which would have to be placed is $\frac{1000}{89}$ = 11.23. Assume that only 11 orders are made and one of the orders makes up the difference between demand of 1,000 units and (89 × 11) = 979 units. This of course is what is referred to in Footnote 8.

Turtle neck value ($6 × 1000)   = $6,000.00
Carrying cost (10% × $267.00) =   26.70
Ordering cost (11 × 2.40)   =   26.40
                Total annual cost $6,053.10

The $6,053.10 figure must now be compared with total annual cost under the alternative quantity discount situation proposed by Style-Rite. If 200 units are bought by the department store in each lot, the cost of each lot would be:

$$(200 × \$6 × .92) = \$1,104.00^{10}$$

If each lot is valued at $1,104.00, average inventory value would be one half or $552.00. The total annual cost, assuming that the store must order five times annually, would be:

Turtle neck value (5 × $1,104.00) = $5,520.00
Carrying cost (10% × $552)   =   55.20
Ordering cost (5 × 2.40)   =   12.00
                Total annual cost $5,587.20

If the firm utilizes the quantity discount, they will save money. They could save over $400.00 by taking advantage of the quantity discount. Since rounding of numbers had to occur in this problem (i.e., 11.44 to 11), the total annual cost figures are only near approximations.

The Limitations of EOQ Models

The most obvious limitation of any of the inventory discussion cited above is that conditions of certainty rarely exist in the real world. In our problem we have assumed that the correct time to order is known. Many times transportation problems, order requisition difficulties, and other related problems make the lead time (i.e., time between placement of an order and actual delivery of the order) a highly unpredictable phenomenon.

The estimation of demand is another problem area. Throughout our discussion demand was stated as a specific amount. The demand for any item at best can only be roughly estimated. There are so many variables—competitors' prices, economic conditions, social conditions, and substitutable items—that can influence demand that stating definitely that it is 1,000 units annually is too specific and definite.

---

[10] The 0.92 is the discount price multiplier or one minus the discount, which in this example is 0.08 or 8%.

The cost components and estimates, such as ordering cost per unit and carrying cost value as a percent of inventory, are only subjectively based figures. Historical cost data, of course, improves the validity of the figures but they are by no means perfectly accurate.

Despite these limitations, the analytical approaches presented can aid the marketing decision maker in reaching more efficient inventory judgments. The reader should recognize that the inventory control methods discussed are analytical approaches which attempt to optimize. The reader should also be aware of the limitations of analytical techniques employed to answer questions under a set of certainty assumptions. This is a basic limitation of deterministic models, such as the break-even, transportation, and inventory models discussed in this chapter.

Inventory Decisions under Conditions of Risk and Uncertainty

As was indicated previously, in most business situations demand for a product and lead time are rarely constant and known in advance by the decision maker. In such a case where these variables are not known we are faced with decision making under conditions of uncertainty. However, not knowing the demand for the product would not really be too serious a problem if we could instantaneously replenish our inventory. This would be necessary if we wished to avoid a stockout. A stockout would occur if the necessary lead time made it impossible to replenish our inventory until after our stock was depleted. Thus, it is the existence of a lead time which causes us a problem. Under conditions of risk or uncertainty the decision maker must maintain safety stocks if stockouts are to be minimized. Here he must be concerned with whether the additional cost of carrying the items will be offset by the savings realized by avoiding lost sales.

There are methods available to deal with inventory control under conditions of uncertainty. These methods will not be discussed here.[11] However, the reader must fully comprehend the material presented here before attempting to cope with inventory control under conditions of uncertainty.

PROBLEMS

1. Discuss the following statements:
(a) "The *EOQ* model can be used to derive answers which are perfectly accurate."
(b) "What characteristics must a problem possess in order for the transportation method to be applicable?"

---

[11] For an excellent discussion of inventory control under conditions of uncertainty, see Richards and Greenlaw, *op. cit.*, pp. 483–490.

(c) "Break-even analysis would be a valuable tool for a marketing manager in a fast moving, dynamic industry."

2. Name particular products which would pose such a list of problems to management that no inventory would be kept. Why do you include these items on your list?

3. Explain the "northwest corner method." Would a "southeast corner method" do the same job?

4. Explain why a firm would need an extremely accurate accounting system to make efficient use of break-even analysis.

5. It is extremely important for the marketing manager to fully comprehend the relationship between costs, revenue, and volume. What effect will the following changes have on the break-even point?

(a) An increase in fixed costs because of the need to operate on a night shift due to breakdowns of machinery and equipment.

(b) An increase in the price of the product with no increase in fixed or variable costs.

(c) Because of the competition for qualified salesmen the firm is forced to increase the commission rate for salesmen in order to maintain a high caliber sales force.

(d) An increase in the sales of the product.

6. The Danjil store, a retailer of children's toys, buys its toys from the Matte Company. The management estimates that next year it will need 4,000 talking dolls. The accountants inform management that the firm's ordering costs are $30.00 per order. Each doll costs the store $8.00. The carrying charge for the dolls is estimated to be 10 percent per year of the value of the average inventory in stock.

(a) Evaluate each of the following order sizes by the tabular procedure. Which is the most economical from a total cost standpoint?

Order size: 40   200   500   1,000   2,000   4,000

(b) Utilizing the *EOQ* formula, find the economic order quantity.

7. The Courtier Supply Corporation is the distributor of canned goods to Independent Grocers of America (IGA) stores in the midwest section of the United States. Courtier owns three warehouses as follows:

Location	Cases in Stock Daily
Chicago	100
St. Louis	30
Cleveland	70

The following customers place orders on the following basis:

Location	Orders
Lafayette	40
Toledo	100
Peoria	60

Delivery costs from each warehouse location to each customer on a per unit basis have been determined by cost accountants to be:

	Demand Destination		
Supply Source	Lafayette	Toledo	Peoria
Chicago	2	3	4
St. Louis	3	5	4
Cleveland	4	2	6

The marketing manager is concerned about minimizing total costs of shipment. Using the "northwest corner method," provide the marketing manager with the optimal shipping cost and transportation network. Show all mathematical computations.

8. The White Chemical Company has developed a new type of hair tonic for men which it feels is far superior to anything currently on the market. However, the management of the firm is not sure how to market the product. Specifically, two alternatives are available. Plan I is to market the product through barber supply houses to barber shops. Plan II is to market the product through wholesalers to retail outlets such as drug, department, variety, and food stores. The firm has collected the following data.

Plan I		*Plan II*	
Production costs (fixed)	$45,000	Production costs (fixed)	$ 45,000
Production costs		Production costs	
(per unit variable)	.37	(per unit variable)	.37
Marketing costs (fixed)	85,000	Marketing costs (fixed)	300,000
Marketing costs		Marketing costs	
(per unit variable)	.03	(per unit variable)	.03
Price to wholesaler	.90	Manufacturers selling price	1.20
Selling price	1.50	Wholesale price	1.50
		Retail price	2.25

After analysis of the market, management has attached the following probabilities to various levels of sales. These estimates are as follows:

Plan I

Level of Sales (Units)	*Probability of Occurrence*
300,000	.10
600,000	.20
900,000	.50
1,200,000	.20

Plan II

Level of Sales (Units)	*Probability of Occurrence*
600,000	.10
900,000	.30
1,200,000	.40
1,500,000	.20

Using the above data, determine which channel the firm should use. Assume that profit is the sole criterion. In your analysis include break-even charts.

9. What happens if the initial assignment in a transportation problem gives less than $r + C - 1$ occupied cells? How is this type of situation handled?

REFERENCES

Elementary treatments of break-even analysis, the transportation model, and the inventory model are found in:

KOTLER, PHILIP. *Marketing Management: Analysis Planning and Control.* Englewood Cliffs, N.J.: Prentice-Hall, Inc., 1967.

NAYLOR, THOMAS H. AND BYRNE, EUGENE T. *Linear Programming, Methods and Cases.* Belmont, Calif.: Wadsworth Publishing Company, Inc., 1963.

More advanced treatments of break-even analysis, the transportation model, and the inventory model are found in:

HADLEY, G. *Linear Programming.* Reading, Mass.: Addison-Wesley, 1962.

HEIN, LEONARD W. *The Quantitative Approach to Managerial Decisions.* Englewood Cliffs, N.J.: Prentice-Hall, Inc., 1967.

KING, WILLIAM R. *Quantitative Analysis for Marketing Management.* New York: McGraw-Hill Book Co., Inc., 1967.

LLEWELLYN, ROBERT W. *Linear Programming.* New York: Holt, Rinehart, and Winston, Inc., 1964.

RICHMOND, SAMUEL B. *Operations Research for Management Decisions.* New York: The Ronald Press Company, 1968.

SHUCHMAN, A. *Scientific Decision Making in Business.* New York: Holt, Rinehart, and Winston, Inc., 1963.

chapter nine

PROMOTION STRATEGY

INTRODUCTION

It is generally agreed that the major objective of promotion activities in a business organization is to generate increased sales of a product or service. No matter how good the widget, the astute marketing manager knows through experience and an understanding of the complexities of the market-place that the consumer will not beat a path to his door without the persuasion and stimulation that promotional activities provide.

The promotional activities of business firms are classified into four broad classifications. These are as follows:[1]

1. *Advertising:* Any paid form of promotion which attempts to inform, educate, and persuade a purchaser.
2. *Personal selling:* Face to face contact with prospective purchasers for the purpose of making a sale.
3. *Sales promotion:* Those activities, other than personal selling, advertising, and free publicity which attempts to inform, educate, and persuade, such as demonstrations and trade shows.
4. *Free publicity:* Nonpersonal stimulation by providing information about a product or service in a published medium that is not paid for by the sponsor.

The application of quantitative techniques in the promotional phase of marketing presented in this chapter will deal only with advertising and personal selling. These two ingredients of a firm's promotional mix lend themselves more readily to quantitative analysis than the sales promotion and free publicity categories.

[1] *Marketing Definitions: A Glossary of Marketing Terms*, compiled by the Committee on Definitions of the American Marketing Association, Ralph S. Alexander, Chairman (Chicago: American Marketing Association, 1960).

The Promotion Mix Program

The exact tools and courses of action to employ in promoting a product, product-line, or service is a crucial decision which faces marketing managers. It is extremely difficult to know with certainty which combination of advertising and personal selling will result in the most optimum payoff for the organization as a whole.

There are a number of major factors which are usually considered before the final promotion mix is created and implemented. First, the amount of money available to carry out specific promotion campaigns must be determined and budgeted. The more money a firm provides to those responsible for making promotion dollar allocations the more flexible and diverse the ultimate program can become. The economist's concept of marginal analysis is a procedure which would aid in ascertaining the dollar allocations in a promotional campaign. Theoretically, the marginal concept assumes that the total promotional budget should be established at a level where the marginal profit from the marginal promotional dollar just equals the marginal profit from using the same dollar in some other nonpromotional activity.[2] The main difficulty, however, is that accurate data on the probable effects of increased investment in promotion versus other sales stimulants are not readily available.

Second, the nature of the market must be considered in developing a promotional program. An initial decision about the economic health of the markets in which the firm hopes to persuade and influence must be gauged. The types of customers or potential purchasers of what the firm has to offer must be delineated. For example, the promotion campaign designed for the industrial purchaser would be significantly different than that specified for the housewife living in a suburban neighborhood.

The location of the market is another consideration that cannot be overlooked. Whether the market is situated in a large urban area or rural area will certainly influence the ultimate strategy decision.

Third, the type of product or service being promoted is an important decision factor. The seller of heavy industrial equipment would place a different emphasis on personal selling than the seller of a household detergent.

Fourth, the stage of a product in its life cycle will influence the promotion strategy choice. At an early phase in the life cycle the key focus would be upon informing prospective purchasers of the qualities of the product. As

---

[2] See Philip Kotler, *Marketing Management* (Englewood Cliffs, N.J.: Prentice-Hall, Inc., 1967), p. 452, for a discussion of this concept.

the product progresses through the various phases in its life cycle, shifts in promotion strategy would occur. The stage of a product in its life cycle and the promotional effort devoted to the product at each stage are interrelated phenomena that must be examined.

Finally, factors external to the firm such as the social, cultural, and legal environment must be considered if sound promotional decisions are to be reached. Promotional activities that are considered in poor taste because of cultural or social constraints should obviously be avoided. These factors must be given special attention in our society today because of the ferment and awareness which exists among various groups.

Any business organization must operate within the guidelines established by the law at the local, state, and federal levels. The nature and scope of the promotion strategy must be reviewed against the legal constraints imposed to protect the public. For example, municipal governments in some regions may regulate door-to-door selling, advertising is subject to a myriad of regulations at all levels of government, and zoning laws may prohibit the intensity of promotion campaigns by not allowing the establishment of a store location in a specific area.

These factors which affect the final promotion strategy are not exhaustive by any means. They do, however, establish a general framework of internal and external constraints which are part of the promotion mix decision process. These factors can be viewed schematically in Figure 9–1.

ADVERTISING

Advertising has been referred to as the mass communication of a promise.[3] It promises the satisfaction of some want to the purchaser of the product(s) or service(s) offered by the firm. Thus, the crux of the advertising effort is to translate the product or service into satisfaction of the prospective purchaser's unfulfilled needs or wants.

The advertising effort of a firm is recognized as an important segment of the seller's promotion mix. This leads us to conclude that the various internal and external factors delineated in Figure 9–1 have a significant influence on the advertising program employed. The success of an advertising program in a simplistic manner may be measured in terms of increased sales volume and sales revenue. This of course is a gross oversimplification of inferred cause and effect relationships. That is, is it valid to assume that advertising effort alone is responsible for an increase in sales revenue?

---

[3] Rollie Tillman and C. A. Kirkpatrick, *Promotion: Persuasive Communication in Marketing* (Homewood, Ill.: Richard D. Irwin, Inc., 1968), p. 191.

FIGURE 9–1

Promotion Mix Framework

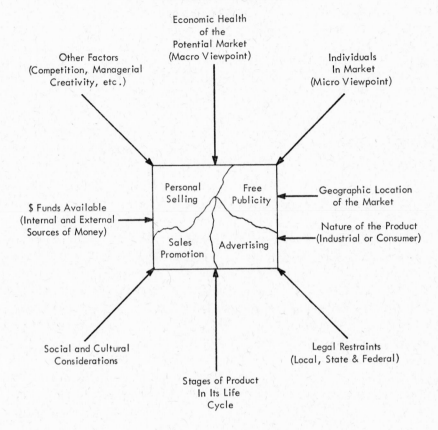

Advertising Decisions

A number of complex and interrelated decisions face those executives attempting to develop and implement a feasible and profitable advertising program. Some of these major decisions in question format are:

1. Is it necessary for the firm to advertise its product or service in order to grow and compete in the marketplace?
2. What type of advertising organizational arrangement would be compatible with the existing firm structure? That is, should advertising be a part of marketing or a separate function entirely?
3. How much money should be spent on the total advertising campaign?
4. When and how should available funds be funneled into the firm's advertising efforts?

5. How should the advertising message be developed to most effectively influence the prospective purchaser's buying habits?
6. Which advertising medium or combination of media should be employed?
7. How effective has the advertising effort been during a particular period of time?

Some of these decision questions lend themselves more readily to quantitative analysis than others. An area in which advanced mathematical procedures have been used in marketing is selecting appropriate media for promotional programs. This area will be given specific attention in this chapter, but it should be remembered that mathematical procedures have also been employed in coping with the other six advertising decision questions.

The Media Selection Problem

The media selection problem is to allocate a scarce resource among a number of alternative uses so that the best possible contribution is made to a central objective.[4] The limited resource is the amount of advertising funds available to the decision maker. The alternative uses of the funds are the advertising units which must be considered before a specific media program is implemented. The objective to be maximized is to achieve the greatest possible impact on an audience with the allocated funds.

In an effort to express the goal of advertising in quantitative terms, several alternative criteria have been suggested. The three proposed criteria are total exposures, frequency (impact), and reach (coverage). A relevant concern in media selection problems is to decide which criterion is to be used to determine the effects of the advertising. The three criteria suggested are relatively easy to measure but are removed from profit and sales results. Reach tends to assure that everyone receives at least one message, whereas frequency is concerned with generating the greatest number of exposures for each person in the target group.[5]

In addition to the controversy involving which criterion to use to measure effectiveness, there are also a number of suggestions concerning what mathematical programming model or economic analysis procedure to employ in developing optimal media schedules. For years traditional marginal analysis has been used to allocate advertising dollars. The common element in the

---

[4] Ralph L. Day, "Linear Programming in Media Selection," *Journal of Advertising Research*, Vol. 2 (June, 1962), pp. 40–44.

[5] David B. Montgomery and Glen L. Urban, *Management Science in Marketing* (Englewood Cliffs, N.J.: Prentice-Hall, Inc., 1969), p. 137.

allocation decision is expressed in three words, "Is it worthwhile?" An alternative method to the marginal analysis technique[6] is provided by linear programming models. The basic linear programming model does not provide the decision maker with a unique solution to media schedule problems, since marginal analysis can be applied to the same problem in many instances. The greatest value of the linear programming model is that it provides an organized and systematic framework for the study of simple and complex relationships. When combined with an electronic computer, the linear programming model provides an efficient way to study simultaneously a large number of interrelated variables.

The Media Mix Model: An Alternative

A growing number of researchers and practitioners have displayed increased interest in using as an alternative to and in combination with marginal analysis, linear programming models.[7] The application of the linear programming model to the media mix problem requires a number of very restrictive conditions. Some of the rigid and at times oversimplified assumptions are:

1. The measure of effectiveness will be total exposure.
2. Responses to media insertions are constant.
3. Costs of media insertions are constant.
4. There are no intermedia interaction effects.
5. The number of insertions is a continuous variable.[8]

With this set of assumptions the media problem is to maximize total exposure of advertisements subject to various cost, budget, rated exposure value,[9]

---

[6] For an excellent discussion of marginal analysis and its limitations see Kenneth E. Boulding and W. Allen Spivey, *Linear Programming and the Theory of the Firm* (New York: The Macmillan Company, 1960).

[7] The following references discuss the linear programming model: F. M. Bass and R. T. Lonsdale, "An Exploration of Linear Programming in Media Selection," *Journal of Marketing Research*, Vol. III (May, 1966), pp. 179–187; Clark L. Wilson, "Use of Linear Programming to Optimize Media Schedules in Advertising," Proceedings of the Forty-Sixth National Conference of the American Marketing Association, Henry Gomez, ed. (Chicago: American Marketing Association, 1963), pp. 178–191; R. D. Buzzell, Chapter 5 in *Mathematical Models and Marketing Management* (Boston: Graduate School of Business Administration, Harvard University, 1964); J. F. Engel and M. R. Warshaw, "Allocating Advertising Dollars by Linear Programming," *Journal of Advertising Research*, Vol. IV (September, 1964), pp. 42–48; Day, *op. cit.*, pp. 40–44.

[8] Montgomery and Urban, *op. cit.*, pp. 143–144.

[9] An "exposure" occurs whenever a prospective buyer becomes aware of a message from a specific medium.

and insertion constraints. This problem can be solved by use of marginal analysis. For example, the *(Va)* rated exposure value in each medium is divided by the cost per insertion *(Ca)* in the medium to derive a rated exposure value per dollar. Then the solution is simply to select the medium with greatest rated exposure value per dollar *(Va/Ca)* and purchase as much as possible in that medium. If the advertising budget is not expended, the decision maker would purchase as much as possible in the medium with the next highest rated exposure value per dollar. This problem can of course be solved with or without a computer or linear programming, following the procedures outlined above. In order, however, for the reader to be able to apply linear programming models to more complex media selection problems in his future work it would be advantageous to examine a simplified media problem in linear programming format. The reader should not conclude that linear programming is the best or the only method that can be used to conceptualize and work this problem. It certainly is not but it is the first step in setting up media problems in programming language and format.

The Mathematical Framework

Assume that the Maxey Corporation, a large producer of athletic exercise equipment, is attempting to determine the most optimum way to allocate advertising funds to promote their product line. The amount of money available *(AF)* is limited and management is considering the possibility of using six media to reach persons responsible for purchase decisions. The symbols used to symbolically establish this problem are as follows:[10]

E = total number of exposures to advertisements

V_1 = the exposure value of an ad in medium (1)

Z_1 = the number of advertisements placed in medium (1)

C_1 = the cost to the firm of placing an ad in medium (1)

AF = the total amount of funds allocated to advertising for the period being considered.

MX_1 = the maximum number of units or space to purchase in medium (1)

MI_1 = the minimum number of units or space to purchase in medium (1)

---

[10] The suggested format for the linear programming model representation in symbolic form is derived from Kotler, *op. cit.*, pp. 477–478; and Day, *op. cit.*, pp. 40–44.

These symbols are formulated into an equation in the following manner:

1. Objective Function (maximize exposure)

$$E = V_1Z_1 + V_2Z_2 + V_3Z_3 + V_4Z_4 + V_5Z_5 + V_6Z_6$$

2. Constraint equations

(Allocated Funds Limitations)

a. $C_1Z_1 + C_2Z_2 + C_3Z_3 + C_4Z_4 + C_5Z_5 + C_6Z_6 \leq AF$

b. $Z_1 \geq MI_1$ $Z_4 \geq MI_4$

$\quad Z_2 \geq MI_2$ $Z_5 \geq MI_5$

$\quad Z_3 \geq MI_3$ $Z_6 \geq MI_6$

c. $Z_1 \leq MI_1$ $Z_4 \leq MI_4$

$\quad Z_2 \leq MI_2$ $Z_5 \leq MI_5$

$\quad Z_3 \leq MI_3$ $Z_6 \leq MI_6$

The appropriate values for each of the items would be substituted into the equations and the simplex procedure could then be used to solve the problem. The greater the number of media being considered and the constraints facing the decision maker the greater the probability that a computer would be used to derive an optimal solution. A complex problem and the computer derived solution are presented below.

The linear programming model as presented raises a number of questions concerning the reality of this type of analysis. These questions are basically in the form of limitations. The major weaknesses of the linear programming model applied to media selection problems are:

a. It does not consider when the advertising effort will occur.
b. It assumes that subjecting an individual to the same advertisement time after time has a constant influence and persuasion effect.
c. It assumes constant media costs (no discounts).

A Systematic Framework for Media Selection

In employing qualitative or quantitative analysis in resolving media selection problems there is one fact that is immediately apparent—the task is difficult. For each medium considered as a possibility in the promotion mix the decision maker must weigh many factors such as cost of the advertisement, the audience reached, the prospective buyers' past purchasing habits, and many other marketplace characteristics. However, before any in depth analyses of such factors occurs, it is the practice of most marketing managers to establish the objective(s) which they hope to achieve by using a particular medium. There are a vast array of potential objectives such as: (1) minimize advertising expenditures; (2) increase sales in a specific market segment; or (3) maximize the number of people that see or hear the promotional message. Thus, the first phase of an organized media selection decision process is to establish in specific terms the objective(s).

After objective(s) have been delineated, it is then necessary to analyze in detail the audience which is the focal point for the advertising message. This can be accomplished by what is referred to as an "audience profile." This profile is a systematic analysis of pertinent demographic characteristics of persons who are the most likely purchasers of the firm's products. The decision maker is faced in media selection situations with attempting to reach as many prospective buyers as possible with every dollar of the advertising budget. Thus, the audience profile serves as a vehicle for acquainting the decision maker with the demographic characteristics of the most likely purchasers of the product or service which is being offered. It also aids the manager in achieving his objective of allocating in the most optimal manner the limited advertising dollars available to him.

A Hypothetical Media Selection Problem

The mathematical framework cited above, which presents in equation format the application of the linear programming model to media selection problems, needs to be placed in a more realistic setting. The realism can be accomplished more readily by using numerical values instead of symbolic notation. Thus, a sample problem using numerical values is presented to highlight the use of linear programming mechanics (see Chapter Six) for media selection decision making.[11]

Assume that the management of the Trumbill Company, manufacturers of cameras and camera equipment, is seeking to allocate as effectively as possible $750,000 to promote their deluxe movie camera in consumer magazines. There are eight possible media choices and the company plans to use full-page ads in these magazines. The objective that management perceives as being most relevant is to reach as many prospective buyers as possible, that is, to get maximum exposure for their ads.

The first order of business is to determine the nature of the market to be cultivated and specify the variables which are of utmost importance in achiev-

---

[11] Based upon the approach presented by Engel and Warshaw, *op. cit.*, pp. 42–48.

ing the objective. Assume that it has been determined by marketing research studies and experience that the significant segment of the market is composed of individuals with the following characteristics: (1) Age: 18–44; (2) Education: high school graduate and above; (3) Family income: $6,700 and above; and (4) residing in a metropolitan area with a population over 150,000.

The next step is to determine what buyers the eight candidates reach. This set of data is then compared with the audience profile which the company has developed. This matching process is often referred to as the "audience profile match." A source such as the Starch Consumer Magazine Report can be employed to determine the readers of advertisements in each of the magazines.

The next process is to give some numerical value to the demographic factors which are considered relevant. This is an objective/subjective process which is heavily influenced by the experience, attitudes, and intuition of the decision

TABLE 9–1

Weighting Scale for Sale of Movie Camera

Factor	Scale
Family income ($6,700+)..........................	.30
High school graduate or above.....................	.25
Age (18–44)......................................	.20
Previous camera purchaser.........................	.15
Metropolitan dweller.............................	.10
Total	1.00

maker. A weighting scale of 0 to 1.00 can be easily utilized for giving numerical values to the demographic characteristics which have been considered important.

After careful deliberation, the Trumbill marketing team decides that a 0 to 1.00 scale is to be employed for weighting five factors considered the most important in the purchase of a Trumbill movie camera. These factors and their assigned weights are presented in Table 9–1.

Of course many other factors could be considered appropriate in developing what can be called an effectiveness rating. For example, the number of children in each family and the time of the last camera purchase may be given more consideration by another team of marketing decision makers. The inclusion of any factor depends entirely on the selection system employed by the decision makers.

After the weighted scale is presented and understood, it is possible to employ a conversion standard. That is, a graduated scale for the five factors which would allow the decision maker to quantitatively derive different weighted scores for the eight magazines. For example, if it were found that a particular magazine had 60 percent of its readers with an education level of at least high school and 75 percent were between the ages of 18 and 44, the decision maker would have to weight these less than perfect audience characteristics. Only if all of the readers of a magazine had a high school education could that medium be given the full weight for that factor which is .25. Thus, some system of graduated weights must be employed to take into consideration the less than perfect match occurrences of desired audience characteristics and the audience reached by a medium. The graduated weighting scale for Trumbill is presented in Table 9–2.

TABLE 9–2

Weighted Conversion Standard for the Five Relevant Factors

Family Income
$6,700+
(0 to .30)

Under 10%	0
11 – 30%	.10
31 – 40%	.20
41 – 60%	.25
Over 61%	.30

Education
(0 to .25)

Under 30%	.05
31 – 40%	.10
41 – 50%	.20
Over 51%	.25

Age 18–44
(0 to .20)

Under 45%	0
46 – 50%	.10
51 – 75%	.15
Over 75%	.20

Previously Purchased Camera
(0 to .15)

Under 10%	0
11 – 15%	.05
16 – 25%	.10
Over 25%	.15

Metropolitan Dweller
(0 to .10)

Under 60%	0
61 – 70%	.04
71 – 75%	.06
Over 75%	.10

The conversion scale (Table 9–2) is used to derive an effectiveness rating for each of the eight media being considered. To illustrate the use of this rating, assume that the data for the X_1 medium is available for the five weighted factors and is presented in Table 9–3. This table informs us that only 56.8 percent of the readers reached by X_1 have a high school degree and only 52.5 percent are between the ages of 18 and 44. The other percentages are interpreted in a similar manner using our factor weighting system in Table 9–2 to make the conversion. The weighted totals for each of the other seven magazines can be derived in a similar manner. However, let us work through in detail our X_1 medium example. The advertising rates per full page color ad for

TABLE 9–3

X_1 Market Data Information and Conversion

Factor	Percentages	Weight
Family income ($6,700+)	46.2%	.25
Education	56.8%	.25
Age (18–44)	52.5%	.15
Previous purchaser	17.1%	.10
Metropolitan dweller	62.1%	.04
Total		.79

TABLE 9–4

Full Page Advertising Rates per Insertion

Medium	Rate per Insertion	Annual Rate for 12 Insertions
X_1	$20,000	$240,000
X_2	28,000	336,000
X_3	32,000	384,000
X_4	18,000	216,000
X_5	10,000	120,000
X_6	5,000	60,000
X_7	12,000	144,000
X_8	13,000	156,000

each of the media are presented in Table 9–4. Note that the rate per insertion for X_1 is $20,000. The size of the audience reached by each of the media are summarized in Table 9–5. The audience totals are multiplied by the weighted scales for each media and the calculation yields the potential audience reached. For example, the total audience reached by medium X_1 is multiplied by the conversion scale developed in Table 9–3. This yields an effective audience reached of 2,975,210, which is shown in Table 9–5. The effective audiences for the other seven media are determined in a similar manner.

After the effective audience is determined, it is possible to begin establishing the linear programming model. The objective function can be formulated by dividing the effective audience totals for each medium by the cost of each full-page advertisement. This calculation provides an effective readership rate per dollar spent. Each of these eight effective readership rates are summarized in Table 9–6.

The readers reached per advertising dollar are presented in the following objective equation which is to be maximized.

TABLE 9-5

Total Audience Reached Multiplied by Conversion Scale
Yields Effective Audience Reached

Medium	Total Audience Reached	Conversion Scale	Effective Audience
X_1	3,766,090	.79	2,975,210
X_2	6,100,000	.50	3,050,000
X_3	2,600,300	.40	1,040,120
X_4	1,985,450	.50	992,725
X_5	2,605,700	.61	1,589,477
X_6	1,900,000	.48	912,000
X_7	3,275,250	.32	1,048,080
X_8	6,100,200	.15	915,030

TABLE 9-6

Effective Readership Rates

Medium	Readers Reached/ Cost of Full Page Ad	Readers Reached per Advertising Dollar Spent
X_1	2,975,210/$20,000	148.7
X_2	3,050,000/$28,000	108.9
X_3	1,040,120/$32,000	32.5
X_4	992,725/$18,000	55.2
X_5	1,589,477/$10,000	158.9
X_6	912,000/$ 5,000	182.4
X_7	1,048,080/$12,000	87.3
X_8	915,030/$13,000	70.3

$$\text{Maximize Exposure } (E) = 148.7X_1 + 108.9X_2 + 32.5X_3 + 55.2X_4$$
$$+ 158.9X_5 + 182.4X_6 + 87.3X_7 + 70.3X_8$$

The total advertising budget constraint is

$$X_1 + X_2 + X_3 + X_4 + X_5 + X_6 + X_7 + X_8 \leq \$750{,}000$$

No negative values are permitted in the final solution and the nonnegatively constraint is presented as:

$$X_i \geq 0 \ (i = 1, 2 \ldots 8)$$

Constraints must also be established which would prevent the assignment of more than 12 insertions (media are published monthly) per year in any of the media. These constraints are written as:

$$X_1 \leq 240{,}000 \qquad X_5 \leq 120{,}000$$
$$X_2 \leq 336{,}000 \qquad X_6 \leq 60{,}000$$
$$X_3 \leq 384{,}000 \qquad X_7 \leq 144{,}000$$
$$X_4 \leq 216{,}000 \qquad X_8 \leq 156{,}000$$

Assume that the company management has reached a conclusion that a specific amount should be spent in three media: X_1, X_5, and X_6. The expenditures must be at least the following amounts:

$$X_1 \geq \$40{,}000$$
$$X_5 \geq 40{,}000$$
$$X_6 \geq 30{,}000$$

This problem cannot be solved simply by observation. It can, however, be solved by use of a simplex computer program. The optimal solution is presented in Table 9–7. The values in Table 9–7, when placed with the objective

TABLE 9–7

Optimal Media Selection Program
for Allocation of $750,000

Medium	Dollars Spent
X_1	$240,000
X_2	330,000
X_3	0
X_4	0
X_5	120,000
X_6	60,000
X_7	0
X_8	0

function, indicate that the number of exposures which occur by allocating the budget on X_1, X_2, X_5, and X_6 would be 101,636,944. To obtain this answer the computer had to perform seven iterations. The greater the number of iterations required to solve a media selection problem the more attention that should be afforded the possibility of utilizing a computer.

Although the basic principle behind linear programming and traditional marginal analysis is essentially the same, the greater value of the linear techniques lies in the fact that the basic limiting inequalities may be more assessible to the marketing decision maker. To some extent this simply follows from their being linear, a linear relationship being the next simplest to a plainly observable characteristic.[12]

---

[12] Boulding and Spivey, *op. cit.*, p. 9.

Some of the other advantages associated with linear programming models applied to media problems include:

1. The development of data which characterizes markets along numerous dimensions.
2. The development of audience profile data is required. The decision maker learns more about relevant demographic characteristics of his potential or current customers.
3. The programming approach requires management to systematize its decision-making process. Instead of a reliance upon hunches and intuition, linear programming and the use of the computer forces a precise definition of variables being considered.

SALES PLANNING

The essence of any promotional activity is communication with potential customers. Often the best method to persuade and influence is to employ face-to-face contact methods. The use of personal selling procedures allows the salesman to get immediate attention from the prospective purchaser and he can then adjust his presentation to follow the mood and attitude of the purchaser.

There are a number of activities common to most personal selling.[13] The time factor is of critical importance in discussing these activities. The salesman must spend time in his dealings with customers in the persuasion, information, and motivation phases of selling. Some customers require more time to sell than others. Thus, adjustments to the salesman's actual selling time schedule are common.

The time required to travel by some mode of transportation from one prospective buyer to another is an additional consideration. Time must also be spent at sales meetings and in training courses learning ways to improve the salesmens' performance and to learn about the new products being contemplated by the firm. Another time consuming activity engaged in by salesmen involves preparing sales reports for their superiors. Finally, salesmen spend time cultivating new customers. That is, finding new contacts and promising sources that can hopefully become purchasers of the firm's product.

A number of quantitative techniques lend themselves to analysis of personal selling problems in such areas as assignment and routing of salesmen. These are, of course, not the only situations that can be analyzed by quantitative methods, but they are the most publicized uses.

[13] These activities are outlined and discussed by Tillman and Kirkpatrick, *op. cit.*, p. 130.

Salesmen Assignment

The assignment of salesmen to cultivate new accounts in a particular geographical area has an impact upon future sales revenue, goodwill, and survival of the firm. If no new accounts are secured, the firm cannot hope to compete effectively in the market. Intelligent assignment and systematic consideration of which salesmen to assign to a territory then has short and long-run implications for the firm.

Many times a situation exists where competitors face a recurring situation in the market. In such a situation, the optimal mixture of profitable marketing strategies can be examined within the conceptual framework provided by *Game Theory*.

For the purposes of this text the present discussion will be limited to a game which involves only two persons and where the gain of one is the loss of the other, that is, the sum of the gains equals zero. This type of game is known as a two-person zero sum game.

Assume that the Tex Insurance Company is considering the assignment of sales personnel to the Houston, Texas metropolitan area. The firm's chief competitor in the area is the Jilly Life Insurance Corporation. An examination of the Tex Company past sales successes and failures in securing new accounts when Jilly salesmen are also attempting to cultivate new purchasers is presented in a payoff matrix format. Table 9–10 illustrates the salesmen's effectiveness in generating new accounts from the viewpoint of the Tex marketing decision maker.

TABLE 9–10

Payoff Matrix for Tex Company and Jilly Corporation
in Terms of Successes and Failures in Generating
New Accounts in Houston

Tex Company Salesmen	Jilly Corporation Salesmen		
	Wilson	*Jason*	*Cobb*
Jones	−2	2	1
Dore	4	−1	−2
Michaels	−1	4	2

The values in the body of Table 9–10 represent effectiveness on the basis of securing new accounts. For example, assume that Tex uses Jones and the Jilly management uses Jason to sell to the same ten prospective customers. In this head to head competition Jones sells six of these prospects and Jason sells four. Therefore, Jones has a gain of two new accounts shown as a positive value. Assume that Dore competes with Cobb in generating sales from ten other prospective buyers. The −2 value indicates that Dore sold four new accounts, while Cobb sold six new accounts. Thus, the value −2 shows that the Tex Company salesman was not as successful as his Jilly Corporation counterpart in nurturing new accounts.

The rest of the values in the table are interpreted in a similar manner. The plus payoffs represent gains for the Tex Company, while the minus values designate a loss to the firm. The executives in the Jilly Corporation view a minus value in a matrix cell as an addition of new accounts and a plus value as a loss.

The executive responsible for assigning Tex Company salesmen must decide upon a strategy to use in order to compete with the Jilly Corporation assignment strategy. A review of Table 9–10 indicates that some salesmen are always more productive in generating new accounts than other salesmen from the same firm. For example, Michaels is always better than Jones. Thus, Jones may be eliminated from consideration. The Jilly Corporation decision maker can see that Cobb is always better than Jason in competing with the sales force of the Tex Company and consequently Jason can be eliminated from the list of possibilities. After these eliminations occur, the revised matrix of possible strategies and payoffs is developed. Table 9–11 is the revised matrix which the managements of both firms must now work with.

TABLE 9–11

Revised Payoff Matrix Tex Versus
Jilly Salesmen

Tex Company Salesmen	Jilly Corporation Salesmen		Maximin
	Wilson	Cobb	
Dore	4	−2	
Michaels	−1	2	2
Minimax	2		

The data presented in Table 9–11 are now used to decide which of the two Tex Company salesmen should be used to compete with the Jilly Corporation representative(s) in the Houston area. Assume that the manager responsible for assignment in the Tex Company is conservative in taking risks. He is an individual inclined to employ a minimax criterion for selection of a salesman. The manager with this philosophy would select Michaels. He would minimize the maximum gain in new accounts by this choice.

If the decision maker responsible for assignment decisions at Jilly is very concerned with minimizing the losses to the Tex Company representative, he would adopt a maximin solution. Thus, he would select Cobb since the maximin value is 2. These choices will lead to a market situation in which for every ten new accounts sold Michaels will sell six and Cobb will sell four.

If Tex's minimax payoff (2) is not the same as Jilly's maximin payoff a, (2) mixed strategy would then have to be employed.[14] That is, the strategy selected by Tex Company is not best suited to compete evenly with that adopted by the Jilly Corporation. This leads to the necessity of developing a mixed strategy or using some combination of the two salesmen in each company as opposed to utilizing only one salesman.

The solution to the mixed strategy problem is derived by using inequalities. First,

Let A_1 represent the frequency of using Wilson to cultivate new accounts.
Let A_2 represent the frequency of using Cobb.
Let B_1 represent the frequency of using Dore.
Let B_2 represent the frequency of using Michaels.

Then

$$\left. \begin{array}{l} 4A_1 - 2A_2 \leq EV \text{ (expected value)} \\ -A_1 + 2A_2 \leq EV \end{array} \right\} \text{Jilly's decision based on these}$$

and

$$\left. \begin{array}{l} A_1 + A_2 = 1 \\ 4B_1 - B_2 \geq EV \\ -2B_1 + 2B_2 \geq EV \\ \\ B_1 + B_2 = 1 \end{array} \right\} \text{Tex's decision based on these}$$

and

The inequalities are established in a manner to denote the fact that Tex is attempting to reach a maximum result and Jilly is attempting to reach a mini-

---

[14] The work of Charvat and Whitman is used to formulate this mixed strategy. For a discussion of their procedures see Frank J. Charvat and W. Tate Whitman, *Marketing Management: A Quantitative Approach* (New York: Simmons-Boardman Publishing, 1964), pp. 285–288.

mum result. The expected value is the payoff anticipated after the salesmen have attempted to generate new sales on a repeat basis. That is, the competition between the representatives of the two companies has transpired over a period of time. If the decision maker lets $P_r = A_1$ and $1 - P_r = A_2$, the following result is generated for the Jilly management:

$$EV = 4P_r - 2(1 - P_r)$$
$$EV = -P_r + 2(1 - P_r)$$

If we set these two equations equal to each other, we get

$$4P_r - 2(1 - P_r) = -P_r + 2(1 - P_r)$$
$$4P_r - 2 + 2P_r = -P_r + 2 - 2P_r$$
$$6P_r - 2 = -3P_r + 2$$
$$9P_r = 4$$
$$P_r = 4/9 = .44$$
$$1 - P_r = .56$$

These findings suggest that the Jilly decision maker should randomly select between Wilson and Cobb to generate new accounts. Wilson should be selected 44 percent of the time and Cobb should be randomly chosen 56 percent of the time.

The same procedures are employed to find the mixed strategy for the Tex Company sales team. Let $P_r = B_1$ and $1 - P_r = B_2$. Then,

$$EV = 4(P_r) - (1 - P_r)$$
$$EV = -2(P_r) + 2(1 - P_r)$$
$$4P_r - (1 - P_r) = -2P_r + 2(1 - P_r)$$
$$4P_r + P_r - 1 = -2P_r + 2 - 2P_r$$
$$5P_r - 1 = -4P_r + 2$$
$$9P_r = 3$$
$$P_r = .33$$
$$1 - P_r = .67$$

Thus, the best strategy for the assignment of salesmen in the Tex Company is to randomly select Dore 33 percent of the time and select Michaels 67 percent of the time.

The payoff matrix can be employed with relative ease when the sizes of the sales teams are reasonably small (i.e., 2, 3, or 4 salesmen from a company versus 2, 3, or 4 salesmen in another company). It is not, however, feasible to employ the procedure with large numbers of salesmen or with numerous competitive sales groups.

Salesmen Routing[15]

The routing of salesmen is one element of sales management that usually receives insufficient attention. Firms often neglect this activity completely or approach it in a shallow, unsophisticated manner. For example, salesmen might be told to cover as many accounts as possible within a given time period, or to eliminate, as far as possible, backtracking. At best they might be told to call only on customers that have the capacity to purchase above a certain sales volume figure.

Quantitative methods advocates have been working for years on a rather intriguing aspect of this area of sales management. This involves solutions to the almost classical "traveling-salesman" problem, which attempts to "find the shortest route (tour) for a salesman starting from a given city, visiting each of a specified group of cities, and then returning to the original point of departure."[16] Essentially, solutions to the traveling-salesman dilemma focus on trying to minimize the distance covered, as indicated above, or on minimizing some other variable, such as travel expense.[17] Certainly these studies have been meaningful. Their value lies chiefly in providing an explicit methodology for minimizing or nearly minimizing some of the variables contained in the routing of salesmen.

Solutions to the traveling-salesman problem, however, suffer from two major deficiencies with regard to their applicability to the real world of sales force routing. First, they do not embrace profit considerations. Since a major objective of business enterprises is the attainment of profit, a more useful approach would be profit oriented. Second, treatments of the traveling-salesman problem do not provide for a time constraint. That is, they assume that the salesman has available sufficient time to complete this most efficient route. In the real world, however, the salesman quite often is faced with the situation in which he cannot possibly cover all accounts within a given time period, and so must make a choice as to which ones he should assign priorities. Consequently, this section of Chapter Nine proposes that Bayesian analysis would be useful in developing a more realistic orientation to salesmen's routing, one that would be both profit conscious and account for the normal time restrictions.

[15] This section was provided by Prof. Richard T. Hise, Associate Professor and Chairman, Department of Business Administration, Shippensburg State College.

[16] G. Dantzig, R. Fulkerson, and S. Johnson, "Solutions of a Large Scale Traveling-Salesman Problem," *Journal of the Operations Research Society of America*, Volume 2 (November 1954), p. 393.

[17] Michael Rothkopf, "The Traveling Salesman Problem: On the Reduction of Certain Large Problems to Smaller Ones," *The Journal of the Operations Research Society of America*, Volume 14 (May–June 1966), pp. 552–553.

An integral part of this proposal, therefore, is the determination of "expected values" for the various customers within the territory to be covered during a specific time period.

Calculation of Expected Value

Expected value for a specific customer is determined by the formula

$$E.V. = [S.V. - (C.G.S. + E)]P$$

where *S.V.* represents an estimate of the *sales volume* that will result given a purchase by the customer; *C.G.S.* is the *cost of goods sold* for that particular sale; *E* is the *expense* incurred in making the sale; and *P* represents the *probability* that the customer will purchase.

To illustrate, assume the following for a specific customer:

$$S.V. = \$10,000$$
$$C.G.S. = \$\ 7,000$$
$$E = \$\ 1,000$$
$$P = .8$$

Placing the figures into the expected value formula, an expected value of $1,600 results:

$$E.V. = [S.V. - (C.G.S. + E)]P$$
$$E.V. = [\$10,000 - (\$7,000 + \$1,000)]\ .8$$
$$E.V. = [\$10,000 - \$8,000]\ .8$$
$$E.V. = [\$2,000]\ .8$$
$$E.V. = \$1,600$$

Application of Expected Value to Salesmen's Routing

As indicated earlier, the basic ingredient for devising an efficient route is the estimate of expected value for all customers within the territory to be covered. Other data needed, however, are the presenting and waiting time (*P.W.T.*) for each account, and the travel time (*T.T.*) required among all accounts.

The above three requirements are diagrammed in a hypothetical situation in Figure 9–2 for nine accounts, A–I. It is assumed that they are to be visited, if possible, within a selling day of 500 minutes, and that the salesman will initiate coverage of his territory from a hotel, which will serve to represent any starting point other than any of the accounts.

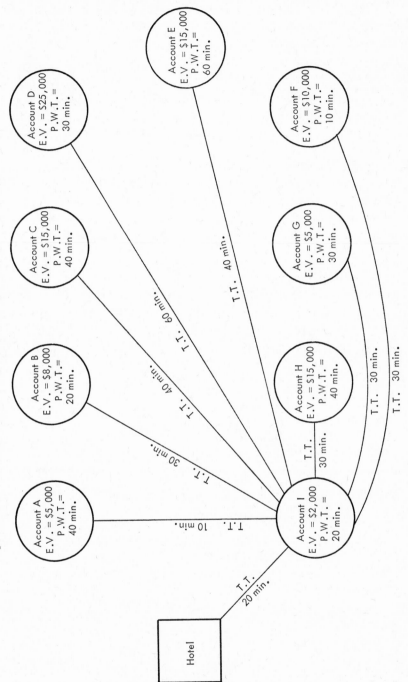

FIGURE 9–2

Input Data for Calculation of Routing Ratio (incomplete except for I ratio derivation)

Account E
E.V. = $15,000
P.W.T.= 60 min.

Account D
E.V. = $25,000
P.W.T.= 30 min.

Account F
E.V. = $10,000
P.W.T.= 10 min.

Account C
E.V. = $15,000
P.W.T.= 40 min.

Account B
E.V. = $8,000
P.W.T.= 20 min.

Account A
E.V. = $5,000
P.W.T.= 40 min.

Account G
E.V. = $5,000
P.W.T.= 30 min.

Account H
E.V. = $15,000
P.W.T.= 40 min.

Account I
E.V. = $2,000
P.W.T.= 20 min.

Hotel

T.T. 40 min.

T.T. 60 min.

T.T. 40 min.

T.T. 30 min.

T.T. 10 min.

T.T. 30 min.

T.T. 30 min.

T.T. 30 min.

T.T. 20 min.

The raw input data necessary to devise a route approaching the optimum one are now available. Although it would be desirable to determine the one best route that would cover the greatest amount of expected value within the time constraint of 500 minutes, this may be almost impossible due to the tremendous number of alternatives involved. For example, 1.3 trillion different routes exist for a fifteen-account problem. For twenty cities, 2.4 quintillion possibilities occur; it would take a computer able to evaluate each route in a millionth of a second 38,000 years of continuous operation to process this size problem.

The procedure next described will demonstrate a relatively uncomplicated approach to salesmen's routing, but one that will enable a route approaching the optimum to be secured. Its very simplicity makes it an effective tool that can be easily employed by sales managers lacking a substantial quantitative background.

Routing Ratio

The rationale for the "routing ratio" is the assumption that as each customer is called on, the salesman wants to *maximize* the expected value while *minimizing* the time involved in so doing. He should cover, then, those accounts that contain the greatest amount of expected value in *relation* to the total presenting and waiting time, and travel time needed.

This relationship is expressed in Table 9–12, the data for which are taken from Figure 9–2 (only the values for Account I are completed because placing all values in Figure 9–2 would create a maze of times which would be confusing). For each account, the total time required in reaching it from each of the other accounts or the hotel is added to the time needed to be spent with each customer, and the total time is divided into the expected value for that particular account. The resultant ratio is called the "routing ratio" and indicates *which* accounts will be contacted, as well as the *order* in which they will be called on.

For example, it takes 30 minutes to go from Account I to Account H; in addition, the salesman estimates that he will spend forty minutes with Account H. The total time, 70 minutes, is divided into the expected value for that account—$15,000. The routing ratio for Account I to Account H is 214.

The salesman is now ready to lay out his route for the day. Since it is assumed that he will begin the day's activities from his hotel, there are nine possible first stops—Accounts A through I. The reader will be able to compute ratios only for Account I. However, the same approach was used for each of the accounts in order to arrive at the ratios included in Table 9–12. As was

TABLE 9–12

Expected Value as Ratio of Selling Time

Account	Account								
	A	*B*	*C*	*D*	*E*	*F*	*G*	*H*	*I*
Ho	63	100	188	278	125	250	100	214	50
A		100	250	357	188	143	83	214	67
B	50		188	500	167	200	100	250	40
C	83	133		278	188	250	71	150	33
D	63	200	150		167	333	71	188	25
E	83	160	250	417		200	100	188	33
F	50	133	214	500	150		56	188	40
G	71	200	188	357	188	143		188	40
H	71	200	150	357	150	200	71		40
I	100	160	188	278	150	250	83	214	

mentioned previously, we have included only the travel times between Account I and the other accounts in order to maintain clarity in Figure 9–2. As revealed by Table 9–12, Account D contains the highest ratio from the hotel, 278; therefore, it will be his first stop. His second call would have to be made to any account other than D and, of course, it would originate from D. Account F is the next stop, as the highest ratio from D, 333, occurs here. The third account to be called on is Account C, since its ratio of 214 is the highest from F.

By following the same procedure for the balance of accounts, the resultant route would be: Hotel–D, D–F, F–C, C–E, E–H, H–B, B–G, and G–I. A total expected value of $95,000 is obtained, with all accounts but A being called on. Total time consumed is 490 minutes. Table 9–13 summarizes the route covered, along with cumulative time and expected values.

TABLE 9–13

Optimum Route through Calling on Accounts with Highest Ratios
of Expected Value to Time

Route	Expected Value	Cumulative Expected Values	Time Involved	Cumulative Time Involved
Ho–D	$25,000	$25,000	90 min	90 min
D–F	10,000	35,000	30 "	120 "
F–C	15,000	50,000	70 "	190 "
C–E	15,000	65,000	80 "	270 "
E–H	15,000	80,000	80 "	350 "
H–B	8,000	88,000	40 "	390 "
B–G	5,000	93,000	50 "	440 "
G–I	2,000	95,000	50 "	490 "

A slight modification of the above process, however, will provide another route that will increase total expected value to $98,000. The rule of thumb describing this modification may be stated: whenever two alternatives from the same departure point yield approximately the same routing ratio, the effect the choice of either would have on the *total* routing ratio should be examined, and the alternative that will maximize this ratio, should be selected. To illustrate, Hotel–D appears, at first glance, to be the best starting point since its ratio of 278 is the highest. But suppose the salesman first called on Account F with a ratio of 250? By doing so he could then contact Account D with a routing ratio of 500. The total routing ratio is 750, which is higher than could be obtained if the salesman first called on Account D, since the ratio

TABLE 9–14

Optimum Route Using Modification Process

Route	Expected Value	Cumulative Expected Values	Time Involved	Cumulative Time Involved
Ho–F	$10,000	$10,000	40 min	40 min
F–D	25,000	35,000	50 "	90 "
D–B	8,000	43,000	40 "	130 "
B–H	15,000	58,000	60 "	190 "
H–E	15,000	73,000	100 "	290 "
E–C	15,000	88,000	60 "	350 "
C–A	5,000	93,000	60 "	410 "
A–G	5,000	98,000	60 "	470 "

of 333 accruing to the next stop (Account F), plus the original 278 from the Hotel to D is only 611.

By following the same reasoning for the remaining customers, the route contained in Table 9–14 is obtained. The reader will notice that the modified approach allows the salesman to cover Account A, not contacted under the first approach, in place of Account I. Since Account A provides $5,000 worth of expected value and Account I is worth only $2,000, there is a net addition of $3,000 to the expected value.

Sources for Input Data

This approach to salesmen's routing depends greatly upon accurate and relevant input data. Obviously, much of the data relies upon estimates. The following discussion of possible sources for input data reveals, however, that meaningful figures may be developed, chiefly through utilization of readily accessible and currently available records.

Sales volume. It should be relatively easy to arrive at a reasonably close approximation of the sales volume figure for individual accounts. Particularly appropriate sources are past sales records, which indicate when accounts are due to purchase and what the average size order is. Such records are a part of most salesmen's normal records.

If new accounts are involved, previous talks with purchasing personnel may have indicated potential sales volume or marketing research studies of account potentials may be available. In some cases, past records may be examined in order to arrive at an average purchase figure for new customers.

Cost of goods sold. This information should be obtainable from the firm's accounting department, particularly the cost accounting area.

Expenses. The accounting section of the firm, through cooperation with marketing, will provide the basis for the necessary allocation of expenses. Firms, of course, will undoubtedly differ as to what specific expenses will be assigned to their customers. Some will prefer to limit their allocations to only *direct* expenses; others may desire to expand the allocation to include *indirect* costs. The latter approach would appear to be preferable, since a *net* profit orientation is achieved. However, a sound basis for the inclusion of indirect expenses should exist.

Probability of completing a sale. The determination of this figure will probably not be as easy as the others, but even so, accurate estimates can be made. Some firms purchase on a regular basis; and the salesman's records may indicate that a purchase is imminent. The number of calls made previously may aid the salesman in assigning a probability figure, for he may know, for example, that the more calls made, the greater the probability of making a sale. Another factor to consider is the number and strength of competitive firms trying to sell to the same company. He can also analyze prospects' reactions to his previous presentations. For example, the presence of a number of favorable buying "signals" would allow for the assignment of a higher probability.

If new prospects are involved, records may be examined as to what percentage of all newly contacted customers ordinarily purchase. If an inquiry was initiated by the prospect, he may be more ready to purchase than if the call were a cold canvass. The employment of "softening-up" devices—such as direct mail literature—may also raise the probability of a purchase; therefore, the salesman should determine the prevalence of such devices for each of the new accounts to be contacted.

Presenting, waiting, and travel times. It should not be too difficult for the salesman to estimate presenting and waiting times. He knows whether he has a definite appointment, what time of the day the prospective buyer can be seen with the least amount of wait involved, the length of a first-time presentation or follow-up call, the number of people he will have to see, the amount of time he usually spends with the buyer, etc. If he has covered the same route before, he should be able to estimate fairly accurately the travel time between accounts. If the route is new, distance between calls and density of traffic could be used to determine travel time.

IMPLICATIONS

What are the implications for a firm and its salesmen if this Bayesian approach to routing is adopted? Undoubtedly, salesmen would be forced to investigate their routing situations in a logical orderly fashion, rather than haphazardly, which is often the case.

Long range routing plans can be developed. For example, a salesman's route for a month could be developed by substituting cities for individual accounts. The total expected value for each city would be the sum of expected values for the individual accounts within the city; waiting and presenting time would likewise be the total time involved with the specific customers. Each city could be linked, then, by the appropriate travel time. In addition, the entire sales force could be routed in a similar manner.

Salesmen should be provided with added incentive to keep accurate and up-to-date records, for they are vital in developing the necessary input data. More effective use of salesmen's time should occur because the more potentially rewarding accounts would be given priority. Additional emphasis on marketing cost analysis should result since allocation of marketing costs to various accounts is needed to secure an accurate picture of their actual expected values.

PROBLEMS

1. Briefly define the following terms:

    a. "A zero-sum game"   b. "Audience profile match"

    c. "Effective readership rates"   d. "Routing ratio"

2. Assume that the Wilding Men's Suit Manufacturing Company is attempting to utilize linear programming in selecting the most efficient media for advertising their men's suits. The company has $200,000 set aside for advertising. A detailed marketing research program provided the company with four factors which are the most relevant for the prospective buyers of suits. These factors are presented in a weighted conversion form in the table below:

TABLE 9–A

Weighted Conversion Standard for Four Factors

1. *College Educated*		2. *Family Income* ($9,000+)	
0 to .40		0 to .30	
Under 40%	.10	Under 20%	.10
41 to 60%	.20	21 to 40%	.20
61 to 70%	.30	41 to 65%	.25
Over 70%	.40	Over 65%	.30
3. *Age* 22–40		4. *Metropolitan Dweller*	
0 to .15		0 to .15	
Under 20%	.05	Under 45%	.05
21 to 50%	.10	46 to 80%	.10
51 to 75%	.12	Over 80%	.15
Over 75%	.15		

There are six media being considered to promote the suits. The advertising rates per insertion are presented in Table 9–B. It is only possible to make six insertions for media sources (M_1, M_3, M_4, and M_6) since these magazines are bi-monthly publications. M_2 and M_5 appear quarterly on the newsstands.

TABLE 9–B

Advertising Rate per Insertion

Medium	*Rates*
M_1	$18,000
M_2	20,000
M_3	9,000
M_4	12,000
M_5	15,000
M_6	17,000

The total audience reached for each medium is summarized in Table 9–C.

Market data information for each medium is collected to determine the nature of the market reached. These data are presented in Table 9–D.

TABLE 9–C

Total Audience Reached
by Each Medium

Medium	*Total Audience Reached*
M_1	1,600,000
M_2	2,200,000
M_3	1,900,000
M_4	1,750,000
M_5	2,200,000
M_6	2,100,000

TABLE 9–D

Market Data on Six Media

	Percentages					
Factor	M_1	M_2	M_3	M_4	M_5	M_6
College educated	68.3	69.6	74.3	66.2	69.8	67.6
Family income	76.2	70.2	88.2	79.2	69.6	50.2
Age 22–40	72.5	80.5	81.6	79.3	84.2	80.6
Metropolitan dweller	90.1	94.1	92.2	86.5	87.8	75.9

The company management would like to spend at least $10,000 in M_1, $20,000 in M_3, and $25,000 in M_6. They are also attempting to maximize the number of exposures.

Set up in mathematical form:

    a. The objective function

    b. The constraint equations

3. Discuss the sources of input data that are utilized in salesmen routing problem decisions. How difficult is it for a marketing manager to secure this information?

4. Discuss the concept of "expected value" as it is related to sales planning. How is it calculated? What are its components?

5. What is the rationale for the "routing ratio" used in routing salesmen? How is it determined?

6. What are the major decisions called for in advertising a product or service?

7. In the discussion of the salesmen assignment problem in this chapter, the following matrix (Table 9–10) was presented:

TABLE 9–10

Payoff Matrix for Tex Company and Jilly
Corporation in Terms of Successes and
Failures in Generating New Accounts
in Houston

Tex Company Salesmen	Jilly Corporation Salesmen		
	Wilson	Jason	Cobb
Jones	−2	2	1
Dore	4	−1	−2
Michaels	−1	4	2

Suppose instead that the original matrix was as shown below:

TABLE 9–E

Payoff Matrix for Tex Company and Jilly
Corporation in Terms of Successes and
Failures in Generating New Accounts
in Houston

Tex Company Salesmen	Jilly Corporation Salesmen		
	Wilson	Jason	Cobb
Jones	−4	4	0
Dore	8	2	0
Michaels	−2	8	4

What would be the salesmen assignment strategies of Tex and Jilly if Table 9–E
possesses the correct payoff values for generating new accounts?

REFERENCES

BRITT, S. H. (ED.). *Consumer Behavior and The Behavioral Sciences.* New York:
John Wiley and Sons, Inc., 1966.

DOUGLAS, J., FIELD, G. A., AND TARPEY, L. X. *Human Behavior in Marketing.*
Columbus, Ohio: Charles E. Merrill Books, Inc., 1967.

ENGEL, JAMES F., WALES, H. G., AND WARSHAW, M. R. *Promotional Strategy.*
Homewood, Ill.: Richard D. Irwin, Inc., 1967.

FERBER, R. AND WALES, H. G. (EDS.). *Motivation and Market Behavior.* Homewood,
Ill.: Richard D. Irwin, Inc., 1958.

GREEN, P. E., AND TULL, D. S. *Research For Marketing Decisions.* Englewood
Cliffs, N.J.: Prentice-Hall, Inc., 1966.

KRETCH, D., CRUTCHFIELD, R. S., AND BALLACHEY, E. L. *Social Psychology.* New
York: McGraw-Hill Book Company, 1962.

MCNEAL, J. U. (ED.). *Readings In Promotion Management.* New York: Appleton-
Century-Crofts, 1966.

MYERS, J. H., AND REYNOLDS, W. H. *Consumer Behavior and Marketing Management.* Boston: Houghton Mifflin Company, 1967.

NICOSIA, F. M. *Consumer Decision Processes.* Englewood Cliffs, N.J.: Prentice-
Hall, Inc., 1966.

ZACHER, R. V. *Advertising Techniques and Management.* Rev. ed. Homewood, Ill.:
Richard D. Irwin, Inc., 1967.

chapter ten

PRICING

INTRODUCTION

Pricing is one of the most important and complex activities with which the marketing decision maker must cope to achieve an efficient and profitable marketing program. Such diverse areas of study as economics, psychology, sociology, mathematics, and engineering have contributed theories, techniques, and programs which purportedly make price setting a systematic procedure. Despite the good intentions and the work of experts in each of these areas, pricing decisions are still made in an atmosphere of uncertainty.

This chapter will not attempt to project the idea that there is one best method for establishing prices. Instead, an analysis of typical pricing techniques will be presented. Also such topics as economics applied to pricing, break-even analysis, decision trees, and competitive bidding models will be analyzed.

The Role of Prices

The role of pricing is vital to the growth and stability of our economic system. There is no simple mathematical formula that firms can adopt to achieve a "best" price. Since goods and services are abundant in our buyers' market economy, the mechanisms for establishing prices are numerous. The range of alternatives within which a pricing decision is made varies widely among different firms and among different products. The market structure within which prices are determined ranges from high degrees of competition to a form of monopoly. Figure 10–1 classifies some industries on a market structure continuum in relation to management's amount of discretion in establishing prices.

Figure 10–1 attempts to illustrate that the firm that produces a standardized product has little discretion about which price is to be charged since competition forces firms to price within a certain range. Firms or professionals selling

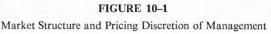

FIGURE 10–1

Market Structure and Pricing Discretion of Management

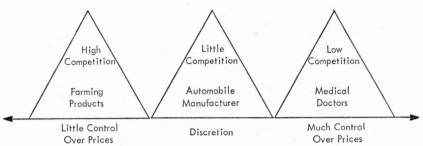

a differentiated or limited product or service generally have more latitude as to the price tag placed on an item or service. In most cases where the firm has some freedom in pricing, the final price decision is based upon what the firm desires to accomplish by its price strategy.

Internal and External Influences upon Price

As is the case in product development, distribution, and promotion, internal and external factors influence pricing decisions. A careful examination of these factors will lead to a better understanding of pricing programs. Some of the factors which should be considered in setting prices are:

1. The cost of producing and selling the product.
2. The nature of the demand for the product or service.
3. The legal environment in which the firm must operate.
4. The type of product or service being made available.
5. The objectives of the firm.

These five factors are, of course, not the only factors that are considered in price setting. They are, however, extremely important to both the short and long-run success of any pricing strategy implemented by a business firm.

Cost of Product

Costs are given consideration in pricing a product or product line, and some form of cost analysis is normally used in reaching a pricing decision. The cost components usually considered include such costs as fixed, semi-fixed, variable, semivariable, direct, and overhead. The first four cost classifications were discussed in our previous discussion of break-even analysis in Chapter Eight. The direct costs of producing and marketing a product are those which can be allocated with certainty to particular products, salesmen, distribution channel, or sales territories. The overhead costs are considered as those which can be allocated only by arbitrary means to a product or some other classification being analyzed.

A manufacturer, wholesaler, or retailer normally will not produce or handle a product unless some portion of his fixed costs are covered. The amount of significance placed upon costs by the marketing decision maker in setting price depends to a large degree upon the time period under consideration. For example, if the manager believes that the life cycle of the product being priced is very short, he would normally be concerned with making money in the short-run. All costs over a short time span are basically sunk. If the time period being analyzed is of a longer duration, then a complete analysis of the six cost components mentioned above is necessary. Thus, the long-run analysis is an in depth project with many possible alternatives for pricing being considered, while the short-run pricing strategy is usually designed to generate large sums of money to recover sunk costs.

The Market Demand

By employing demand analysis, the decision maker attempts to ascertain the amounts or quantities of a product that can be sold over a range of prices at some specific point in time. Every product except a new one has a pricing history which is used in establishing prices at different points in time.

In economic analysis, the response of customers to price changes is associated with price elasticities. In examining the nature of the demand for a product, whether the price is elastic, inelastic, or unitary elastic has a major impact on the effects which price changes have upon the total revenue generated from sales.

A number of factors such as consumers' wealth, social and psychological preferences, and demographic characteristics should be analyzed. The incomes of prospective purchasers can be determined but the preferences of consumers are difficult to measure. Despite these difficulties, a thorough understanding of the demand for a product is not possible unless something is known about the relationship between price, income, and preferences.

The Legal Environment

The marketing decision maker in firms that control a significant share of their market must in establishing prices consider the government reaction to the pricing program. For example, if a pricing decision will lead to a large firm acquiring an even greater percentage of the market, it may be beneficial to not make this planned price change. The government has established broad generalizations on what constitutes a monopolistic share of the market and it is advantageous to learn about these government standards before undertaking a pricing program.[1]

There are other forms of legal constraints which forbid price fixing and certain forms of price discrimination. Laws such as the Sherman Act of 1890, the Clayton Act of 1914, and the Robinson-Patman Act of 1936 place constraints on pricing actions open to business firms. A clear understanding of these laws allows the decision maker to reach pricing decisions within a legal framework established by the government.

The Type of Product

The nature of the product being marketed influences the price strategy adopted. For example, insulin, a product used by diabetics, could be priced at a high level since the product is a necessity, i.e., its demand is inelastic. On the other hand, a farmer setting a price on potatoes knows that if he sets a high price his competitors will benefit because customers can purchase the same product from his competition at a lower price.

Whether the product is a consumer good or an industrial good also plays a role in price setting. The location in which the product is marketed and whether it is a seasonal product (e.g., automobile anti-freeze) are also factors that should be given consideration.

Organizational Objectives

It is frequently assumed that a firm's pricing program should be designed to maximize profits. This contention is too simplistic and too much of a generalization to provide a realistic perspective of the goals of a particular price strategy. The ultimate goal of pricing is to earn a profit but the means for achieving this desired end result are different. At least five specific pricing objectives which are cited in the marketing literature are discussed below.[2]

1. *Satisficing price objective.* A number of companies of all sizes designate that their pricing objective is to achieve a satisfactory rate of return on

---

[1] See P. J. Verdoorn, "Marketing From the Producer's Point of View," *Journal of Marketing*, Vol. 20 (January, 1956), pp. 221–235.

[2] A. D. H. Kaplan, Joel B. Dirlam, and Robert F. Lanzelloti, *Pricing in Big Business* (Washington, D.C.: Brookings Institute, 1958). For a synopsis of these five objectives see Philip Kotler, *Marketing Management* (Englewood Cliffs, N.J.: Prentice-Hall, Inc., 1967) pp. 357–358.

capital investment. The determination of the level of this return depends upon the perceptions, goals, and philosophy of those setting prices. What is a satisfying return to one decision maker may not be to another. The key to understanding this concept is that the managers responsible for price setting are satisfied with their return on the sale of a product, product line, or service. The price established may not be the maximum or the minimum possible but it is that which provides the price setting team with satisfaction. In a strict sense this objective should be analyzed and discussed by employing psychological concepts.

2. *Product line price promotion objective.* In some instances business firms attempt to set a price that will enhance the sales revenue generated from the sale of the entire product line, rather than yield a high profit on the sale of one item. Supermarkets employ what is called loss-leader pricing so that customers are exposed to a product line by purchasing one item in that line at an attractive price. Theoretically, by charging a low price for a product the customer traffic and purchases of the item will increase. Thus, the purchase of the loss-leader today supposedly leads to purchases of the entire product line in the future.

3. *Skimming the market price objective.* Many consumers are willing to pay a higher price for some products than for others because, for some reason, the product has a high present value to them. This value may be functional, economic, symbolic, or psychological in nature. The objective of "skimming" is to attract as many buyers as possible at a high price and then gradually reduce the price at different time intervals to attract other segments of the market. Because of this gradual reduction in price, the "skimming" technique is perceived as being a form of price discrimination over time. This type of pricing strategy is most applicable when there is a sufficient market segment that is willing to pay a high price, when there is little danger that a high price will cause more competing firms to begin producing and marketing the product, and when the cost of producing a small volume of an item is not so much higher that it eliminates revenues generated by charging a high "skimming" price. Best selling novels are often priced this way, beginning with higher priced hardbound copies and moving toward lower priced paperbound copies.

4. *Market penetration price objective.* A strategy used by many firms is to establish a relatively low price in order to stimulate present and future growth of the market. The implication is that a lower price will attract more prospective buyers and that the firm charging the lower price will attract a significant portion of these new buyers. The success of this strategy depends to some extent upon the nature of the market. A lower price and a larger market could

possibly lead to increased competition with more firms entering the industry because of the size of the potential market.

5. *Quick return price objective.* A firm in financial difficulty may develop a pricing program permitting it to generate cash quickly. The same reasoning may be employed by a single-product firm which realizes that the product being sold has a short life cycle and the firm is only going to produce and sell this one item (e.g., fad items). These financial and life cycle considerations could lead to many different price strategies depending upon the product being sold.

Not all firms have the above pricing objectives; some may pursue only a single one, some pursue a combination of these goals or other goals. The truth of the matter, however, indicates that stating the pricing objectives of any firm as profit maximization is not only misleading but is an incomplete interpretation. It is not complete because it fails to consider loss-leader pricing, quick return pricing, and other pricing strategies. To acquire a more in depth understanding of pricing, it is worthwhile to consider the traditional price competition model proposed by economists. This model does not unravel all of the mysteries of pricing but it provides insight into the relationship between the internal and external factors which are considered in pricing and the basic objectives of a pricing program. After the economic concepts are understood, some of the quantitative methods used in pricing will appear to be logical and not as theoretical as the economists' perception.

ECONOMICS APPLIED TO PRICING

Economists have developed several simplified models to explain price setting. One such theoretical model is applied to a market situation in which pure competition exists. Economists usually attempt to distinguish between pure and perfect competition by specifying a number of necessary conditions in order for perfect competition to exist. These are:

1. *Homogeneity of product.* The product sold by seller A is identical to that sold by sellers B, C, and D. If four sellers exist and they produce identical products, then there is no valid reason why the product of one of the firms will be preferred to that of any other firm.

2. *Buyers and sellers are relatively small.* Each buyer and seller in the market must be so small in relation to the total market that he has no significant impact upon the price charged for the item in the market.

3. *No artificial barriers.* There must be no restrictions of demand for, supply of, and price of the ultimate product marketed. The price must be

flexible to move in response to supply and demand factors. There must be no price fixing among suppliers, purchasers, or governmental institutions.

4. *Freedom of movement.* There must be a completely free atmosphere for goods, resources, and firms to operate. New firms must be allowed to enter the industry producing the product without any penalty. The resources and goods must be allowed to move to each supplier or purchaser who is willing to pay the desired price.

5. *Complete knowledge.* All economic units possess complete knowledge of the economy under perfect competition. The differences in prices, if they exist, among sellers will be known accurately and immediately by all buyers and they will purchase at the lowest price. If purchasers are willing to pay different prices for the product, sellers know exactly what they are willing to pay. The product will be sold to the purchaser who pays the highest price.

The first four conditions cited above are usually considered as requirements for pure competition to exist. There are few economists who contend that perfect or pure competition exists in our society.[3] This truism, however, does not diminish the value of studying the pure competition model in price setting situations. The concepts discussed in the purely competitive model enable us to analyze the relationships which exist between demand, supply, and price. To study and understand the theory of pure competition price setting does not mean that we necessarily believe that marketing managers ever operate in a purely competitive environment. It is simply the most logical starting point for acquiring an understanding of how quantitative analysis is applied in price setting.

Product Demand

The demand for a product can be defined as the various quantities of it that purchasers will take off the market at different price levels. The quantity that buyers will purchase is affected by a myriad of factors, the most important being (1) the price of the product, (2) the income levels of prospective purchasers, (3) the purchasers' preferences, (4) the price of closely related products, and (5) the range of products available for consumption.

A demand schedule and curve are used to depict the quantities of the product that purchasers will take at different prices. Table 10–1 illustrates the demand schedule for a product being sold in a perfectly competitive market.

---

[3] The stock market and agricultural markets are probably the closest approximations to perfect competition found in the United States.

A demand curve may be constructed from the values presented in Table 10–1. The demand curve is presented in Figure 10–2. The horizontal axis in Figure 10–2 illustrates the quantity, while the vertical axis depicts the price charged by the seller. Note that for Product *XX* an inverse relationship exists between price and quantity sold.

TABLE 10–1

Demand Schedule for Product *XX*

Price of One XX	Quantity Purchased
$1.00	20
.90	25
.80	30
.70	35
.60	40
.50	45
.40	50

FIGURE 10–2

Demand Curve For Product *XX*

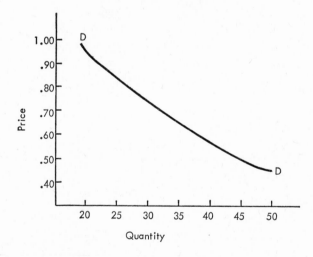

The economist makes a clear distinction between a movement along a demand curve and a change in the demand for a product. In Figure 10–3, an increase in price from P to P' decreases quantity purchased from Q to Q'. This decrease should not be viewed as a change in demand since it occurs on a specific demand curve.

A change in some of the factors which affect demand such as the prospec-

FIGURE 10–3

Movement Along a Demand Curve

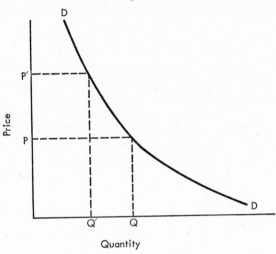

FIGURE 10–4

Upward and Downward Shifts in Demand

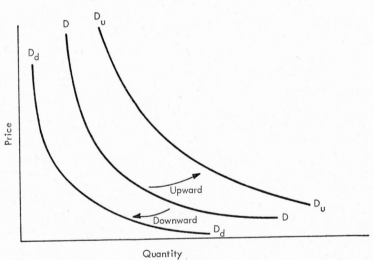

tive buyers' income levels or the market segments product preferences can shift the entire demand curve to the right or left. For example, higher incomes may cause the purchasers of Product *XX* to increase their rate of purchase at each alternative price. The shift in demand in both directions is illustrated in Figure 10–4. Thus, a shift in the demand curve means that more or less of the product (depending upon the direction of the shift) will be purchased at the same price.

Product Supply

The supply of a product is defined as the various quantities of the product that sellers are willing to market at different levels of price. Economists discuss supply schedules and supply curves in a manner similar to that used in discussing demand schedules and curves. The typical supply curve is illustrated in Figure 10–5. It can be readily seen that a higher price will induce a seller to place more of the product on the market.

FIGURE 10–5

Typical Supply Curve

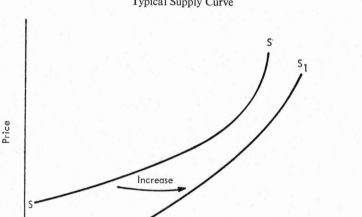

A shift in the total amount supplied can be illustrated as a downward or upward shift in the supply curve. These shifts in supply are interpreted differently than is the case with demand. For example, a shift in supply illustrating an increase in the total supply would be shown as a *downward* shift of *SS* to the right in Figure 10–5. This means that more goods will be supplied at the same prices.

Market Price

The demand curve and supply curve for a particular product can be illustrated in a single diagram to illustrate the variables which influence the market price. The demand curve depicts what the buyers are willing to purchase, while the supply curve illustrates what the sellers of the product are willing to supply.

The demand curve and supply curve combination is presented in Figure 10–6.

FIGURE 10–6

Demand Curve and Supply Curve Combination
for Market Price Determination

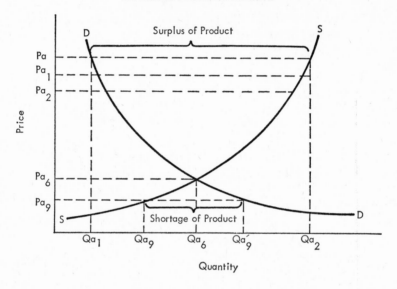

At a price level such as Pa the purchasers are demanding or are willing to take Qa_1 quantity of the product. The seller, however, at the Pa price is willing to produce and place a Qa_2 quantity of the product on the market. The difference between the quantity demanded and the quantity supplied forms into a surplus of the product if the Pa price is set by the seller. If each seller perceived the surplus as accumulated, he would assume that he could sell a greater quantity of the product if the price level were reduced below Pa. Thus, there is an incentive to cut prices to Pa_1, Pa_2, and other lower price levels. Eventually, when and if the price is reduced to Pa_6, the purchasers would buy all of the product that the seller is willing to place on the market at that particular price level.

If the sellers initially set a price of Pa_9 for the product, the purchasers would be willing to purchase Qa'_9 quantity of the product. The sellers, however, would only place a Qa_9 quantity of the product on the market at the

Pa_9 price level. This difference in willingness to produce more and the intense demand for the product would theoretically force the purchasers to bid against each other to purchase the product. The bidding would stop at the Pa_6 price level.

The Pa_6 price is referred to by economists as the equilibrium price. The logic employed is that if the price deviates from Pa_6, forces are set in motion to drive the price down to or up to the Pa_6 level. A price set above Pa_6 will create a surplus because the purchasers are not willing to take every item off the market at a level which they perceive as being too high. This condition will cause prices to decrease. A price set below Pa_6 will create a shortage because the sellers are not willing to produce and place more of the product on the market. This condition will cause prices to rise.

Changes in the Market

As previously mentioned, changes can occur in the market which lead to a shift in supply and/or demand for a product. For example, an intense advertising campaign with elaborate promotional gimmicks can bring about a distinct shift in the demand for a product. If the supply of the product remains

FIGURE 10-7

Advertising Campaign Causing an
Increase in Demand for the Product

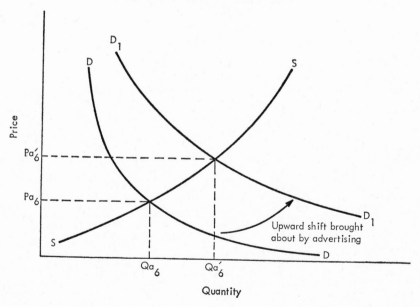

constant when demand is increasing, changes in what constitutes the equilibrium price will occur. Figure 10-7 illustrates the effects of our hypothetical advertising program upon demand in general and the equilibrium price in particular.

Before the intense advertising efforts, Pa_6 was charged for the product and Qa_6 was purchased. The campaign allowed the sellers to increase their price to Pa'_6 and at this higher price a greater quantity of the product Qa'_6 was purchased in the market.

FIGURE 10–8

Poor Quality Product Leading to Poor Industry Image and
a Decrease in Demand for Product

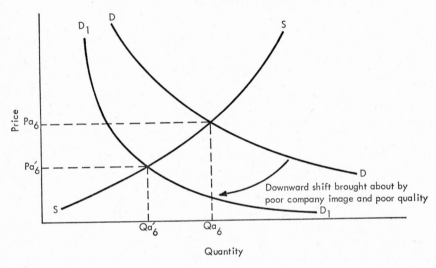

Quantity

A decrease in demand brought about because of a low quality product being placed on the market and the resultant poor image of the products of the industry would lead to a downward shift in demand. This shift is illustrated in Figure 10-8.

Before the public became displeased with the industry's product, they were willing to purchase Qa_6 quantity at the Pa_6 price level. After the product was used by some consumers with poor results, prospective purchasers became aware of the low quality and the equilibrium price level decreased to Pa'_6 and the quantity demanded to Qa'_6.

Shifts in supply can also be brought about leading to changes in the price charged and quantity demanded. Suppose that the introduction of a new adapting device improves the efficiency of a group of machines, resulting in an increase in the supply of the product. Figure 10–9 illustrates this increase in supply and the effect on the equilibrium price. The shift leads to a decrease in price and an increase in the quantity demanded. A decrease in supply brought about by some restriction set by the government on resources needed

FIGURE 10–9

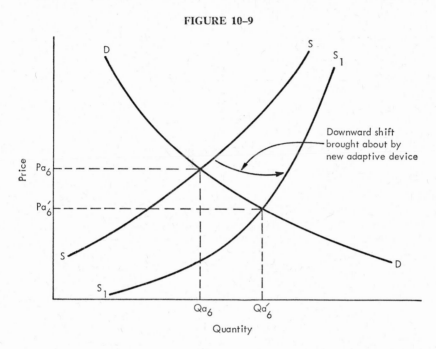

for production or because of an increase in the prices for raw materials would be represented by an upward-left shift in supply. These types of conditions would lead to an increase in the equilibrium price and a decrease in the quantity demanded.

Price Elasticity of Demand

Earlier in our discussion of market demand the concept of price elasticity was introduced. Price elasticity is defined as the responsiveness of the quantity of a product that purchasers are willing to buy to changes in the price charged, given the demand curve for the product. If the quantity purchased is very responsive to price changes (i.e., elastic), a decrease in price may increase the total amount of income spent on the product and an increase in price may decrease the total amount of income spent on the product. If the quantity purchased is not very responsive to price changes (i.e., inelastic), a decrease in price may bring about a decrease in the total amount of income spent on the product and an increase in price may bring about an increase in the total amount of income spent on the product.

Algebraic Formulation of Elasticity

The British economist Alfred Marshall defined elasticity as the percentage change in quantity taken divided by the percentage change in price when the price change is small.[4] In mathematical notation the elasticity concept appears as[5]

$$E = \frac{\Delta Q/Q}{\Delta P/P}$$

This formula can be visualized by illustrating a small percentage change in price and its corresponding influence upon the quantity demanded. These changes are presented in Figure 10–10. The decrease in price from P_1 to P_2 is

FIGURE 10–10

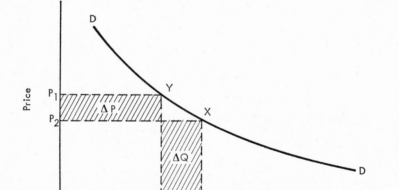

represented by the area ΔP, while the change in quantity from Q_1 to Q_2 is illustrated by the area ΔQ. When elasticity is computed between points such as x and y on the demand curve, it is referred to as arc elasticity. If it is cal-

---

[4] Alfred Marshall, *Principles of Economics* (London: MacMillan & Co., Ltd., 1920), chapter IV.

[5] ΔQ designates a change in quantity from Q to Q_i and ΔP designates a change in price from P to P_i.

culated by using a single point on the demand curve, it is known as point elasticity. Point elasticity is simply arc elasticity when the distance between two points on a curve approaches zero.

Elasticity of Demand for a Product

Suppose that the Williams Electric Company would like to determine the elasticity of demand for a product. The demand schedule for the product is presented as follows:

Price	Quantity Demanded
$10	100
9	115
8	135
7	160
6	200
5	250

FIGURE 10–11

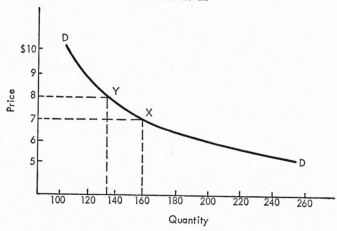

The demand schedule is converted into a demand curve in Figure 10–11.

Suppose that management is interested in the arc elasticity between the area y and x or what the elasticity is if price decreases from $8 to $7. The coordinates of these points are as follows:

	Dollars	Quantity
At point y	$8.00	135
At point x	$7.00	160

Substituting into our elasticity formula, we get

$$E = \frac{\dfrac{\Delta Q}{Q}}{\dfrac{\Delta P}{P}} = \frac{\dfrac{25}{135}}{\dfrac{-\$1.00}{\$8.00}} = \frac{.19}{-.13} = -1.5$$

However, if we move in the opposite direction from x to y, we get the following elasticity coefficient.

$$E = \frac{\dfrac{\Delta Q}{Q}}{\dfrac{\Delta P}{P}} = \frac{\dfrac{-25}{160}}{\dfrac{\$1.00}{\$7.00}} = \frac{-.16}{.14} = -1.1$$

The computations in the y to x and x to y direction indicate that the arc elasticity between two different points on a demand curve must be approximated. To avoid the differences in calculating arc elasticity, let us use the following elasticity formula:[6]

$$E = \frac{\dfrac{\Delta Q}{QL}}{\dfrac{\Delta P}{PL}}$$

The quantity QL is the lower of the two quantities and the price PL is the lower of the two prices. Utilization of this formula for our problem yields a coefficient of demand elasticity of

$$E = \frac{\dfrac{25}{135}}{\dfrac{-1.00}{7.00}} = \frac{.19}{-.14} = -1.35$$

The modified formula provides us with an approximation of the average of the two results previously calculated. Note the coefficient is negative since price and quantity change in opposite directions. However, when economists discuss elasticity, they ignore the minus sign. That is, an elasticity coefficient of minus two is greater than an elasticity coefficient of minus one.

Three Forms of Elasticity

The decision maker concerned with price setting is interested in the influence which price changes have upon quantity purchased in relation to total

---

[6] This formula which attempts to approximate arc elasticity is suggested by Richard H. Leftwich, *The Price System and Resource Allocation* (New York: Holt, Rinehart and Winston, 1965), pp. 35–36.

revenue. There exist three classifications of elasticity related to total revenue. When the elasticity coefficient is greater than one, demand is said to be *elastic*. When the coefficient is equal to one, demand is interpreted as being *unitary elastic*. Finally, when the elasticity coefficient is less than one, demand for a product is said to be *inelastic*.

If the demand for a product is elastic, a small decrease in price will bring about a greater increase in quantity demanded and a small increase in price will bring about a greater decrease in quantity demanded. However, if the demand for a product is inelastic, a small decrease in price will bring about a smaller increase in the quantity demanded and a small increase in price will bring about a smaller decrease in quantity demanded. These conditions are such that if elastic portions are analyzed for a price decrease, it can be seen that the total revenue increases since enough additional units of the product are sold at the lower price to more than make up for the price reduction. If the inelastic segment is considered, it can be seen that the additional units sold at the lower price do not make up for the price reduction, and total revenue decreases. A problem will emphasize the total revenue test of elasticity. The data for the sale of a product are presented in Table 10–2.

TABLE 10–2

Elasticity of Demand and the Total Revenue Criterion

Quantity Demanded	Price per Item	Total Revenue Generated	Elasticity Coefficient
2000	$.50	$1,000	
			4.00 = Elastic
4000	.40	1,600	
			2.25 = Elastic
7000	.30	2,100	
			1.14 = Elastic
11000	.20	2,200	
			.45 = Inelastic
16000	.10	1,600	

Table 10–2 indicates that for portions of the demand curve that are elastic, a drop in price will lead to more total revenue for the company and an increase in price will lead to less total revenue. However, for the segment of the demand curve that is inelastic, a drop in price will lead to less total revenue and an increase in price will lead to more total revenue. The factors cited above as internal and external influences must be considered when the seller is attempting to learn about the elasticity of demand for a product at different price levels.

Another concept that provides insight into the price mechanism in a competitive market is supply elasticity. This concept is handled in a similar manner to that employed to clarify the elasticity of demand procedure.[7]

Firm Price and the Competitive Environment

The manager of a small grain farm faces a very simple pricing decision. All he does is contact the local grain elevator to determine the price which reflects the interaction of industry supply and demand in the Chicago grain market. Thus, Figure 10–6 discussed previously illustrates the derivation of industry price in such a situation. If the individual farmer were interested in maximizing his short-run profit, he would sell that quantity at the industry price where the marginal cost of producing another unit is equal to the marginal revenue obtained from its sale.

Economists have also described price determination in imperfectly competitive markets and in monopolistic market environments. Again, however, these models indicate the theoretical short-run profit maximization combination of price and quantity which would result if the firm were able to calculate its marginal cost and marginal revenue data at any given instance of time. Since it is not our purpose here to delve into economic theory, the reader is encouraged to consult the references cited in footnote 7.

The Economic Models in Practice

A major limitation of the economic models presented above is that they are a gross oversimplification of actual business practices. Despite this shortcoming, the economic models serve to systematically organize the approach to price setting. The interaction of economic price theory and business price setting serve to provide a starting point and a conceptual framework for pricing programs. Neither the economic models nor the business models are perfectly valid models but together they complement each other.

There appear to be three broad classifications of pricing policies that are followed by businessmen. These are cost-oriented models, demand-oriented

---

[7] If the reader is interested in refreshing his memory about such concepts as elasticity of supply, cross elasticity of supply or demand, and other economic concepts, see the following excellent sources: Alfred W. Stonier and Douglas C. Hague, *A Textbook of Economic Theory* (New York: John Wiley & Sons, Inc., 1964); William J. Baumol, *Economic Theory and Operations Analysis* (Englewood Cliffs, N.J.: Prentice-Hall, Inc., 1965); John F. Due and Robert W. Clower, *Intermediate Economic Analysis* (Homewood, Ill.: Richard D. Irwin, Inc., 1961); and M. M. Bober, *Intermediate Price and Income Theory* (New York: W. W. Norton & Company, Inc., 1962).

models, and competition-oriented models.[8] In the cost-oriented models, the firm establishes its price, based largely upon costs. Such practices as mark-up pricing and target pricing are assumed to be cost-oriented pricing techniques.[9]

The *cost-oriented* techniques depend upon some form of markup over costs and/or an acceptable level of profits. The *demand-oriented* concept, however, focuses upon the level of demand for a product. If the market demand for a product is weak, the strategy would then be to place a low price tag on the product so as not to discourage those current purchasers and hopefully attract a greater number of purchasers. A high price would be placed on a product when the market demand is great. A pricing technique that is considered a demand-oriented procedure is price discrimination. Here, a different price is attached to a product because of different product features, time of sale, place of sale, and purchaser of the product.

If a business firm sets its prices on the basis of what its major competition is charging, its policy is referred to as being *competition-oriented*. The key concept to qualify a pricing program as competition-oriented is that the major consideration in price setting is not the costs incurred in producing and marketing the product or the market demand for the product, but is instead the actions of competitors. Going-rate and sealed-bid pricing are considered competitive oriented pricing techniques.

The use of quantitative procedures to highlight cost-oriented, demand-oriented, and competition-oriented pricing are appearing in greater numbers in modern marketing literature. The exact models and techniques used have not been separated and presented in a fashion which illustrates that they are applicable to more than only specific types of pricing situations. Some of the models and techniques being employed by marketing decision makers are presented and discussed below.

THE BREAK-EVEN MODEL APPLIED TO PRICING

The break-even model presented in Chapter Eight is a method which considers demand and cost components in price setting. Assume that the Jackson Supply Company is concerned with their short-run profit position because of financial difficulties. The firm is considering a number of alternative prices for a new electronic inspection device they have manufactured. Cost

---

[8] These classifications are proposed and discussed by Kotler, *op. cit.*, pp. 351–385.

[9] For a thorough classification and discussion of marketing pricing techniques, see the following: Thomas A. Staudt and Donald A. Taylor, *A Managerial Introduction to Marketing* (Englewood Cliffs, N.J.: Prentice-Hall, Inc., 1965); William J. Stanton, *Fundamentals of Marketing* (New York: McGraw-Hill Book Co., 1967) and Eugene J. McCarthy, *Basic Marketing: A Managerial Approach* (Homewood, Ill.: Richard D. Irwin, Inc., 1968).

accounting data, market demand information, and demand estimations are analyzed together and the result of this managerial effort is summarized in Table 10–3.

The typical mathematical procedure used to calculate the break-even point in units for each of the nine different price levels can be found as follows:

$$B.E.P. \text{ units} = \frac{TFC}{P - VC}$$

$$B.E.P. \text{ units (\$20 Price)} = \frac{350}{20 - 6} = 25 \text{ units}$$

$$B.E.P. \text{ units (\$40 Price)} = \frac{350}{40 - 6} = 10.3 \text{ units}$$

TABLE 10–3

Price, Variable Cost, Fixed Cost, and Contribution Data as Estimated for Electronic Inspection Device

Per Unit Price	Variable Cost Per Unit	Contribution to Fixed Cost and Profit/Unit	Total Fixed Costs
$10	$6	$ 4	$350
15	6	9	350
20	6	14	350
25	6	19	350
30	6	24	350
35	6	29	350
40	6	34	350
45	6	39	350
50	6	44	350

The other seven break-even points can be found in a similar manner. The typical break-even chart used to provide an orderly visual reference point for the manager presents the decision maker with the number of units that must be sold for each selling price. Figure 10–12 presents the break-even chart for a selling price of $20 per unit.

The break-even representation in Figure 10–12 is rather incomplete since there are nine possible price levels that should be considered. It would be more informative to the decision maker to present break-even charts showing more than one price level and their relation to break-even and costs. This larger viewpoint of break-even levels is presented in Figure 10–13, which shows four different break-even points for four different price levels.

Although the data represented in Figure 10–13 is more informative than

FIGURE 10–12

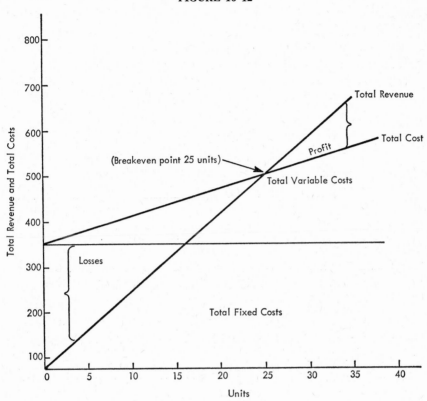

that illustrated in Figure 10–12, it is only applied to situations in which an un-limited amount of the product can be sold at the four prices. This type of analytical framework is similar to the pure competition model offered by economists. Thus, although traditional break-even analysis has a business orientation, it still is not completely realistic because it does not include what the firm can actually sell at each price level. Although the break-even point at the $15 per unit price level is approximately 39 units, this does not mean that purchasers will buy 39 of the electric inspection devices. The market may only take 34 units at this price level.

A procedure used to minimize some of the unrealistic assumptions in-cluded in break-even analysis is to estimate the total demand which would exist at the different price levels. Estimating the demand schedules at different price levels is a very difficult task. Each of the popularly used methods such as questionnaire methods, consumer panels, regression analysis, and market ex-

FIGURE 10–13

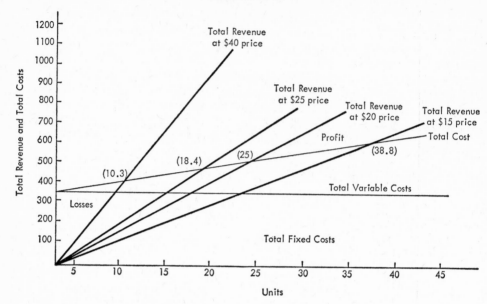

perimentation possess major limitations.[10] Despite these limitations use of one or more of these estimation techniques provides a more realistic set of data for analyzing price levels and break-even points.

Let us assume that the management of the Jackson Company employs some method of demand estimation and this demand data is presented in Table 10–4.

TABLE 10–4

Price per Unit	Estimated Demand (Total)
$10	36
15	34
20	31
25	28
30	25
35	20
40	13
45	12
50	8

[10] The questionnaire, regression, and experimentation procedures are discussed in Wroe Alderson and Paul E. Green, *Planning and Problem Solving in Marketing* (Homewood, Ill.: Richard D. Irwin, Inc., 1964), pp. 238–268.

The demand estimation data can be combined with break-even, total cost, total revenue, and total profit data as shown in Table 10–5. This type of tabular format provides the decision maker with ready comparisons of pertinent information for reaching price decisions.

TABLE 10–5

Market Demand Information Included with Break-Even Data for Electronic Inspection Device

Price per Unit	Estimated Demand (Total)	Total Revenue	Total Cost	Total Profit	Break-Even Point (units)
$10	36	$360	$566	− $206	87.5
15	34	510	554	− 44	38.8
20	31	620	536	84	25
25	28	700	518	182	18.4
30	25	750	500	(250)	14.6
35	20	700	470	230	12
40	13	520	428	92	10.3
45	12	540	422	118	8.9
50	8	400	398	2	7.9

The data presented in Table 10–5 is more complete than the previous charts representing break-even points for one price level or four price levels. Based upon the demand and cost estimations, the price that should be charged by the Jackson Company if profit is the main objective is $30 per unit. At this price level the total profit expected to be earned would be $250.

We do not claim that the break-even model is the perfect pricing device for businessmen to employ. The major limitations, such as acquiring accurate estimates of demand, knowing what the various costs are, and assuming that costs are static, definitely limits what management can do with break-even information. These limitations, however, should not lead the reader to dismiss break-even models as an informative and systematic pricing tool. There is a need for further refinements in constructing break-even models and these will come about with the use of more sophisticated mathematical procedures.

THE DECISION TREE IN PRICE SETTING

The decision tree procedure was previously presented in Chapter Four. The decision tree analysis can also be employed in pricing decision making.[11]

---

[11] An excellent decision tree discussion and analysis is found in William R. King, *Quantitative Analysis for Marketing Management* (New York: McGraw-Hill Book Company, 1967), pp. 323–331.

A sample problem which emphasizes a competitive environment will illustrate how the decision tree can be utilized in price setting situations.

Assume that the Ogan Toy Manufacturing Company is considering the possibility of charging $1.59 or $1.69 for a new toy tractor. The new tractor has no present substitute on the market because of a number of new electrical mechanisms which have not yet been developed by the chief competitor of Ogan, the Double A Toy Corporation. The marketing research team believes that Double A will not be able to duplicate the electronic mechanisms on the tractor for at least three months. Despite the knowledge that Double A cannot immediately duplicate the product, it is not known with certainty how much of the market Ogan will capture over a one year period of time. Of course they would like to capture as large a share of the market as possible.

With the present price alternatives, it is possible to construct a sample decision tree. The decision tree is presented in Figure 10–14. The segments labeled Double A in Figure 10–14 suggest that the next meaningful event is for Double A to introduce at some point in time a new tractor which is very similar to the Ogan model. The price alternatives available to Double A are also $1.59 and $1.69. These prices are used in order to simplify decision tree calculations which will be made. However, the prices of Ogan and Double A do not have to be identical when using decision tree analysis.

The upper branch of the decision tree presented in Figure 10–14 indicates that when Ogan sets an initial price of $1.59, the reaction of Double A could be to match this price or charge $1.69. After Double A responds to the Ogan initial price of $1.59, it is then Ogan's move to respond. This is shown by the branches which indicate that Ogan can charge $1.59 or $1.69 after Double A has responded to the initial $1.59 price of Ogan.

The lower branch of the tree is related to the initial Ogan price of $1.69. Once again the Double A Company could respond by charging either $1.59 or $1.69 after learning about the Ogan initial price. Then the Ogan Company would take some kind of pricing action in response to the Double A price program.

The results of the pricing actions and responses of the Ogan Company and the Double A Company are categorized as (1) the market captured, and (2) the market lost to Double A. The market captured relates to the share of the total market which Ogan has secured. The market not captured refers to a situation in which the anticipated profit for Ogan is below that which is achieved when the market is captured. The two-classification system is of course an oversimplification, used so that the decision tree analysis is not cluttered with outcome possibilities.

FIGURE 10–14

Decision Tree for Ogan
Price Setting on New Tractor

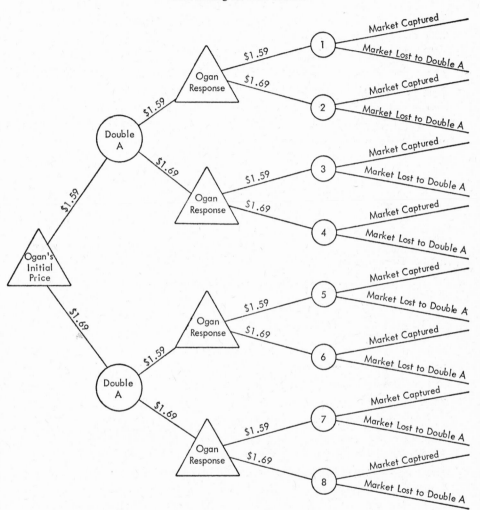

The Pricing Program

The management of Ogan has a number of different price programs which they can adopt. The programs are influenced by the initial price, the competitor's response, and the response of Ogan to the competitor's pricing program. One program is depicted by following the upper branch. For example, if the initial price of Ogan is $1.59 and the response price of Ogan is $1.69, this $1.59–1.69 combination is perceived as a possible program. This program, however, is incomplete because the Double A response price of $1.59 is not illustrated. Thus, a complete price program involves the three prices: $1.59 (Ogan), $1.59 (Double A), and $1.69 (Ogan).

For the problem being considered there are eight potential programs. This is true because there exist three possible prices—initial, competitors' response, and Ogan's response and two alternative prices for each, $1.59 and $1.69. Thus, 2^3 yields the possibility of eight different price programs. Review of Figure 10–14 clearly indicates that eight potential price programs exist. For the upper branch the combinations are:

1. $1.59(O),[12] 1.59(A),[13] 1.59(O)
2.   1.59(O),   1.59(A),   1.69(O)
3.   1.59(O),   1.69(A),   1.59(O)
4.   1.59(O),   1.69(A),   1.69(O)

The lower branch of Figure 10–14 yields the other four price programs which are as follows:

5. $1.69(O),   1.59(A),   1.59(O)
6.   1.69(O),   1.59(A),   1.69(O)
7.   1.69(O),   1.69(A),   1.59(O)
8.   1.69(O),   1.69(A),   1.69(O)

These eight programs are summarized in an orderly format in Table 10–6.

The Ogan management team must still select one of the eight programs. This task would not be difficult if the size of the total market and the size of the market which Ogan is likely to capture if a particular program is adopted were generally known. Other information which would make the selection of a price program easier would be to know the probabilities of occurrence of a particular response of Double A to the initial price and to know the probability that Ogan is likely to capture a particular share of the market when a particular price program is adopted. The probabilities of occurrence will of course be based on a combination of objective and subjective estimates. Such factors as the decision maker's overall experience, intuition, and experience dealing with Double A as a competitor in the past will affect the probabilities assigned.

The Ogan management team, after careful consultation and a review of

---

[12] The *O* is used to designate a price by Ogan.
[13] The *A* is used to designate a price by Double A.

TABLE 10–6

Eight Pricing Programs Available

Program (P_i)	Ogan Initial Price	Ogan Response if Double A Charges 1.59	Ogan Response if Double A Charges 1.69
P_1	$1.59	$1.59	$1.59
P_2	1.59	1.59	1.69
P_3	1.59	1.69	1.59
P_4	1.59	1.69	1.69
P_5	1.69	1.59	1.59
P_6	1.69	1.59	1.69
P_7	1.69	1.69	1.59
P_8	1.69	1.69	1.69

past dealings in the market in which they are competing with Double A, constructs a table of possible profits under each potential program. These profits are presented in Table 10–7.

While profit outcomes were determined, it was also decided what the probabilities of Double A's response to the initial price would be and the probabilities that Ogan will capture each share of the market for each profit level to be realized. It is decided that there is a .80 probability that if Ogan charges

TABLE 10–7

Profits Anticipated for Each Outcome Node

Node (N_i)	Profit Outcome (Market Captured MC and Market Not Captured MNC)
N_1	$64,000 ($MC_1$) 36,000 ($MNC_1$)
N_2	60,000 (MC_2) 44,000 (MNC_2)
N_3	71,000 (MC_3) 59,000 (MNC_3)
N_4	75,000 (MC_4) 61,000 (MNC_4)
N_5	78,000 (MC_5) 60,000 (MNC_5)
N_6	68,000 (MC_6) 60,000 (MNC_6)
N_7	51,000 (MC_7) 50,000 (MNC_7)
N_8	43,000 (MC_8) 41,000 (MNC_8)

$1.59 as their initial price, the price response of Double A will be $1.59 and a .20 probability that the Double A response to the initial price of $1.59 will be $1.69. The probabilities that the market is captured or not captured by Ogan if they respond to the $1.59 price of Double A are, respectively, .60 that they will capture the market as they desire and .40 that they will not capture the size market they hope to. These probabilities are incorporated into the appropriate paths of the decision tree. The abbreviated portion of the decision tree illustrating the probabilities is shown in Figure 10–15.

FIGURE 10–15

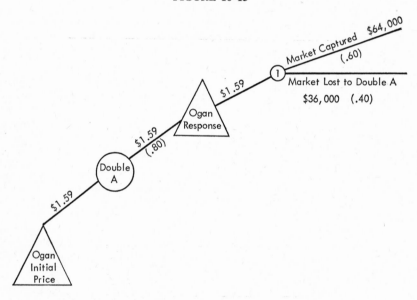

The (.80) probability in Figure 10–15 is the probability that Double A will respond to a $1.59 initial price of Ogan by charging $1.59. Similarly, the (.60) probability for the market captured indicates that the decision-maker believes there is a .60 chance that the market will be captured in such a manner that a profit of $64,000 will be earned.

A complete decision tree illustrating every probability and all of the potential profits is shown in Figure 10–16.

The best of the eight price programs from a profit viewpoint can be determined by ascertaining the expected profit for each program. For example, if we are concerned with P_1 and analyze the paths in the decision tree associated with setting an initial price of $1.59 and maintaining that price regardless of what Double A charges, we have four paths to examine. These paths

FIGURE 10–16

Complete Decision Tree for
Eight Price Strategies

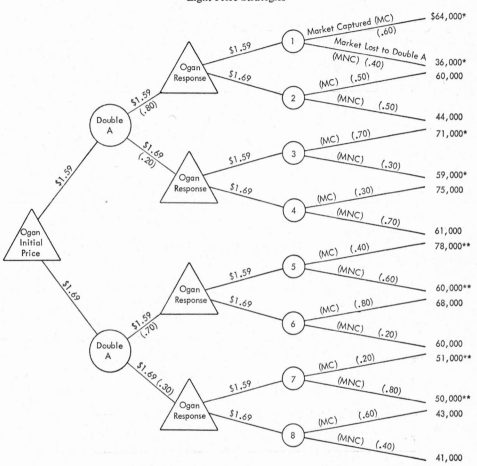

are identified by the single asterisks in Figure 10–16. Thus, no matter what the Double A response is to the initial price of $1.59, Ogan's response is $1.59, which is indicated by the terminal nodes 1 and 3 in Figure 10–16.

The probability of arriving at node 1 (market captured or market lost to Double A) and node 3 (market captured or market lost to Double A) is the product of the probabilities along these paths. Thus, the $64,000 profit will be achieved under P_1 with probability (.80) × (.60) or .48. It is also found that P_1 may lead to a $36,000 outcome, $71,000 outcome, or a $59,000 outcome. The probabilities for these outcomes are presented in Table 10–8.

TABLE 10–8

Probabilities for P_1 Outcomes

Branch	Double A Price & Probability	Node Probability	Product Probability	Profit
Upper	1.59 (.80)	MC (.60)	.48	$64,000
Upper	1.59 (.80)	MNC (.40)	.32	36,000
Upper	1.69 (.20)	MC (.70)	.14	71,000
Upper	1.69 (.20)	MNC (.30)	.06	59,000

The total expected profit for the four possible P_1 outcomes is calculated by multiplying the combined probabilities for each branch by the profit and then adding the individual expected profits. The expected profit for P_1 is then

$$EP\ (P_1) = (.48)(\$64,000) + (.32)(\$36,000) + (.14)(\$71,000)$$
$$+ (.06)(\$59,000)$$

or

$$EP\ (P_1) = \$30,720 + \$11,520 + \$9,940 + \$3,540$$
$$EP\ (P_1) = \$55,720$$

Similarly, suppose Ogan is also interested in the P_5 strategy and that after an initial price of $1.69 they will charge $1.59 no matter what Double A's response is to the first price. These paths are indicated by a double asterisk (**) in Figure 10–16. The combined probabilities for the profit outcomes are presented in Table 10–9.

TABLE 10–9

Probabilities for P_5 Outcomes

Branch	Double A Price & Probability	Node Probability	Product Probability	Profit
Lower	.70	.40	.28	$78,000
Lower	.70	.60	.42	60,000
Lower	.30	.20	.06	51,000
Lower	.30	.80	.24	50,000

Once again the expected profit of the program being analyzed (P_5) is determined by the following calculations:

$$EP\ (P_5) = (.28)(\$78,000) + (.42)(\$60,000) + (.06)(\$51,000)$$
$$+ (.24)(\$50,000)$$
$$EP\ (P_5) = \$21,840 + \$25,200 + \$3,060 + \$12,000$$
$$EP\ (P_5) = \$62,100$$

The other six expected profit figures for the price programs can be found in the same manner that the P_1 and P_5 figures were determined. The eight expected profit figures are presented in Table 10–10.

Examination of Table 10–10 indicates that pricing program P_5 yields the greatest expected profit. The expected profit of $62,100 is achieved if the decision maker at Ogan initially charges $1.69, and if Double A responds by charging $1.59, the Ogan response is $1.59. If the Double A response to the initial $1.69 price is $1.69, the Ogan response is a price of $1.59.

The decision tree procedure has enabled the Ogan decision makers to introduce objective/subjective based probabilities into the pricing analysis. This is a more realistic method of pricing than considering market place occur-

TABLE 10–10

Expected Profits for Eight Price Programs

Program	Expected Profit
P_1	$55,720
P_2	55,280
P_3	55,080
P_4	54,640
P_5	62,100
P_6	59,700
P_7	61,540
P_8	59,140

rences as being known with certainty. In the future it is expected that more managers concerned with pricing will employ decision tree procedures in reaching specific price programs. Despite the use of decision trees and other more sophisticated techniques, it should not be assumed that any simple and completely accurate approach to optimal price setting is only a few years away.

COMPETITIVE BID PRICING MODEL

A form of price strategy is the program that must be adopted by a firm that must bid on a contract for a particular job. For example, in the defense industry, firms normally bid on contracts to manufacture items needed by the military complex of the United States. In the typical bidding situation each firm must submit a sealed bid, and the firm that submits the lowest bid is usually awarded the contract to complete the particular project.[14]

---

[14] For an excellent and concise analysis of competitive bidding, see David W. Miller and Martin K. Starr, *Executive Decisions and Operations Research* (Englewood Cliffs, N.J.: Prentice-Hall, Inc., 1963), pp. 223–238.

The specific bidding strategy adopted by a firm depends upon the objective of the firm. In the discussion utilized to introduce competitive bidding, we shall assume that the firm is primarily concerned with maximizing short run profits. Other objectives such as cost minimization, capturing a larger share of the market, and meeting competition would necessitate a different approach to and discussion of competitive bidding.

Monetary Bid and Cost Relationship

In developing any bid which is to be submitted in sealed form for consideration, the firm must analyze profit and costs of performing the work necessary to complete the project. Profits earned by a firm are determined by the difference between the sealed bid (SB) and total costs (TC) or

$$\text{Profit or } \pi = SB - TC$$

The administrative costs of developing the bid are not considered in our analysis since they are incurred by a firm whether a bid is made or not.

The expected value procedure which is used widely in decision theory is a valuable concept in studying bid and cost relationships in competitive bidding situations. There is only a chance that a firm will be awarded a contract. It is logical to assume that the higher the sealed bid submitted the lower the probability that the firm will win the contract. To illustrate a competitive bid situation employing expected value, let us examine a sample problem.

Assume that the cost of developing an advertising campaign is $78,000. The decision maker in the advertising agency believes that a bid of $108,000 has a probability of .4 of being awarded the advertising job and a bid of $95,000 has a probability of .6 of winning the contract. The profits for both bids are as follows:

$$\pi = SB - TC \tag{1}$$
$$\pi = \$108,000 - \$78,000$$
$$\pi = \$30,000$$
$$\pi = SB - TC \tag{2}$$
$$\pi = \$95,000 - \$78,000$$
$$\pi = \$17,000$$

When $\pi = \$30,000$, the expected return is calculated as

$$\text{Expected Profit } (EP) = \$30,000\,(.4) + \$0\,(.6)$$
$$EP = \$12,000 + 0$$
$$EP = \$12,000$$

If $\pi = \$17,000$ the expected profit is calculated as

$$EP = \$17,000 \,(.6) + \$0 \,(.4)$$
$$EP = \$10,200$$

The largest expected profit is realized if the bid of $108,000 is submitted. Thus, if the firm is interested in maximizing short run expected profit, they would submit the larger bid. The expected profit is the average return that is expected if the probabilities of winning the contract remain the same and the same bid is submitted on a similar contract a large number of times. It is clear that expected profit can be determined if the probability of the firm's winning the contract with different bid amounts is known.

Let us expand our advertising problem to include a number of different size bids and probabilities of winning the job. Assume that the cost of com-

TABLE 10–11

Bid Size and Cumulative Probabilities of
Winning Award

SB (*Selected Bid Amount*)	*Probability of Winning* (Pr_w)
$108,000	1.00
109,000	.90
110,000	.80
111,000	.60
112,000	.40
113,000	.10
114,000	.00

pleting the advertising job remains at $78,000. In Table 10–11 the relationship between the probabilities of winning the job and the size of the bid are presented in a cumulative distribution format.

Note that the probability of being awarded the advertising job gets smaller and smaller as the bid amount increases. The cumulative probability information in Table 10–11 indicates that a bid of $108,000 would certainly win the contract but a bid of $109,000 has only a .9 chance of winning the contract. The reason for the .9 chance for the $109,000 bid is that there is a 1.00 − .90 = .10 chance that a bid of $108,000 would be submitted which would beat the higher $109,000 bid. Similarly, the probability that a bid of $112,000 will be submitted is .40 − .10 = .30. Thus, by a process of successive subtractions of the probabilities illustrated in Table 10–11, the probability of each bid being submitted is calculated. These are shown in Table 10–12.

TABLE 10–12

Bid Probabilities

SB (Sealed Bid)	Probability of Bid
$108,000	.10
109,000	.10
110,000	.20
111,000	.20
112,000	.30
113,000	.10
114,000	.00

The presentations of probability information shown in Tables 10–11 and 10–12 are simply two different procedures for presenting the same information.

Using the same procedures followed in illustrating expected profit calculations above, we can calculate the expected profit for each bid. Previously it was implied that the expected profit for each bid is determined by

$$\text{Expected Profit} = P(SB - TC) + 1 - P(0)$$

or

$$EP = P(SB - TC)$$

Thus, the expected profit for a bid of $112,000 is .40($112,000 − $78,000) = $13,600. The expected profits for all seven bids are presented in Table 10–13. The largest expected profit is coincidentally realized if a bid of $108,000 is submitted. This amount is then the bid that on the average under identical circumstances would yield the largest return to the firm.

TABLE 10–13

Expected Profit Using Cumulative Probabilities

SB (Sealed Bid)	Expected Profits
$108,000	1.00(108,000 − 78,000) = 30,000
109,000	.90(109,000 − 78,000) = 27,900
110,000	.80(110,000 − 78,000) = 25,600
111,000	.60(111,000 − 78,000) = 19,800
112,000	.40(112,000 − 78,000) = 13,600
113,000	.10(113,000 − 78,000) = 3,500
114,000	0(114,000 − 78,000) = 0

Cost Estimates and Bidding Procedures

In a real life situation there is a need to analyze the bidding action of competitors if known. This can be done by analyzing the bids of competitors in relation to our firm's cost estimates. We assumed in our sample problem that costs of completing a project were known with certainty. These costs are not the actual expenditures but only the estimated costs. Let us assume that our firm, the Lakich Aircraft Company, has calculated a frequency distribution for the ratio of our chief competitor's bids, the Callahan Corporation, to our cost estimates. For example, for hypothetical contracts the following ratios are derived:

Plane Engine	Lakich Estimated Cost	Callahan Bid	Ratio
Contract 1	$10,000	$14,000	1.4
Contract 2	8,000	16,000	2.0
Contract 3	9,000	9,000	1.0
Contract 4	8,000	4,000	.5

The ratios are simply Callahan's bids divided by Lakich's cost estimates.

The data in Table 10–14 are derived over an extended period of time by the Lakich management.

Table 10–14 is read that 8 percent of the time Callahan has submitted bids on contracts, which were .8 times Lakich's cost estimate for the contract. The other probabilities are interpreted in a similar manner.

As stated in discussing the data presented in Tables 10–11 and 10–12, for each probability distribution there is a corresponding cumulative probability

TABLE 10–14

Lakich Analysis of Callahan Bids

Ratio of Callahan Bids to Lakich Cost Estimates	Number of Times Occurring	Probability of Occurrence
.8	8	.08
.9	12	.12
1.0	20	.20
1.1	24	.24
1.2	16	.16
1.3	12	.12
1.4	8	.08
Total	100	1.00

distribution. Therefore, from the data presented in Table 10–14 we can determine the cumulative probability distributions for the ratios represented. This distribution will illustrate the probability that a particular sealed bid, expressed as a multiple of Lakich's cost estimate, will be lower than the bid of Callahan. For example, a bid of .8 times the cost estimate will be lower than the bid of Callahan with probability of $1.00 - .08 = .92$. These values would enable the possibility of tie bids because of the large intervals we have used in presenting the ratios (i.e., 0.1). To eliminate tie possibilities we can lower each bid slightly (e.g., .01). Thus, we can say that a bid of .79 times the cost estimate (Lakich) will be lower than Callahan's bid with a probability of 1.00. A bid of .89 times the cost estimate will be lower than Callahan's bid

TABLE 10–15

Bids as Multiple of Cost Estimate
and Probabilities (cumulative)

Bid, as Multiple of Cost Estimate	Probability of Bid Lower than Callahan Bid
.79	1.00
.89	.92
.99	.80
1.09	.60
1.19	.36
1.29	.20
1.39	.08
1.49	.00

with a probability of $1.00 - .08 = .92$. A bid of 1.29 will be lower than Callahan's bid with a probability of $1.00 - .08 - .12 - .20 - .24 - .16 = .20$. The bids as a multiple of cost estimates and the probability that the Lakich bid is lower are illustrated in Table 10–15.

Table 10–15 provides us with information about the probability of being awarded the contract as a function of the amount bid. Having this type of information and employing expected profit information, the decision maker should be able to maximize his profit if Callahan is the only competitor.

Let us designate C as the cost estimate on the contract. Then if the Lakich decision maker bids $1.29C$ on the contract, there is a .20 probability that he will win the contract. If he wins the contract, he will make a profit of $1.29C - C = .29C$. This is simply the $(SB - C)$ we previously employed above, where $SB = 1.29C$. We know that the expected profit is found by $P(SB - C)$ and in this case $.20 (.29C) = .058C$. The expected profits for each of the bids if Callahan is the only competitor are presented in Table 10–16.

TABLE 10–16

Expected Profits when Callahan Is the Only Competitor

Bid, as Multiple of Cost Estimate	Expected Profit
.79	$1.00(.79C - C) = -.210C$
.89	$.92(.89C - C) = -.101C$
.99	$.80(.99C - C) = -.008C$
1.09	$.60(1.09C - C) = .054C$
1.19	$.36(1.19C - C) = .068C$
1.29	$.20(1.29C - C) = .058C$
1.39	$.08(1.39C - C) = .031C$
1.49	$.00(1.49C - C) = 0$

Examination of Table 10–16 shows that a bid of $1.19C$ gives the maximum expected profit of $.068C$. If we use as an estimate of cost $78,000, this would mean a bid of $92,820 and an expected profit of $5,304.

Two-Competitor Bidding Situation

In many bid situations the decision maker must be concerned with the bids of two competitors. Let us assume that the Lakich Company normally bids against Callahan and McLaughlin. The same procedures would be followed in obtaining information about McLaughlin as we did for Callahan. The complete cumulative probability distribution information is presented in Table 10–17.

From Table 10–17 we can conclude that a bid of 1.29 times the cost estimate has a probability of .20 of being lower than Callahan's bid and a .36

TABLE 10–17

Cumulative Probability Distribution for Callahan and McLaughlin

Bid, as Multiple of Cost Estimate	Probability That Bid of Lakich Is Lower than Bid of	
	Callahan	McLaughlin
.79	1.00	1.00
.89	.92	.96
.99	.80	.84
1.09	.60	.58
1.19	.36	.48
1.29	.20	.36
1.39	.08	.10
1.49	.00	.00

TABLE 10–18

Joint Probabilities

Bid, as Multiple of Cost Estimate	Probability that Bid is Lower than Bids of Callahan and McLaughlin Simultaneously				
	Callahan		McLaughlin		
.79	1.00	×	1.00	=	1.00
.89	.92	×	.96	=	.88
.99	.80	×	.84	=	.67
1.09	.60	×	.58	=	.35
1.19	.36	×	.48	=	.17
1.29	.20	×	.36	=	.07
1.39	.08	×	.10	=	.01
1.49	.00	×	.00	=	.00

probability of being lower than the sealed bid of McLaughlin. By using the logic and procedures followed in solving joint probability situations, we can determine the probabilities that the bid of Lakich will be lower than both the Callahan and McLaughlin bids. For example, the probability that a bid of 1.29 times the cost estimate will be simultaneously lower than the Callahan and McLaughlin bids is found as follows:

Callahan Bid Probability   *McLaughlin Bid Probability*
at 1.29 of Cost Estimate   *at 1.29 of Cost Estimate*
.20   .36

$.20 \times .36 =$ Probability of Bid That is Lower Than Bids
of Two Competitors
$P = .072$

Proceeding in a similar manner, it is possible to derive the probabilities for each bid that would be simultaneously lower than the Callahan and McLaughlin bids. These calculations are summarized in Table 10–18.

TABLE 10–19

Expected Profits when Callahan and McLaughlin
Are Only Competitors

Bid, as Multiple of Cost Estimate	Expected Profit
.79	$1.00(.79C - C) = -.210C$
.89	$.88(.89C - C) = -.097C$
.99	$.67(.99C - C) = -.007C$
1.09	$.35(1.09C - C) = .031C$
1.19	$.17(1.19C - C) = .032C$
1.29	$.07(1.29C - C) = .020C$
1.39	$.01(1.39C - C) = .004C$
1.49	$.00(1.49C - C) = .000$

With the information presented in Table 10–18 we can once again employ the expected profit analysis procedures previously employed. This methodology is summarized in Table 10–19. The maximum expected profit of .032C would be realized from a bid of 1.19C. If costs were $78,000, this would mean bidding $92,820, which yields an expected profit of $2,496.

The procedures used to analyze the bidding situation with two known competitors can be employed for any number of known competitors. The more competitors being considered the more cumbersome become the necessary calculations. However, the calculations can be handled quickly and efficiently by automated devices.

Bidding when Competitors Are Unknown

There are situations in which the bidding competitors are not known with certainty. The decision maker would have to employ less than perfectly accurate data concerning the unknown competitors. Data regarding the average competitor is normally utilized. That is, the past behavior of previous competitors is gathered and developed into a framework which would depict the action of an average competitor. The probability distributions of past competitors such as Callahan, McLaughlin, X Company, Y Company, and Z Company would be combined to derive an overall cumulative probability distribution. The result of this combining effort is presented in Table 10–20.

The table is interpreted as follows: For a bid 1.09 times the cost estimate, the probability is .70 that it would be lower than the bid of any single competitor selected at random.

If the decision maker knows that 2, 3, 4, or any number of bidders will be involved, he can use the joint probability procedures previously presented. For example, suppose that the Lakich decision maker knows that three firms

TABLE 10–20

Cumulative Distribution of Average Competitor Based on Previous Bidding Behavior of Opposing Bidders

Bid, as Multiple of Cost Estimate	Probability That Bid Is Lower Than Bid of the Average Competitor
.79	1.00
.89	.90
.99	.80
1.09	.70
1.19	.60
1.29	.30
1.39	.10
1.49	.00

other than his own will be bidding on a contract but does not know the names of the three firms. He would then construct Table 10–21.

The expected profits would then be calculated in the same manner followed in the other examples presented in this section.

TABLE 10–21

Three Unknown Bidders

Bid, as Multiple of Cost Estimate	Probability That Bid Is Lower Than Bid of Three Unknown Firms
.79	$1.00 \times 1.00 \times 1.00 = 1.00$
.89	$.90 \times .90 \times .90 = .73$
.99	$.80 \times .80 \times .80 = .51$
1.09	$.70 \times .70 \times .70 = .34$
1.19	$.60 \times .60 \times .60 = .22$
1.29	$.30 \times .30 \times .30 = .03$
1.39	$.10 \times .10 \times .10 = .001$
1.49	$0 \times 0 \times 0 = .00$

PROBLEMS

1. Briefly discuss the following terms or concepts:
A. "External influences upon prices"
B. "Satisficing price objective"
C. "Homogeneity of product"
D. "Demand elasticity"
E. "Demand estimation"

2. Discuss the major limitations of break-even analysis as applied to price setting problems.

3. Discuss the differences between the following combinations of concepts:
A. Demand curves versus demand schedules
B. Movement along a demand curve vs. shift in total demand
C. Inelastic price versus unitary elastic price
D. Skimming price versus market penetration price

4. Discuss the following statement:
"Advertising managers of the Mayflower Manufacturing Firm believe that an intense advertising effort will cause a downward to the left shift in the demand curve for their dishwashing detergent. A top level executive, however, believes that the advertising personnel meant to state that an upward to the right shift in demand is the hoped for result."

5. The management of the Concord Products Corporation believes that a price program can be adopted for their men's after shave lotion if a decision tree procedure is employed. The main competitor of Concord is Jade Westy. Table 10–A presents eight potential pricing programs that can be adopted by Concord.

TABLE 10–A

Concord Price Program

Program	Concord Initial Price	Concord Response If Jade Westy Charges $1.09	Concord Response If Jade Westy Charges $1.19
P_1	$1.09	$1.09	$1.09
P_2	1.09	1.09	1.19
P_3	1.09	1.19	1.09
P_4	1.09	1.19	1.19
P_5	1.19	1.09	1.09
P_6	1.19	1.09	1.19
P_7	1.19	1.19	1.09
P_8	1.19	1.19	1.19

A. Construct a decision tree which will clearly illustrate the eight price programs presented in Table 10–A.

The Concord management team of course would like to penetrate as much of the potential market as possible. However, some of the market will not be penetrated by Concord's after shave product. Whether the market is penetrated as desired or not, management anticipates a profit for each program and market penetration circumstance. The anticipated profits are presented in Table 10–B.

TABLE 10–B

Anticipated Profits

Node	Profit Outcome	Market Penetrated As Desired (MP) Market Not Penetrated as Desired (MNP) Probability of Outcome
N_1	$ 80,000(MP_1)	.3
	38,000(MNP$_1$)	.7
N_2	70,000(MP_2)	.4
	29,000(MNP_2)	.6
N_3	100,000(MP_3)	.5
	95,000(MNP_3)	.5
N_4	80,000(MP_4)	.5
	30,000(MNP_4)	.5
N_5	81,000(MP_5)	.4
	80,000(MNP_5)	.6
N_6	98,000(MP_6)	.6
	60,000(MP_6)	.4
N_7	102,000(MP_7)	.3
	90,000(MNP_7)	.7
N_8	50,000(MP_8)	.2
	20,000(MNP_8)	.8

It is also expected that if Concord's initial price tag on the after shave is $1.09, there is a .6 probability that the Jade Westy response price will be $1.19. However, if the initial Concord price is $1.19, there is a .7 probability that the Jade Westy response will be $1.09.

B. Complete the decision tree developed in response to question A by incorporating the correct probabilities for each path and profit outcome. Then develop a table showing the expected profits for each price program. If the Concord decision maker's main objective is to maximize expected profit, which price program should he choose? Which price program is the worst from an expected profit standpoint?

6. The Carter Manufacturing and Distribution Corporation has carefully collected cost information and demand data for a children's swing set. The information is presented in tabular format in 10–C.

TABLE 10–C

Pertinent Cost and Demand Data

Price per Unit	Variable Cost per Unit	Total Fixed Cost	Estimated Demand
$18	$14	$600	165
19	14	600	163
20	14	600	160
21	14	600	156
22	14	600	150
23	14	600	145

A. Construct a table similar to that shown in Table 10–5 in the chapter which clearly presents total revenue, total cost, total profit, and break-even (units) data.

B. Present on the same break-even graphical chart the break-even points for the product if it is sold for $18, $20, $21, and $23.

C. If total fixed costs increase by $200, what would happen to the break-even points for each of the six prices? Indicate the break-even points in a table similar to that constructed to answer Question A above.

D. Present the break-even graphical chart showing break-even points for the product if it is sold at $19 and $22. Employ the $800 total fixed costs for this analysis.

7. Comment on the correctness of the following statements.

A. "Price is the focal point of all other actions which a firm takes in producing and marketing a product."

B. "New product pricing is relatively simple and a quick return price objective is usually the rule."

C. "Competitive bidding models can be effectively applied to the pricing program developed for a consumer item."

D. "A firm must make a profit on every item which it carries in its product line since profit is so essential to the survival of a business enterprise."

8. The Miles Aircraft Corporation is interested in winning a large helicopter contract from the federal government. The main competitor of Miles is the Steve Defense Systems Manufacturing Company. It is estimated that the cost of completing the helicopter contract would be $500,000. Since the only competitor is the Steve Company and Miles has previously competed against this company, they are able to construct a bid probability table.

TABLE 10–D

Bids as Multiple of Cost Estimates and Probabilities

Bid, as Multiple of Cost Estimate	Probability of Bid Lower Than Steve Bid
.99	1.00
1.09	.99
1.19	.98
1.29	.96
1.39	.78
1.49	.76
1.59	.74
1.69	.60
1.79	.44
1.89	.24
1.99	.00

A. Employing expected profit analysis, compute the bid that Miles should submit in order to win the helicopter contract.
B. What is the maximum expected profit realized if the optimal bid is submitted?
C. Assume that a second competitor enters the picture after the first sealed bids are submitted. The new competitor is the Jax Aircraft Corporation. The historical record of the company provides the probabilities (cumulative) shown in Table 10–E.

TABLE 10–E

Bids as Multiple of Cost Estimate and Probabilities

Bid, as Multiple of Cost Estimate	Probability of Bid Lower Than Jax Bid
.99	1.00
1.09	.98
1.19	.97
1.29	.89
1.39	.86
1.49	.78
1.59	.70
1.69	.68
1.79	.40
1.89	.20
1.99	.00

D. Present in tabular format the probabilities for each bid of Miles that would be simultaneously lower than the Steve and Jax bids.

E. Using the probabilities presented for the table developed to Answer D above, perform the expected profit analysis. What is the maximum expected profit realized if an optimal bid is submitted? Assume that the cost of completing the contract is still $500,000.

REFERENCES

ACKOFF, RUSSELL L., AND SASIENI, MAURICE W. *Fundamentals of Operations Research.* New York: John Wiley & Sons, Inc., 1968.

KING, WILLIAM R. *Quantitative Analysis For Marketing Management.* New York: McGraw-Hill Book Co., 1967.

KOTLER, PHILIP. *Marketing Management.* Englewood Cliffs, N. J.: Prentice-Hall, Inc., 1967.

LEFTWICH, RICHARD D. *The Price System and Resource Allocation.* New York: Holt, Rinehart and Winston, Inc., 1966.

MILLER, D. W., AND STARR, M. K. *Executive Decisions and Operations Research.* Englewood Cliffs, N. J.: Prentice-Hall, Inc., 1960.

MULVIHILL, DONALD F. AND PARANKA, STEPHEN. *Price Policies and Practices.* New York: John Wiley & Sons, Inc., 1967.

WATSON, DONALD S. *Price Theory and Its Uses.* Boston: Houghton-Mifflin Company, 1963.

PART IV

Computers and simulation in marketing

chapter eleven

MARKETING INFORMATION SYSTEMS

INTRODUCTION

The tremendous growth of the United States economy is attributed in great part to the physical processes of manufacturing. Throughout the growth period management has always sought better tools, techniques, and methods in order to produce more and to produce it more efficiently. However, throughout this period of growth one area, information management, has been consistently overlooked and as a result, business firms in the United States today face a monumental problem. This problem is a result of the capability of our business enterprise system to produce massive amounts of information and data. In fact this era has often been described as the "Age of Information." Why then do so many executives complain that they have insufficient or inappropriate information on which to base their everyday operating decisions? Specifically, marketing decision makers' complaints usually fall into the following categories:[1]

1. There is too much marketing information of the wrong kind, and not enough of the right kind.
2. Marketing information is so dispersed throughout the company that great effort is usually needed to locate simple facts.
3. Important information is sometimes suppressed by other executives or subordinates, for personal reasons.
4. Important information often arrives too late to be useful.
5. Information often arrives in a form that provides no idea of its accuracy, and there is no one to turn to for confirmation.

---

[1] Philip Kotler, "A Design for the Firm's Marketing Nerve Center," *Business Horizons,* Vol. 9 (Fall, 1966), pp. 63–74.

Actually, we can compare this situation with a similar problem faced by managers a few decades ago. At that time the United States industrial complex was unable to produce enough to meet the needs of consumers. Through careful study and technological developments American business is today capable of producing far beyond the subsistence needs of the population.

Historically, business executives did not have to deal with an overabundance of information. Instead, they gathered a bare minimum of data and hoped that their decisions would be reasonably good. In fact, marketing research to a large extent came to be recognized as an extremely valuable staff function in the 1930's and 1940's because it provided information where previously there had been little or none and thus alleviated partially the paucity of information for marketing management. Today, by contrast the business executive often feels "buried" by the deluge of information and data that comes across his desk. Thus, as with our production problems, it appears that we are now able to produce far beyond our "subsistence" needs for information.

The Need for a Marketing Information System

The means for greater productivity are available. New computers and various other information handling equipment are being developed at a rapid rate. In addition, new techniques of analysis are being developed which improve the quality of the information while at the same time reduce the cost of producing it. However, executives still complain of information losses, delays, and distortion. It appears that ironically managers have been so concerned about advancing technology, the abundance of new computers, and new analytical techniques and their potential that they have overlooked the planning necessary for the effective use of these new developments. This has happened to such an extent that some people believe the gathering, storing, manipulating, and organizing of information for management costs as much or more than does direct factory labor.[2]

Many companies today are faced with the serious problem of utilizing the capabilities of computers. Unfortunately in some firms computers are not being utilized effectively in providing management with the best information for decision making. There are many nonmeasurable (but extremely important) costs of this problem. This is because the ability of the firm to compete effectively in the marketplace of today is more often than not at the mercy of

---

[2] Marshall K. Evans and Lou R. Hague, "Master Plan For Information Systems" *Harvard Business Review*, Vol. 40 (January–February, 1962), pp. 92–103.

the executive's marketing information. In the dynamic environment of today's market the need is great for swift and effective decisions. Most business firms are involved in many more markets and selling many more products than ever before. Competitors are capable of moving swiftly, and such external environmental factors as technology, economics, legal, social, and cultural are undergoing rapid change.

However, in most firms the marketing research department supplies only a small proportion of the total amount of information needed. As a result, executives must search for their information from highly dispersed sources both internal and external to the firm. The problem appears to be that the marketing information requirements of today's marketing manager have changed greatly in the past two decades but the basic information arrangements within the firm have remained essentially the same. The problem of generating the right information at the right time must now be viewed in a much broader perspective than previously has been the case. The task of generating effective decision data for marketing management must be seen as the function of a *"marketing information system"* rather than as solely the function of a marketing research department.

The Systems Approach

Before examining the concept of a marketing information system we shall discuss two related ideas: the "systems" concept and the concept of the firm as an information-decision system. An understanding of these two ideas will provide the conceptual framework within which the concept of a marketing information system can be developed as well as an appreciation for the role of information flows in the overall organizational system.

The idea of a business organization as an operating or functioning whole or "system" is gaining wide acceptance among both businessmen and scholars. The idea of a "system" is primarily a way of thinking about a particular phenomenon. Advocates of the "systems approach" view phenomena in holistic terms, emphasizing that systems (e.g. a business organization and the human body) are comprised of numerous interrelated elements but the behavior of these elements is influenced by and can only be understood in light of the system as a whole. In fact, we can define a system as an assemblage of objects which are united by some interaction or interdependence. Using this definition, we see that many phenomena can be viewed as a system. Thus, the systems concept is actually a way of thinking. It provides us with a conceptual framework for visualizing the internal and external factors as an integrated whole. Generally speaking, the basic structure of a system will include the following elements:

1. Input. Anything that is taken into the system can be considered input. Thus, for the firm we can consider raw materials as an input while oxygen is one of the many inputs into the human body system. Major inputs into the marketing system of the firm are a saleable product and information.

2. Output. Anything generated outward from the system can be considered output. The products that are produced are the output of the firm while the morale of its employees is one output of the firm's management system, which is one of the many subsystems which comprise the overall organizational system. Two major outputs of the marketing system are sales and information.

3. Processor. Obviously, the system under study is the processor. The manufacturing process in a production system transforms the inputs (raw materials, labor, etc.) into output (a finished product).

4. Feedback. Any system to function effectively must have feedback on the results of past decisions in order to correct errors which otherwise might go unnoticed. The quality control function provides feedback to correct errors in a production system. Marketing research often provides information feedback to enable adjustments in the marketing system of a firm.

FIGURE 11–1

Basic Structural Elements of a System

The basic elements of a system are illustrated diagrammatically in Figure 11–1.

An advantage of the "systems approach" is that it allows us to recognize the existence of and proper place and function of subsystems. Subsystems are the various systems which comprise the total system. For example, the nervous system and digestive system are subsystems of the overall human body system. The firm as a system is also comprised of numerous subsystems. The production system, financial system, marketing system, distribution system, and personnel management system are just a few of the subsystems which comprise the total system. Finally, the firm is a subsystem of an even larger system—perhaps an industry which is a subsystem of our total economic system. Thus, the reader can recognize the integrated nature of specific systems, including the recognition that every system has both inputs and outputs and can be viewed as a self-contained unit or as part of a larger total system. Thus, the systems approach in marketing provides us with a way of thinking or a way to organize the marketing system of a firm as being composed of numerous subsystems each with its own inputs and outputs.

The Firm as an Information-Decision System

One of the numerous subsystems that contributes to an effectively functioning total business system is the flow of information and the analysis necessary to facilitate decision making. When viewed as the conversion of information into action through the process of decision making, the firm can be thought of as an *information-decision system*. The success of management depends largely on the availability and timely utilization of information at all levels of the organization. In this context the firm can be viewed as an open system in continuous interaction with its operating environment, composed of numerous interdependent and interacting subsystems, vital to which are management decisions designed to bring about action to fulfill previously determined objectives and which are linked together by feedback and information flows.

The concept of information flow is essential in the development of systems concepts. In our definition a system requires interrelationships and interaction among parts and subsystems to comprise the whole; a system of information flow would link the various subsystems by providing information and feedback throughout the various subsystems. The importance of an information-decision system can be seen in the following statement from Johnson, Kast, and Rosenzweig:

Information-decision systems should be considered in conjunction with the fundamental managerial functions: planning, organizing, and controlling. If organization is to implement planning and control, if organization is tied inextricably to communication, and if communication is represented by an information-decision system, then the key to success in planning and controlling any operation lies in the information-decision system. Its importance cannot be overemphasized.[3]

---

[3] Richard A. Johnson, Fremont E. Kast, and James E. Rosenzweig, *The Theory and Management of Systems* (New York: McGraw-Hill Book Company, Inc., 1967), p. 107.

The term *information-decision system* is also used to stress the importance of only generating that information which is needed in order to facilitate effective decision-making throughout the organization. The flow of information should be such that the entire organization becomes an effectively functioning integrated whole.

THE MARKETING INFORMATION SYSTEM

The information subsystem of a total firm system is itself comprised of many different specific information subsystems. For example, there is an accounting information system, a logistics information system, a personnel information system, and a financial information system. In this text we are concerned with only one of these subsystems, the *marketing information system*. We shall define a marketing information system as:

A structured, interacting complex of persons, machines, and procedures designed to generate an orderly flow of pertinent information, collected from both intra- and extra-firm sources, for use as the bases for decision-making in specified responsibility areas of marketing management.[4]

From the outset, however, it must be made clear that the majority of United States firms have not as yet established any kind of formal marketing information system. In fact, as of 1964, an extensive study[5] of the 1,000 largest corporations in the United States indicated that only 80 had established a formal marketing information system. By formal marketing information system we mean a carefully developed plan for information flow, with stated objectives and a place in the formal organization.

However, the number of firms which have such systems is increasing each year as management comes to realize the gains that result from a well planned marketing information system. These firms recognize the need for a more carefully integrated and directed flow of marketing information. They realize that marketing management must get the information needed to manage the marketing mix in the most effective way and this can only be achieved through an effectively functioning marketing information system. More and more companies in the future will take advantage of this approach that has such great potential for marketing management and where the technical aspects no longer pose a barrier.

---

[4] Samuel V. Smith, Richard H. Brien, and James E. Stafford *Readings in Marketing Information Systems* (New York: Houghton Mifflin Company, 1968), p. 7.

[5] "Marketing Intelligence Systems: A DEW Line for Marketing Men," *Business Management* (January, 1966), p. 32.

MARKETING INFORMATION FLOWS

Two types of information flows in a marketing information system can be distinguished. An *external-information flow*, which is information which flows to the organization from its outside environment (intelligence information) or from the firm to its outside environment (promotional communications), and an intra-firm flow, which is information which flows within the boundaries of the organizational system.[6]

External Information Flows

As we have indicated, the external flow proceeds from the firm to the market and from the market to the firm. We shall call the inward flow marketing intelligence.

Marketing intelligence includes data on the various elements in the firm's operating environment such as consumers, competitors, channel members, and information the government supplies for use in evaluating short-run trends in the immediate marketing environment. It also includes long-run strategic information on the economic environment such as consumer income trends and spending patterns as well as developments in the social and cultural environment of consumers. This type of information has a longer-run significance to the firm and aids in long-range planning.

Promotional communications flows outward from the firm to the market. It generally consists of advertising messages and personal selling efforts. In both cases the content of the communications is controlled by the firm. Although an important marketing information flow, promotional communications is an outward flow with which we will not be concerned in this discussion.

Intra-Firm Information Flows

When marketing intelligence data enters the organizational boundaries, it must reach the right executive in order to be useful. Thus, information must flow through as well as to the organization. In addition, information generated within the organization must be channeled to the right executive.

Unfortunately, there are many executives who feel that somehow information within the organization will find its way to the proper individual at the

---

[6] For excellent discussions of marketing information flows, see William T. Kelley, "Marketing Intelligence for Top Management," *Journal of Marketing*, Vol. 29 (October, 1965), pp. 19–24 and Kotler, *op. cit.*, pp. 66–68.

right time. However, this is not always true. It must be recognized that within every organization there are vertical (both upward and downward), horizontal, and informal communication flows. These flows must all become part of the master plan of a marketing information system and not be allowed to function without a formal scheme and direction.[7]

We can illustrate the marketing information flows diagrammatically in Figure 11–2.

FIGURE 11–2

Marketing Information Flows

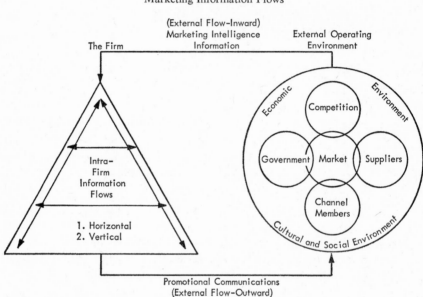

THE MARKETING INFORMATION CENTER

Most experts agree that a single, separate marketing information center must exist in the firm in order to make one person responsible for the marketing information within the firm.[8] This is necessary because both the users and suppliers of such information are scattered throughout the organization and some unit is needed to oversee the entire operation. These experts believe that

---

[7] See Gerald S. Albaum, "Horizontal Information Flow: An Exploratory Study," *Journal of the Academy of Management*, VII (March, 1964), pp. 21–33 for a study of what happens to internal information in an unmanaged system.

[8] Kenneth P. Uhl, "Better Management of Market Information," *Business Horizons*, Vol. 9 (Spring, 1966), pp. 75–82. Also see Kotler, *op. cit.*, pp. 70–74 and Kelley, *op. cit.*, pp. 21–22.

a basic structural weakness in most marketing organizations has been the absence of a central entity for the collection and processing of marketing information. Specifically, it will be necessary for such firms to do the following in order to better manage their marketing information:[9]

1. Scattered information activities must be identified throughout the organization.
2. These components must be recognized as being parts of a whole.
3. The components must be both perceived and managed as an information unit through a single, separate and centralized office.

The objective of this organizational unit will be to improve and upgrade the accuracy, completeness, and timeliness of information for marketing management. Kotler describes this entity as the "marketing nerve center" for the firm which will provide instantaneous information and develop analytical and decision aids for marketing management. Specifically, he sees this new organizational unit providing marketing management with three major information services: gathering, processing, utilization, and numerous constituent services.[10]

1. *Information gathering* is concerned with locating information which is needed by or is relevant to the tasks of marketing management. It consists of three constituent services.

The first is *search* activity based upon management's requests for certain types of marketing information. Search activities can range from locating already published data to conducting full-scale marketing studies.

Scanning is the second information gathering service. This relates to the responsibility of the unit to assemble general marketing intelligence data. This involves scanning trade journals, reports, magazines, newspapers, and any other source which may provide useful information pertinent to the executive's task. This also relieves executives from this time consuming activity.

The third information gathering service is *retrieval*. This involves storing and retrieving information when needed. Many of the modern information retrieval techniques can be used here.

2. *Information processing* is designed to improve the overall quality of the information. Here there are five supporting services.

The first is *evaluation*, which involves determining how much confidence can be placed in a given piece of information. Such factors as source credibility, reliability, and validity of the data must be determined.

The second information processing service is that of *abstraction*. This in-

---

[9] See Uhl, *op. cit.*, pp. 75–77.
[10] Kotler, *op. cit.*, pp. 71–73.

volves editing and condensing incoming information in order to provide the executive with only that information which is relevant to his particular task.

Once information has been gathered, the service of *indexing* is very important. The purpose of indexing is to provide classification for storage and retrieval purposes.

The fourth information processing service is that of *dissemination*, which entails getting the right information to the right decision maker at the right time. Indeed, this is the overriding purpose of an information system.

The final information processing service is that of *storage*. Every information system must provide efficient storage of data in order that it can be used again if needed. Many of the modern information storage techniques can be used here.

3. *Information utilization* dictates that the marketing information unit must assist in more than just information gathering and processing. It must provide additional support in aiding the executive in utilizing the information. This means that the organizational unit must include specialists in statistics, psychology, econometrics, and operations research in order to determine executive needs and interpret research results.

In this section we have stated the need for a centralized marketing information unit within the business organization for the purpose of facilitating marketing information flows both to and within the firm. An approach such as this will insure that any data gathered will be pertinent. It is a waste of both time and money to collect redundant or superfluous information. The marketing information unit within the organization does not focus on specific problems. Instead, it acts as a thermostat that monitors the external operating environment and facilitates intra-firm information flows to enable the firm to better adjust itself to changes that occur in its operating environment. Specifically, this organizational unit must be responsible as a consultant, coordinator, and controller for the three basic marketing information components of gathering, processing, and utilization. In order to justify its existence, it must facilitate better management through more and better information availability and use. This can only be achieved through company-wide management of all the various marketing information components.

MARKETING RESEARCH AND THE MARKETING INFORMATION SYSTEM

By now the reader has probably asked two questions. Where does marketing research fit into this view of marketing management? Can the marketing research department be expanded to include the management of marketing information flows?

At first glance it would seem that the most obvious headquarters for the marketing information function would be the existing marketing research department. After all, this department is concerned with marketing information and its head usually has personal contact and communicates with the marketing vice-president. As logical as this may seem, most experts feel that this should not be done. The reasons for this relate to the nature of marketing research and the objectives of a marketing information system.

Marketing research usually focuses on a specific marketing problem. As such, marketing research projects have a beginning and an end. As we noted previously, the marketing information system does not concentrate on specific problems. Marketing research gathers data, while the marketing information system gathers, processes, and utilizes data. It coordinates and integrates the information system with the day-to-day operating of the business. Thus, the problem of generating data for marketing decision making must be examined from a broader perspective than solely being thought of as marketing research.

The primary purpose of the marketing research department is to conduct field studies and present reports. This is not to deter from the important role that marketing research plays in the marketing process. However, in this chapter we are speaking of a real *information center*. The marketing research department generally lacks such a conception of itself. Thus, the marketing information center concept is in reality an expansion of the marketing research department, which includes several additional tasks.

We have already stated that a marketing information system, in order to be effectively integrated into the firm's marketing program, must be a centralized system. A single, separate marketing information office must be created in order to make one individual responsible for all the marketing information within the firm. This office must oversee the entire area of marketing information.

If it is desirable to separate the marketing information center from marketing research, where then, should this office be located? Because of the newness of the entire idea of a marketing information system, this question is not an easy one to answer.

THE MARKETING INFORMATION CENTER
AND THE OVERALL ORGANIZATION

Probably the greatest cause for the relatively slow application of the information systems concept is the determination of the place such a unit should assume in the organization structure in order to implement the concept.

In the previous section it was indicated that the information center should in most cases be separated from the marketing research department. If this is the case, there are only two remaining locations.[11] One of these—the merchandising office—is located within the marketing structure while the other—a central information office—is located outside the marketing structure.

Merchandising Office

Since we have eliminated marketing research as the possible location point for the information center, the only remaining possibility within the marketing structure is the merchandising office. In most firms this office is usually responsible for the direction, coordination, and control of the activities of product or brand managers. Many firms have been extremely successful in utilizing the brand manager form of organization structure. In such cases it may be possible to expand the merchandising office into the marketing information center. This would be an alternative in firms where no central information office exists.

Central Information Office

Earlier in this chapter we indicated that there were several information subsystems within the overall information system of the firm. We noted there were accounting, personnel, financial, and logistics information systems in addition to the marketing information system. In some firms which have become "information-oriented" there has been the development of a separate, centralized, company-wide information office. Obviously, in firms where such an office exists the marketing information center should be located as part of this office. This arrangement is ideal and offers several advantages such as increased efficiency and more effective use of information. All computer facilities, knowledge, and storage and retrieval facilities become available to the marketing function as well as all other functions. In such firms the various information subsystems must be coordinated and integrated. This type of system is illustrated diagrammatically in Figure 11–3.

However, regardless of the specific organization decided upon, the major issue is that the firm as a whole or each operating unit in a large decentralized firm both perceive and manage the marketing information function as an

---

[11] Uhl, *op. cit.*, pp. 80–81.

entity. The collection and storage of marketing information must be concentrated at some central point where it will be available to marketing executives and executives from other parts of the company.

Only a handful of companies are pioneering in the development of more effective marketing information systems. These organizations are dissatisfied with the quantity and quality of their marketing information. These firms are realizing that to develop an effectively functioning marketing information system involves a great deal more than expanding or automating the data gathering process.

FIGURE 11–3

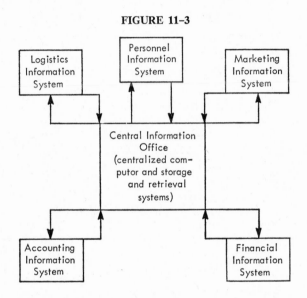

One of the major reasons for the increased interest in the concept of information systems has been the rapid growth in information handling and technology. However, as we have seen in this chapter, the study of information systems is *not* the study of computers. The study of marketing information systems is part of a much larger task, the study of more efficient methods for marketing management.

The discussion in this chapter is more a description of things to come than a description of what is. Marketing information systems cannot be developed overnight. It will undoubtedly be more of a process of evolution as management is able to conceptualize the firm as an information-decision system linked together by information flows.

PROBLEMS

1. In your own words explain what the "systems approach" means to you. What is your opinion of the concept?

2. If the firm can be considered a "system" and the human body can be considered a "system," then they must have some basic structural similarities. What are these similarities?

3. Many people like to view the firm as an information-decision system. In your own words explain what this view of a business organization means to you.

4. Evaluate the following statement. "There can never be such a thing as too much information for decision-making."

5. Firms never really gave much thought to their information systems until the use of computers became widespread. Why do you think they both developed simultaneously?

6. If the study of information systems is not the study of computers, then what is it?

7. In what ways does marketing research differ from the concept of a marketing information system?

8. Evaluate the following statement. "A marketing information system, in order to be effectively integrated into the firm's marketing strategy, must be a centralized system."

REFERENCES

Periodicals

ALBAUM, GERALD S. "Horizontal Information Flow: An Exploratory Study," *Journal of the Academy of Management*, VII (March, 1964), pp. 21–33.

BERENSON, CONRAD. "Marketing Information Systems," *Journal of Marketing*, Vol. 33 (October, 1969), pp. 16–23.

DANIEL, D. RONALD. "Management Information Crisis," *Harvard Business Review*, Vol. 39 (September–October, 1961), pp. 111–121.

DEARDON, JOHN. "How to Organize Information Systems," *Harvard Business Review*, Vol. 43 (March–April, 1965), pp. 65–73.

EVANS, MARSHALL K. AND HAGUE, LOU R. "Master Plan for Information Systems," *Harvard Business Review*, Vol. 40 (January–February, 1962), pp. 92–103.

KELLEY, WILLIAM T. "Marketing Intelligence for Top Management," *Journal of Marketing*, Vol. 29 (October, 1965), pp. 19–24.

KOTLER, PHILIP. "A Design for the Firm's Marketing Nerve Center," *Business Horizons*, Vol. 9 (Fall, 1966), pp. 63–74.

UHL, KENNETH P. "Better Management of Market Information," *Business Horizons*, Vol. 9 (Spring, 1966), pp. 75–82.

Books

BUZZELL, ROBERT D., COX, DONALD F., AND REX V. BROWN. *Marketing Research and Information Systems.* New York: McGraw-Hill Book Company, Inc., 1969.

JOHNSON, RICHARD A., KAST, FREMONT E., AND JAMES E. ROSENZWEIG. *The Theory and Management of Systems.* New York: McGraw-Hill Book Company, Inc., 1967.

SMITH, SAMUEL V., BRIEN, RICHARD H., AND JAMES E. STAFFORD. *Readings in Marketing Information Systems.* New York: Houghton-Mifflin Company, 1968.

chapter twelve

SIMULATION

INTRODUCTION

The marketing decision maker is faced on many occasions with problems that are so complex and detailed that popular analytical procedures such as linear programming, inventory models, and PERT are impotent in achieving feasible solutions. In such instances, the decision maker may employ a technique known as simulation. The simulation procedure has been particularly useful in studying the characteristics of complex systems (e.g., marketing, production, and economic). In this chapter the use of simulation in marketing problem solving will be examined in both a descriptive and analytical manner.

The Nature of Simulation Models

Simulation involves constructing and employing an abstract model which replicates some aspect of the organization's operations.[1] The simulation models currently used in business organizations are typically much more complex than those models which we have previously analyzed in the text. Typically, simulation models are utilized to acquire a thorough understanding of the system under study, to predict future outcomes, and/or to suggest feasible marketing strategies to decision makers.

Some writers classify simulation models as nonanalytical in nature in contrast to the linear programming model and other operations research models which are considered analytical.[2] This classification provides a clear distinct categorization for nonanalytical simulation models and analytical operations research models. The nonanalytical models utilize an experimental approach,

---

[1] See Max D. Richards and Paul S. Greenlaw, *Management Decision Making* (Homewood, Ill.: Richard D. Irwin, Inc., 1966), for an excellent discussion of simulation.
[2] *Ibid.*

which hopefully yields satisficing solutions rather than the typical optimizing solutions.

The Experimental Nature of Simulation

The process of simulation has an experimental overtone. If a marketing manager is attempting to describe and evaluate some characteristic of a given system, he may experiment with changes in inputs and study the resultant outputs. The first order of business in this type of operation would be to construct a model which represents the relevant aspects of reality. In developing the simulation model, it is necessary to describe the relevant aspects of each component that is involved in the experiment.

The second order of business involves the operation of the constructed model. This necessitates a generation of output data. For example, we might systematically experiment by altering inputs to the model in order to determine how the output characteristics are affected. The final purpose, of course, is to infer from the output data generated by each experiment how the corresponding real-world system would operate under similar variations in inputs.

Through such experimentation a large number of input combinations and their impact upon output can be carefully scrutinized. The ability to perform the experimental procedure allows the decision maker to test his theories and plans of marketing action on a simulation model instead of on the firm's ongoing marketing system. Thus, a marketing strategy or strategies can be tested without disrupting the marketing operations.

TYPES OF SIMULATION PROCEDURES

During the past decade, simulation has been increasingly applied to a growing number of marketing problems. The application spectrum includes: predicting media exposure, evaluating advertising effectiveness, pricing, information systems design and evaluation, and physical distribution, among others.[3] In spite of this increased usage, there is no universally accepted method for classifying simulation methods. One of the most reasonable methods is that offered by Richards and Greenlaw.[4] They believe that the most systematic general categorization for simulation processes is (1) hand, (2) machine, and (3) man-machine.

If the decision maker is employing a hand simulation method, all neces-

---

[3] Harold Weitz, "The Promise of Simulation in Marketing," *Journal of Marketing*, Vol. 31 (July, 1967), p. 28.

[4] Richards and Greenlaw, *op. cit.*, p. 503.

sary mathematical calculations are performed by individuals either by hand or by using adding machines or other calculating equipment. Machine simulations are those in which calculations are carried out by a computer system. Finally, man-machine simulation methods are those in which individuals perform as active participants in the operation. This involves placing individuals in the simulated system being studied.

Hand simulation.   The hand simulation method is typically utilized to study relatively simple marketing problems. These may involve considering only a small number of input variables. Because of the simplicity, it may not be economically feasible to purchase a computer or computer time. In some complex machine simulations, a form of hand simulation is used to "debug." For example, the first phase of a complex machine simulation problem involves performing hand calculations.[5] This is an example of utilizing hand calculations to "debug" before the more complex machine method is utilized.[6]

Machine simulation.   The more complex the problem facing the marketing decision maker the more mandatory becomes the utilization of a computer. Large-scale computers have facilitated integrated-system simulation, which has lead to improved problem solving efforts in the areas of designing better marketing systems and understanding the working of operative systems.

Man-machine simulation.   The man-machine method is employed when (1) it is important to simulate certain aspects of human behavior if the simulated results are to have relevance; (2) the expense of or accuracy of developing a program to simulate human behavior on the computer is excessive. It is difficult to program simulated behavior for a computer.

A Marketing Oriented Classification of Simulation Models

There are a number of simulation models which have particular relevance to problems which typically face the marketing decision maker.[7]

Marketing mix models.   This type of model is used to examine and describe the impact of alternative marketing strategies on sales and profits. A number of business games are examples of this form of model. The games which are utilized vary in their degree of sophistication and complexity. In some games the player has to set prices, establish promotion budgets, consider and attempt to minimize distribution costs, develop budgets for research

---

[5] Gordon B. Davis, Howard Ambill and Herbert Whitecraft, "Simulation of Finance Company Operations for Decision Making," *Management Technology*, Vol. 2 (December, 1961), pp. 87–89.

[6] *Ibid.*, p. 89.

[7] The discussion of models in this section is developed primarily from and based upon the presentation of Philip Kotler, *Marketing Management* (Englewood Cliffs, N.J.: Prentice-Hall, Inc., 1967), pp. 238–241.

and development expenditures for new products, and consider the overall marketing plan of action. This type of marketing mix simulation, however, is the exception rather than the rule. Typically, the games which are available only superficially treat the overall marketing mix program developed by the corporation that is being studied.

Market models. These types of models attempt to study a sample of customers which is being influenced by alternative marketing mixes. An example of this type of model is the Simulatics Corporation.[8] This hypothetical company was designed to deal with approximately 3,000 persons representing a cross-section of the American population. These hypothetical consumers were exposed to alternative media schedules for an extended period of time. The computer was utilized to assess which consumers in each classification being examined viewed the various media schedules. From this assessment an audience profile is provided to the advertiser that is concerned about which consumer segment is being exposed to which media schedule.

Competitive response models.   These models are constructed so that the responses and reactions of competitors in the market place can be examined. Cyert and March[9] have developed a duopoly model in which each duopolist evaluates different marketing strategies, forecasts competitive behavior, and stipulates a profit goal, among other things. The process used in this particular model ends when the duopolist finds some plan which will attain his original profit objective or a revised profit program.

Specific Simulation Methods Used in Marketing

The three broad classifications of simulation models cited above are useful in that they specifically describe the areas in which simulation has been used most extensively in marketing. A more detailed discussion of some marketing applications of simulation models will add detail to the more general categorization of marketing mix, market, and competitive response models.

Marketing Games

A number of marketing games have been used in the classroom and in management development programs as simulation devices. The Carnegie Institute of Technology MATE simulation (Marketing Analysis Training Exercise) is an example of a fairly realistic marketing game.[10] In this simulation,

[8] Philip Kotler, "The Competitive Marketing Simulator—A New Management Tool," *California Management Review*, Vol. VII (Spring, 1965), pp. 49–60.

[9] Richard M. Cyert and James G. March, *A Behavioral Theory of the Firm* (Englewood Cliffs, N.J.: Prentice-Hall, Inc., 1963), pp. 83–97.

[10] David B. Montgomery and Glen L. Urban, *Management Science in Marketing* (Englewood Cliffs, N.J.: Prentice-Hall, Inc., 1969), p. 31.

consumer demand is determined by use of a mathematical formula for each time period being investigated. Once the total market demand for a product is ascertained, it is then allocated among a number of competing brands. The allocation of the total demand depends upon brand loyalty and brand shifting. The practice of brand shifting is simply the demand that remains in the total market over and above the habitual repurchases (loyalty) of the brands in the market. The marketing programs of the competitors influence the loyalty and shifting structures that eventually emerge in the model. Such factors as price, advertising, characteristics of the competing brands, and personal consumer preferences are incorporated in the MATE game.

Another realistic marketing game is the Total Market Environment Simulation (TOMES).[11] This game synthesizes total demand as the sum of the demand from individual customers. The consumers in this game are considered in elaborate detail. The attitudes and preferences of consumers are considered in addition to various retailer preferences.

A One-Page Game[12]

The best introduction to marketing games is to play one. The following is a very simple version of a game that can be played with paper and pencil between two players (or two teams could be formed). This game is fun as well as being competitive and educational.

Assume that you are the proprietor of a novelty stand at the Washington Senators ball park. Your only product is a miniature Senator. Your only competitor stations himself at the opposite end of the stands from you. Both of you have an agreement with the Senators that you will pay them $10 each game for the privilege of selling that product in their park, plus $5 for rent of the booth. The only remaining stipulation is that you submit your price for that game to the management in secret. As alternative employment to selling, you are offered the job of taking tickets at $10 per game. The miniature Senator costs you $2, and all unsold units may be returned for a full refund.

Step 1. Set your price in secret, one game at a time.
Step 2. Match your price and your competitor's price with the noncompetitive price index shown in Table 12–1 (e.g., a price of $4 will yield a noncompetitive price index of 1.2).

[11] A. E. Amstutz and H. J. Claycamp, "The Total Market Environment Simulation," *Industrial Management Review*, Vol. 5 (Spring, 1964), pp. 47–60.

[12] The authors wish to thank Robert E. Schellenberger, Chairman, Department of Management, Southern Illinois University for permission to use his one page game.

TABLE 12–1

Price	Noncompetitive Price Index
$2.00	1.6
2.50	1.5
3.00	1.4
3.50	1.3
4.00	1.2
4.50	1.1
5.00	1.0
5.50	0.9
6.00	0.8
6.50	0.7
7.00	0.6
7.50	0.5
8.00	0.4
8.50	0.3
9.00	0.2
9.50	0.1

Step 3. Compute the competitive price index for your score by the following formula:

$$CI_1 = I_1 + 4\left(\frac{2I_1}{I_1 + I_2} - 1\right)$$

where CI_1 is the competitive price index for Stand 1, I_1 is the noncompetitive price index for Stand 1, and I_2 refers to Stand 2.[13]

Step 4. Multiply the competitive price index by the potential for that game found in Table 12–2 to get total unit sales (drop partial units).

Step 5. Complete the income statement.

TABLE 12–2

Game	Potential or Base Demand
1	50
2	45
3	30
4	30
5	40
6	35
7	30
8	25
9	20
10	30

[13] Stand 2 computes CI by using I_2 instead of I_1.

TABLE 12–3

	Game 1	Game 2	Game 3	Game 4	Game 5	Game 6	Game 7	Game 8	Game 9
1. Total sales									
2. Fixed expenses									
3. Variable expenses									
4. Net profit									

The income statement contains only four lines:

1. Total dollar sales (total units sold times price)
2. Less fixed expenses $25 (includes $10 opportunity loss because you did not sell tickets)
3. Less variable expenses (total units sold times $2)
4. Equals net income before taxes

You might arrange these items as in Table 12–3.

For example, assume that Stand 1 sets a price of $3, and Stand 2 sets a price of $4. Then the results could be as shown in Table 12–4.

Now, verify for yourself that if Stand 2 had set a price of $5 instead of $4, Stand 1 would have made a profit of $78 and Stand 2 a profit of $23.

In playing the one-page game or any business game, the participants usually experience significant emotional involvement in attempting to beat the competition. This spirit of competition in many individual cases forces the participant to guage what their competitors will do. This systematic analysis of competitive actions and variables included in the game is one of the major advantages of using games.

TABLE 12–4

Stand 1	*Stand 2*
Step 1. 1.4	Step 1. 1.2
Step 2. $1.4 + 4\left(\dfrac{2(1.4)}{1.4 + 1.2} - 1\right)$	Step 2. $1.2 + 4\left(\dfrac{2(1.2)}{1.4 + 1.2} - 1\right)$
Step 3. 1.708(50) = 85	Step 3. 0.892(50) = 44
Step 4. Total sales = 85($3).....$255	Step 4. Total sales = 44($4).....$176
Fixed costs............ 25	Fixed costs............ 25
Variable costs 85($2)..... 170	Variable costs 44($2)..... 88
Net profit............$ 60	Net profit............$ 63

Market Simulations

The more realistic market simulation models have been used to study the dynamics and complexities of market structure so that more efficient marketing strategies can be developed. An excellent simulation of a market was developed by Balderston and Hoggatt.[14] This study simulated the patterns of trade and business operations among members of a channel of distribution in the lumber industry (i.e., manufacturers, wholesalers, and retailers). It is typical in the lumber business for transactions between members in the

FIGURE 12–1

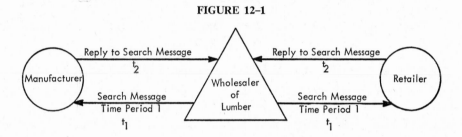

channel to be negotiated by a number of buyers. The normal transaction would be initiated with a wholesaler sending a search message to a manufacturer to determine the manufacturer's offer price and quantity available at that price. At the same time, the wholesaler would send a message to a retailer and obtain the retailer's bid and quantity required. This procedure is presented in Figure 12–1.

The replies received by the wholesaler provide information which is analyzed by considering the profitability of dealing with the manufacturer and retailer specified in Figure 12–1. If the decision maker decides that the transaction between parties will be profitable for him, an order would be placed with the manufacturer and a promise message sent to the retailer.

The Balderston-Hoggatt model contains approximately 16,000 variables. Thus, a giant computer must be utilized to perform the necessary simulations. Through simulation, the behavior of the market arrangement associated with different input data (e.g., costs of messages and nature of decision rules) can be observed.

---

[14] Frederic E. Balderston and Austen C. Hoggatt, *Simulation of Market Processes* (Berkeley, California: Institute of Business and Economic Research, University of California, 1962).

Stochastic Simulation Models

In designing stochastic simulation models, it is necessary to provide some procedure for coping with probabilistic variables. One commonly used method for dealing with probabilistic variables in simulation models is the Monte Carlo technique.[15] Before examining an elaborate Monte Carlo simu-

TABLE 12–5

Past Daily Demand and Lead Times for White Shirts

Daily Demand (shirts)	Probability of Occurrence*	Lead Time (days)	Probability of Occurrence
40	.10	1	.30
41	.15	2	.50
42	.30	3	.20
43	.25		
44	.15		
45	.05		

* The probabilities are assumed to be the same, regardless of the day of week.

lation, let us utilize a simplified example to highlight the mathematical operations involved.[16]

Suppose that the Johnson Men's Shop wants to develop a policy for ordering men's white dress shirts. The consumer demand on any given day and the lead time required between ordering and receiving the shirts is variable. Elaborate records have been kept so that probability distributions for both average daily demand and lead time are available. These distributions are presented in Table 12–5. The marketing decision maker can utilize this probability data and simulate numerous days and determine the impact of changing the ordering procedures upon such important variables as inventory levels and number of orders to be placed.

The Johnson management decides to test over a ten day period the following two ordering rules:

---

[15] For an excellent discussion of this procedure, see J. M. Hammersley and D. C. Handscomb, *Monte Carlo Methods* (New York: John Wiley and Sons, 1964).

[16] This type of approach is suggested by Richards and Greenlaw, *op. cit.*, pp. 512–518.

1. When shirt inventories at the beginning of the day have fallen to a level of 70 or below, reorder 70 shirts.
2. When shirt inventories at the beginning of a day have fallen to a level of 100 or below, reorder 100 shirts.

In actual practice, of course, the management team would try out more than two decision rules and may want to simulate for more than 10 days. The selection of only two rules and a 10-day simulation was arbitrarily selected so that the Monte Carlo procedure could be examined.

The problem facing management is that values which represent the range of demand 40–45 and lead time 1–3 are needed. One method of performing the necessary iterations of the model is to utilize random number tables which would represent the demand and lead times in proportion to the frequency that each of these conditions is expected to occur in the real world. Before this procedure is discussed, let us examine another procedure that is widely used in classrooms.

A classroom procedure which can be used to simulate the demand distribution and the lead time is to utilize two urns with 100 slips of paper in each. In Urn 1 the following is the case:

1. *Urn 1 (demand simulation)*—100 slips of paper each with only one number, either 40, 41, 42, 43, 44, or 45. On 10 slips of paper there is the number 40, on 15 slips the number 41, on 30 slips the number 42, on 25 slips the number 43, on 15 slips the number 44 and on five slips the number 45. The frequencies of the number on the slips of paper correspond with the frequency of the daily demand for shirts shown in Table 12–5.

In Urn 2 the following is the case:

2. *Urn 2 (lead time simulation)*—100 slips of paper each with only one number, either 1, 2, or 3. On 30 slips of paper there is the number 1, on 50 slips the number 2, and on 20 slips the number 3.

We could then proceed to draw a piece of paper from Urn 1, record the number on this slip, and replace it in the urn. This would constitute a simulation of the demand for the first day. This procedure would be followed so that 10 days of simulation can be generated.

Employing the two decision rules would also allow us to simulate lead times each time it is necessary to place an order. The same replacement process would occur when it is necessary to draw from Urn 2.

TABLE 12–6

Number Assignment to Demand Requirements and Lead Times

Daily Demand (shirts)	Probability of Occurrence	Assigned Numbers to Occurrence	Lead Time (days)	Probability of Occurrence	Assigned Numbers to Occurrence
40	.10	1–10	1	.30	1–30
41	.15	11–25	2	.50	31–80
42	.30	26–55	3	.20	81–100
43	.25	56–80			
44	.15	81–95			
45	.05	96–100			

It is not practical to employ urns when simulating demand or lead time. The assignment of numbers to the occurrence of each event in our problem would allow us to carry out our simulation in a more convenient manner. Thus, we would assign to the numbers 1–100, daily demand and lead times. These assigned numbers are illustrated in Table 12–6. A number from 1 to 100 is generated randomly for each demand and lead time iteration and the event assigned to the number generated is considered as having occurred for that particular simulation.[17] The random selection of assigned numbers can be accomplished by use of a table of random numbers (See Appendix A).[18]

The various phases of the Monte Carlo procedure are presented qualitatively in Figure 12–2.*

TABLE 12–7

Generation of Demand Levels and Lead Times

Simulated Day	Random Number Selected	Represents Demand Level of	Order	Random Number Selected	Represents Lead Time of
1	12	41	1	10	1
2	24	41	2	58	2
3	70	43	3	96	3
4	65	43	4	40	2
5	40	42	5	02	1
6	02	40	6	27	1
7	19	41	7	69	2
8	68	43			
9	56	43			
10	40	42			

---

[17] *Ibid.*, p. 514.

[18] The reader should be familiar with a table of random numbers from a basic statistics course. If necessary, he can consult any basic statistics text to refresh his memory.

FIGURE 12–2*

Phase 1: Stochastic Relationships

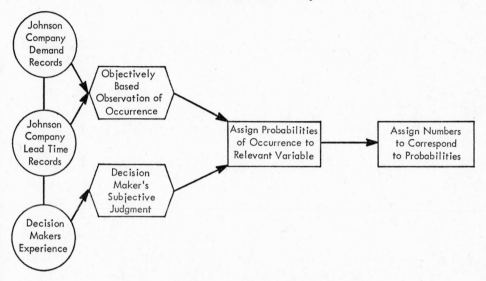

Phase 2: Monte Carlo Process to Obtain Simulations

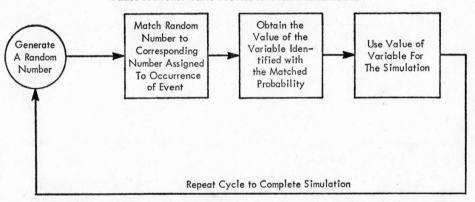

* The model for this specific problem is based upon a general model developed by Richards and Greenlaw, *op. cit.*, p. 515.

Suppose that by utilizing a table of random numbers we generate the data illustrated in Table 12–7.

If the store begins with an inventory of 70 and we are investigating the first ordering rule that when the inventory falls to a level of 70 or below we re-order, the simulations generated would be schematically represented as shown in Figure 12–3.

FIGURE 12–3

Simulation with 70-Shirt Reorder Schedule

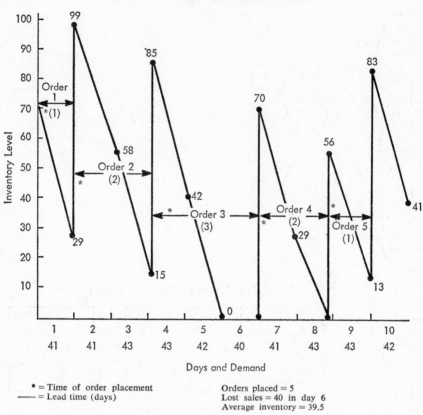

Days and Demand

* = Time of order placement
—— = Lead time (days)

Orders placed = 5
Lost sales = 40 in day 6
Average inventory = 39.5

The average inventory is calculated by making ten observations of the inventory level. In the 70-shirt reorder schedule the observations yield the following: $99 + 29/2 = 64$, 58, 50, 42, 0, 35, 29, 28, 48, and 41. This totals 395 and is divided by 10 observations to yield an average inventory of 39.5.

The second ordering rule simulation is presented schematically in Figure 12–4. In order to compare the two preestablished ordering rules, management would have to define the costs involved in this type of problem. Let us assume that the administrative costs of placing an order with the manufacturer is $9; that the cost of a lost sale is subjectively estimated (through experience and personal opinion) to be $1.75; the carrying costs associated with the in-

FIGURE 12–4

Simulation with 100-Shirt Reorder Schedule

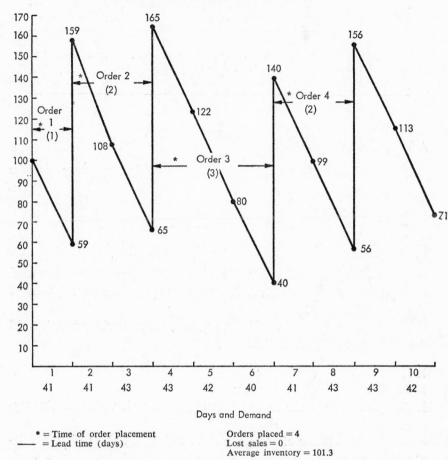

Days and Demand

* = Time of order placement
—— = Lead time (days)

Orders placed = 4
Lost sales = 0
Average inventory = 101.3

ventory of shirts is approximately \$.16 for each shirt of average inventory in the storeroom. The computation of costs associated with the two ordering rules is summarized in Table 12–8.

A review of the data presented in Table 12–8 indicates that if the choices available to the decision maker involve the 70-shirt reorder or the 100-shirt reorder, it would be most favorable from a monetary standpoint to adopt the 100-shirt reorder rule. The sample of only 10 simulations is considerably small and if a more accurate picture of the actual inventory situation is required, it would certainly be necessary to increase the sample size.

TABLE 12-8

Comparisons of Two Order Rules (70-shirt reorder and 100-shirt reorder)

	70-Shirt Reorder	*100-Shirt Reorder*
Ordering costs	$9 × 5 = $ 45.00	$9 × 4 = $36.00
Average inventory costs	39.5 × $.16 = $ 6.32	101.3 × $.16 = $16.21
Lost sales costs	40 × $1.75 = $ 70.00	–0–
Total costs	$121.32	$52.21

A Marketing Monte Carlo Simulation

In an elaborate Monte Carlo simulation involving numerous variables and iterations, it is advantageous to employ computer simulation procedures. Claycamp and Amstutz employed a detailed Monte Carlo simulation process to develop marketing strategies for drug firms.[19] The overall objective of the project was to develop a complete simulation of the prescription-drug market that would enable management to investigate in a synthetic environment the implications of (1) alternative strategies and (2) alternative policies without allocating financial and human resources required for investigations of this order in the real world.

In developing specifications for the system, the researchers were hopeful that the model could do the following:

1. Evaluate media effectiveness.
2. Evaluate sales force effectiveness.
3. Test particular policies and strategies for products in various market segments.
4. Evaluate the success of new products at their initial phase of market development.
5. Appraise the validity of management's understanding of the prescription-drug marketing system.

In developing a simulation of competitive market behavior, the firm and its competitors are viewed as input generators to the model. The external-market simulation is then developed to duplicate the response characteristics

[19] Henry J. Claycamp and Arnold E. Amstutz, "Simulation Techniques in the Analysis of Marketing Strategy," a paper presented at Purdue University, July 1966, at a symposium on the Applications of the Sciences in Marketing. Reprinted in Frank M. Bass, Charles W. King, and Edgar Pessemier, editors, *Applications of the Sciences in Marketing Management* (New York: John Wiley & Sons, Inc., 1968), pp. 113–149. The description which follows concerning the prescription drug simulation was developed by Claycamp and Amstutz.

of comparable real-markets to the inputs generated by the competing firms.

The preliminary conception of the prescription-drug environment is diagrammatically presented in Figure 12–5. This is a rather crude interpretation but it is an initial starting point in analyzing the problem. The lines connecting the various parties indicate the companies' interest in personal and promotional interactions between the relevant market elements.

FIGURE 12–5

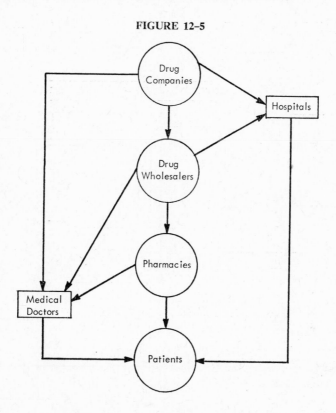

Figure 12–6 represents a more thorough specification of the system being studied. It is referred to as the macro specification for the prescription drug market. The flows of information are indicated by the connecting lines between parties, while *O* indicates orders, *P* designates prescriptions, and *I* designates information.

Some of the data sources for the model include monthly audits of drugstore invoices, weekly audits of prescriptions written, quarterly reports from panels of doctors who recorded treatment of patient illnesses, direct mail promotions, and salesman details used for promoting particular drugs.

FIGURE 12-6

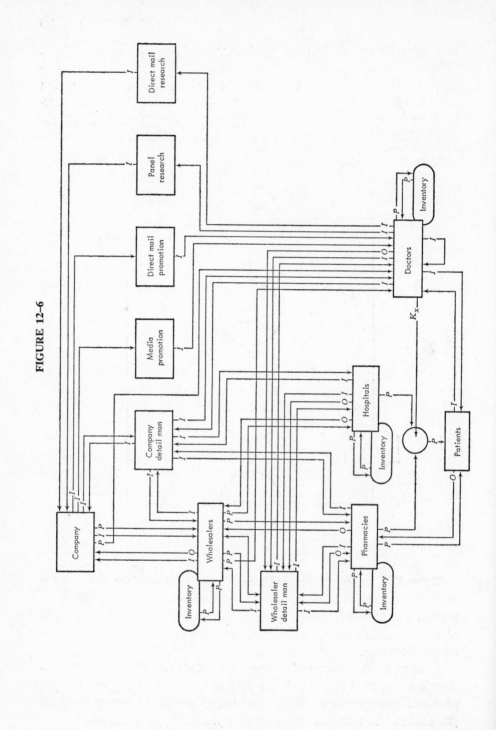

Instead of dealing with the macro specification in its entirety, let us discuss the basic logic of the details illustrated in Figure 12–6. This can be done by describing the simulation process employed in tracing the product flow from the company to the wholesaler and finally to the doctor.

The actual simulation involving medical doctors consists of a population of doctors, each of whom is represented on a computerized magnetic tape that includes such data as his area of specialty, patient load, probability that he will receive and be exposed to various promotion influences from companies, and geographical area in which the doctor's practice is located.

Each doctor's behavior is simulated at a specific time, in the manner summarized in the following paragraphs. Once the last doctor in the population has been processed, a summary report is provided which yields such measures as drug usage by company and brand that resulted from the particular configuration of inputs (e.g., advertising message, number of calls by detail men) for each drug firm as well as the configuration of illnesses that occurred during the time period being analyzed.

1. *Drug file input data.* Each simulated doctor is described by the content of a doctor file record. Doctor files are recorded on tape (computer) sequentially by geographic region. A single doctor file is held in core (computer) at a given point in time. After simulating the doctor's activity for a specified period of time (e.g., one week, two weeks, or one month), the file is updated to reflect his experiences, and recorded on tape. A new doctor is then read into core, and the procedure is repeated. This continues until the entire doctor population is considered.

2. *The time loop.* The system is structured so that time is moved past each doctor in turn. This organization is necessitated by the large size of the doctor-file record, which makes it impractical to move doctors in and out of core or to maintain more than one doctor in core at a given point in time.

For most simulation runs, the period considered is one simulated year. The time step is one week and the time index (IT) proceeds sequentially from one through 52.

3. *Doctor response to media promotion.* During each week in simulated time, the publication frequency of each relevant journal is tested to determine whether it is published during the week under consideration. If a particular journal appears, the probability of the doctor then under consideration being exposed to that journal is developed. If, on the basis of this probability, it is determined that the doctor will be exposed to the journal, each advertisement appearing in an advertising schedule table for that journal is examined to determine whether or not the doctor will be exposed to and assimilate any new

information. When an advertisement is assimilated, the doctor's response to the message is established and his memory updated to take account of information content. This process is continued for all media messages and doctors at each point in time.

4. *Direct-mail response.* The handling of direct-mail response is structured in a manner analogous to media promotion. During each simulated period of time, a comparison is made to determine whether any direct-mail pieces appear. If a direct-mail piece is being sent during the week in question, exposure probabilities are developed to determine whether the particular doctor being considered will be exposed to the specified mailing. If exposure occurs, assimilation probabilities are generated and if, on the basis of these probabilities, it is determined that the doctor will assimilate portions of the communication, his response is determined and his memory updated.

5. *Response to salesman detail.* In developing a representation of the doctor's response to salesman communication, the probability of exposure is first determined on the basis of parameter values in the doctor-file record that establish the probability that the doctor will receive a call from a salesman representing any one of the relevant companies. If the doctor is exposed to a salesman from a particular company, the schedule of details (sales messages for a specific drug) presented by that salesman is examined to determine which details are being presented to doctors of the indicated specialty during the week under consideration. If a particular detail is presented and assimilation occurs, the doctor's memory is updated. As in the case of all other communication response loops, this procedure continues until all sales messages have been considered.

6. *Response to convention activity.* Exposure to presentations at a convention is based on a convention schedule that specifies the probability of a doctor of a particular specialty and residence attending a convention held at a particular time. In keeping with the previously established procedure, the convention schedule is examined once during each simulated period of time to determine whether a convention is being held. If a convention is being held, the probability of the doctor then in core (computer) attending that convention is determined and, if the doctor is found to have attended the convention, procedures similar to those outlined above are used to determine exposure to and assimilation of relevant information.

7. *Response to word-of-mouth communication.* Within the structure of the simulation, messages generated by doctors in a particular region are accumulated along with descriptors of the generating doctor in a table of word-of-mouth messages. Thus, when a particular doctor is in core (computer), messages generated at various points in time by doctors preceding him are

available in the word-of-mouth table. This table is referenced in a manner analogous to the schedule and content table discussed for other media. The probability of interaction between the doctor in core (computer) and the message-generating doctor who preceded him is established. If the doctor is exposed to the word-of-mouth communication, the probability of assimilation is developed in a manner analogous to other communication functions and the doctor's memory is updated to reflect the word-of-mouth interaction.

8. *Treatment of patients.* The simulated doctor is exposed to patients from an artificial patient population that is supplied as an input to the simulation. An average patient load parameter in each doctor-file record determines how many patients will be treated in a given week. In treating a patient, the simulated doctor determines what drug or drugs, if any, will be prescribed for the patient.

Once treatment has been decided upon, the probability that it will achieve desired results is established on the basis of clinical data. If it is determined that the treatment undertaken will not prove effective within a specified period of time, the patient is maintained in a backlog of patients who will return to the doctor at some time in the future. If the outcome of medical treatment is successful, the patient is, for all practical purposes, dropped from the model. In either instance, the trial and outcome (including possible side effects) of a particular treatment is noted.

After the first simulated period of time, the doctor has two sources of patients: (1) patients in the population from which his original patient group was drawn; and (2) patients who require continuing treatment. During subsequent time periods, the doctor's first source of patients is the returning-patient file. After all patients previously treated and scheduled to return have been treated, the doctor considers new patients from the outside population.

9. *Generation of word-of-mouth communication.* As the doctor considers various drugs in context of the treatment during the simulated period, a record of his attitude toward his experiences is maintained. Following completion of the treatment cycle for a particular simulated period, this record is examined to determine whether the doctor will generate word-of-mouth communication regarding some aspect of his recent treatment experience. If such word-of-mouth communication is generated, communication content is established, dated, and stored in the word-of-mouth communication file for later referencing by other doctors.

10. *Forgetting.* At certain prescribed time intervals, the doctor's memory is examined to determine whether forgetting would have occurred during the lapsed time period. The memory record for each drug is examined and if forgetting has occurred, the record is reduced.

11. *Time cycle combination.* The basic process described above is repeated for each period (week) in the simulated year for each doctor in the artificial population. Once the final simulated period for a particular doctor is completed, an activity report is generated and the doctor file is updated to reflect his experiences during the simulated year. This record is then written on tape to serve as an input for simulation of future time periods.[20]

Once the prescription drug simulation is developed to a point where it is able to produce and generate artificial behavior, the emphasis shifts to testing. Specifically, the reliability and validity of any simulation model should be ascertained before it is used as an operational device.[21]

The Claycamp-Amstutz simulation model is an example of a detailed simulation process which has tremendous potential for marketing decision makers. It allows them to analyze complex interactive systems and decision processes.

FACILITY PLANNING (QUEUING THEORY)

The store manager, the warehouseman, the barber, and other business managers are occasionally faced with situations in which their customers have to wait for service. Such situations are often described in terms of customers arriving at a service facility (e.g., check-out counter in a supermarket) and waiting in line for service. The waiting lines that form at a service facility are referred to as queues. While our discussion of queuing theory could have been appropriately placed in Chapter Eight (Distribution), we have decided to defer it until now, where the reader will have a greater appreciation of simulation.

The marketing manager is usually concerned with the development of queues because slow service may often lead to a loss of sales. The customer being a part of a dynamic and fast moving society such as ours, places a premium value on promptness of service. Those firms or stores that are not providing prompt service find that customers often will go elsewhere. The marketing manager's dilemma is one of bringing about some degree of balance between the cost of lost sales and the cost of providing additional service facilities.

In the supermarket checkout problem, if the manager wants to reduce the length of waiting time that occurs at a single checkout counter, he can add another cash register and checkout facility. Each addition of equipment and personnel adds to expense, but at the same time it reduces the waiting line at each service facility. Thus, there is a limit on how much can be spent to reduce queues and the manager must weigh this against customer ill will.

---

[20] *Ibid.;* paper is quoted with slight revisions.
[21] *Ibid.*

Queuing Terminology

As is the case in algebra, linear programming, statistics, and other areas employing mathematics, queuing theory has its own unique language. Before the mathematical procedures employed in studying waiting lines are presented, it is desirable to become familiar with the basic terminology. Some basic terms which are widely utilized are presented below.

The *arrival rate* refers to the average rate at which people or items (e.g., trucks at a loading dock) arrive at a service facility. This rate is usually expressed as a rate of arrival per unit of time. That is, it could take the form of nine housewives per hour arriving at a checkout facility in a supermarket.

The *service rate* designates the rate at which the particular service facility can handle the incoming calls for service. It is expressed as a rate per unit of time. For example, Mary Smith, at Checkout Register 8 can process five average orders per hour or Loading Team A can load five trucks per hour.

The manner in which arrivals and servicing times are distributed has a significant impact on resolving waiting line problems. For example, arrivals can be random over time or the arrival of people or items can be uniform in that they do not vary. A *random arrival* situation exists if there is no logical pattern of arrival of customers requiring service. That is, in the first hour of business, 50 customers arrived at the service facility, the second hour 18 customers arrive, the third no customers appear, and the remainder of the day the pattern continues to fluctuate each hour. Arrival rates that are *uniform* have a logical consistency. For example, through the period of time being considered five customers arrive every hour. In most business situations involving queues, the arrivals are usually *randomly distributed*.

The amount of time necessary to service a customer or a machine can be either *randomly or uniformly distributed*. The fact that servicing times are randomly distributed is caused by the type of service required. For example, a warehouse loading crew may have to load boxcars and trucks. The times required to service these modes of transportation depend on such factors as the size of the truck or boxcar, the type of items being loaded, the number of men in the loading crew, and the distance between the loading site and the place where the items are stored.

The servicing rates may also be uniformly distributed. That is, each person or item which requires service takes the same amount of time as every other person or item. An example of uniform service rates would be found in the inspection of items being mass produced. In inspection of color television tubes there is no valid reason why the inspection of one tube should take any longer than the inspection of other tubes.

A Waiting Line Problem

To highlight the terminology and concepts used in queuing theory, a sample problem is used. Assume that the Farley Distribution Corporation is concerned with randomly distributed arrival and service times at its warehouse loading department. The company loads from its warehouse two-ton trucks which distribute their loads throughout Chicago. The loading expenses are a part of a spiraling distribution cost picture which the company is trying to control. A method that can be employed in analyzing the truck queues that develop daily is to simulate the random arrivals at the loading dock. This can be accomplished by use of random number tables (See Appendix A). By use of random number tables it is possible to simulate the random arrival of trucks at the loading dock. These data can then be utilized to assign warehousemen in optimum numbers so that a balance between service time and waiting time is achieved.

The Farley Company has assigned six warehouse men to load trucks. The number of trucks that appear for loading on a daily basis averages 10. It has been noticed that occasionally trucks are lined up waiting to be loaded. Management is considering the possibility of increasing the size of the warehouse crew responsible for loading trucks.

For a period of three months the loading dock operations are observed for two-hour periods each day. These observation periods are randomly selected during the day in order to acquire a representative sample of the loading dock's activities. The following data is collected over the three-month study period.

A. Total number of trucks to be
    loaded (observed)   = 100
B. Average time between arrivals = 40 minutes
C. Different times for loading:

60 minutes	20
65 minutes	30
70 minutes	40
75 minutes	10
Total observations	100

A percentage distribution of the loading times is calculated as follows:

$$20/100 = 20\% \text{ (60 minutes)}$$
$$30/100 = 30\% \text{ (65 minutes)}$$

$$40/100 = 40\% \text{ (70 minutes)}$$
$$10/100 = 10\% \text{ (75 minutes)}$$

The weighted average of loading times can be calculated as follows:

$$20\% \times 60 \text{ minutes} = 12.00$$
$$30\% \times 65 \text{ minutes} = 19.50$$
$$40\% \times 70 \text{ minutes} = 28.00$$
$$10\% \times 75 \text{ minutes} = \underline{7.50}$$
$$67.00 \text{ minutes}$$

The data collected and analyzed allows the decision maker to simulate the operation of the loading dock. The first task is to simulate the arrival of trucks at the dock. We know that there is a high probability that there will be one or more arrivals within any given 40-minute period. We will use a random number table (see Appendix A) to simulate the number of arrivals in each 40-minute period. The average work day is approximately 11 hours, which means that 15 40-minute periods have to be examined. The workers have a 40-minute paid snack break and a 30 minute nonpaid lunch break. Since there is better than a 50 percent chance that a truck will arrive every 40 minutes, we can use the first two columns (10 digits) in the random number table. We can select a digit (perhaps 4) and let it represent an arrival. The values in the first two columns which are used to simulate the 15 40-minute periods are reproduced as follows:

		Number of 4's Appearing
31827	80191	0
92204	68347	2
72608	47319	1
71171	34112	1
30238	58381	0
97806	63153	0
68901	15231	0
51517	35148	1
96035	69002	0
40704	12590	2
99130	52082	0
71335	76694	1
13116	26616	0
97727	69749	1
55499	59891	1

The number of 4's we find in each 10-digit random number represents the number of trucks arriving at the loading dock during a normal 11-hour working day (recall that there is better than a 50 percent chance that a truck will arrive each forty minutes).

The above analysis using random numbers has simulated the truck arrival times. Now it is necessary to simulate the loading times. Assume the service times are distributed randomly in the following manner:

Time for Loading	% of Time
60 minutes	20%
65 minutes	30%
70 minutes	40%
75 minutes	10%

Because we are using a random number table with 10 digits, we can analyze our simulated loading times in the following manner:

A. Let 0 and 1 designate the probabilities of a loading time of 60 minutes (note that there is a two in 10 chance that it will take 60 minutes to load).
B. Let 2, 3, and 4 designate the probabilities of a loading time of 65 minutes.
C. Let 5, 6, 7, and 8 designate the probabilities of a loading time of 70 minutes.
D. Let 9 designate the probability of a loading time of 75 minutes.

TABLE 12–9
Simulated Arrivals

40-minute Periods	Simulated Arrivals (random numbers)	Service Time for Each
1	0	
2	2	65 min. and 70 min.
3	1	70 min.
4	1	65 min.
5	0	
6	0	
7	0	
8	1	60 min.
9	0	
10	2	65 min. and 70 min.
11	0	
12	1	70 min.
13	0	
14	1	65 min.
15	1	70 min.

Because we have two chances in 10 of getting a 0 or 1, it represents a .2 probability. Because we have three chances in 10 of getting a 2, 3, or 4, it represents a .3 probability. The other digits are analyzed in a similar manner in deriving the probabilities. The simulated arrivals of trucks for each of the 15 periods are presented in Table 12–9. To simulate the service times we utilize the first digit in Column 3 of the table of random numbers in Appendix A. The digits are related to the probability discussion on the previous page.

Now both the arrival and loading times have been simulated and the decision maker now must determine the optimum number of warehouse men. The management of Farley is concerned with minimizing the total cost of warehouse operation plus time lost (idle time for the truck drivers) by waiting in line for loading.

The standard loading rule of first-come-first-loaded is strictly practiced. The following guidelines are utilized in analyzing the waiting line problem:

1. If there is one arrival, it will be assumed to occur at the beginning of the 40-minute period.
2. If there are two arrivals, one will be assumed to arrive at the beginning of the 40-minute period and the other at the beginning of the twenty-first minute.

FIGURE 12–7

Schematic Presentation of Arrival, Loading, and Waiting Times,
8:00 A.M. to Lunch

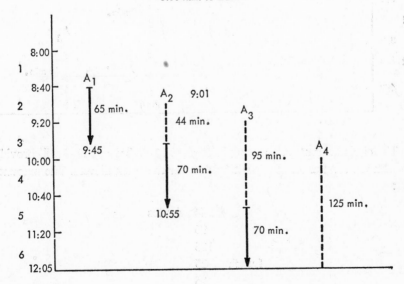

The simulation is begun at 8:00 A.M. From 8:00 until 8:40 A.M. there are no arrivals. The entire 15 periods can be illustrated in schematic format in three separate diagrams. In each diagram the following symbols are used:

$$A_i = \text{arrival}$$

= being loaded

= waiting

FIGURE 12–8

Schematic Presentation of Arrival, Loading, and Waiting Times
(after lunch) 12:30 P.M.–4:50
(coffee break and snack)

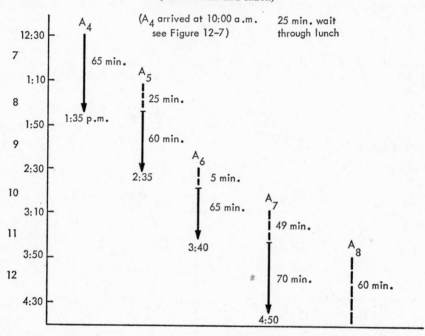

The circled minutes appearing in Figures 12–7 through 12–9 will provide us with the total amount of waiting time for the truck drivers. The amounts are:

44 minutes
95
125
Lunch   25
25

$$
\begin{array}{r}
5 \\
49 \\
60 \\
\text{Snack}\quad 40 \\
30 \\
\underline{55} \\
\text{Total waiting time}\quad 553
\end{array}
$$

Thus, the average waiting time is $\dfrac{\text{Total Waiting Time}}{\text{Number of Arrivals}} = \dfrac{553}{10} = 55.3$ minutes.
This is the average idle time for each truck driver. The time the truck driver spends during loading is not idle time since he is aiding the warehouse crew in the loading activities.

FIGURE 12–9

Schematic Presentation of Arrival, Loading, and Waiting Times 5:30 P.M.–7:30 P.M.

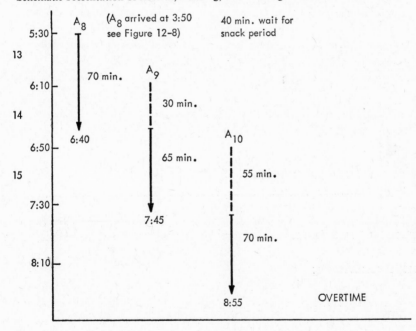

The warehouse crew is paid $4.00 an hour for regular time and $6.00 per hour for any time worked after 7:30 P.M. Thus, the total wage costs of warehousemen are:

Regular Wage: $6 \times \$4.00 \times 11\text{-hour work day} = \$264.00$
Overtime Wage: $6 \times \$6.00 \times 1.42 \text{ overtime} \quad = \quad 51.12$

The 1.42 represents the difference between 7:30 P.M. and 8:55 P.M. (1 hour and 25 minutes) which is 1.42 hours.

The trucking firms have agreed with the Farley management that the trucking firms will receive a waiting time reimbursement based upon the average waiting time calculated in the simulation. Each driver then is entitled to a reimbursement based upon 55.3 minutes of waiting time. Since the drivers are all

FIGURE 12–10

Schematic Presentation of Arrival, Loading, and Waiting
Times 8:00 A.M. to 11:30, Two Crews

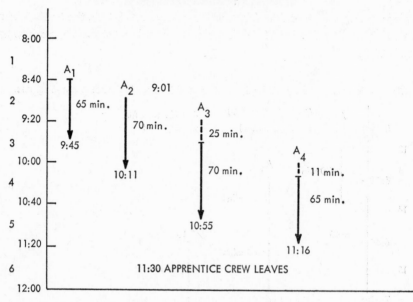

union members, the rate is based upon an hourly wage and inconvenience fee which totals $30.00 per hour or $.50 per minute. The driver reimbursement rate is calculated as:

$$10 \times 55.3 \times \$.50 = \$276.50$$

The total costs of the present arrangement are:

A. Regular wage	=	$264.00
B. Overtime wage	=	51.12
C. Trucker reimbursement	=	276.50
	Total	$591.62

The Farley management believes that using an apprentice crew of warehousemen in the morning can reduce the wage and waiting line expenses incurred by the company. The apprentice group works at the same efficiency

FIGURE 12–11

Schematic Presentation of Arrival, Loading, and Waiting Times
(After Lunch) 12:30–4:30 . .
(coffee break and snack)

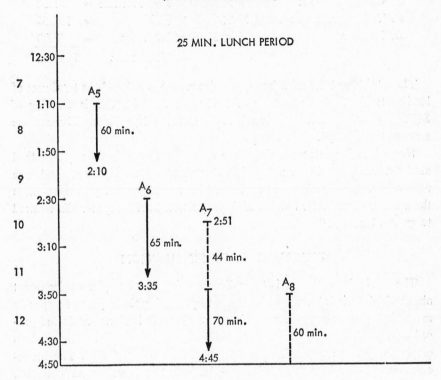

level as the journeymen loading group but are paid only $2.00 per hour be-
cause they are not full-fledged union members. Figures 12–10 and 12–11 illustrate the arrival, loading, and waiting time situation when two crews are
utilized. There is enough dock space to accommodate two crews loading two
trucks at the same time.

The remainder of the times remain the same since the one journeyman crew
is utilized. The second crew in the morning reduces the total waiting time from
a total of 553 minutes to 265 minutes.

$$\text{Figure 12–10} \begin{cases} 25 \\ 11 \end{cases}$$

$$\text{Figure 12–11} \begin{cases} 44 \\ 60 \end{cases}$$

$$\text{Figure 12–9} \begin{cases} 40 \text{ snack} \\ 30 \\ 55 \end{cases}$$

The average waiting time is now $265/10 = 26.5$. The total costs for the two crew alternative are calculated as follows:

A. Regular wage: $6 \times \$4.00 \times 11$ hours $= \$264.00$
B. Overtime wage: $6 \times \$6.00 \times 1.42$ overtime $=$ 51.12
C. Trucker reimbursement $10 \times 26.5 \times \$.50$ $=$ 132.50
D. 2d crew $6 \times \$2.00 \times 3.5$ hours $=$ 42.00

                                                    Total costs $\$489.62$

The addition of the morning apprentice crew has reduced the total cost of loading trucks from an average of \$591.62 to \$489.62. This is a saving of \$102.00 per day. On an annual basis of 250 working days this would constitute a savings of \$25,500.

Not all waiting line problems are currently amenable to mathematical analysis. The procedure employed in this chapter can only be utilized with relatively simple distribution problems. Like so many other problems, when the number of variables reaches high proportions, the computer can be used to great advantage.[22]

EVALUATION OF SIMULATION

The marketing manager is typically operating in a complex environment about which little is known with respect to predicting the impact of a specific marketing strategy or program decision.[23] Such optimization models and procedures as linear programming frequently utilize gross simplifications such as employing linear relationships between variables being studied. The break-even analysis requires accurate information about costs, prices, and demand. It, however, does not take into consideration a series of cost, price, and demand changes over an extended period of time. Many of the other models and techniques previously discussed in the text resort to similar oversimplifications of complex environmental and organizational phenomena.

The major problem associated with oversimplifying is that the analytical model and its outputs do not consider some important real life parameters. This of course leads to results that deviate significantly from real world circumstances. The use of simulation models hopefully interjects more realism into the analyses and the outcomes. It is assumed by simulation advocates that once a simulation model has been adequately developed and tested, ob-

---

[22] For an additional discussion of queuing theory, see Richard I. Levin and C. A. Kirkpatrick, *Quantitative Approaches to Management* (New York: McGraw-Hill Book Company, Inc., 1965), Chapter 12.

[23] Weitz, *op. cit.*, p. 30.

servations of the model can be used to derive and test new theories and hypotheses.[24]

There have been numerous advantages of using simulation in marketing decision making cited by scholars and practitioners. Some of the purported advantages are:

1. Simulation procedures can be used to explore the validity and implications of the marketing managers' perceptions about environmental factors. The marketing team of an organization and others working on marketing problems can pool their talents and data about consumers, products, markets, and other related phenomena and study specific marketing programs. The result of the pooling effort can be transmitted to the management scientist (operations researcher) who will put them into a simulation format. The ultimate result of these efforts will hopefully be a simulation model that can predict outcome(s).[25]

2. Simulation provides the marketing decision maker with a method for performing experimentation even where precise input data is not available. It enables one to conduct a series of experiments by hand, hand-machine, and/or machine, using the simulation model to describe some process without disrupting the ongoing operations of a firm.[26]

3. Simulation models can be used to integrate in an orderly manner large quantities of information obtained from past marketing research studies and secondary sources. The simulation process aids the marketing decision maker in integrating isolated bits of information and this procedure often increases the value of the model to the decision maker.

4. A simulation model which has been accepted as a reasonable representation of the relevant aspects of the real world can be used as a guide for future research activities. If the developer of the model has confidence in the structure of the system, he can perform sensitivity analysis[27] with respect to various component characteristics. The various sensitivity tests will help to indicate what kinds of additional empirical or theoretical research will have the greatest impact upon the overall accuracy of the model.

5. Once a simulation process has been validated to the satisfaction of the personnel working with the model, the method of artificial experimentation

---

[24] George W. Morgenthaler, "The Theory and Application of Simulation in Operations Research," in Russell L. Ackoff, editor, *Progress in Operations Research* (New York: John Wiley and Sons, Inc., 1965), p. 367.

[25] Claycamp and Amstutz, *op. cit.*

[26] Weitz, *op. cit.*, p. 30.

[27] The purpose of sensitivity analysis is to determine the parameters and inputs to which the simulation model output is most sensitive. For an excellent discussion of sensitivity analysis, see Montgomery and Urban, *op. cit.*, pp. 47–52.

can be utilized to derive forecasts of sales levels, profits, or other criteria variables conditioned upon alternative specifications of the elements of the firm's marketing mix. The model can act as a kind of synthetic test and can be used to screen alternative strategies.[28]

6. There are a number of computer programs available which, because of their simplicity, can be readily employed with simulation models. For example, SIMSCRIPT is widely used throughout the United States and is relatively easy to understand and learn. These languages allow both experts and nonexperts in computer applications to deal with simulation models.

Despite this impressive list of advantages, which is definitely not exhaustive, there are a number of disadvantages which are commonly associated with simulation. The use of simulation models poses a number of problems and limitations to the marketing decision maker. Some of the most often cited disadvantages are the following:

1. The use of simulation models that are sophisticated and realistic are time consuming. This is due to the numerous simulation runs that are required to study the behavior of the system under investigation. As the number of input variables increases, the number of interrelationships and outcomes increases at a factorial level.

2. The sophisticated simulation model which includes many variables can be expensive. For example, computer time, researchers to develop the model, computer programmers, and researchers to test the model cost money. A recent survey of the level of expenditures for simulations of social, political, and economic systems provides some idea of the costs involved. Of 41 projects for which financial data was available, 20 were reported to have cost between $10,000 and $100,000, and 17 over $100,000. Some of the projects reported cost in excess of $2,000,000.[29] Thus, if an organization is short of funds, they may find that expenditures for simulation models do not yield favorable short-run results.

3. The publicity provided simulation models in recent years has led some over zealous advocates to conclude that simulated outcomes are always more valid than analytical results. This type of philosophy can lead to inappropriate utilization of simulation models. It would be beneficial to place simulation models in proper perspective. A simulation model should only be utilized where it is more efficient than employing an analytical technique.

4. Formidable problems are present in testing simulation models. Most

---

[28] The advantages cited in numbers 3, 4, and 5 were specified originally by Claycamp and Amstutz, *op. cit.* and are slightly revised.

[29] Clark C. Abt, et al., *Survey of the State of the Art: Social, Political, and Economic Models and Simulations* (Cambridge, Mass.: Abt Associates, November, 1965), pp. 64–65.

models contain so many parameters that it is impossible to do sensitivity analyses on all possible combinations of values. Thus, the researcher must use judgment or a formal technique (e.g., random sampling) to select specific values to be included in sensitivity tests—and hope that feasible, but untested, values will not cause the model to behave in an erratic fashion.[30]

5. Ascertaining the validity of a simulation model is also a complicated task. The researcher must decide which aspects of the system under investigation are to be used as evaluative criteria and how close the simulation model output must be before it can be said to be valid. This type of decision is difficult and involves highly subjective conclusions.[31]

THE NEXT ERA OF SIMULATION EVOLUTION

In this chapter a number of existing marketing simulation models have been briefly introduced. Most of these are relatively simple in comparison to what some experts are predicting will be the next phase of development. There is currently a trend toward the development and testing of more sophisticated, complex, and mathematically oriented models. An example of the possibilities in various marketing areas would be in moving from conceptualization to the operational level in market share analysis.

Market Share Predictions

There are a number of brand loyalty and brand switching models which are currently utilized by marketing decision makers. They basically involve employing Markov analysis and various stochastic models. In most of the existing models such factors as competition and promotional strategies are not treated.

A conceptual model developed by Barton[32] deals with sales predictions over a short period of time. This type of conceptual analysis can be expanded into an operational model for predicting short term sales and relating these sales to various promotional strategies.

The prediction model would view a consumer at two different points in time: prior to the point of sale, and at the point of sale. The environmental factors influencing the purchaser are termed consumer momentum, customer

---

[30] Claycamp and Amstutz, *op. cit.*

[31] *Ibid.*

[32] Samuel G. Barton, "A Marketing Model for Short Term Prediction of Consumer Sales," *Journal of Marketing*, Vol. 29 (July, 1965), pp. 19–29.

intention to change, share of shelf space, and consumer-deal offerings.[33] For example, the factors influencing a consumer's intention to change his purchase patterns include among other things the following:

1. Share of general advertising by company.
2. Share of shelf and display stocks company is able to receive.
3. Share of new product announcements company is responsible for.

There are other areas in marketing in which simulation will grow in importance. Among these will be advertising, evaluation of the effectiveness of sales training programs, market planning, market structure, information systems, and competitive gaming.

PROBLEMS

1. Briefly define the following terms:
A. Analytical model
B. Nonanalytical model
C. Input data (simulation model)
D. TOMES
E. Marketing games

2. In a marketing problem involving stochastic variables, would it be practical to utilize the Monte Carlo technique? Why?

3. What are the major differences between hand, machine, and man-machine simulation procedures?

4. Would you classify the prescription-drug simulation discussed in this chapter a hand procedure? Why?

5. Utilizing the demand and lead time data presented in Table 12–7 from the Monte Carlo simulation:
A. Simulate the effect of each of the following ordering rules for a 10-day period. Whenever inventories at the beginning of a day have fallen to:
   1. A level of 60 or below, reorder 60.
   2. A level of 110 or below, reorder 110.
B. For each of the above rules construct a schematic diagram such as those illustrated in Figures 12–3 and 12–4.
C. Determine what total costs would be incurred for each ordering rule if the following cost data applies:

> 1. Cost of placing an order = $12
> 2. Average inventory costs = $.09
> 3. Lost sales cost/unit   = $.97

6. What would be some of the input variables you would consider if you were working with a simulation model concerned with introducing new products into the marketplace?

---

[33] This move from conceptualization to operationality is suggested by Weitz, *op. cit.*, p. 32.

7. What is the major advantage (one) of utilizing simulation models?

8. What is the major disadvantage (one) of utilizing simulation models?

9. How would you assign numbers to the occurrence of the following events in conjunction with the Monte Carlo technique?

Number of Salesmen Required to Sell 100 Units	Frequency of Occurrence Percent
1	8
2	11
3	14
4	16
5	15
6	18
7	10
8	3
9	3
10	2

A. Assign numbers to the occurrence of the events.

B. Describe how you would use a table of random numbers to generate 15 simulation runs.

10. The Mackman Supply Distribution Company operates one supply window for customers who drive up in their cars for repair parts. Currently Mr. William Jannotta is the only employee servicing these drive up customers. The arrival of customers for service is found to be at a uniform rate of 20 per hour, and Jannotta is able to handle these requests at a uniform rate of 19 per hour.

(a) How much waiting time is likely to be generated in four hours; six hours; and 10 hours?

(b) If the uniform arrival rate increases to 21, what would be the waiting time generated after four hours; six hours; and 10 hours?

11. Describe the characteristics of a table of random numbers. What are the uses of a table of random numbers in quantitative decision making?

REFERENCES

BALDERSTON, F. E. AND HOGGATT, AUSTEN C. *Simulation of Market Processes.* Berkeley: Institute of Business and Economic Research, University of California, 1962.

BONINI, CHARLES P. *Simulation of Information and Decision Systems in the Firm.* Englewood Cliffs, N.J.: Prentice-Hall, Inc., 1963.

BONINI, C. P., JAEDICKE, R. K., AND WAGNER, H. M. *Management Controls: New Directions in Basic Research.* New York: McGraw-Hill Book Company, Inc., 1964.

COHEN, K. J., DILL, N. R., KUEHN, A. A., AND WINTERS, P. R. *The Carnegie Tech Management Game.* Homewood, Ill.: Richard D. Irwin, Inc., 1964.

FORRESTER, J. W. *Industrial Dynamics.* Cambridge, Massachusetts: and New York: The M. I. T. Press and John Wiley & Sons, Inc., 1961.

GREENLAW, P., HERRON, L., AND RAWDON, R.   *Business Simulation.* Englewood Cliffs, N.J.: Prentice-Hall, 1962.

GUETZKOW, H. (ED.).   *Simulation in Social Science: Readings.* Englewood Cliffs, N.J.: Prentice-Hall, Inc., 1962.

ORCUTT, G. H., GREENBERGER, M., KORBEL, J., AND REVLIN, A. H.   *Microanalysis of Socio-Economic Systems.* New York: Harper & Row, 1961.

SCHELLENBERGER, R.   *Managerial Analysis.* Homewood, Ill.: Richard D. Irwin, Inc., 1969.

Simulatics Media-Mix: Technical Description.   New York: The Simulatics Corporation, 1962.

TOCHER, K. D.   *The Art of Simulation.* Princeton, N.J.: Van Nostrand Company, Inc., 1963.

chapter thirteen

THE FUTURE OF ANALYTICAL METHODS IN MARKETING

INTRODUCTION

As indicated previously, both marketing scholars and practitioners have been eye witnesses to a growing movement toward the use of analytical methods in marketing. Such terms as "operations research," "mathematical models," "systems analysis," and "model building" have been widely used with a myriad of claims and counterclaims made for each with respect to its impact on the field of marketing. In this chapter we shall attempt to take an objective look at the future expectations of analytical methods in marketing.

The Growth of Management Science

While some individuals would probably claim that the field of management science has been with us for centuries, we take the view that management science has formally existed for the last twenty years. We take this viewpoint because it was during this period that such professional societies as The Institute of Management Sciences and The Operations Research Society of America were formed. The activities of these groups have been characterized by an emphasis on the mathematical modeling of systems. Their approach and techniques, however, have been drawn from a wide variety of fields, including psychology, mathematics, economics, and statistics.

While management science has grown tremendously, the early efforts of those utilizing quantitative methods seems to have been directed toward other areas of business with little emphasis on marketing. An examination of the management science literature reveals a prolific outpouring of applications and models for problems in production scheduling, equipment replacement, inventory control, equipment maintenance, and waiting lines. However, during the decade 1950–1960 only 3 percent of some ten thousand manuscripts were devoted to applications for marketing problems.[1] Although this was definitely a slow start, there has been a definite trend during the 1960's toward increased interest in marketing applications on the part of the management scientist. Thus, it is safe to say that during the 1970's as the field of management science matures as a discipline, we can expect more attention being focused on marketing problems.

Types of Problems Studied

In Chapter Two a continuum was developed along which types of problems could be placed depending upon their degree of complexity and the types of variables involved. It was stated that the majority of marketing problems lean toward the right side of the continuum, that is, they are "complex and disorganized" containing many stochastic variables. For the convenience of the reader this continuum is reproduced as Figure 13–1.

FIGURE 13–1

Problem (Simple-Complex) Continuum

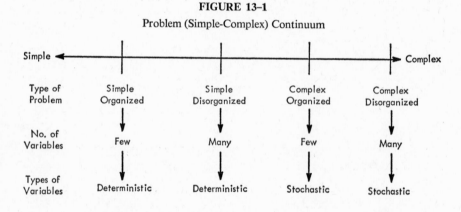

It seems reasonable to conclude that during the 1950–1960 decade, management scientists directed their efforts toward relatively well-defined problem areas such as inventory control and various scheduling problems, where somewhat straightforward relationships appeared to exist among a small number of variables. In other words, the problems analyzed were those which leaned toward the left end of the continuum, that is, were "simple and organized" and contained a small number of deterministic variables. In fact, two writers made the following comment in 1958:

[1] Michael Halbert, *The Meaning and Sources of Marketing Theory* (New York: McGraw-Hill Book Company, Inc., 1965), p. 128.

Operations research has made large contributions to those management decisions that can be reduced to systematic computational routines. To date, comparable progress has not been made in applying scientific techniques to judgmental decisions that cannot be so reduced.[2]

Thus, we can conclude that in general the early models developed by management scientists tended to be of static, deterministic systems. The less structured problems (those leaning toward the right side of the continuum) received relatively little attention. Early marketing applications were concerned with such problem classifications as physical distribution and inventory control, which are relatively static, deterministic, and controllable in nature.

The paucity of early management science applications to marketing does not imply, however, that no substantive contributions were made. The initial impact was more subtle and indirect. It created an awareness in many individuals of the great need to become more explicit in the formulation of marketing problems. Thus, this interest and curiosity in the early days of management science was to make its impact at a later date with a more highly quantified approach to marketing problem solving.

In recent years, management science activity can be summarized by noting two significant trends:[3]

1. A break with the "algorithm consciousness" of earlier management science efforts and an increased effort to develop techniques to cope with less structured problems.

2. Extensions of earlier analytical techniques to deal with the type of time-dependent, interactive world faced by the marketer.

These trends have important implications for marketing decision makers. As time passes, we can expect more attention being devoted to problems which are more complex and probabilistic in nature. In other words, management scientists will begin analyzing those types of problems which lean toward the right end of the simple-complex continuum. As we move along the continuum, more and more attention will be given to solving less structured problems which are probabilistic and dynamic in nature. As we mentioned previously, most problems faced by marketing decision makers are of this type. Halbert summarizes the implications of these trends as follows:

. . . it appears that management science is at last attempting to come to grips with the behavioralistic elements, interdependencies, and variability which characterize marketing (and other) currently ill-structured systems. (We need only remember

---

[2] H. A. Simon and A. Newell, "Heuristic Problem Solving," *Operations Research*, VI, 1 (January, 1958), p. 3.

[3] Halbert, *op. cit.*, p. 130.

that "ill-structured" is a relative term which could have been applied to inventory control, say, twenty years ago.)[4]

In addition to management science, such fields as econometrics, systems engineering, and the various social and behavioral sciences are also making progress in coping with the complexities of man-machine systems. In the future, we can expect the interdisciplinary approach of studying business problems to continue and intensify.

The reader should not construe the above as an indication that analytical methods in marketing are widely utilized in all business organizations. In fact, Kotler has stated that, "Over 99% of all marketing decisions in the country are still made on the basis of intuitive judgment unaided by any advanced mathematical analysis."[5] However, in a small but increasing number of firms the traditional ways of making marketing decisions (intuition and experience) are giving way to more analytical methods for marketing decision making.

Evidence of this growing ferment can be seen by examining marketing literature. By the late 1960's the published literature had grown to include a bibliography which listed over 200 marketing articles of a mathematical nature and several collections of readings.[6] In addition, there are a variety of other indicators. For example, there is an increasing number of universities which sponsor short summer courses in analytical methods in marketing. These programs have received wide support from the business community. Finally, in 1966 The Diebold Group, Inc. sent a detailed questionnaire to business organizations and scholars. One of the purposes was to determine what analytical techniques appeared most promising for marketers. Their study concluded that the most promising techniques appear to be (in descending order): simulation, modeling, Monte Carlo methods, linear programming, and the various network methods such as PERT and CPM.[7] In the remaining part of this chapter we shall attempt to forecast into the future and examine some expected developments in the application of quantitative methods in marketing.

THE FUTURE

Throughout this text we have examined a number of models now being used as decision aids by marketing managers. However, there are a number of

---

[4] *Ibid.*, p. 137.

[5] Philip Kotler, "Operations Research in Marketing," *Harvard Business Review*, Vol. 45. (February, 1967), p. 30.

[6] *Ibid.*, p. 31.

[7] *Ibid.*, pp. 31–32.

models still in the developmental stages which, when they finally reach operational status, are expected to prove extremely valuable to marketing decision makers. Two of these new developments are *market simulators* and *rote marketing*.[8]

Market simulators. Some business organizations are showing a great interest in developing total marketing decision models rather than separate models for advertising, pricing, distribution, and so forth. These are computerized models of the firm's markets which serve as a basis for testing and predicting responses to alternative marketing policies.

The most advanced of these market simulators are micro-behavioral in nature. They include (1) a representative group of final customers distributed geographically, (2) a representative group of channel members (i.e., wholesalers and retailers), and (3) a specified group of competitors. As such, the model encompasses the firm's best understanding of the structure, nature, character, and behavior of the market in which it sells. The advantages of such a model accrue when management is developing a new marketing strategy. The various alternatives can be tried out on the market simulator and the expected results determined without disrupting the ongoing operations of the firm. This experimental nature of simulation was emphasized in Chapter Twelve.

Some of the well known firms which have market simulators in various stages of development are Pillsbury (cake market),[9] Lever Brothers (detergent market),[10] and General Electric (flashbulb market).

Rote marketing. In many firms, analysts have been searching for semi-routine decisions in the marketing area which can be turned over to a rote marketer—the computer. This search has been encouraged by the success which has been achieved with automated inventory systems. In such systems, the computer assumes full responsibility for determining order points and issuing reorders similar to the inventory model presented in Chapter Eight. Work has also been undertaken in some universities to automate higher level marketing decisions. However, much of this work is still in the research and development stage.

Undoubtedly, the reader can imagine how useful a computer can be when attempting to utilize the various models and techniques presented in this text. In some of the problem situations presented in this text where the number of

---

[8] The discussion of market simulators and rote marketing is provided by Kotler, *op. cit.*, p. 44.

[9] "Pillsbury Finds a New Mix That Pays," *Business Week*, June 25, 1966, p. 178.

[10] Alfred A. Kuehn and Doyle L. Weiss, "Marketing Analysis Training Exercise," *Behavioral Science*, Vol. 10 (January, 1965), pp. 51–67.

variables or activities were few, the models and techniques could be manipulated by hand. However, in many real-life situations where there are numerous variables, the reader can well imagine the usefulness of a computer. It would be beneficial for us, because of the computer's tremendous capabilities, to examine some of the expected contributions of the computer as a facilitating tool in marketing analysis in the future.

MARKETING ANALYSIS AND THE COMPUTER

As we have seen throughout this text, the computer has been one of the primary causes of the increased use of analytical techniques in marketing. Its extreme data handling capabilities and computational ability make it an extremely valuable aid when utilizing various models and techniques. In this section we shall examine several specific areas of marketing and discuss the future contributions of the computer in each area.

Distribution

As was noted in Chapter Eight, management has recently paid greater attention to problems of distribution. In this process they have discovered the vast wealth of information provided by the computer which can lead to better service, faster deliveries, and more efficient inventory management. They have come to realize that they have a strong stake in seeking more efficient distribution of their product because while promotion generates sales demand, distribution provides utility by placing the goods in customers' hands. Actually then, the manager has a set of conflicting objectives. At the same time he would like to minimize distribution costs and maximize customer service. The ability of the computer to aid managers in striking a balance between these two seemingly conflicting objectives is perhaps its greatest appeal.

According to a recent study, *Sales Management Magazine* found that automation of the order-processing cycle, inventory management, and physical handling of goods are the three most widely used computer applications in distribution.[11] What the computer provides management with in such instances is time in the form of shorter order cycles. In addition, in the future, as a firm's operations become more geographically dispersed, the mating of computers and communications technology will provide marketing management with an even faster updating of information and greater ability to speed inventory turnover and to react to changing environmental factors.

[11] "The Computer in Marketing: Distribution," *Sales Management*, December 1, 1968, p. 45.

Sales Forecasting

One of the basic foundations of a sound marketing plan is a sales forecast. As marketing planning becomes even more indispensable to success in marketing, the need is greater for an accurate, timely sales forecast.

The reader is undoubtedly aware of the various techniques used in sales forecasting so there is no need to review them here.[12] These techniques have been used without the aid of a computer. However, the tremendous ability of the computer to digest information and to calculate at high speeds has enabled marketing management to make greater and more efficient use of the tried and tested techniques for sales forecasting. Whatever the technique used, there is no doubt that the computer can do it faster and more accurately. In addition, the computer enables us to forecast in greater detail. More variables can now be incorporated at both the input and output points of the forecast spectrum. In this respect, therefore, the computer provides us with a better forecast than would ever be feasible by hand. Besides reducing the cost and time involved in manually preparing forecasts, the computer also greatly reduces the chances of error that are present when several individuals are involved in preparing forecasts manually.

With all of its great data handling and computational ability, the computer has not reduced the need for human judgment decisions in sales forecasting (and in many other areas). It is a human mind which decides what the input variables shall be and what type of output is desired. From this standpoint, the use of higher mathematical techniques may place heavier demands on the judgment of forecasters than ever before.[13]

Advertising

Asked to comment on the state of advertising in 1985, one agency executive has stated that computerized information systems will be "the single most pervasive change that will affect productivity in advertising agencies."[14] In these systems will be stored all the necessary research data and media information as well as complete histories of campaigns, copy, and illustrations for

---

[12] The techniques used for sales forecasting are covered in most elementary business statistics courses. If the reader is unfamiliar with these techniques, he should consult any basic business statistics text.

[13] For an excellent discussion of the use of the computer in sales forecasting, see "The Computer in Marketing: Sales Forecasting," *Sales Management*, January 7, 1966, pp. 45–52.

[14] "The Computer in Marketing: Advertising," *Sales Management*, July 15, 1966, p. 57.

both the client and his competitors, which he will view on cathode ray tubes. In addition, there will be taped records of customer purchases by brand and price gathered at store checkouts which will replace the data currently gathered by retail audits and consumer panels. Finally, a steady inflow of current information will constantly update the system.

To gain some idea of the future of the computer in advertising, one need only examine some of the more advanced systems in use at the present time by various advertising agencies.[15]

HAMM. The advertising agency of Young and Rubicam has been one of the pioneers in applying the computer to advertising. They currently have between 50 and 100 computer programs for advertising problems. One of the most widely used is HAMM (High Assay Media Model). The purpose of this program is to allocate a client's budget in such a way that most of the budget is spent in the medium that is most likely to provide the greatest return. The remaining funds are allocated to the second-best medium, and so on. The inputs into this model include consumer purchasing behavior and media behavior. Built into this model are the purchase cycles of the product (local buyers, brand-switchers, potential buyers, and buyers who move into and out of the market). This data is provided from Young and Rubicam's population profile. The profile contains 540 demographic variables such as age, sex, family size, and family income. Once the potential market for the particular product is determined, it is matched with potential media audiences.

SIMAD. The advertising agency of Batten, Barton, Durstand, and Osborn (BBDO) uses a mathematical model, SIMAD (System for the Integration of Marketing and Advertising Data) to choose the "best" or "optimum" combination of media elements given certain constraints. Each candidate medium is screened to determine its comparative effectiveness in delivering maximum advertising exposure to the people most likely to purchase the product. Each individual audience is then analyzed to determine what ratio of the audience is likely to be exposed to a certain advertisement. Then agency officials assign qualitative judgment values in the form of numerical ratings for the impact each advertisement in each medium is likely to have. Combining all of these factors, the agency develops what it calls Rated Exposure Units (REU) delivered per advertisement and per medium. This gives an indication of the effective audience of prime prospects which are likely to be exposed to the advertisement. The REU's are the basic input data for the analytical model in addition to costs and discount structures for each candidate medium and budget limitations. This is similar to the media mix model discussed in Chapter Nine.

---

[15] *Ibid.,* pp. 59–63.

The two models presented here are only two of many such applications. They are provided to make the reader aware of the wide-scale use of computer models in advertising.

HEURISTIC PROGRAMMING

One development which is expected to make a great contribution to improving the efficiency of marketing decision making is heuristic programming. Heuristic programming combines the great data handling capabilities of the computer with human problem solving techniques in order to improve the speed and quality of marketing decisions. In effect, what is done is that the computer is programmed to analyze a problem in the same manner that an executive might go about solving the problem on the basis of his experience and judgment if he had the weeks or months of time needed to do the job.[16] In a heuristic model the analyst makes use of heuristics or "rules of thumb." These rules of thumb, can shorten the time needed to find a reasonably good solution. For example, in a model designed to select potential market areas, a heuristic used might be, "Only consider market areas with cities over 250,000 population." Thus, there is an attempt to program the computer with the thinking capabilities of the human being. Programs designed to enable the computer to play checkers and chess are examples. The heuristics used amount to the common-sense procedures used by the actual players or decision makers.

Using this approach, a problem need not be "well structured" in order to program it for decision making. Thus, the combination of the heuristic method of human problem solving and the computer opens up a vast area of relatively unstructured marketing problems where the heuristic approach may possibly make significant contributions. Heuristic programming has great promise as an aid in decision making.[17] However, how great its contribution will be is something that cannot be accurately determined at this time.

MARKETING INFORMATION SYSTEMS

Marketing information systems will have a great impact in the future for marketing decision makers. As these systems and their closely related data

---

[16] See Alfred A. Kuehn "Heuristic Programming: A Useful Technique for Marketing," in Charles H. Hindersman, ed., *Proceedings of the Forty-Fifth National Conference of the American Marketing Association*, 1962, pp. 162–170.

[17] For an example of the heuristic approach, see Alfred A. Kuehn and Michael J. Hamburger, "A Heuristic Program for Locating Warehouses," *Management Science*, Vol. 9 (July, 1963), pp. 643–666.

banks develop, they will expand greatly the information base for marketing management decisions. Marketing decision makers will be able to collect, store, retrieve, analyze, and manipulate great quantities of data much more easily and at lower costs than ever before. However, these developments present two possible dangers.

The first is that as more and more data is generated there will be a greater need for bringing this data together and assimilating it in such a way that it proves useful in the decision-making process in the firm. There will be a great need for individuals who can put these powerful new information tools to use in decision making.

The second danger is that with such a vast array of data, there is the possibility that the marketing manager will be faced with an information overload. In other words, the manager will be bombarded with data to such a great extent that he will be unable to make effective use of the data. Obviously, if such a situation occurs, the basic purpose of a marketing information system will be defeated. The development of marketing information systems must be accompanied by careful observation, analysis, and evaluation of how these systems are functioning.

The Computer Utility and Marketing Information Systems

One future development which is expected to have a great impact on marketing information systems is the growth of the time-shared computer. A time-shared computer is one which can be used simultaneously by several users. Each user communicates with the computer through a remote console. As such the time shared computer has made possible the development of "computer utilities." A computer utility would be much like the electric utilities we are all familiar with. Such a utility would maintain a time-shared computer and firms would purchase computing time according to their needs. The computer utility would be responsible for all maintenance aspects while the user would only be concerned about his own programs. This enables the user to gain the full advantage of a full scale computer facility without committing himself to the huge investment in computer software, hardware, and the personnel necessary to staff such an operation. The user would purchase only what he needs.

It is easy to imagine the effect that the computer utility concept will have on marketing information systems. This will make possible the development of full scale information systems in small and medium size firms which ordinarily would not be able to afford such systems. It is also highly probable that the growth in computer utilities will result in a faster evolution of the type of marketing information system discussed in Chapter Eleven.

To operate efficiently in an environment which is becoming more complex and dynamic, the marketing decision maker is going to need the aid of various analytical methods. It appears that the surface has only been scratched in applying mathematical tools and techniques to marketing problems. As the mathematical training of future business managers is increased, we can expect that these men will approach marketing problems in a different manner than their predecessors. Armed with analytical techniques and models will not preclude the need to make difficult marketing strategy choices in the future. The choices, however, will be made by using the traditional approaches of experience and intuition in addition to the analytical techniques discussed in this book.

PROBLEMS

1. Such terms as "operations research," "mathematical models," "systems analysis," "model building," and "management science" have been widely used to describe a similar movement in the solution of business problems. What do all of these terms have in common?

2. Why did management scientists devote a great deal of their early efforts to developing models for problems in production scheduling, equipment replacement, inventory control, equipment maintenance, and waiting lines?

3. In the chapter we discussed two significant recent trends in management science activity. Discuss these trends as to their probable effects on the solution of marketing problems.

4. "Since 99% of all marketing decisions are still made on the basis of intuition, there is little need to study analytical methods in marketing since it is obvious that they have had no impact." Discuss this statement.

5. Discuss some of the anticipated influences that the computer will have on marketing problem analysis.

6. What is heuristic programming? Why is it expected to aid marketing problem solving?

7. Discuss the concept of a "computer utility" and its probable impact on marketing information systems.

REFERENCES

Periodicals

"Computers Begin to Solve the Marketing Puzzle," *Business Week* (April 17, 1965), pp. 114–138.

GARRETSON, ROBERT C. AND MAUSER, FERDINAND F. "The Future Challenges Marketing," *Harvard Business Review*, Vol. 41 (November–December, 1963), pp. 168 ff.

VANDELL, ROBERT F. "Management Evolution in the Quantitative World," *Harvard Business Review*, Vol. 48 (January–February, 1970), pp. 83–92.

"Who'll Boss the Computer," *Sales Management* (October 16, 1964), p. 76.

Books

FRANK, RONALD E. AND GREEN, PAUL E. *Quantitative Approaches to Marketing* (Englewood Cliffs, N.J.: Prentice-Hall, Inc., 1967).

HALBERT, MICHAEL. *The Meaning and Sources of Marketing Theory* (New York: McGraw-Hill Book Co., Inc., 1965).

MONTGOMERY, DAVID B. AND URBAN, GLEN L. *Management Science in Marketing* (Englewood Cliffs, N.J.: Prentice-Hall, Inc., 1969).

APPENDIXES

APPENDIX A: Table of Random Numbers

31827	80191	43585	20270	74558	48961	90052	02750	82718	27982
92204	68347	84735	32061	47876	42152	89344	82877	44440	61944
72608	47319	85449	66261	38104	76120	66105	86843	17467	79969
71171	34112	21904	22894	46802	68360	67676	37401	50290	46941
30238	58381	06203	10840	07664	84061	78870	19046	94038	74214
97806	63153	46986	88540	26772	51091	60122	13542	29098	02527
68901	15231	70325	54459	74210	33550	67053	03497	00764	50007
51517	35148	82482	85693	34742	79244	54316	59097	05238	71302
96035	69002	34342	01936	91700	87950	36445	27181	94249	35572
40704	12590	78982	10013	72214	98454	63763	75478	24327	74597
99130	52082	16513	04318	44844	62677	52651	92644	60732	8278[1]
71335	76694	81253	49676	62672	77020	33251	77045	66312	2003[8]
13116	26616	14165	91983	19943	51068	33249	54613	76240	9918[0]
97727	69749	70411	30598	83133	74098	05019	92651	23968	39257
55499	59891	93900	73882	25113	59388	43088	23301	32577	52791
68114	62784	03503	02342	33585	79067	62339	67327	50998	48054
10644	70253	87979	40870	51988	92913	41660	58484	48654	81809
63563	42705	55463	28808	32994	93355	85549	85878	05904	85119
50696	67283	43473	16233	06090	37524	02533	41551	86849	63729
38518	61790	07851	50846	59824	61794	38329	16693	74317	87486
29835	05742	96097	41131	44163	56513	17119	69346	05420	06509
81722	66318	35983	03825	65327	00154	32181	50676	88628	92081
76493	58045	96750	07129	28694	35174	95039	09874	53959	79355
49335	20556	69838	18227	50454	68776	00591	81476	95160	32618
32626	25525	16767	87974	58254	09435	16945	70276	45279	49740
31413	49624	17412	92485	88605	17066	49553	43131	83541	54640
30882	36088	10376	15157	23479	92796	08852	98101	43943	44458
41294	09786	32189	23352	72569	43449	42922	91977	57528	49302
17888	24568	43374	48671	62219	17537	23896	10865	64795	21522
84534	85628	24040	62091	52814	00627	38812	37041	53031	62065
84770	38718	43464	28531	51519	98086	26105	98067	75599	05821
57412	03967	67914	47176	77597	98660	53675	83472	08001	75477
64826	46172	01491	06483	17601	86795	48441	79485	38864	89016
76411	41221	57763	52366	06071	32907	65560	31382	38259	13439
52345	55303	85463	56129	92052	58633	91461	13864	56921	23004
89904	07019	11723	27044	91405	04809	58411	56670	09970	31461
79283	35627	79392	14301	64037	26769	21626	82401	36774	88633
48682	88664	43008	32795	31584	98842	23352	88054	24483	93679
76037	32852	87414	96027	98954	42626	80580	93418	71767	88077
17517	46860	09293	41303	06117	13912	46878	38007	08537	27855
83388	12208	91115	21707	13677	90780	32243	09065	21672	39205
55719	99276	72750	18190	51008	70429	34917	50515	86410	87268
24435	18058	05772	72162	34936	62984	78068	06540	12552	72151
54699	57233	62385	34763	55021	47298	60832	32583	42662	00155
10678	53085	81841	14499	40856	34563	60072	28619	65728	72342
59680	53378	61676	67807	03084	19757	93934	80627	44152	21253
44014	55930	28617	75065	82315	92855	00405	22571	77823	38423
33995	38895	35776	76418	62458	17011	44858	56450	38343	31087
75524	91815	79153	32915	41471	14944	69944	17231	15667	48228
68239	39427	42908	78396	31568	38097	68515	14236	46656	90676

Source: Boyd L. Nelson, *Elements of Modern Statistics* (New York: Appleton-Century-Crofts, Inc., 1961).

APPENDIX B: Table of Areas under the Normal Curve

z	.00	.01	.02	.03	.04	.05	.06	.07	.08*	.09
0.0	.0000	.0040	.0080	.0120	.0160	.0199	.0239	.0279	.0319	.0359
0.1	.0398	.0438	.0478	.0517	.0557	.0596	.0636	.0675	.0714	.0753
0.2	.0793	.0832	.0871	.0910	.0948	.0987	.1026	.1064	.1103	.1141
0.3	.1179	.1217	.1255	.1293	.1331	.1368	.1406	.1443	.1480	.1517
0.4	.1554	.1591	.1628	.1664	.1700	.1736	.1772	.1808	.1844	.1879
0.5	.1915	.1950	.1985	.2019	.2054	.2088	.2123	.2157	.2190	.2224
0.6	.2257	.2291	.2324	.2357	.2389	.2422	.2454	.2486	.2517	.2549
0.7	.2580	.2611	.2642	.2673	.2704	.2734	.2764	.2794	.2823	.2852
0.8	.2881	.2910	.2939	.2967	.2995	.3023	.3051	.3078	.3106	.3133
0.9	.3159	.3186	.3212	.3238	.3264	.3289	.3315	.3340	.3365	.3389
1.0	.3413	.3438	.3461	.3485	.3508	.3531	.3554	.3577	.3599	.3621
1.1	.3643	.3665	.3686	.3708	.3729	.3749	.3770	.3790	.3810	.3830
1.2	.3849	.3869	.3888	.3907	.3925	.3944	.3962	.3980	.3997	.4015
1.3	.4032	.4049	.4066	.4082	.4099	.4115	.4131	.4147	.4162	.4177
1.4	.4192	.4207	.4222	.4236	.4251	.4265	.4279	.4292	.4306	.4319
1.5	.4332	.4345	.4357	.4370	.4382	.4394	.4406	.4418	.4429	.4441
1.6	.4452	.4463	.4474	.4484	.4495	.4505	.4515	.4525	.4535	.4545
1.7	.4554	.4564	.4573	.4582	.4591	.4599	.4608	.4616	.4625	.4633
1.8	.4641	.4649	.4656	.4664	.4671	.4678	.4686	.4693	.4699	.4706
1.9	.4713	.4719	.4726	.4732	.4738	.4744	.4750	.4756	.4761	.4767
2.0	.4772	.4778	.4783	.4788	.4793	.4798	.4803	.4808	.4812	.4817
2.1	.4821	.4826	.4830	.4834	.4838	.4842	.4846	.4850	.4854	.4857
2.2	.4861	.4864	.4868	.4871	.4875	.4878	.4881	.4884	.4887	.4890
2.3	.4893	.4896	.4898	.4901	.4904	.4906	.4909	.4911	.4913	.4916
2.4	.4918	.4920	.4922	.4925	.4927	.4929	.4931	.4932	.4934	.4936
2.5	.4938	.4940	.4941	.4943	.4945	.4946	.4948	.4949	.4951	.4952
2.6	.4953	.4955	.4956	.4957	.4959	.4960	.4961	.4962	.4963	.4964
2.7	.4965	.4966	.4967	.4968	.4969	.4970	.4971	.4972	.4973	.4974
2.8	.4974	.4975	.4976	.4977	.4977	.4978	.4979	.4979	.4980	.4981
2.9	.4981	.4982	.4982	.4983	.4984	.4984	.4985	.4985	.4986	.4986
3.0	.4987	.4987	.4987	.4988	.4988	.4989	.4989	.4989	.4990	.4990

INDEX

Index

*This book has been set in 10 point Times New Roman,
leaded 3 points, and 9 point Times New Roman,
leaded 2 points. Part numbers and titles are in 24
point Times New Roman. Chapter numbers and
titles are in 18 point Times New Roman. The size
of the type page is 27 by 45 picas.*